Held... ...alled Earlier

From Opportunity to Entitlement

From Opportunity to Entitlement

The Transformation and Decline of Great Society Liberalism

Gareth Davies

University Press of Kansas

Published by the University Press of Kansas (Lawrence, Kansas 66049),
which was organized by the Kansas Board of Regents and is operated and
funded by Emporia State University, Fort Hays State University, Kansas
State University, Pittsburg State University, the University of Kansas, and
Wichita State University

Library of Congress Cataloging-in-Publication Data

Davies, Gareth.
    From opportunity to entitlement : the transformation and decline of
Great Society liberalism / Gareth Davies.
       p.   cm.
    Includes bibliographical references and index.
    ISBN 0-7006-0757-9 (alk. paper)
    1. Public welfare—United States—History.   2. Liberalism—United
States—History.   3. Individualism—United States—History. 4. United
States—Social policy.   I. Title.
HV91.D3524   1996
361.973—dc20   95–46919
                                          CIP

British Library Cataloguing in Publication Data is available.

Printed in the United States of America

10 9 8 7 6 5 4 3 2 1

The paper used in this publication meets the minimum requirements of
the American National Standard for Permanence of Paper for Printed
Library Materials Z39.48-1984.

For Martha Derthick and Byron Shafer

CONTENTS

Contents

ACKNOWLEDGMENTS

Since this is my first book, I begin by acknowledging the three people who did most to stimulate my early interest in history: my father, Michael Heale, and the late Geoffrey Holmes. At Oxford, Duncan Macleod and Gillian Peele helped me to define a D.Phil topic, while the St. Catherine's College M.C.R. and its members provided a thoroughly congenial respite from research. I was lucky enough to spend the middle year of my studies at the University of Virginia and can't imagine a more pleasant introduction to American life, not least because Charlottesville is where I met my future wife, Liz Bergmann.

In writing my dissertation I benefited enormously from the generosity of Nuffield College and from the model supervision of Nigel Bowles. I would also like to thank Andrew Adonis, David Butler, Jim Sharpe, and Jonathan Tritter, all of Nuffield. Joyce Appleby, Jessica Gienow, Bill Harbaugh, the late Sar A. Levitan, Bill Merkel, Jack Pole, and Lelia Roeckell all read and improved parts of the manuscript, and two thorough but humane examiners, Tony Badger and David Goldey, made my *viva* an unexpectedly pleasant experience.

I have found American librarians and archivists to be uniformly helpful, but I would like to express my particular gratitude to the excellent staff of the Lyndon B. Johnson library in Austin. And although I cannot thank all the people who have shown me hospitality during the course of the American research for this book, I should mention Steve Mansfield and Wendy Braje, John Buckner, Maureen Krug, Mavis and Harold Evans, and Tom and Vivi Liverman. Above all, I want to express my gratitude to Otto and Anni Bergmann, who provided meatloaf, walks, and much else during my trips to Washington, D.C.

The final version of this book was improved immeasurably by the suggestions and corrections of Edward D. Berkowitz, Nigel Bowles, Jean Day, David Hamilton, Tom Jackson, Russell Price, and Doris Youdelman. Although I have not always followed their advice, they will all see the evidence of their contribution in the pages that follow. I am also grateful to Fred Woodward and his colleagues at Kansas for their professionalism and support.

I owe a good deal to all my former colleagues in the Department of American Studies at Manchester University, and I benefited also from the fine resources of the John Rylands University Library. I would also like to acknowledge the friendly welcome that I have had from my new colleagues in the Politics Department at Lancaster. More generally, the warmth and good humor of my friends has indebted me in ways that I can neither quantify nor adequately acknowledge. That is even more the case with my family: Liz, Mary and Mervyn Davies, and Kate.

This book is dedicated with gratitude to the two friends and mentors whose encouragement and intellectual inspiration did most to shape it: Martha Derthick of the University of Virginia, and Byron Shafer of Nuffield College, Oxford.

INTRODUCTION

Continued dependence upon relief induces a spiritual and moral disintegration fundamentally destructive to the national fiber. To dole out relief in this way is to administer a narcotic, a subtle destroyer of the human spirit.
　　　　　—President Franklin D. Roosevelt, Budget Address, 4 Jan. 1935

[Welfare is] degrading, causing a deterioration of the human spirit, because it destroys the sense of purpose and meaning of life and living.
　　　　　—Senator Terry Sanford (D-N.C.), Senate Finance Committee Hearings on
　　　　　　　　　　　　　　　　　the Family Security Act, 14 Oct. 1987

On 13 October 1988, President Ronald Reagan signed into law a welfare reform bill whose stated purpose was to promote personal independence and self-advancement. Its principal legislative sponsor had been Daniel Patrick Moynihan, the Democratic senator from New York. Two weeks earlier, both houses of Congress had approved the bill by overwhelming margins: 347 to 53 in the House of Representatives; 96 to 1 in the Senate. In signaling his approval, Reagan extolled "reform that will lead to lasting emancipation from welfare dependency."[1]

In arriving at a rough consensus on welfare policy, legislators had endorsed Lawrence Mead's notion that "the most vulnerable Americans need obligations, as much as rights, if they are to move as equals on the stage of American life."[2] Governor Bill Clinton (D-Ark.), testifying before Congress on behalf of the National Governors Association (NGA), envisaged a "New Covenant" between the welfare recipient and the state, "setting forth not only the recipient's right to receive benefits but responsibilities

1

that go along with those benefits." Among the obligations favored by the NGA was "an enforceable commitment to pursue an individualized course of education, training, and work leading to independence."[3]

On the floor of the House, liberal congressmen such as Thomas Downey of New York joined more conservative colleagues in demanding alternatives to what Byron L. Dorgan (D-N.D.) termed "the dead-end road of institutional welfare." Mike Espy, a black Democrat from Mississippi, acknowledged that the existing welfare system had not been "entirely ineffective" if its purpose had been simply to "maintain millions of Americans at or below the federal poverty level." It had, however, manifestly failed to deliver if the objective of public policy was "to move these people out of poverty and onto self-support." Espy argued, "As much as we must include the element of compassion, the design and structure of our welfare reform must include accountability and attractive incentives that urge participants to become self-supporting. What can be more motivating than the self-dignity that is the light at the end of the welfare tunnel?"[4]

OPPORTUNITY LIBERALISM

In historical terms it is striking that the liberal component of the 1988 welfare reform coalition should have presented the ideals of personal responsibility and self-support as some bold philosophical innovation. In a narrow sense this was a legitimate claim, since the perennial American quest for welfare reform had never yet succeeded in devising authoritative and effective expressions of the nation's dominant individualism. In another sense, however, when Senator Moynihan spoke of "citizenship" and "the idea of mutual obligation,"[5] he merely restated a proposition that had undergirded a whole series of rehabilitation-oriented welfare reform initiatives ever since the 1950s. Considering the great social reform eras of the twentieth century more generally, it soon becomes clear that the most successful reform-minded politicians have been those who responded to changing social and economic conditions by adapting rather than replacing the language of individualism. The language of opportunity has remained central to American discourse about economic security, and in this context Moynihan's proposal was entirely unexceptional. Like Lyndon Johnson and Franklin Roosevelt, he understood that a liberal political agenda could not be advanced unless it was seen to respect the nation's dominant social philosophy.

However, there is one major exception to this tradition of opportunity-centered liberalism, and its development provides the subject for this book. The principal reason why traditional and authentically liberal notions of self-help and personal independence sounded novel or conservative in the 1980s and 1990s is that these ideals largely disappeared from liberal discourse during the late 1960s and 1970s. In their place came radical notions of income by right, and American liberalism remains associated in the public mind with an entitlements doctrine that in reality lies outside its broader political tradition. Although the history of twentieth-century reform does indeed include the extension of new entitlements to deprived or otherwise deserving populations, the notion of an unconditional right to income clearly exceeds the bounds of that tradition. Accordingly, when Democrats today employ the language of obligation, it is wrong to depict them as representatives of a new breed, freed from the permissive doctrines of New Deal—Great Society liberalism.[6]

THE RISE OF ENTITLEMENT LIBERALISM

In 1964, when President Johnson unveiled his War on Poverty, liberal legislators enthusiastically endorsed its individualistic approach. For reasons both of convenience and conviction, the Economic Opportunity Act characterized welfare as part of the poverty problem rather than as a mechanism for eliminating want. Eight years later, Senator George McGovern, soon to be chosen as the Democratic presidential candidate, sponsored a $6,500 guaranteed-income proposal drafted by the National Welfare Rights Organization. According to the new orthodoxy, which the NWRO proposal embodied, the federal government had an immediate obligation to raise all poor Americans above the poverty level by guaranteeing them an income, no questions asked. By the time of McGovern's ill-fated quest for the presidency, the dominant strain of American liberalism had come to share this view, and to denigrate those who made demands on the poor of the sort that had won universal approval in 1964. When President Richard Nixon proposed a Family Assistance Plan (FAP) that would have significantly reduced the inequities of the New Deal welfare state, his bold initiative was assailed by supporters of the new liberal orthodoxy as punitive and medieval. This book asks how American liberals came to repudiate a venerable and politically valuable individualist tradition, in favor of radically "un-American" definitions of income entitlement.

3

EXPLAINING THE GUARANTEED INCOME MOVEMENT

Most explanations for the rise of the guaranteed income movement start with the failure of the more traditional approaches to alleviating poverty employed by the Johnson administration. In an environment of acute social tension and political dislocation, it is argued, previously unattractive income redistribution schemes acquired new appeal.[7] Characteristic of much of this scholarship is the belief that the "income strategy," for all its seeming novelty, represented a logical outgrowth of the earlier initiative. Antipoverty officials, according to this view, were drawn to the income strategy from an early stage, motivated by the manifest insufficiency of the Economic Opportunity Act as a response to structural poverty.[8]

Lawrence Mead has found the same basic philosophies of permissiveness and entitlement, the same aversion to reciprocal responsibility, in each response to poverty. Great Society liberals, in his view, were challenged by the disappearance of the more obvious racial and economic barriers to self-help, but the momentum of reform led them to dream up new obstacles. Both the Economic Opportunity Act and the various guaranteed income proposals of later years embodied the view that the poor remained victims of social injustice and were thus entitled to the unconditional largesse of the federal government. The guaranteed income movement may have represented a peculiarly advanced manifestation of this tendency, but the 1964 program had also excused its would-be beneficiaries of any significant obligation.[9]

An important aspect of the failure of the War on Poverty to achieve its goals was the development of a supposed "welfare crisis." Three elements of this widely identified but variously defined crisis were the rapid growth of the unpopular Aid to Families with Dependent Children program (AFDC), continued inequality of benefits between states, and the growing incidence of single parenthood in the ghetto. Radicals, liberals, and conservatives alike were drawn to the idea of a radical overhaul of the welfare system, and each could find some merit in the guaranteed income strategy. Scholars have described the relationship between the welfare crisis and the rise of the guaranteed income in various ways. For some, the political establishment was forced to embrace the cause of reform by the new militancy of the poor and by the incipient bankruptcy of existing matching grant programs.[10] Others place rather more emphasis on the effect that longstanding, monotonous policy failure had in finally persuading policymaking elites

4

to abandon tired and discredited notions of rehabilitation and prevention. Particularly striking in this respect was the influential role of professional economists in placing the guaranteed income on the agenda, and the way in which general bureaucratic momentum propelled it to the top of that agenda during the Nixon years.[11] In each case, politicians belatedly endorsed the logic of "an idea whose time had come."

INCOME ENTITLEMENT AND THE NEW POLITICS

Whether these various explanations emphasize fiscal crisis, ghetto militancy, or the intellectual conversion of policymaking elites, they all share one limiting attribute: All view the rise of the income strategy as unremarkable in the context of the times. This contention has validity up to a point. It is not surprising that activists in the black and antipoverty movements—confronted with racial and economic obstacles to self-advancement, and armed with an alternative language of justice—should have lost patience with the language of reciprocal obligation. Nor is it peculiar that federal bureaucrats, confronted with policy failure and the discontent of those whom the War on Poverty was intended to benefit, should have been drawn to expanded notions of entitlement. And equally comprehensible is the enthusiasm so many academics felt for a negative income tax approach (the most widely touted form of guaranteed income) that could eliminate the problem of cash poverty overnight, provide the recipient with a continuing incentive to work, and at the same time avoid the legion pitfalls of the Johnson administration's antipoverty program.

The problem with existing analyses of the guaranteed income movement is not so much that they are wrong as that they leave an important question unanswered, important territory unexamined. They explain why activists, bureaucrats, social workers, and academics were drawn to the income strategy; in each case, conviction was matched by political interest (or, in the case of academics, by the absence of political constraints). But they *fail* to explain why American liberalism was drawn to such radically unpopular versions of that strategy as the Adequate Income Act of 1972. It is important to distinguish the income strategy of Richard Nixon—motivated by efficiency, concern for the working poor, and hostility to New Deal-Great Society bureaucracies—from that of George McGovern—fueled by extravagant definitions of income by right. Why did pragmatic and ambi-

5

tious liberal politicians such as McGovern, Fred Harris, and Eugene McCarthy come to embrace ideas of unconditional entitlement that never commanded more than marginal popular support and, indeed, attracted widespread public hostility? On the face of it, their advocacy revealed a suicidal disregard for popular sensibilities: Polled in 1969, even the poor had expressed their opposition to the guaranteed income concept.[12]

In narrow terms, this book seeks to illuminate the unique transformation in liberal perspectives on entitlement and dependency that occurred during the Great Society era. It also hopes to expose the dynamics of a broader ideological and tactical shift that had profound political consequences. To understand why liberal politicians (mostly, but not exclusively, Democrats) chose to abandon an individualist tradition that enjoyed mass support in favor of manifestly unpopular definitions of income by right, a useful place to begin is with the epochal shifting of national political gears that took place during the late 1960s and early 1970s.[13]

In retrospect, it is clear that the decline of the New Deal coalition after the mid-1960s facilitated the rise of the right to political dominance. At the time, however, many liberals found reason for hope in a phenomenon that came to be labeled the New Politics. Committed to the politics of protest, and fundamentally hostile to traditional liberalism, New Politics radicals seized control of the Democratic Party nominating process during the early 1970s. Writing on the period after 1968, Byron Shafer highlights "the rise of an alternative coalition of Democratic elites, different in social background, political experience, and policy preference from the coalition which had previously dominated the national Democratic elites."[14]

The growth of entitlement liberalism, and the corresponding decline of its opportunity-oriented predecessor, provides a fascinating instance of what Shafer terms the "circulation of elites." In this particular case study, the process left the Democratic Party astonishingly distant from the work ethic of Middle America. But an examination of the changing politics of race, patriotism, or civil liberties during this period, would expose a parallel process of detachment, nourished by the same underlying dynamics: acute political dislocation and perceived political self-interest.

In general, scholars of the War on Poverty have been slow to consider the wider political context within which liberal perspectives on poverty and dependency were transformed (in some cases this reflects a belief that no such transformation took place). The black struggle for racial justice has been widely acknowledged as a dynamic of radicalization, one that gave powerful impetus to a more general preoccupation with group rights.[15] But other ingredients combined with race to produce the climactic crisis of American liberalism during the 1960s. If the seemingly misguided entitlements advocacy of Senator McGovern is to be understood, the War on Poverty must be placed in the broader context of an embattled New Deal-Cold War Democratic tradition and an emergent New Politics. Accordingly, analyzing the politics of welfare policy during the 1960s sheds new light on the domestic political consequences of the Vietnam War.

The work that best captures the assumptions of the entitlements movement is Lawrence Mead's *Beyond Entitlement*. But where Mead sees income by right as an approach that came to dominate federal policy during the 1960s, this book presents it as a largely unsuccessful challenge to a social welfare system that has remained wedded to the connection between economic security and employment. In terms of historical understanding, Mead's is a flawed analysis that demonstrates only a limited comprehension of twentieth-century liberalism. In his view, Great Society programs "tended to shield their recipients from the usual demands of American society, as the New Deal had not." Neglecting substantial evidence to the contrary, Mead asserts that "policy after 1960 seldom assumed that government clients could support themselves, either individually or collectively." The poor, he continues, "were assured a secure, if depressed, place in American society almost without reference to behavior."[16]

Mead mistakes for Great Society liberalism an ideology that emerged primarily in *opposition* to the Johnson program. The principal ambition of the War on Poverty was to ensure that Mead's "government clients" ceased to be dependent on federal largesse. If many methods and ambitions of the Economic Opportunity Act were imprecise and unrealistic, it yet remains that their intention was directly opposite to that which Mead has adduced. And if, as he maintains, these programs were largely noncoercive in nature, then it is also true that their intended benefits were reserved for those prepared to seize opportunities.[17]

In tracing the evolution of liberal perspectives on poverty and dependency during the Great Society era, this book exposes itself to a number of serious potential objections, not least concerning the nature, extent, and practical relevance of American individualism. It departs from most recent works on the United States' welfare state in viewing popular individualism as a more consistently powerful determinant of social policy than race, gender, or dynamics internal to an autonomous state.[18] Even if popular ideology *is* important, how can it be considered remarkable that welfare dependents and their political allies should identify a basic right to income, given the centrality of "rights talk" to American history and political discourse?[19] Lawrence Mead asserts that "in a society as individualistic as the United States, so prone to asserting rights against government, the idea of obligating people to function is inherently problematic."[20] In this context, guaranteed income advocacy could easily represent a classic example of "uncompromising individualism" rather than its antithesis.[21] By contrast, the Economic Opportunity Act's service strategy could conceivably be portrayed as "un-American" in its paternalism.

The problem of what constitutes individualism becomes still more complex if one considers the broader ideological perspectives of the two categories of liberal who feature in this case study. In some senses, the forces of insurgency (advocates of a New Politics) appear more concerned with the individual, more suspicious of state power, while the old liberalism seems bureaucratic and impersonal by comparison.[22] In his biography of the antiwar activist Allard Lowenstein, William H. Chafe characterizes his subject as "a profound individualist" who believed in the "sanctity of individual over group identity and allegiance."[23] In such a context, how plausible can it be to view his enemy, Lyndon Johnson, as an embattled defender of liberal individualism?

These substantial points emphasize the need for some definition of terms at this stage. When this book refers to Lyndon Johnson as a liberal individualist and George McGovern as a deviant from the individualist tradition, it is within the specific context of national attitudes toward dependency and work. An examination of the history of United States antipoverty policy reveals both a persistent tendency to denigrate dependency and elevate self-help, and a remarkable paucity of alternative visions. The assertion of an unconditional and universal entitlement to income *does* clearly lie outside the individualist tradition, thus defined. Accordingly, the guaranteed income movement represented a striking deviation from the nation's dominant social philosophy, and liberalism's embrace of the cause of universal income entitlement amounted to a similarly dramatic departure in political philosophy.

Notions of mutual obligation and restricted definitions of income entitlement have always been crucial to national discourse concerning welfare and work. The extent and orientation of both private and public relief to the poor have characteristically been guided by a simple question, namely "Who is expected to work?" In the nineteenth century, stern responses to this question meant that the able-bodied poor were frequently entitled only to workhouse relief. Subsequently, a welfare state did develop for those deemed worthy of support by token of age, youth, disability, family responsibilities, or work history. But just as these have been the "deserving poor," only rarely have significant numbers of Americans questioned the assumption that there also existed an "undeserving poor," not entitled to public support.

Both government policies and popular attitudes have upheld the conviction that employment should be a prerequisite for economic security in most cases; only infrequently has the abandonment of this link been seriously proposed. The tenacity of the national work ethic is evidenced by American perspectives on public policy toward the jobless. On the one hand, the unemployment compensation system remains unusually limited, presumably reflecting disquiet at the notion of supporting inactive, able-bodied adults. But on the other hand, opinion poll data reveal a high level of public support for the alternative principle that the federal government should be the employer of last resort. In December 1968, 62 percent of those polled by Gallup opposed a $3,200 per annum guaranteed income, but as many as 79 percent favored (only 16 percent opposed) the idea of the government guaranteeing a job to all Americans.[24] How did entitlement liberals come to abandon the link between income and work, at a time when the public's devotion to the link was so obvious? This book explains the remarkable process by which disaffected Great Society liberals were propelled along a road that had been almost universally rejected in 1964. The political consequences of this development are apparent to this day.

CHAPTER 1

Historical Context of the War on Poverty

THE INDIVIDUALIST TRADITION IN AMERICA

The concept of individualism presents significant philosophical problems in terms both of definition and realization.[1] Such key tenets as self-help and equality of opportunity may be seen to contradict one another if either is construed in undiluted form, while the creed's moral foundations may struggle to restrain baser human instincts released by the acquisitive impulse that it elevates. Alexis de Tocqueville, an early user of the term, associated individualism not simply with rugged autonomy and flinty integrity but also with a paradoxical tendency toward conformity. Worried by the civic consequences of an excess of individualism, he was reassured by the thought that traditions of mutuality and voluntary association would have a corrective influence.[2]

Certain nineteenth-century religious persuasions also viewed the burgeoning impulse as one that subverted rather than embodied the founding principles of the American Republic.[3] Ralph Waldo Emerson might announce that "America is another word for opportunity,"[4] but neither Transcendentalism nor the democratic spirit of Jacksonian America, nor even the sense of boundlessness unleashed by westward expansion, could altogether erase persistent doubts about the animating philosophy of the New World, although each encouraged Americans to view the goal of self-help as being eminently practicable. And as the twentieth century approached, a new generation of novelists, social scientists, and reformers scorned as absurd the posited relevance of Horatio Alger to industrial America.

Yet while acknowledging all of this, both the tenacity of America's individualist ethos, and the uniformity with which spokesmen for all manner of reformist and reactionary causes have enunciated its problematical tenets, remain striking. Numerous historians have exposed aspects of the American credo that appear to have imperfect application to the nation's actual experience.[5] But none has discovered a countertradition of sufficient intensity to displace or even seriously challenge an all but consensual attachment to the *principle* of self-help. The specter of dependency, and the indignity of charity, concerned William Jennings Bryan and Eugene Debs, as well as Benjamin Franklin and Andrew Carnegie.

Pondering this phenomenon, J. R. Pole has observed that even where reformers have declared their dissatisfaction with the dominant social orthodoxy, "the strains of protest often seem to have been muted by the partial acceptance of assumptions which in themselves conflict with the ideal of achieving an equal society."[6] One can therefore acknowledge the importance of conflict and dissent in American history while remaining sensible to important consensual elements in the American experience. Richard Hofstadter observed that "however much at odds on specific issues, the major political traditions have shared a belief in the rights of property, the philosophy of economic individualism, the value of competition; they have accepted the economic virtues of capitalist culture as necessary qualities of man."[7]

An abundance of literature exists documenting the history of equality and the individualist creed in America, and an extended treatment of the historical basis for Lyndon Johnson's individualism lies beyond the proper scope of this chapter. To understand the social philosophy and the political equation that produced President Johnson's War on Poverty, attention should focus on the legacy of New Deal liberalism. But before moving on to consider the genesis and principles of the welfare state that emerged during the 1930s, a number of features of the earlier period are worth noting.[8]

The concern for the morality of the poor, which animated both Franklin Roosevelt and President Johnson and which followers of George McGovern found so distasteful, has a long pedigree in American history. Reformers and philanthropists concerned with the plight of the poor have, since the early years of the Republic, been anxious to distinguish between the deserving and the undeserving poor. The early nineteenth-century views of custodians of the poor in Beverly, Massachusetts, are representative. These worthies declared themselves anxious lest carelessly distributed relief might prevent the slothful from recognizing "the just consequences of their idleness."[9] A similar anxiety animated post-1870 advocates of "scientific philanthropy," such as S. Humphreys Gurteen, who feared the consequences of a false generosity that would injure the pauper by "destroying all self-respect and independence and ambition" while encouraging "idleness and unthrift and improvidence."[10] The socialist Robert Hunter, in his book *Poverty* (1904), maintained the same moral distinction between the working man, with his "dread of public pauperism," and the paupers "who live more or less contentedly on rubbish and alms."[11] He feared that "support in idleness and dependency does an additional injury to a class already unfairly treated."[12]

The insistence that entitlement should derive from honest labor has been common to Americans with very different political agendas. The tenacity and consensual character of the individualist tradition is remarkable, especially when viewed in the context of the wrenching forces of economic modernization that transformed American society during the late nineteenth century, rapidly distancing the nation from its Jeffersonian past. Despite prominent and intoxicating images of the frontier and of the self-made man, the Gilded Age was also the period when the industrial worker's loss of autonomy became acute. Yet it was during this same Gilded Age that the individualist credo reached its zenith, not simply in the exhortations of John D. Rockefeller and the novels of Horatio Alger but in the People's Party platform of 1892 and in the speeches of Samuel Gompers.[13]

It may well have been the willingness of Progressive Era reformers to confront the problems associated with radical individualism (social distress, economic inequality, corruption, and poor municipal services) that allowed a modified version of the same creed to survive and shape twentieth-century attitudes toward entitlement. These reformers disparaged as outmoded the laissez-faire doctrines of the previous generation; yet they retained their insistence on self-help. As William Harbaugh has observed, even Eugene Debs "never abandoned his faith in individualism."[14] The distinctive quality of Progressive individualism was the claim that laissez-faire capitalism *impeded* self-advancement. The dependent poor were victims of unregulated combination rather than personal immorality.

The key point is that dependency remained an ignoble condition. For Woodrow Wilson, the New Freedom meant deploying public power and new knowledge "for the purpose of recovering what seems to have been lost . . . , our old variety and freedom and individual energy of development."[15] In rejecting the dogma of the immediate past, Wilson looked back to the transcendant virtues of the preindustrial age, but did so with the buoyant conviction that historic values could yet be made compatible with the new economic order. Similarly, Theodore Roosevelt declared that his

New Nationalism sought "not to destroy but to save individualism" from the twin specters of socialism and plutocracy.[16]

In considering matters of poverty and dependency, early twentieth-century critics of rugged individualism typically preached a doctrine of opportunity and work rather than one of entitlement. As with Lyndon Johnson's War on Poverty a half century later, such a stance reflected both opportunism and conviction: reformers understood the political value of respecting a creed that in any case they shared.

NEW DEAL LIBERALISM AND THE INDIVIDUALIST INHERITANCE

On the face of it, the New Deal welfare state fits neatly into this tradition of liberal individualism. Many of its key principles and prejudices appear to have been inherited from the Progressive Era, and they can also be espied in the subsequent antipoverty initiatives of the Great Society period. Yet the notion of a linear political tradition, connecting these three reformist eras and respectful of popular individualism, is problematic. A number of scholars have seen in postwar liberal ideology a constricted vision that they contrast (nearly always unfavorably) to the supposedly social democratic credo of the later New Deal.

According to this version, Great Society liberalism was the enfeebled product of the *failure* of New Deal planners to realize their statist designs.[17] Nelson Lichtenstein believes that the postwar political settlement "may well have foreclosed the possibility of a more progressive approach to American capitalism's chronic difficulties." The constricted vision of postwar liberals "stood counterposed to the once hopeful effort to expand the welfare state and refashion American politics along more 'European,' explicitly social democratic lines."[18] In order to assess the merits of this view, one must consider both the substantive legislative legacy of the New Deal, and the reform agenda that emerged after 1937, in the wake of its loss of momentum.

In terms of social welfare policy, the most important legacy of the permanent New Deal was the Social Security Act of 1935, the founding legislation of the modern American welfare state. This legislation enshrined a "melting away" orthodoxy that was to have considerable staying power, and according to which prosperity and the extension of social insurance would eliminate most reasons for welfare dependency.[19] Despite the economic environment in which it was conceived, the Act left primary long-term responsibility for ensuring an adequate safety net with the private sector: the extension of the social insurance principle and the return of full employment were expected to provide a moral basis for work remaining the fundamental source of entitlement. When the system of social insurance was complete—and Roosevelt viewed the Social Security Act as being "by no means complete"[20]—all working Americans and their dependents would be insured by the federal government against old age, disability, and unemployment.

In the meantime, the federal government would also contribute to the cost of state programs for those needy citizens not covered by social security who were nonetheless deemed deserving of support. The 1935 Act restricted such public assistance to three narrow categories: the indigent aged, the blind, and widows with dependent children. Other needy Americans unable to work were required to rely upon the uncertain largesse of state and local governments, private charity, or family. James T. Patterson observes that "the new order" was in fact underpinned by the "age-old distinction between the deserving and the undeserving poor."[21]

Given the subsequent popularity of social security, the reasons for its adoption in 1935 might seem sufficiently apparent to obviate further analysis. Why, given the nation's attachment to a powerful work ethic and its corresponding aversion to dependency, would Roosevelt even have contemplated an economic security system that detached entitlement from employment? But in 1935, the principle of social insurance singularly lacked the appeal that it would possess by mid-century; indeed, the Social Security Act passed despite rather than on account of its Old Age Insurance (OAI) provision.[22] Martha Derthick observes that "left to itself, the Democratic majority would have enacted something else. That it approved old age insurance was due to the executive's influence."[23]

The relative unpopularity of OAI had a number of sources, but most were connected to its failure to meet immediate social and economic needs. During the Depression, with state and charitable coffers empty, a fifth of the population out of work, and Townsend Clubs agitating for universal $200-per-month old-age pensions, need-based general assistance represented a much more popular option than did contributory schemes. OAI was regressive, deflationary, and only dimly related to need. Moreover, it was not scheduled to deliver its first benefit check until 1942, although payroll taxes were to begin in 1937. Alf Landon, campaigning against Roosevelt in 1936, echoed the sentiment widespread among both conservatives and liberals that social security was "unjust, unworkable, stupidly drafted and wastefully financed."[24]

14

The Roosevelt administration's rejection of general assistance on the basis of need is particularly striking in view of the fact that, prior to 1935, the Federal Emergency Relief Administration (FERA) had been dispensing direct cash grants on precisely that basis. Rexford Tugwell, one of the more planning-oriented members of the Brain Trust, believed in 1934 that "the divorce of work from income, as an economic principle, had been firmly adopted."[25] Instead, Roosevelt chose to retreat from FERA's break with precedent and reinstated an older tradition of federal disengagement.

In explaining the orientation of the Social Security Act, which in this light appears socially harsh, politically perverse, and economically inappropriate, one must consider two factors. First, Roosevelt had a personal aversion to relief which, in important respects, overrode short-term political exigencies. Far from endorsing the "divorce of work from income," Roosevelt had, during the first two years of his presidency, been alarmed by the dramatic growth of dependency; in Baltimore, for example, 30 percent of the population was now dependent on welfare. Edward D. Berkowitz observes that "massive relief of this sort made President Roosevelt uneasy."[26]

In his famous state of the union address of January 1935, the president warned that "continued dependence upon relief induces a spiritual and moral disintegration fundamentally destructive to the national fiber. To dole out relief in this way is to administer a narcotic, a subtle destroyer of the human spirit." With Harry Hopkins urging the distribution of emergency general assistance as a matter of right, and with Tugwell advocating a "permanent relief and public works system," Roosevelt elected to announce instead that "the Federal Government must and shall quit this business of relief."[27] Together with the abolition of general assistance, 1935 would see the introduction of a $5 billion public works program, funded by the largest appropriation in the nation's history and driven by Roosevelt's conviction that "we must preserve not only the bodies of the unemployed from destitution but also their self-respect, their self-reliance and courage and determination."[28]

In this respect, the orientation of the Social Security Act owed something to the impact of the Depression on relief rolls. But in other respects, the planners of the Social Security Act seem to have been remarkably insensitive to the economic environment in which they deliberated. In a speech delivered in 1940, Grace Abbott, former head of the Children's Bureau, condemned the ending of federal general relief as "a tragedy for all the destitute," further observing that it was "simply not possible . . . for employment to be guaranteed to all who are unemployed."[29] Yet the body that drew up the Social Security bill, the Committee on Economic Security (CES), appeared to ignore this practical judgment. Instead, as one recent study has concluded, the CES had as its "central conception" the view "that every employable person would have the opportunity to be self-supporting."[30]

This leads on to the second reason for the 1935 Act's emphasis on social insurance: both Roosevelt and the experts who designed the social security system had a commitment to its long-term survival. Their calculations were shaped by the assumption that with the return of prosperity, popular individualism would also be restored. They were intent on building an edifice that would survive the vagaries of political fortune and would be avowedly responsive to central national principles. Martha Derthick remarks that social security policy executives began with the assumption that "a program for the poor is a poor program" that "would degrade the beneficiaries" and "lack sufficient public support to command a substantial share of public resources." According to Derthick, these same policymakers "assumed that the poor in the United States are despised by themselves and by others, and that a government program designed for their benefit would be despised too."[31]

Nowhere was this long-term calculation more evident than in the debate over how social security should be financed. Such was Roosevelt's determination that OAI be spared the political uncertainty associated with any program dependent on the federal treasury that he insisted on its being entirely self-financing.[32] That way, OAI could be presented as being just another actuarially sound pension scheme that happened to be administered by the federal government. Participants, through their contributions (rather than taxes), made a contractual claim on the social security trust fund. In intellectual terms, this characterization was absurd, but Derthick sums up its political value: "In the mythic construction begun in 1935 and elaborated thereafter on the basis of the payroll tax, social security was a vast enterprise of self-help in which government participation was almost incidental."[33]

ECONOMIC PLANNING AND THE LATER NEW DEAL

The example of the Social Security Act, therefore, would appear to add weight to the notion of a linear tradition of liberal individualism rooted in the national experience and shaped by both opportunism and conviction. President Roosevelt inherited that tradition from the Progressive Era, adapted it to the exigencies of the Depression years, and bequeathed a revivified version of the same to his Democratic successors. The Great Society agenda of Lyndon Johnson was rooted in this same social and political philosophy, and for good reason: for all the profound changes that America had undergone during the previous half century, the connection between entitlement and employment had retained its popular appeal. In this context, the subsequent endorsement by McGovernite liberals of the guaranteed income principle represents a striking deviation from tradition.

But this version may be too simple, for there is strong evidence to support the argument that after 1935 the New Deal moved in a different and more social democratic direction, not so much in terms of substantive legislative accomplishments but rather in terms of defining agendas for the future. The recent historiography of the New Deal has been preoccupied with the nature and historical importance of this shift. Although contributors to the debate seem to disagree as to the precise timing of the "social democratic moment," they share the sense that it distanced American liberals from the individualist, antistatist tradition of their forebears. By the end of the 1930s, New Dealers such as Alvin Hansen, Mordecai Ezekiel, and Henry Wallace were disillusioned with American capitalism and drawn to ideas of centralized economic planning, which clearly lay outside of any sensibly defined tradition of liberal individualism. What significance should be attached to their disaffection, and to the brand of full-employment liberalism it produced? Perhaps two New Deal legacies can be identified—a substantive one, typified by the Social Security Act and individualistic in character, and an unrealized liberal agenda, much more critical of the individualist tradition. If so, this would alter the historical context of the later guaranteed income movement.

What is the evidence for this social democratic potential? Alan Brinkley contends that support for a fundamental break with the individualist tradition mounted during Roosevelt's second term. In particular, he demonstrates that the sharp economic downturn of 1937–1938 produced a strong reaction against the perceived selfishness and irresponsibility of concentrated economic power.[34] (Such New Dealers as Robert Jackson and Harold Ickes believed that big capitalism's machinations were responsible for the so-called Roosevelt Recession.) In a rerun of Progressive Era arguments, some antimonopolists favored breaking up conglomerates, while others accepted bigness but advocated strong regulation. More

17

generally, there was emerging within the administration a certain disdain for the eternal verities of American individualism and a parallel impatience with the president's seeming reluctance to break with economic orthodoxy.

Examining this period of profound economic anxiety, Brinkley pays particular attention to Thurman Arnold, the young Yale lawyer whom Roosevelt appointed in 1938 to head the Justice Department's Antitrust Division.[35] In his acerbic and witty book, *The Folklore of Capitalism* (1937), Arnold mocked the absurdity of that creed labeled "the American Way." Somewhat like the Progressives, he believed that laissez-faire capitalism had effects quite at odds with those that its exponents celebrated. In reality, he observed, "the use of the individualistic ideal to justify dictatorial business institutions is one of the greatest obstacles to considering the real problems of freedom of the individual."[36] Arnold, however, was convinced that "this folklore is on the way out."[37] Predicting that the views of the rugged individualists would soon be of interest only to anthropologists, he argued that "we have reached a time when men are beginning to realize their complete interdependence."[38] From this recognition, he believed, must come a new acceptance of the activist state, regulating the private sector in the interests of the worker and the consumer.

During the dispiriting middle years of Roosevelt's second term, liberal impatience with individualism gained added weight from Alvin Hansen's mature-economy thesis. A Harvard economist with close New Deal connections, Hansen feared that American capitalism had permanently exhausted its capacity to generate economic growth and meet societal needs. Unless governmental economic and social policies responded to this fact, and addressed the particular problem of chronic underconsumption, basic structural defects would go uncorrected.[39] Two responses commended themselves. First, the state could intervene much more strongly than hitherto in the workings of the private economy, regulating production and pricing decisions, preventing collusion, and generally ensuring that the national interest prevailed over the selfish designs of the monopolist. Second, the federal government could prevent crippling downturns such as the 1937–1938 recession by engaging in massive public expenditure programs designed to boost demand to a level that would produce full employment.

For Brinkley, the first course most clearly evokes "the celebration of the state that . . . marked liberal thinking in the late 1930s."[40] But during the war years, the prospect for regulatory liberalism rapidly waned, due to the return of prosperity, the restored standing of big business, popular conservatism, and a perceived kinship between statism and totalitarianism. In the midst of wartime mobilization and full employment, there was no immediate need for the planned, Keynesian spending strategy that Hansen had envisioned. But Americans of all political stripes remained anxious lest the nation slip back into depression and mass unemployment once the stimulus of wartime demand had ceased. Consequently, during the early 1940s, organized labor, business groupings such as the Committee on Economic Development, and government agencies such as the National Resources Planning Board (NRPB) devoted much attention to the future challenge of sustaining prosperity under peacetime conditions.

The result of the NRPB's initial deliberations was a 1941 report entitled *Security, Work, and Relief Policies*. Together with a second report, *Post-War Plan and Program* (the two were released simultaneously in 1943), this document has interested numerous scholars seeking to characterize the agenda of the later New Deal.[41] Edwin Amenta and Theda Skocpol are among those who believe that the findings of the 1941 report presaged "an American full employment welfare state that might have emerged after World War II, had the New Deal planners achieved their aims."[42] They pay particular attention to its call for "an 'American Standard' of economic security as a *right* of every citizen."[43] This new right of citizenship was to be conferred by various means, but particularly arresting were the committee's recommendations that the federal government acknowledge and guarantee fundamental new rights to employment and shelter. As far as the Social Security Act of 1935 was concerned, the report favored national welfare standards and general assistance in place of a system that currently limited federal relief to narrowly defined categories and allowed states to set their own benefit levels. The "melting away" orthodoxy was nowhere to be seen.

These same themes of a federal commitment to full employment and a permanent, expanded welfare state found subsequent expression in the second NRPB report, but with a different emphasis. John Jeffries demonstrates that while the earlier document's preoccupation with relief revealed the continued influence of the mature-economy thesis, its successor was infused with a new optimism about the future. By 1943–1944, he shows, interest in welfare measures was in decline, while full employment dominated liberalism's domestic agenda.[44] Although the unpopularity of the NRPB's clarion call with the right was evident from the board's congressionally ordered dissolution, its advocacy of an Economic Bill of Rights found expression in Franklin Roosevelt's final reelection campaign and in the proposed Full Employment Act of 1945.[45]

Anticipating the rebirth of the reformist impulse once peace returned, the president urged "a second Bill of Rights under which a new basis of security and prosperity can be established for all—regardless of status, race, or creed." Such rights should include equal access to medical care and education, the "right of every family to a decent home," and the right "to earn enough to . . . provide adequate food and clothing and recreation."[46] Reviewing the themes of the 1944 campaign, one historian has found Roosevelt's new liberal agenda "staggering to contemplate."[47] Another, more skeptical, suggests that FDR's bold statements during this period were "no more than isolated rhetorical gestures."[48] Either way, we need to contemplate the subsequent fate of full-employment liberalism, together with the relative fortunes of the New Deal's more individualist strain, if we are to discover their respective historical significance.

THE LEGACY OF THE LATER NEW DEAL

Liberalism remained on the defensive after the war, just as it had been throughout the latter half of Roosevelt's presidency, and an early casualty was the Full Employment Act of 1945. Far from formalizing a new right to employment, the Employment Act merely committed the government symbolically to the vaguely defined goal of maximum employment. But it was not just a case of the conservative politics of the Truman years preventing the planning agenda from reaching the statute books. Additionally, the remarkable success of American capitalism during the postwar period made planning seem unnecessary or unattractive even to many liberals, especially in Congress.[49] Planning had come to the fore in response to a mature-economy thesis that was subsequently invalidated; with the economy still booming despite the return of peace, sometime stagnationists developed new confidence in the future. Thurman Arnold—onetime scourge of the monopolists—now found happiness "representing the business interests he had attacked during wartime."[50]

By 1952, J. K. Galbraith was articulating the conventional liberal wisdom when he proclaimed that American capitalism "works, and in the years since World War II, quite brilliantly."[51] In his book *American Capitalism*, Galbraith observed that growing wealth tends to act as a solvent for both "mistakes" and "grave social strains." Whereas in Britain "social reform . . . has been at the fairly direct expense of the privileged," in the United States "no measure for the assistance of any group," other than emancipation, "has brought an *identifiable* reduction in the income of any other group."[52] In America, moreover, while "in principle the American is controlled, livelihood and soul, by the large corporation, in practice he seems not to be completely enslaved." In response to this paradox, Galbraith posited that "private economic power is held in check by the countervailing power of those who are subject to it."[53]

Prosperity, full employment, and conservatism combined to produce a liberal vision very different from that of the late 1930s and the war years. It would be quite wrong, however, to suggest that full-employment liberalism left no mark on the postwar agenda. What remained from the campaign for full employment was a commitment to "compensatory" Keynesianism and economic growth. No longer very interested in class, or in the distribution of power and wealth, American liberals still envisioned an expanded role for the state, one "that would, they believed, permit it to compensate for capitalism's inevitable flaws and omissions without interfering very much with its internal workings."[54] Leon Keyserling, as chairman of President Truman's Council of Economic Advisors, was perhaps the most prominent advocate of growth liberalism, while its most important policy accomplishment was the tax cut of 1964.

Great Society liberalism can be seen to be a logical product of this postwar orthodoxy. Little interested in the redistribution of wealth, its adherents were convinced of the basic efficacy of American capitalism but had an activist commitment to compensate for its problems, one of which was the persistence of poverty. Had the legacy of full-employment liberalism been a stronger one, it is possible that the War on Poverty might have adopted the jobs strategy favored by Lyndon Johnson's secretary of labor, rather than the individualistic approach of the Economic Opportunity Act.[55] And had full-employment liberalism retained at least a somewhat higher profile, the failure of the War on Poverty might not have resulted in a brand of liberalism that separated income entitlement from employment. Perhaps a guaranteed jobs movement might have emerged in its place.

In this sense, the odyssey and fate of wartime liberalism help us to understand the contours of social reform during the postwar era. In 1945 there were two brands of work-oriented liberalism on the agenda: the liberal individualism embodied by the Social Security Act and the full-employment liberalism of the later New Dealers. But with the latter so enfeebled during the postwar period, the former prevailed. And however interesting it might be to ruminate about what might have been, the scholar of the American welfare state should be more concerned with the activities of the Social Security Board (SSB) than with the marginalized deliberations of the NRPB.[56]

In fact, the program executives who oversaw the development of the social security system after 1935 were successfully undermining the influence of the NRPB, even during the earlier period of supposed social democratic promise. *Security, Work, and Relief Policies,* after all, advocated the general assistance orientation that Congress would have preferred to social security in 1935 but that the authors of the Social Security Act had successfully opposed.[57] The SSB was preoccupied throughout the late 1930s and 1940s with consolidating a still vulnerable social insurance principle.[58] Arthur Altmeyer, chairman of the SSB, would later recall that "we felt that there were many shoals there and that the ship of state had to be steered pretty carefully to avoid them."[59] Programs other than OAI for which the board had responsibility (such as public assistance and unemployment compensation) were, as Derthick points out, "regarded as inferior programs." By contrast, "Social insurance was the shining star in the constellation of social programs."[60]

Advocates of a redistributionist welfare state found the SSB unsympathetic; the Congress of Industrial Organizations, for example, won influence only in 1943, when it abandoned its advocacy of a welfare system designed to correct "the present mal-distribution of income."[61] Indeed, such was official indifference to public assistance during this period that key program executives like Douglas Brown were quite prepared to stoke congressional hostility to relief in order to generate greater support for OAI. During the formative years of social security, policymakers learned the value of incrementalism and the importance of respecting the nation's central individualist creed. It was this, and not the NRPB's ideas for general assistance, that shaped the politics of social policy during the postwar period. By 1950, as Berkowitz maintains, "Social Security had completed a reassuring transformation," becoming "a productive and noncontroversial program."[62] More broadly, the New Deal welfare state of 1935, politically embedded in traditional assumptions about entitlement and self-help, had become part of the mid-century consensus.

EMERGENCE OF THE WELFARE PROBLEM

The "melting away" myth remained central to the strategy of the insurance-minded policymakers who directed the consolidation and expansion of the New Deal welfare state. Arthur Altmeyer explained in 1949 that "this public assistance is a residual program to help needy persons who are not adequately protected by the various forms of contributory social insurance." He was pleased to reassure legislators that "if we have a comprehensive contributory social insurance system . . . in time the residual load of public assistance would become so small in this country that the States and the localities could reasonably be expected to assume that load without Federal financial participation."[63] Some observers recognized at an early stage that this view was implausible, resting as it did upon a chimerical faith in the peculiar perfectibility of American capitalism. In 1938, for example, William Haber penned an article entitled "Relief: A Permanent Program."[64] Yet Gilbert Steiner observes that Haber was an exception, for "assertions as to the permanency of public assistance as a major federal obligation were infrequent during the period up to 1953."[65]

The political rationale for Altmeyer's glib prediction can readily be adduced, in part from material that is already familiar. Until the 1950s, the future of social security was by no means assured; yet for the program executives who also had responsibility for public assistance, the social insurance principle possessed the appeal of a religious dogma and was defended with theological devotion. To advance their ambitious agenda, they held out the promise of a dramatically reduced public assistance burden. The problem here was that legislators did not in fact view public assistance as a burden. OAA, by far the largest program, distributed its largesse to millions of constituents who were not expected to work.[66] In order to secure the future of social insurance, Altmeyer and others emphasized that OAI pensions were superior by token of their having been earned and paid for. Whereas OAA benefits were akin to charity and not conferred by right, insurance payments represented a contractual entitlement.

Douglas Brown, a former staff member of CES, told the House Ways and Means Committee in 1939 that OAI was a distinctly American alternative to "dependency." Whereas welfare involved "mounting dependency and the impairment of independence and incentive," OAI maintained the "dignity of human personality," a quality that the nation "certainly needed in these days of totalitarianism."[67] The triumph of social security, and the

23

withering away of public assistance, would attest to the superiority of the American way.

In large part, this type of appeal was expedient rather than deeply felt, yet it does epitomize a sensitivity to political reality characteristic of the social welfare bureaucracy's efforts to consolidate and expand the Social Security Act. Brown had no particular aversion to dependency, and, in intellectual terms, his notion that OAA impaired independence while OAI fostered dignity was problematic. Moreover, in 1935 executive policymakers had sought to attach no such stigma to OAA; as Berkowitz points out, public assistance programs were conceived of as pensions rather than as an ignoble form of relief or dependency.[68] But if the expansion of the preferred vision of social insurance was impeded by the popularity of public assistance, then Brown and Altmeyer were quite prepared to conceive the notion of a race between OAI and OAA. In 1949, Brown appeared again on Capitol Hill, warning that welfare was "fast winning the race," and that America risked being led down "the primrose path of state paternalism."[69] By this time he was on the verge of winning his political case, for in that year the key Ways and Means Committee too "echoed the executive's litany in celebration of insurance."[70]

Between 1939 and 1954, the insurance principle was extended successively to survivors, the disabled, farmers, and the self-employed, while sharp increases in benefit levels improved the popularity of the program still further. The most serious reverse came in 1943, when health insurance was defeated by the conservative 78th Congress. As late as 1953, as anxious executives and program partisans contemplated the prospect of the first Republican presidency in two decades, the future of social security remained a matter of concern.[71] Yet by then a 1950 increase in social security benefits had done much to ensure the program's political future and had also produced a welcome success for the "melting away" orthodoxy. The number of OAA recipients had finally begun to decline.

This success, however, presaged a new political problem that would come to bedevil defenders of the welfare state in the mid-1950s and, in fact, has persisted to the present day. In 1957, Aid to Dependent Children replaced Old Age Assistance as the largest public assistance program. More significantly, as the profile and cost of ADC increased, its popularity deteriorated. In part this reflected the extent to which Congress and the public had absorbed the "melting away" doctrine. Steiner cites the case of Congressman Winfield K. Denton, a mainstream Democrat from Indiana, who in 1957 registered his "disappointment" at the persistence of ADC, and who regularly reminded bureaucrats that "in 1951 . . . your department told me that the welfare problem would end."[72]

But in the main, aversion to ADC reflected the changing characteristics of the dependent population. Together, the expansion and transformation of the program compelled policymakers to produce a more activist conception of "melting away," one founded on doctrines of rehabilitation and social engineering that had been largely absent from the New Deal agenda.

ADC had been conceived as a noncontroversial and modest safety net for fatherless children; in most early cases, the cause of dependency was the death of the principal breadwinner. Yet by 1956, 57 percent of a considerably expanded caseload arose from illegitimacy, desertion, and divorce, and the proportion was expected to rise as high as 85 percent by the 1980s.[73] The political and philosophical issues raised by this change featured prominently in a series of Faculty Seminars on Income Maintenance convened by Wilbur J. Cohen in 1956.

Cohen had been intimately involved in the development of the Social Security Act under three presidents and had only recently left the Eisenhower Administration to take up a position with the University of Michigan. He retained intimate ties to the Democratic Party, the federal bureaucracy, and the social welfare lobby, and would return to the Department of Health, Education and Welfare (HEW) in 1961. Much as he preferred social insurance to welfare, Cohen shared with other partisans of the Social Security Act an abiding aversion to political controversy and a particular fear of incipient assault from the right. Moreover, as William Haber had predicted in 1938, most of those currently covered by welfare had no realistic alternative. At one of the Ann Arbor seminars, Cohen outlined the sources of his concern, both political and moral: "This change . . . raises a number of problems: Can benefits be increased without encouraging illegitimacy? Will the character of the program alienate public support? How can aid to unmarried mothers be awarded in a constructive manner?"[74]

The records of the Ann Arbor group reveal a striking insensitivity on the part of its academic contributors to the external dynamics of poverty and dependency. One participant observed that poverty was in important respects a cultural problem, with income deprivation but "one of a constellation of social defects, to be found in the individual and his immediate community." He further explained that these defects "prevent the individual from securing opportunities available to others in the community." Cohen echoed this sentiment, pondering "the extent to which family disorganization . . . will reduce family income and cause dependency."[75]

Such thinking represented an important shift away from the perspective of Depression era liberals who, as Berkowitz notes, "had tended to conceive of social problems in economic terms."[76] Amid the prosperity of the postwar years, it became increasingly fashionable to explain the persistence of unemployment and poverty by referring to the deviant cultural traits of its victims. Yet, in two other senses, there is a conspicuous continuity in the American welfare tradition. First, Cohen and his colleagues shared with previous generations a common concern with the behavior and morality of the poor, a concern that would persist into the 1960s with President Johnson's antipoverty initiative. Central to that concern was the sense that dependency was a fundamentally "un-American" condition. Second, postwar experts contemplating this specter of dependency believed that they had the power and duty to reform the poor. Rehabilitation and prevention, concepts that had been so central to the settlement house movement of the Progressive Era, had again come to the fore.

The notion that policymakers should rehabilitate welfare recipients emerged with the conviction that dependence upon public assistance was a problem. The conviction gained strength during wartime, as labor shortages gave a boost to vocational rehabilitation programs aimed at training and hiring the disabled.[77] And during the Cold War that followed, restoring welfare recipients to productivity remained a crucial patriotic objective. Citing the example of Operation Knoxville, a joint public-private venture in which the tools of psychiatric social work were deployed in a bid to "put the old, blind, disabled, and welfare mothers to work," Berkowitz and McQuaid observe: "If the armed forces needed complicated weaponry to keep America secure from outside attack, so the social welfare experts needed the wide-ranging methods of psychiatry and labor market analysis to turn back welfare, the persistent enemy that attacked America from within."[78]

Soon, rehabilitation was on its way to becoming all things to all men. Steiner, writing in the mid-1960s, observed that "a kind of happy marriage has taken place between state groups concerned with low taxes and those who consider themselves 'welfare-oriented.'" Both groups were happy to join the valiant struggle against dependency.[79]

In 1964, this community of interest between conservative and liberal groups, each with its reasons for resisting the specter of dependency, would contribute powerfully to the political appeal of President Johnson's War on Poverty. As will be discussed in the next chapter, Johnson's initiative was characterized by its allies as a historic bid to restore the dependent poor to self-sufficiency. Great Society liberals were much impressed by the novelty of the crusade they commended to the nation. But the War on Poverty, for all its activist zeal, was rooted in anxieties inherited from the previous decade.

In this connection, the parallels between the little-known War on Poverty that Averell Harriman, Democratic governor of New York, declared in January 1956 and Lyndon Johnson's more celebrated initiative are instructive. The governor's staff included a young social scientist, Daniel Patrick Moynihan, who subsequently assisted in planning the Economic Opportunity Act and has had a ubiquitous presence in the area of welfare policy ever since. Initially, Harriman's crusade focused on the straightforward structural problem of unemployment (a nagging problem during the 1950s), but its focus swiftly shifted from poverty to dependency. At a 1957 conference, the director of New York's Bureau of Public Assistance reported that only 30 percent of general relief recipients were looking for work and asked, "What can we do to restore this group to a condition of self-support?" She had her own answer: "Possibly the best chance of waging a successful war on poverty rests with helping the children . . . get a decent start in life so they won't perpetuate the dependency pattern. Other states may not have announced war on poverty but every state is concerned over its dependent families."[80]

This concern about poverty was shared by the Committee on Economic Development, which in 1956 commissioned from Wilbur Cohen a report on the reasons for its persistence.[81] Although the Eisenhower administration showed little inclination to declare its own war on poverty, the Social Security Amendments of 1956 revealed similar preoccupations regarding the orientation of ADC.[82] The 1956 proposal authorized funds for services "to help maintain and strengthen family life and to help such parents or relatives to attain the maximum self-support and personal independence consistent with the maintenance of continuing parental care and protection."[83] Commending the new service strategy to social workers the following year, Eunice Mincer of the Bureau of Public Assistance observed that the Eisenhower administration had "put new life into public welfare" by emphasizing "strengthened family life, self-support and self-care."[84]

RACE AND THE CHANGING POLITICS OF WELFARE

It is hard to find any interested party during this period who dissented from the proposition that restoring the dependent poor to self-sufficiency and Middle American values was both desirable and practicable. Yet ADC remained a problem, and by 1960 it was the racial context of dependency and family instability that was causing most alarm among defenders of this embattled component of the New Deal welfare state. Elaine Burgess, of the American Public Welfare Association (APWA), articulated a growing concern when she identified a disturbing assault on "specific racial groups who deviate from certain norms regarding family structure and marriage patterns."[85]

The political impact of this new pattern can best be illustrated with reference to the Newburgh affair of 1961.[86] The upstate New York town of Newburgh had recently received an influx of poor southern blacks, described by Joseph Mitchell, the city manager, as the "dregs of humanity." The disproportionate presence of these new arrivals on welfare rolls was grist to Mitchell's political mill. Despite the fact that welfare spending was lower in his town than in much of the state, Mitchell declared that "it is not moral to appropriate public funds to finance crime, illegitimacy, disease, and other social evils." Henceforth, he decreed that all dependent, able-bodied males in Newburgh (according to James T. Patterson, there were as many as ten) must work for their benefits. Furthermore, unmarried mothers who had additional children would lose their benefits, and no welfare mother would be able to claim relief for more than three months in any one year.

The "Battle of Newburgh" was soon over, Mitchell's various edicts all being ruled illegal. Yet this seemingly trivial incident generated national publicity, together with evidence that the city manager's determination to clamp down on welfare was shared by much of the population. Responding to support for Mitchell, Barry Goldwater declared, "I don't like to see my taxes paid for children out of wedlock. I'm tired of professional chiselers walking up and down the streets who don't work and have no intention of working." The *Saturday Evening Post* issued a heartfelt protest, declaring: "Surely a community should have some defense against Bankruptcy by Bastardy."[87]

Social welfare professionals were aghast at the Newburgh furor: their existing campaign to confer legitimacy upon a reoriented ADC program had suddenly become even more difficult. Liberal politicians were similarly challenged, but they sensed an opportunity as well as a threat. Eisenhower's earlier commitment to the principle of rehabilitation was now all but forgotten, and the new Kennedy administration had a chance to claim for itself the mantle of warrior against dependency. In so doing, it could perhaps do more than simply insulate itself from welfare-baiting; it could also confer new legitimacy on a program that seemed increasingly unlikely to melt away in the near future. Secretary of Health, Education and Welfare Abraham Ribicoff responded to the challenge by repackaging some familiar themes. One idea he favored was changing the name of the Bureau of Public Assistance, perhaps to the Bureau of Family Rehabilitation. He told a meeting of welfare professionals that "the word 'family' should definitely be in," even if "I don't know as yet just how."[88]

The occasion for this visionary suggestion was the submission by his Ad Hoc Committee on Public Welfare of the 1962 Public Welfare Amendments, which were designed to advance the twin goals of prevention and independence by extending federal grants for retraining and other rehabilitative services. Ribicoff was impressed by their potential, reminding the committee that "the public thinks . . . we are trying to have more and more on relief. If the public thinks we are trying to get people off public welfare, our popularity will increase."[89]

Appearing before the House Appropriations subcommittee in defense of the 1962 Amendments, Ribicoff denied that he was simply demanding more money "for a stale old policy that everybody was unhappy with." Instead, he claimed that "we have . . . finally brought in a new change and a new philosophy in welfare."[90] The political success of his bid to "interest both liberals and conservatives" in the Public Welfare Amendments of 1962 was demonstrated by the proposal's easy passage.[91] American liberals had demonstrated to potential adversaries that the New Deal welfare state remained solidly grounded in the nation's central individualist ethos. They had done so, as would Lyndon Johnson in 1964, by dedicating themselves to a new version of the "melting away" myth. A relieved Arthur Altmeyer, who had been alarmed by the implications of Newburgh, praised Wilbur Cohen in fulsome terms for his "miracle" in "channeling congressional emotions along constructive lines."[92]

CHAPTER 2

War on Dependency: Liberal Individualism and the Economic Opportunity Act of 1964

Today, for the first time in our history, we have the power to strike away
the barriers to full participation in our society. Having the power, we have the duty.
—President Lyndon B. Johnson, War on Poverty message to Congress,
16 March 1964

Scholars pondering the doctrine of and motivation for the War on Poverty tend to follow well-worn tracks. In terms of doctrine, the historiography tends to focus upon the respective importance of cultural and structural explanations for poverty in shaping the Economic Opportunity Act. Regarding strategy, commentators have for three decades highlighted the Johnson Adminstration's preference for rehabilitative and preventive services over simple redistribution of wealth: the service strategy, as opposed to the income strategy. Seeking explanations for the initiative, historians and social scientists have explored the political interests of Presidents Kennedy and Johnson, the racial and economic contexts of their deliberations, and the way in which such prior concerns as juvenile delinquency and regional underdevelopment found expression in the new program.

The territory covered may be familiar, but scholars remain sharply divided in their understandings of the War on Poverty. The extent to which the initiative was stimulated by short-term political opportunism, crusading liberal optimism, or fear of incipient racial rebellion is unresolved. For present purposes, an analysis of the sources of the Economic

Opportunity Act can most profitably be directed toward two objectives. First, in emphasizing and recapturing the authentic optimism and energy with which Lyndon Johnson's administration pursued its quest in 1964, the subsequent transformation of American liberalism during the 1960s can be placed in appropriately sharp relief. There is an unfortunate tendency in much of the existing literature to read into the political landscape of 1964 considerations that entered the equation at a later stage, albeit not much later. Second, locating the War on Poverty within the tradition of liberal individualism can act as a useful corrective to the current conservative tendency to associate the program with some radical deviation from national tradition.

The antipoverty debate of 1964 was influenced profoundly by the assumptions of postwar liberalism, and most notably by the sentiment expressed in John F. Kennedy's axiom that "a rising tide lifts all boats." American liberalism remained contentedly wedded to that faith in the nation's capacity to resolve class conflict through growth that had been so central to the postwar economic doctrine of Leon Keyserling. Presenting the War on Poverty not as an exercise in income redistribution but as an opportunity to extend to all Americans the promise of the American dream, Lyndon Johnson married ideological conviction to the politics of the liberal consensus.[1] The intellectual credibility of this nonconfrontational all-American initiative derived from the authentic, if misguided, faith of New Frontier-Great Society liberals that human ingenuity could engineer universally beneficent social change through economic expansion, complemented by the increasingly familiar doctrines of rehabilitation and prevention.[2] Sargent Shriver, Johnson's antipoverty "czar," provided a typical exposition of this philosophy in explaining the mission of the Economic Opportunity Act: "It is a war for the benefit of all Americans, poor and rich, because every time we help a poor man we help a rich man, too."[3]

In substantial measure, the War on Poverty was a classic product of that postwar liberal spirit whose constricted and enervated character has disappointed so many recent scholars.[4] Its preoccupation with rehabilitating the dependent poor was little more than an extension and repackaging of a concern that was by now a decade old. More broadly, the orientation of the program derived from an older historical tradition, namely that creed of liberal individualism from which the guaranteed income movement would shortly deviate. And it also owed much to the individual who formally declared war on poverty, in particular to the way in which Lyndon

31

Johnson's immediate political needs complemented his identity as a classic representative of that tradition.

LYNDON JOHNSON AND LIBERAL INDIVIDUALISM

Johnson's commitment to education and government as agencies for redistributing opportunity, together with his faith in the "log cabin" myth, owed much to his upbringing in the Texas hill country, and was reinforced by his formative political experience as a New Deal administrator.[5] The political scientist James L. Sundquist, who participated in the task force that designed the antipoverty program, recalls that Johnson "could talk feelingly of his first-hand knowledge of poverty in the Texas hills,"[6] and even Robert Caro's venomous account of Johnson's early years concedes that his brief experience as a teacher at a deprived Mexican school in the late 1920s revealed a genuine concern for the poor.[7]

But it is Johnson's performance as Texas director of President Roosevelt's National Youth Administration in 1935–1937 that attests most strongly to the early appeal of principles that would subsequently underpin the War on Poverty. Johnson's devotion to Franklin Roosevelt is too familiar to require extended treatment at this point.[8] Suffice it to say that during his very first week as president, Johnson told Walter Heller, his chief economic adviser, that he was "an FDR New Dealer,"[9] and shortly thereafter he recalled that Roosevelt's first inaugural address "gave me an inspiration that has carried me all through the years since."[10]

The NYA's mission was to provide the young with income through work that would help them to stay in school. Such an objective must have had particular appeal to Johnson; Robert Dallek observes, "Throughout his life, nothing in politics appealed more to him than marrying his ambition to help for the poor."[11] As he drove through Texas entreating conservative businessmen, journalists, and civic groups to support his program, Johnson demonstrated another lifelong passion—an obsession with "blunting potential criticism." The NYA, he told one group, was an apolitical venture "based strictly upon American traditions."[12] Another audience was reminded that the agency was "Constructive, Beneficial, American."[13]

Similar themes manifested themselves through Johnson's congressional career, which began in 1937 with his election to the House of Representatives. A staunch New Deal Democrat, he believed that government must be an agent for helping the poor escape the ravages of depression, ignorance, and free market capitalism. This activism was allied to the same preference for work over relief that marked his political mentor. Once prosperity had returned in the 1940s, Johnson added to these ideals a commitment to equality of opportunity that would remain with him throughout his political career. This faith coexisted with a consistent aversion to "advanced" liberal positions that offended unnecessarily the values of key constituencies. Reflecting on the unhappy fate of his liberal ally Maury Maverick, whose aggressively progressive identity alienated his Texan constituency, Johnson opined, "There's nothing more useless than a dead liberal."[14] This set of convictions made President Johnson an implacable opponent of the guaranteed income movement that gathered strength after 1965.

The central objective of the War on Poverty, equalizing life chances, had little immediate relevance to New Dealers confronting the massive social and economic dislocation of the 1930s. Toward the end of that decade, and throughout the war years, policymakers across the political spectrum turned their attention to the long-term problems of American capitalism. Johnson contributed to this debate in January 1944, the same month that the president commended an Economic Bill of Rights to the nation. Like Roosevelt, Johnson responded to the failings of the free market by highlighting the need for more government. Addressing the Texas legislature, he outlined a philosophy of government that would continue to animate him two decades later: "I want to substitute for free enterprise *equal opportunity*. Every man who has gone through a living Hell for you and for me, and comes out with scars on his body and his soul to show for it, shall have an equal opportunity to get a job when this is over."[15] Were local communities and the private sector unable or unwilling to deliver such equality, Johnson announced, he expected "to vote for whatever legislation is necessary to let the Federal Government do it. If that be enlarging the power of the Federal Government, and if that be centralizing more power in Washington, make the most of it."[16]

At the NYA, Johnson once boasted that his agency had "touched the lives of over 30,000 youngsters" but "didn't give them one red cent they didn't work for and earn for themselves."[17] His vision of a new range of federal stimulants to self-advancement a decade or so later attested to the same aversion to "doles." Those who worked with Johnson during the 1960s were struck (and frequently frustrated) by the remarkable tenacity of his liberal individualist faith. James C. Gaither, a White House assistant to Johnson, remarks upon his lifelong faith in education and the "log cabin" myth:

I think there's one basic philosophical strain that's seen through almost everything that the President has done . . . and that is a very deep conviction that everybody in this society should be given a full and complete chance to make his own way. . . . I have never sensed any great interest on his part in the welfare program or any other that is a basic subsidy kind of approach. He feels that if you let people start off on an equal footing . . . then this society will get along all right and we won't have poverty; people will pull themselves up.[18]

Other colleagues agree that Johnson never lost his deep and instinctive hostility to "welfarism." Robert Lampman, an economist who advised both the Kennedy and Johnson administrations, recalls that Johnson was always "very hostile" to the notion of a guaranteed income.[19] And Charles Schultze, head of Johnson's budget bureau, believes that "it is clear he sincerely, deeply, fundamentally believed in . . . the basic concept of providing opportunities. Or, put another way . . . he is all for doing a lot of things for the deserving poor."[20]

THE ECONOMIC OPPORTUNITY ACT OF 1964

The rise of the welfare problem during the 1950s, and the simultaneous emergence of rehabilitation as its solution, are familiar from the last chapter. By 1964 rehabilitation was just one part of a vaunted "knowledge revolution" whose cumulative effect was to persuade liberal policymakers that poverty and dependency could be solved without adversely affecting the economic interests of the more affluent. Each of the Economic Opportunity Act's six titles reaffirmed the central and traditional objective of extending opportunities for individual initiative. (Johnson instructed a young economic adviser, Lester Thurow, to comb the text of the bill and remove any portion that could be viewed as a cash support program. Similarly, Bill Moyers, a key domestic aide until 1966, was ordered: "You tell Shriver, no doles."[21]) Its opening "Declaration of Purpose" announced that the War on Poverty aimed "to eliminate the paradox of poverty in the midst of plenty" by "opening to everyone the opportunity for education and training, the opportunity to work, and the opportunity to live in decency and dignity."[22] The commitment to eliminate poverty was dramatic and new, but the rights of the poor were to opportunities, not outcomes.

The two most important programs were the Job Corps and the Community Action Program. The first (Title I of the Act) was intended to "increase the employability of youths aged from sixteen through twenty-one by providing them in residential centers with education, vocational training [and] useful work experience."[23] President Johnson told Congress that the Job Corps would recruit youths "whose background, health and education" made them "least fit for useful work.[24] By implication, even the most hardened juvenile delinquent could be brought within the opportunity structure of the affluent society. Senator Hubert H. Humphrey (D-Minn.), soon to become Johnson's vice president, celebrated "an opportunity to break the chain of self-perpetuating defeats and failure, and substitute in their place the unique experience of accomplishment and self-fulfillment."[25]

The Community Action Program (Title II) was designed "to provide stimulation and incentive for urban and rural communities to mobilize their resources . . . to combat poverty." The proposed Office of Economic Opportunity would award "special consideration to programs which give promise of effecting a permanent increase in the capacity of individuals, groups, and communities to deal with their problems without further assistance."[26] Strong emphasis was placed on the need for local solutions to local problems—a sharp contrast with the subsequent liberal judgment that poverty was a national problem that must be tackled at a national level. Title II also included a small Adult Education Program whose purpose was to reduce illiteracy, thus making its beneficiaries "less likely to become dependent on others."[27]

The remaining titles of the Economic Opportunity Act established projects for rural areas (Title III), small business loans (Title IV), and a work experience program for welfare recipients (Title V). Senator Humphrey believed that Title III would assist those who in the past had "found their way to the cities, only to become misfits and new entries on the welfare rolls." Similarly, he viewed Title V as "an effort to break the pattern of poverty by fighting family disintegration and abandonment of children, and by promoting the ability and habit of self-support in those who need it so desperately."[28] Later in the decade, the dominant strain of American liberalism regarded self-support as an excuse for denying dependents their basic rights, but in 1964 it seemed axiomatic that declining dependency would provide an indication of success in the war against poverty. The omission of any income-maintenance proposal reflected widespread faith in the service strategy as well as a strong element of political opportunism.

SOURCES OF LIBERAL ACTIVISM

If liberal adherence to self-help and equal opportunity owed much to inherited intellectual and political traditions, then the remarkable enthusiasm with which the individualistic orthodoxy was espoused during the early 1960s reflected economic prosperity and the intoxicating spirit of President Kennedy's New Frontier.

The dramatic shift from the noninterventionist governmental philosophy of the Eisenhower years to the activist approach of the New Frontiersmen was epitomized by the New Economics, and in particular by the tax cut of February 1964. The affluence of the postwar period had, until 1960, been tarnished by regular recessions (three during the 1950s) and by persistently high unemployment, but President Eisenhower's economic messages typically featured strong attacks on "constant stirring or meddling" in the economy.[29] During the 1960s, however, a preoccupation with balancing the federal budget was replaced by the Keynesian conviction that government could and should "fine tune" the economy so as to eliminate the tiresome pattern of "boom and bust." President Kennedy's proposal to cut taxes by $11.5 billion would, it was believed, produce accelerated and noninflationary economic growth, despite a significant budget deficit and rising federal expenditure.

The New Frontier's faith in Keynesian techniques of fiscal management both reflected and encouraged a growing spirit of social activism. Walter Heller later recalled that the importance of the tax reduction lay in the stimulation of "a better economic setting for financing a more generous program of federal expenditures."[30] Another Johnson administration economist, Henry Aaron, contends that poverty had previously been "considered to be largely outside the proper realm of public policy"; however, with the advent of New Frontier-Great Society liberalism, "the view that solutions . . . were the proper business of government gained currency and temporarily became dominant."[31]

New economic techniques could create conditions in which the elimination of poverty became a feasible objective, but President Johnson warned that "we cannot leave the further wearing away of poverty solely to the general progress of the economy."[32] This view was shared by the Senate Labor and Public Welfare Committee. "We will certainly continue to enjoy economic growth and an increase in our general well-being," the committee predicted, but inattention to the residual problem of poverty "would condemn substantial millions of our citizens to continue leading a life of deprivation and dependency for decades to come."[33]

36

The conviction that continued economic expansion would not eliminate deprivation stemmed largely from an uncomfortably high rate of unemployment (5.5 percent in January 1964),[34] much of which had a structural rather than a cyclical character. Unemployment had preceded poverty as a matter of public concern and, although the two problems were far from identical, it seemed clear that any federal attack on poverty must confront the causes of unemployment. This was an insight of considerable significance, for simply providing the victims of structural unemployment with income support would not enhance their capacity to meet the changing requirements of the labor market. If, however, the long-term unemployed could be equipped with the relevant skills and motivation, then a dynamic economy could offer them opportunities for self-advancement—a far more American concept than public assistance. The more direct approach would have been a public employment program. Adam Yarmolinsky, a member of the antipoverty task force, explains that both conviction and cost underpinned the decision to concentrate on "preparing people for jobs" rather than on "finding jobs for people."[35]

While the basic dynamic for the War on Poverty was the boundless optimism of its liberal sponsors, concern about persistent joblessness also played its part.[36] Reference to the antipoverty debate of 1964 reveals widespread fears surrounding the problem of automation, a phenomenon that seemed to reduce opportunities for the poor even as the majority population enjoyed unprecedented affluence. The celebrated Swedish social scientist Gunnar Myrdal spoke of an emergent "underclass," contending that "something like a caste line is drawn between the people in the urban and rural slums, and the majority of Americans who live in a virtual full-employment economy."[37]

This theme was taken up with enthusiasm by both conservative and liberal supporters of the Economic Opportunity Act. More than one seemed to echo the sensibilities of the Progressive Era, on the one hand raising anxieties about a closing frontier and on the other assuming that new knowledge could be used to open up fresh opportunity. Congressman Phil Landrum (D-Ga.), for example, recalled that during his youth it had been possible to deal with poverty on "an individual or small group basis." Now, however, "the frontiers such as existed for our forbears and for us as young men simply do not exist any more."[38] Senator Ralph Yarborough, a Texas liberal, echoed his conservative colleague, recalling "the early days when the will to work and a strong back, or a fertile imagination and a great deal of energy, were all that one needed to get ahead." Both remained optimistic that the ideal of equal opportunity could again be realized, but only if America provided education and training to complement the traditional national virtues of "energy and imagination."[39] Sargent Shriver, the president's choice to head the proposed federal antipoverty agency, adopted a similar line:

> Certainly, in the early days of our country . . . "America, the land of opportunity" was really true, I guess, for nearly everybody in it. But there are some people, sad to say, today, who are caught and they can't get out. They are flat on their backs. They don't have the capital to move. They have responsibilities where they are. It is for these people that we are trying to open up exits.[40]

In retrospect, these fears seem overstated. The following five years saw a remarkable decline in unemployment, despite the expanding labor force, and Allen Matusow observes that attempts to combat automation represented a "cure for a disease that did not exist."[41] Nevertheless, the "automation problem" was a broad concern in 1964—Congressman James Roosevelt (D-Cal.) went so far as to speak of "industrial dust bowls"[42]—and provided important justification for the War on Poverty.

This theme of a jobless underclass highlighted the shortcomings of public policy in the United States, but few liberals doubted that ready solutions lay at hand. The conviction that America's poor could be rehabilitated despite automation and structural unemployment owed much to one archetypal New Frontier theme, namely the knowledge revolution. At an early meeting with his economic *troika*, Lyndon Johnson unveiled his faith that "any problem could be solved."[43] Within a short period of time, such confidence would seem utterly facile, but in 1964 it was widely shared, underpinning the Vietnam War and the Apollo project, as well as the War on Poverty.[44] Senator Humphrey celebrated the intoxicating new "discovery" that, once identified, any problem had a solution. In his 1964 book, *War on Poverty*, the future vice president reported the view of former Assistant Secretary for Defense John H. Rubell that "the new knowledge can literally solve any problem if there is what he calls the 'social need.'" Humphrey believed that "only if we wait passively for the future to come will we be its victims rather than its masters. . . . For no matter how complex the world might be, it is still *our* world, and its complexity is in great part *our* creation."[45] In a remarkable article in *Public Interest*, Daniel Patrick Moynihan celebrated the imminent victory over poverty: "The prospect that the more primitive social issues of American politics are at last to be resolved need only mean that we may now turn to issues more demanding of human ingenuity than that of how to put an end to poverty in the richest nation in the world."[46]

The War on Poverty, then, was a war born of optimism. Abundance created the conditions in which a successful campaign might be launched, while new knowledge encouraged the belief that the causes—and not merely the consequences—could be eliminated. The apparent political genius of the Economic Opportunity Act lay in its congruence with the individualist ethos. The War on Poverty promised a hand up, not a handout. Whereas the liberals of the late 1960s and early 1970s identified an unqualified entitlement to income that was wholly at odds with the social philosophy they had inherited, the 1964 position constituted a celebration of American values and a reaffirmation of the nation's belief in equality of opportunity.

POVERTY AND DEPENDENCY

So strong was the bipartisan national commitment to the American creed of equal opportunity in 1964 that many liberal commentators defined poverty as the absence of such opportunity rather than the presence of material hardship. Congressman Richard T. Hanna (D-Calif.) told the House of Representatives that "poverty is only incidentally a condition of low income," observing that it was possible to be materially deprived but not impoverished. "The poverty we are here addressing ourselves to is the impoverishment of opportunity."[47] Walter P. Reuther, the fiery leader of the United Auto Workers, addressed Adam Clayton Powell's War on Poverty subcommittee in similar terms. He feared that, while the United States was "more richly blessed than any country in the world," that poverty which remained constituted "a much more serious problem than the poverty of Africa in terms of what it does to the persons involved."[48]

The key here was the absence of any sense of participation or dignity, and the essence of opportunity was access to the economic system which had allowed other Americans to fulfill their individual potential. The Republican minority's response to President Johnson's 1964 Economic Report implicitly endorsed the philosophy of the War on Poverty, demanding that it "accentuate and extend the vast successes of our system in order to realize the promise of the free and open society for all our people."[49] The confidence with which legislators across the political spectrum insisted on the attainability of equal opportunity reveals an optimism that, in subsequent years, came to be seen as naive in the extreme; liberals debating welfare reform in 1969 and 1970 were openly scornful of the notion that rehabilitation could be facilitated in the absence of a comprehensive income-maintenance approach.

In 1964 the notion of income redistribution exerted little appeal. The War on Poverty recognized that everyone was born equal, but this did not confer an entitlement to an equal reward but rather to an equal opportunity to fulfill individual potential. Redistribution was the antithesis of this creed, decried by Congressman Hanna as "an immoral exercise of taking from the rich and giving to the poor in a vain attempt to equalize."[50]

Whereas liberal legislators of the late 1960s were to find it difficult to hold any of the poor responsible for their condition, their position in 1964 was less determined by fears of blaming the victim. Essentially, the traditional distinction between the deserving and the undeserving poor was still seen as valid. Once the Economic Opportunity Act had provided the necessary tools for self-advancement, the structure of the national economy would permit the deserving poor to prosper. (Later liberals protested that such tools could not be provided and that, in any case, the nation's economic system was fundamentally flawed.) Senator Humphrey acknowledged that "there will be a few loafers and freeloaders—there always are,"[51] while his colleague Warren Magnuson (D-Wash.) regretted that "there are some people who do not possess either the will or desire to lift themselves out of poverty, even when given a better opportunity."[52]

Such rhetoric might seem vacuous, formulaic, and anodyne, but the historian should not discount it on this basis. It is precisely the ritualistic quality of these bromides about opportunity and self-help that demonstrates the political sensitivity of the average liberal Democrat, circa 1964. The abandonment of this lexicon toward the end of the decade may have been intellectually refreshing, but in political terms nothing could compensate for the loss of the ability to articulate the deeply held faith of key Democratic constituencies.

The corollary of the equal opportunity creed was a uniform aversion to welfare dependency. Here again, the opportunities for identifying American liberalism with popular values were boundless. President Johnson was eager to tap antiwelfare feeling, which, in any case, he shared. In language reminiscent of Franklin Roosevelt's rhetoric in 1935, Johnson rejected the notion of doles:

> This [measure] is not in any sense a cynical proposal to exploit the poor with a promise of a handout or a dole. We know—we learned long ago—that answer is no answer. . . . [T]he purpose of the Economic Opportunity Act of 1964 is to

offer opportunity, not an opiate. . . . We are not content to accept the endless growth of relief rolls or welfare rolls.[53]

To extend an assured income to a group or individual that realistically could take advantage of the tools Johnson sought to supply would be to stifle the essential genius of the individualist tradition. Charity seemed a terribly patronizing and defeatist response to material deprivation, and no response at all to the spiritual malaise that beset the American poor. William Ryan (D-N.Y.), one of the most outspoken liberals in the House of Representatives and in 1968 sponsor of the first ever guaranteed income bill, had no doubts about the debilitating effects of welfare:

> Public assistance is necessary for those who have no place else to turn. But it provides subsistence only. It deadens the spirit. It provides no encouragement, no incentive, no room for growth. [Training] . . . will give new hope to those who are desperately poor, encouraging them to develop the skills that will enable them to make their own way in our increasingly complex society.[54]

Among supporters of the Economic Opportunity Act, antipathy to the specter of dependency was as uniform as it was familiar. It may only have been two years since the federal government had last promised to reorient the Aid to Dependent Children program in the direction of rehabilitation and prevention, but in 1964 President Johnson was allowed to present the tired, old "opportunities, not doles" theme as a refreshing break with the past. Similarly, when Secretary for Health, Education and Welfare Anthony Celebrezze enthusiastically predicted, "Welfare costs can go down if our theories are right," no one observed that Abraham Ribicoff had made exactly the same pledge in 1962, and to the same body.[55] As with President Clinton's proposed Work and Responsibility Act of 1994, the shortness of the nation's collective political memory, together with the evergreen appeal of the anti-dependency issue, concealed the familiarity of his message.

A number of books published in the early 1960s attested anew to a widespread national faith that income support was more a manifestation of the poverty problem than a means to its resolution. In 1960 Julius Horwitz, a welfare consultant to the State of New York, published *The Inhabitants,* a novel that features strikingly unnuanced depictions of the degradation associated with dependency. In one of many melodramatic episodes, a social worker (the narrator) warns a prospective client of the dangers of relief, prophesying, "You'll be a dog in six months on welfare." Responding to the client's suggestion that she might claim relief "just to get started," while she looks for work, the caseworker elaborates his earlier claim: "'Look,' I told her, 'I've seen second-generation mothers like you on welfare. The mother is on welfare, the daughter grows up on welfare, then she gets a baby and she graduates to her own separate case. If you don't apply now, then maybe you can beat it.'"56

For the War on Poverty's more conservative supporters, the Aid to Families with Dependent Children program (ADC had been rechristened in 1962) was a major irritant, and the 1964 Act's cosponsor Phil Landrum promised not to "add another layer of icing on an already heavily coated welfare cake."57 Although the implication that America's public assistance program was excessively generous was arguable, this popularly held conviction was nevertheless extremely useful to the Economic Opportunity Act's liberal advocates.58 Most, it is true, appeared anxious to avoid the ugly stereotypes that characterized popular attitudes about the dependent poor: for Congressman Ryan and such senators as Jacob Javits (R-N.Y.), and Pat McNamara (D-Mich.), AFDC was a necessary but cumbersome device that failed to match the promise of American ideals. Yet such advocates were acutely conscious of the political risk of being too closely associated with unpopular welfare programs. Presumably for this reason, a recent and sensation-seeking investigation by Senator Robert Byrd (D-W.Va.) into welfare fraud in the District of Columbia had elicited the enthusiastic support of Hubert Humphrey.59

As with partisans of social security during the 1940s, some members of the Johnson administration were prepared to risk fueling antiwelfare sentiment in order to advance their political ends. In February of 1964, for example, Daniel Patrick Moynihan—now working for Secretary Willard Wirtz in the Department of Labor—made a speech in which, according to the *Washington Post,* he accused welfare of "rotting the poor," especially poor blacks. A prominent social welfare activist complained that such remarks seemed almost calculated to reignite the destructive flames of Newburgh. A defiant Moynihan told his boss that he did not recall having made the offending remark, and that, in fact, he fully accepted the indispensability of welfare programs. However, he did take the opportunity to alert Wirtz to the favorable response his alleged comments had elicited from the Republican right. Thomas Curtis, a highly conservative Senator from Nevada, reproduced the *Post* article in the *Congressional Record* and pronounced himself "delighted to hear so responsible and well-informed a view from a high-ranking official of the Johnson administration." Moynihan professed himself "embarrassed" by the article, but nevertheless suggested to Wirtz that "we should take advantage of the reaction from Curtis and others."60

In the congressional debate of 1964, Senator McNamara, who had little ideological affinity with his cosponsor, Congressman Landrum, nevertheless echoed the Georgian's anxiety about the alarming cost of this unloved program, solemnly warning colleagues that "the visible cost of not adopting this program, in terms of direct public assistance payments alone, is $5 billion per year."[61] Congressman Roman Pucinski (D-Ill.) went considerably further, asking, "Is there a member in this House who does not have in his congressional district, local, township, county, or State, governments whose resources are not taxed beyond all ability because of the rising cost of public relief?"[62]

Faced with arguments such as this, opponents of the War on Poverty struggled in their bid to label it another Democratic handout. Their task was made still more difficult by the way in which supporters of the War on Poverty identified their cause with national pride. Congressman Sam Gibbons (D-Fla.) exploited the patriotism card to the full: "There is a great national purpose to this legislation, that we raise up every American not by a handout, not by a giveaway, not by any magic hocus-pocus, but by the same fine American principles that have supported this country."[63]

The same buoyant pride in America recurs time and again in the antipoverty debate of 1964. For Senator William J. Fulbright, it was "a tribute to our democracy that in a time of relative prosperity the Senate should now be considering legislation to strike at the roots of poverty."[64] Administration officials testifying on behalf of the bill were predictably quick to wrap themselves in the flag. Secretary of Labor Willard Wirtz told Adam Clayton Powell's antipoverty subcommittee of the "warmth, satisfaction, and . . . pride" he felt when he considered America's standing in the world. He went on to insist that the War on Poverty must respect "the individualist ethic in this country."[65] It is not necessary to take all this rhetoric at face value in order to appreciate its political function.

EXTERNAL SOURCES OF THE WAR ON POVERTY

In 1961 the newly elected president, John F. Kennedy, stated, "Before my term is ended, we shall have to test anew whether a nation organized and governed such as ours can endure. The outcome is by no means certain."[66] Cold War tensions added a note of menace and urgency to the dominant mood of patriotism and self-congratulation. Their contribution to the decision to declare war on poverty should not be understated. In 1960, when President

Eisenhower's Commission on National Goals issued its report, *Goals for Americans,* the problem of poverty only appeared once, and the context was the nation's need to demonstrate to the Third World the superiority of American individualism. The report insisted that "every American is summoned to extraordinary personal responsibility, sustained effort, and sacrifice." America was imperiled by dictators "for whom the state is everything, the individual significant only as he serves the state." Among the greatest dangers was "the specious appeal of Communist doctrine to peoples eager for rapid escape from poverty."[67] Four years later, Congressman Edward Patten (D-N.J.), a supporter of the Economic Opportunity Act, warned that poverty "darkens America's image throughout the world."[68] Congressman Hugh Carey (D-N.Y.), fearing the sheer numbers of the Communist enemy, observed, "[To] contend with that giant we have to develop every young American to carry his share of the burden of freedom."[69] Winning the war against domestic poverty, therefore, was a matter of national security. Adam Yarmolinsky, a leading member of the antipoverty task force whose background was in defense, felt that even the conquest of poverty at home would not be sufficient. He envisioned a still broader Great Society agenda, featuring the "rebuilding of cities, not only in the United States but throughout the world."[70]

By the end of the decade, the idea that the "victims" of American society had any duties at all was deeply distasteful to many liberal Democrats. The notion that such obligations had an international context was positively obscene, given the emotions of shame and guilt that America's commitments in Southeast Asia then inspired. Far from seeking to sell the virtues of rugged individualism abroad, such liberals were beginning to reexamine their own support for outmoded assumptions and look to more social democratic nations for guidance on public policy. In 1964, however, America's global mission was perceived by liberals as a noble one, and in such a context the War on Poverty was, in the words of Congressman Charles Weltner (D-Ga.), "a challenge worthy of the finest minds and most dedicated spirits."[71]

RACE AND THE WAR ON POVERTY

According to some scholars, the principal threat to which the War on Poverty represented a response was neither Cold War anxiety nor automation but racial imperatives.[72] Allen Matusow provides one version of this argument: "The government did not undertake a War on Poverty because Michael Harrington wrote a book. A constituency both aggrieved and vocal had first to demand it. In the spring of 1963 the civil rights movement took a mass dimension, creating that constituency overnight."[73]

These scholars are right to argue that the struggle for racial equality played a critical role in creating and shaping the liberal reformist spirit of the 1960s.[74] Furthermore, influential black leaders within the liberal coalition insisted from an early stage that theirs was a struggle for economic as well as legal equality. The 1963 March for Jobs and Freedom in Washington, and the pronouncements of such civil rights leaders as the Reverend Martin Luther King, Jr., and Whitney M. Young, Jr., acted as a reminder to white America that more was at stake than the collapse of the segregationist South.[75]

Nevertheless, the available evidence suggests that white liberals remained insensitive to the economic plight of black America during the planning phases of the War on Poverty. President Johnson's Secretary of Labor, Willard Wirtz, observed that "for most Americans the strongest visual image of poverty is that of the miners and hill-folk of Eastern Kentucky and West Virginia."[76] Reference to the media reports of the time tends to confirm this analysis: organs ranging from *Newsweek* to *Look* were replete with investigations into the "invisible poverty" of whites in Appalachia. And Homer Bigart's series for the *New York Times* on the desperate conditions to be found in Eastern Kentucky generated considerable interest within the Kennedy Administration.[77] The papers of such key domestic policymakers as Theodore Sorensen and Walter Heller suggest that it was this type of poverty that provided the initial political rationale for the program. A month before Kennedy's assassination, Heller justified the proposed initiative on the grounds that disadvantaged groups "other than Negroes" deserved help.[78]

The War on Poverty would come to be viewed by liberals as an arm of the civil rights struggle, but in 1964 this was manifestly not the case. Committed individualists in a time of great optimism, they favored the color-blind approach that both philosophical conviction and political expediency demanded. Robert Kennedy addressed the economic needs of the ghetto in passionate and urgent tones but emphasized that his concern went "far beyond the question of civil rights." Observing that blacks comprised only a minority of the poor population, he stressed that "we are equally interested . . . in all the people in this nation who live without opportunity."[79] In an address before the NAACP, Sargent Shriver reminded his audience, "Eighty percent of the poor people in America are white."[80]

45

Participants in the presidential task force that drew up the Economic Opportunity Act of 1964 confirm that race was not uppermost in their minds. Daniel Patrick Moynihan recalls that "at this time the American poor, black and white, were surpassingly inert."[81] Adam Yarmolinsky concurs, remarking that in 1964 "the whole problem of the northern ghetto was still not seen in anything like its full depth and complexity."[82] Some black leaders were beginning to argue that African-Americans deserved special treatment because of a legacy of racism, but this claim was explicitly and repeatedly repudiated by white liberals. Even so fervent a campaigner for civil rights as Gunnar Myrdal warned that "this demand for a discrimination in reverse, i.e., to the advantage of the Negroes, is misdirected."[83] Black leaders, too, were cautious about advocating a course of racial preference, having historically associated the concept with white supremacy.[84]

Politically, the War on Poverty did have an important racial dimension, but it did not center on any incipient or actual ghetto revolt or the need to avert civil disorder. Rather, it centered on the need to *avoid* associating the issues of poverty and racial disadvantage in the public mind. This need had both a national and a sectional context. In national terms, the political value of the Appalachian "poster child" was well understood: a war on black poverty would struggle to gain the same degree of public enthusiasm.[85] Still more important, a racial dimension was injected into the antipoverty debate by Southern anxiety that federal insistence on racially mixed Community Action Programs and Job Corp camps would hasten the demise of segregation. Howard "Judge" Smith, the crusty and reactionary Virginian who presided over the powerful House Rules Committee, issued the following warning: "I want to say to the Members from the South who are going to vote for this bill—and I know that there are a lot of them—that they are voting to implement the civil rights bill that they opposed and voted against."[86]

Smith's offensive was a worrying and dangerous one, given that Republican opposition to Johnson's election-year program made the support of Southern Democrats for the Economic Opportunity Act critical. Congressman Jack Flynt (D-Ga.) told one administration official of distressing GOP charges in his district to the effect that the proposed legislation was "another device to foster racial integration without real regard for poverty."[87] In a similar vein, Congressman John McMillan of South Carolina wrote to Johnson explaining that, despite his sympathy with the bill's objectives, he felt constrained to oppose it because of Goldwaterite sentiment in his district.[88]

Ultimately, however, as many as sixty Southern Democratic congressmen were to support the Economic Opportunity Act. Some, such as Charles Weltner (D-Ga.) of Atlanta and Sam Gibbons (D-Fla.) of Tampa, represented a new, urban and moderate South, and sought to build new voting coalitions that included newly enfranchised blacks. Many more were influenced by the weighty sponsorship of Phil Landrum, who was attracted by the opportunity approach and remained a loyal supporter of the program. Landrum's impregnable electoral base made him invulnerable to attack from the likes of Judge Smith or Barry Goldwater. Moreover, he had since the 1950s been vilified by liberals on account of his sponsorship of the anti-labor Griffin-Landrum Act, and thus held impeccable conservative credentials. President Johnson's success in persuading Landrum to shepherd the Economic Opportunity Act through the House of Representatives significantly increased the credibility of the legislation with the right.

It is understandable that scholars preoccupied with the catastrophic ghetto violence of the "long, hot summers" should seek racial explanations for a War on Poverty that came to be viewed largely as a response to black discontent. But neither archival sources, the public record, nor the recollections of the antipoverty warriors support the contention that the Economic Opportunity Act was prompted by racial exigencies. To the contrary, the authors of the Economic Opportunity Act explicitly repudiated notions of racial targeting in favor of a highly optimistic social philosophy predicated on the notion that all the poor needed was individual opportunity.

OPPORTUNISM OR CONVICTION?

To date it has been argued that opportunism combined with a powerful strain of authentic optimism in the antipoverty debate of 1964. This is not to say, however, that the liberal community, either within or without the government, was uniformly satisfied with the Economic Opportunity Act. A number of prominent intellectuals were troubled by the changing role of work in modern society and felt that Johnson had not adequately confronted the challenge of automation. In 1964 they combined to form the Ad Hoc Committee on the Triple Revolution. This short-lived but much-publicized body, founded by the British economist Robert Theobald, included such luminaries as Michael Harrington (whose 1962 book, *The Other America*, had done much to focus political attention on the problem of poverty), Gunnar Myrdal, the civil rights leader Bayard Rustin, and Irving Howe of *Dissent* magazine. Contending that "the traditional link between jobs and incomes" was "being broken," the committee argued that society must respond by making "an unqualified commitment" to provide "every individual and every family with an adequate income as a matter of right."[89] One signatory, the political scientist Michael Reagan, warned that while "it may be easy to scoff at the A.H.C. proposals," such a response would reflect a destructive unwillingness to "face up to the problem of automation."[90]

Doubts about the philosophical basis upon which war had been declared were not confined to the intellectual community. Walter Reuther, of the United Auto Workers (UAW), attacked the myth that poverty could be defined in absolute terms and that, by inference, the poor could attain economic security without the redistribution of income. Reuther conceded that maldistribution of wealth was a "painful" issue to confront but told Adam Clayton Powell that he intended "to keep talking about it, because someday this country will wake up to the real test of the twentieth century."[91] Similarly, Ernest Hollander, of the Americans for Democratic Action (ADA), reminded legislators that, regardless of the merits of the "culture of poverty" argument, "the poor are poor . . . because they have too little money, and whatever else is done they will remain poor until they have enough."[92] The National Social Welfare Assembly was anxious to dispel the attractive yet ultimately unrealistic notion that the War on Poverty would obviate public assistance. It warned the Senate Committee on Labor and Public Welfare that "the public must not be led to expect that [the Economic Opportunity Act] will reach all poor people or that it will solve the problem of poverty."[93] In a Cincinnati speech, the assembly's leading political lobbyist Elizabeth Wickenden urged, "We must master our mistrust of government as an instrument of common welfare." Bluntly expressing sentiments that were rarely heard in 1964, she stated, "We are all too confused and frightened by a bogey we call the 'welfare state,' [a] term of pride in most parts of the world but one which sends respectable politicians scurrying for cover here at home. . . . Let us never forget that the basic answer to poverty is income and for millions of our fellow-citizens income means social security, pensions, and [public] assistance."[94]

A certain skepticism in some quarters about American myths, and doubts about the practicality of the administration's ostensible objectives, do not justify the contention that the Economic Opportunity Program evaded a "real" war on poverty because of political considerations. It is significant that many of those who detected flaws in the 1964 Act shared the conviction that poverty was a complex and partly cultural condition, impervious to an unadorned income strategy. This formulation had little in common with the subsequent liberal belief that the poor were separated from the mainstream solely by their lack of money. The ADA and the UAW evidenced more than a hint of confusion in their critiques of the War on Poverty. Even as Reuther urged Congress to recognize that a principal goal of any such "war" must be "to assure incomes to provide an adequate living . . . for all Americans," he characterized "social and spiritual impoverishment" as "the most difficult and deep-seated aspect of the problem," and expressed the fear that many of today's poor were "permanent wards of the welfare state."[95] Similarly, while emphasizing the need for income redistribution, the UAW urged Johnson not to treat poverty symptomatically. At its Atlantic City convention, the union adopted a highly orthodox resolution: "The nation's war against poverty must focus mainly on eradicating its causes and not on relief for its symptoms. Obviously, the poor need immediate assistance and should receive it. But, above all, they need help in lifting themselves and their children out of poverty."[96]

At least two signatories to the Ad Hoc Committee's declaration, Michael Harrington and Gunnar Myrdal, shared views on poverty that owed far more to the prevailing liberal orthodoxy than to Robert Theobald's proposed entitlement revolution. In *The Other America*, Harrington flatly rejects the notion that poverty can be defined in strictly economic terms:

> There is, in a sense, a personality of poverty, a type of human being produced by the grinding, wearing life of the slums. The other Americans feel differently than the rest of the nation. They tend to be hopeless and passive, yet prone to bursts of violence; they are lonely and isolated, often rigid and hostile. To be poor is not simply to be deprived of the material things of this world. It is to enter a fatal, futile universe, an America within America, with a twisted spirit.[97]

Harrington was convinced that, in addition to income-based measurements, "poverty should be defined psychologically in terms of those whose place in the society is such that they are internal exiles who, almost inevitably, develop attitudes of defeat and pessimism and who are therefore excluded from taking advantage of new opportunities."[98]

Myrdal, in approving the thesis of the Ad Hoc Committee, seemingly endorsed the principle of income entitlement. But in *Challenge to Affluence* he provides a ringing defense of the traditional work ethic, emphasizing "how unhealthy and destructive it is for anybody . . . to go idle and live more or less permanently on doles." Work, he continues, is "the basis for self-respect and a dignified life."[99]

But even if members of the Ad Hoc Committee *had* possessed a distinct and coherent alternative to the prevailing orthodoxy, it would still be a mistake to accord much significance to their views. After all, most commentators who worried about the consequences of automation in 1964, far from advocating entitlement, viewed economic modernization as justification for opportunity-based liberalism. Theobald's views had little impact on the antipoverty debate, despite efforts by one Republican to associate the national Democratic Party with the Ad Hoc Committee.[100]

Even the Economic Opportunity Act's more radical critics appear to have shared Johnson's basic conviction that curing poverty implied something more than simply cash support. Indeed, the most radical voices in the debate belonged to the strongest supporters of the opportunity theory, such as David Hackett and Richard Boone, who had worked for President Kennedy's juvenile delinquency committee and developed a crusading faith in the empowering potential of community action.[101] Matusow observes that even Hackett and Robert Kennedy had no interest in the redistribution of income.[102] The key to eliminating poverty lay instead in transforming individual opportunity through community development. In terms of entitlement, the almost universal convictions that deprivation was in part a spiritual condition, and that America should confront its sources, rather than simply ameliorate its consequences, excluded the guaranteed income solution. Government's obligation was not to identify new rights for the poor but to give relevance to those rights which, in principle, they already shared with the rest of the population.

But if few dissented from the objectives and principles of the War on Poverty, it remains the case that the vigor with which the "bootstraps" message and the colorblind orthodoxy were sold owed much to political opportunism. In private, some key administration officials nourished significant doubts about the likely impact of the Economic Opportunity Act. Willard Wirtz warned that unless the proposed legislation were amended to include public works programs it would "be very weak on employment-creating measures, and the war on poverty will simply not appear as big as it can and should."[103] Daniel Patrick Moynihan favored greater recognition of the unique character of black poverty.[104] Even Sargent Shriver shared private qualms about the program with Whitney Young, Jr., of the National Urban League, who felt moved on one occasion to commend him for his aplomb at defending the War on Poverty in public.[105] Wilbur Cohen, assistant secretary at HEW, was particularly blunt when he shared with Theodore Sorensen his fear that "the anti-poverty bill has been all messed up."[106]

But the role that political opportunism played in generating the extravagant promises that Johnson and others made on behalf of the Economic Opportunity Act in no way diminishes the fact that its self-help orientation and service strategy were widely supported. Whatever flaws administration figures may have found in the 1964 legislation, it is clear that the general backdrop of new knowledge, liberal self-confidence, and economic abundance generated a genuine faith in the administration's capacity to reduce poverty, and to do so without resorting to divisive income redistribution schemes. Wirtz, Moynihan, and Cohen each had bureaucratic and institutional reasons for opposing legislation that centered the drive against poverty in a new, rival agency, the Office of Economic Opportunity.[107] By contrast, none had any philosophical quarrel with rehabilitation, although organized labor preferred a new job creation initiative.[108] Wilbur Cohen, for example, had been a devotee of the rehabilitative principle for a decade, and doubted the value of income redistribution as an antipoverty strategy.[109] Willard Wirtz, too, was a strong supporter of vocational education and retraining initiatives, provided they were administered by his department.

The findings of a confidential 1964 task force on income maintenance highlight the genuine strength of the antidependency impulse. Task force members were told by Charles Schultze, director of the Bureau of the Budget, that they "should not be bound by what seems immediately practicable," but rather "should look ahead to 1975 or 1980."[110] But despite this invitation to boldness, the task force's report and its preceding deliberations revealed few breaks with tradition or the public orthodoxy of the Johnson administration. In a discussion paper entitled "Criteria for Income Maintenance Programs," Arthur Smithies, professor of political economy at Harvard University, observed that the redistribution of $11 billion per year would bring all poor families above the poverty line, but he unequivocally denied that this would solve the problem: "If we believed that such an annual expenditure could be a permanent cure for poverty, we would unhesitatingly recommend it. But we do not believe that a policy of that kind would be workable. We have little doubt that a government guarantee against poverty of this kind would expand the welfare rolls to an intolerable extent."[111] For Smithies, the "fundamental cures for poverty" lay "outside the field of cash income support." Nevertheless, he did not share HEW Secretary Anthony Celebrezze's view that "[if] we really get to the root causes of poverty and discrimination . . . many of our welfare programs would disappear."[112] To the contrary, Smithies and his colleagues felt that public assistance programs would remain an integral part of the safety net. The group's final report warned that "in any modern society many persons suffer from risks beyond their control which interrupt or destroy their opportunities to work, to earn, and thus to support themselves and their families."[113] Moreover, without income support programs, the War on Poverty's bid to rehabilitate the poor would come to little: as Smithies observed, "A hungry family is unlikely to take full advantage of its educational opportunities."[114]

Task force members, therefore, were concerned that the long-term indispensability of public assistance be acknowledged. Additionally, they were exercised by the wide discrepancies in benefit levels. The final report observed that "public assistance programs in many states still are inadequate and follow policies which do not protect the dignity and independence of individuals."[115] Nevertheless, both in tone and in substance, the findings of the group had far more in common with the self-help orientation of the Economic Opportunity Act than they did with the guaranteed income movement that was to take off within little more than a year. The task force report stressed the link between "productive work" and "economic security," spoke of the value of "thrift and self-reliance," and emphasized that "the preferable method of providing income security is through contributory social insurance."[116] Smithies found it "hard to believe that the availability of relief does not encourage a carefree attitude toward having or supporting children" and argued, "Eligibility standards must be tightened in order to avoid 'abuses.'"[117] Welfare experts, even in their private deliberations and recommendations, remained wedded to the core values that animated Lyndon Johnson's War on Poverty.

CONCLUSION

Political considerations alone would have provided reasons enough for the Johnson administration to reject the income strategy in favor of a program of rehabilitative services. The Economic Opportunity Act helped to place the new president's vision of a Great Society firmly within America's core individualist tradition, and further marginalized Barry Goldwater's inherently unattractive brand of extreme Republicanism. Additionally, it was an initially inexpensive program, consistent with Johnson's perceived political need to keep the federal budget below $100 billion while cutting taxes by $11.5 billion.

But the fact that the Economic Opportunity Act's social philosophy made political sense does not mean that its liberal supporters were merely engaged in some kind of cynical electoral gambit. Tactical considerations provide only a partial explanation for the philosophical orientation of the program. Liberals declined to define bold new conceptions of entitlement for the simple reason that they continued to uphold the very different New Deal tradition which they had inherited. If the president was sensitive to the political advantages of the antipoverty program, there can be no real doubt that his faith in education and opportunity, and his antipathy to "welfarism," were genuine.

The philosophical appeal of equal opportunity, liberal identification with a Cold War in which the furtherance of individualism was a patriotic duty, the incumbency of a president identified with the New Deal's work-oriented ethos, and—not least—the impact of affluence and the "knowledge revolution" on the prospects for success, all served to make the Economic Opportunity Act an attractive vehicle for traditional liberal ideals. In 1964, the paradox of poverty was not that deprivation existed (some would always spurn possibilities for self-advancement) but rather that millions of Americans were deprived of an equal opportunity in a nation historically committed to that ideal. In a war which sought to tap the buoyant optimism and idealism of the American people, the guaranteed income, far from representing the triumph of liberalism, would have been considered the ultimate admission of its defeat.

CHAPTER 3

Race and Poverty: Redefining Equality, 1964–1965

Of the various factors that enervated a seemingly entrenched tradition of liberal individualism after 1964, none was more powerful than race. Ghetto violence and a mounting white backlash injected urgency and rancor into a political debate over the extent and dynamics of black disadvantage that transformed perspectives on antipoverty strategy. From the outset, however, liberal optimism about race was far stronger within the executive branch of the federal government than it was elsewhere. Few big city politicians nourished many illusions about the profound difficulties presented by the black struggle for equality outside of the South. At an economic level, employment opportunities for low-skilled urban blacks had in many instances declined. Meanwhile, militant black activism was gaining both strength and profile: the Muslims preached a doctrine of separatist nationalism, parents agitated against de facto segregation in schools, and the Congress of Racial Equality (CORE) protested the hiring practices of Northern businesses.

Politically, these sundry sources of tension were manifested in mayoral elections: in 1963, both James H. Tate, of Philadelphia, and Richard M. Daley, of Chicago, having ceased to enjoy the confidence of a majority of whites, were reelected by black voters.[1] In Newark, Mayor Hugh Addonizio struggled to keep afloat a listing black-Italian coalition.[2] The housing issue was especially divisive; indeed, Chicago had for well over a decade been the scene of violent protests by white ethnic residents who resisted the penetration by black families into their neighborhoods.[3] President Kennedy's decision to delay issuing an executive order to bar discrimination in federally assisted housing until after the midterm elections of 1962 owed much to the discomfort of Northern pro–civil rights congressmen alarmed by the bitter antagonism of their white constituents.[4]

Yet, for all these ructions at the grass-roots level, federal policymakers during the early 1960s were remarkably sanguine about the prospects for racial equality. Nicholas Lemann observes that "conditions in the big-city black slums were an obsessive local issue that somehow did not rise to the level of national concern."[5] In part this reflected institutional features of the executive branch (and of the Senate, where the same pattern was to be found), and in further part, the manner in which the intensity of the Southern civil rights struggle obscured profound difficulties elsewhere. But also significant, if impossible to quantify, was the transcendant mood of liberal optimism: even where problems were acknowledged, they were frequently converted into welcome challenges.

Illustrations of this sense of overriding optimism abound in the academic literature of the time, as might be expected, given the important role that academic experts then played in the formulation of federal policy. In their 1963 book, *Beyond the Melting Pot,* Nathan Glazer and Daniel Patrick Moynihan were keen to expose the assimilationist myth by highlighting the tenacity of ethnicity in New York City, together with the persistence of economic and political competition between different groups. Glazer's chapter on black New Yorkers catalogs the woes that confronted this latest wave of migrants to the city. The author observes that "it is pointless to ignore the fact that the concentration of problems in the Negro community *is* exceptional."[6] Yet this is followed by the arresting contention that "New York has good race relations," a contingency that Glazer ascribes in part to the "mellowness" of the city's Irish and Italian populations.[7] His prognosis is optimistic: "New York will very likely in the end be an integrated city—or rather something even better, a city where people find homes and neighborhoods according to income and taste, and where an area predominantly of one group represents its positive wishes rather than restricting prejudice. We see the signs everywhere."[8]

Having dismissed pious talk of assimilation, the authors embraced the virtues of pluralism in a fashion that soon seemed at least equally naive. In the preface to the second edition of *Beyond the Melting Pot,* written in 1970, they ruefully recall having viewed Southern-style violence as "hardly possible." It had seemed as if New York blacks were already becoming just another ethnic group, "part of the game of accommodation politics."[9]

By the time that President Johnson left office in 1969, this basic optimism about poverty and race had long since vanished. Attendant problems but dimly understood by liberal politicians in 1964 had meanwhile moved to center stage, in the process transforming perspectives on entitlement and responsibility. This chapter considers the critical initial phase of this shift, during which the rationale for a colorblind War on Poverty was significantly undermined by the changing character of the black struggle for equality.

BLACK POVERTY AND THE STRUGGLE FOR CIVIL RIGHTS

Although the period from June 1963 to July 1965 was dominated by the battle to enact civil rights legislation to outlaw de jure discrimination in the South, black leaders were forthright in addressing issues that transcended the legal question. In a statement issued 9 June 1963, the National Urban League urged "a crash program of special effort to close up the gap between the conditions of Negro and white citizens," before it was too late:

> Current demonstrations in the South by Negro citizens seeking elementary and fundamental rights . . . are mild in comparison with those on the verge of taking flame in the tinder-box of racial unrest in Northern cities. . . . In these teeming Northern ghettos, hundreds of thousands of Negro citizens . . . are reaching the breaking point.
>
> These are the unemployed, the ill-housed, the disillusioned. It is they who are seething with the lava of deprivation and denial, out of which violence and bloodshed can erupt at any moment unless swift and realistic effort is exerted to prevent it.[10]

That same year, Bayard Rustin and A. Philip Randolph conceived a March for Jobs and Freedom designed to highlight the battles that still lay ahead once formal racial equality had been accomplished. To the annoyance of these two leaders—the first a socialist intellectual and close associate of the Rev. Martin Luther King, Jr., the second a veteran black labor activist—this protest turned out to be little more than a rally for the Civil Rights Bill. Nevertheless, they persevered, stimulated by a rising tide of black militancy that threatened their own authority. In May 1964, Randolph proposed a one-day strike and prayer vigil whose purpose, as outlined in a resolution at once prolix and urgent, was "to awaken, arouse and challenge the conscience of America concerning the tragic economic plight and widespread and deepening depths of grinding poverty into which Negroes have fallen and from which they must be rescued by our affluent American society if the country would avoid increasing frustrations, if not desperation, with consequent explosive racial convulsions in the darkening slums of metropolitan America."[11]

Other members of the mainstream civil rights leadership shared, to a greater extent than Rustin or Randolph, the classic objectives of American individualism: an unfettered opportunity for self-advancement. Yet the impeccable orthodoxy of their objectives was in a sense misleading, and those who identified a community of perspective as well as interest between white liberalism and the civil rights movement were to this degree mistaken.

The source of divergence came as reformers defined the barriers to black self-advancement. Publicly at least, President Johnson, Hubert Humphrey, and other liberals were convinced that formal, legal discrimination lay at the heart of black America's peculiar economic plight. Legal equality would create a level playing field and legitimize a colorblind War on Poverty, that is, one in which race was irrelevant. Black leaders, by contrast, believed that both past and present discrimination would, for many years to come, continue to cast lengthy shadows over the efforts of the minority poor to live the American dream. Accordingly, the logic of liberalism's own objective (equality of economic opportunity) and the dictates of morality (recompense for past injustice) made necessary a period of positive discrimination on behalf of the black American.[12]

Martin Luther King, Jr., and Whitney Young, Jr., were among those who sought to persuade the nation that existing definitions of equality of opportunity were not sufficient. Motivated both by liberal complacency and by the challenge to established black leadership from more militant groups, each produced an ambitious blueprint for economic equality between the races. Young's National Urban League released a ten-point Marshall Plan for the American Negro, while King issued a similarly conceived G.I. Bill of Rights for the Disadvantaged. Both schemes combined a call for positive discrimination with the claim that poor whites, too, would benefit from this next stage in the struggle for black equality. King observed that it was "a simple matter of justice that America, in dealing creatively with the task of raising the Negro from backwardness, should also be rescuing a large stratum of the forgotten white poor."[13] And Young remarked that while "we have to have immediate programs to relieve a disaster situation which is unique to the Negro," his "more idealistic" vision was for the "kind of situation where all poor people, whatever their color, will be given a better break in this society." In a revealing interview, Young suggested:

[I]f the poor white person were smart today he would keep quiet. The Negro happens to have the political leverage to get something from this crash effort. Certainly the Government is not going to provide benefits for the Negro alone. Whites will also benefit. The poor white is not an organized bloc, however, and so he might well be able to ride in on the coat-tails of the Negro.[14]

The tone of these manifestos is impassioned and challenging, but each is suffused with a desire for inclusion, an enthusiasm for America's stated ideals, and a belief that citizenship brings with it duties as well as rights. Young insisted that it was "not enough to man the machinery of protest," and that "participation in the responsibilities and opportunities of full citizenship in our democracy" was, if anything, more critical.[15] And King came across less as a moderate dissenter from American ideals than as a militant true believer, determined that the promise of those ideals should finally be realized. Outraged by the hypocrisy of those who counseled patience on the part of black America, he marveled at "the amazing assumption that society has the right to bargain with the Negro for the freedom which inherently belongs to him."[16]

LIBERAL PERSPECTIVES ON POVERTY AND RACE

Ample evidence existed to support the contention that blacks throughout the nation—and not simply in the South—suffered from race-specific problems that, by definition, could not be corrected by a colorblind War on Poverty. But through much of 1963–1964, liberal sentiment remained stubbornly attached to narrowly legalistic conceptions of black disadvantage. The seeming naïveté of liberals on the Northern race question paralleled the simple faith in rehabilitation they tended to reveal in debating the Economic Opportunity Act. Invited by filibustering Dixiecrats to contemplate the unhappy plight of their own black constituents, liberal friends of the Civil Rights Bill preferred to accentuate the positive. Senator Richard Russell (D-Ga.) professed himself infuriated by the "sanctimony or holier-than-thou attitude [of] the professional reformers in the East" who excoriated and demonized the South, even as they neglected their own racial crisis.[17]

Even when Northern legislators considered the rancorous issue of de facto segregation in schools, their public remarks betrayed striking complacency. In cities such as New York, Boston, and Chicago, recent demographic patterns, together with discriminatory housing practices and heavy white enrollment in private and parochial education, had generated a high degree of de facto segregation in many urban neighborhood schools. The pedagogical impact of this development was controversial, but ever since *Brown v. Board of Education,* pressure had been mounting within the black community for governmental efforts to rectify imbalance. Nowhere was the racial tension generated by such efforts more acute than in New York, but the state's senior senator, Jacob Javits, downplayed the ongoing conflict, celebrating "New York, where the whole climate and the people are in favor of correcting racial imbalance in schools."[18] Rebuking Senator Sam Ervin (D-S.C.) for having attempted to exploit the North's racial problems, Javits expressed the hope that desegregation in the South would occur as "quickly and effectively" as in his own state.[19]

Racial tension in New York persisted, however, and in April 1964 the Brooklyn chapter of CORE threatened to disrupt the opening of the New York World's Fair. Responding to the group's plan to mount demonstrations and stage a stall-in to disrupt traffic, Senator Javits protested that his city did "not deserve" civil disorder.[20] Two liberal Republican colleagues, Senator Kenneth Keating and Congressman John V. Lindsay, shared his sense that the source of black frustration in the North was the continuing filibuster of the Civil Rights Bill. These legislators seemingly were unable to appreciate that such legislation was all but irrelevant to Northern blacks because they already enjoyed the legal rights that the proposed federal legislation would secure. (The threatened "stall-in" did not materialize, a fact Javits attributed to his state's willingness to address black grievances. In his view, this was "a proud day for New York in many ways."[21])

Equally noteworthy, in terms of the North's tendency to view the struggle for black equality in purely sectional terms, was the response of the liberal community to the surprising success of Governor George Wallace (D-Ala.) in three Northern presidential primaries. It had seemed improbable that the staunchly segregationist governor would make significant inroads outside of his native South. The *New Republic*'s TRB doubted that "an all-out racist" with an "electric-prod-stick mentality" could successfully tap Northern anxieties.[22] But ultimately, Wallace succeeded in mustering 34 percent of the vote in Wisconsin, 30 percent in Indiana, and 43 percent in Maryland.[23] After all three primaries, liberal senators downplayed Wallace's performance, often ascribing it to mischievous, racist disinformation disseminated by opponents of the Civil Rights Bill. Again, the existence of profound sources of racial tension indigenous to the North was only rarely acknowledged.

During the spring of 1964, most liberal legislators were either insensitive to, or unwilling to acknowledge, the scale of the incipient racial crisis that was brewing outside the South. Their failure had a number of sources. First, Northern legislators were beginning to enjoy the heady feeling of enacting the unfinished liberal agenda of the Truman, Eisenhower, and Kennedy years. Legislative achievement rather than policy implementation was the emphasis, and—at a time of great optimism and relative social tranquillity— liberals were not looking for reasons to be skeptical. Axiomatic to postwar liberalism was the conviction that, thanks to the promise of American indi- vidualism and the continuing expansion of the national income, a thought- fully constructed, philosophically sound legislative program could assist all groups in society. Hence employers would benefit from federal aid to edu- cation in deprived areas, the poor would gain from middle-class tax cuts, Southern whites would come to appreciate the positive effects of the Civil Rights Act, and the War on Poverty would bind society together.

Second, the self-help ethos of the Economic Opportunity Act allowed grand goals to be pursued with very modest financial outlay. White liberals, who were anxious to avoid the vast and politically unpopular financial com- mitment that an emergency Marshall Plan for black America would require, were less keen than their allies in the civil rights movement to acknowledge the desperate racial crisis of the Northern ghetto. (The same pressures con- tributed to Lyndon Johnson's decision not to include a public works pro- gram in the Economic Opportunity Act, despite the role that unemploy- ment had played in focusing concern on poverty.)

Third, liberal legislators, prior to the summer of 1964, were so preoccu- pied with securing passage of the Civil Rights Act that they betrayed an understandable tendency to view equal opportunity in a predominantly Southern context. The flagrant denial of even basic rights in the South con- trasted markedly with the plethora of state human rights commissions, fair employment regulations, and open-housing ordinances in the North, and contributed to the reassuring conviction that the problems of the Northern black were not predominantly racial in character.

But the most significant factor that deterred Northern liberal senators from embracing demands for a Marshall Plan or a black bill of rights was constituency sentiment. During the autumn of 1963, there had been talk in the media of a white backlash against black demands for equality. Legisla- tors who were obliged to sustain a heterogeneous electoral coalition were necessarily concerned by this possibility, for it would undercut both their political strength back home and the civil rights cause to which they were committed. During the first half of 1964, such talk had subsided somewhat, despite the radical protests and school controversies to which Senator Javits had been compelled to respond. Nationally, support for President Johnson's handling of civil rights was encouragingly high: a February 1964 poll revealed that only 28 percent of Americans felt his administration was pushing integration "too fast"; three months later, 65 percent of Northern whites reported a preference for candidates who "took a strong stand on civil rights."[24] Liberal senators such as Jacob Javits, Joseph Clark (D-Pa.), and Clifford Case (R-N.J.) felt assured that publicity generated by civil rights advocacy enhanced their standing with black voters and the civil rights leadership, and was unlikely to antagonize white constituents.[25]

However, Wallace's performance and other poll data suggested that were civil rights legislation to be seen as affecting race relations in the North, a backlash would indeed swiftly emerge. A 1964 Harris survey indicated to its authors that while the white man's "intellect tells him that the Negro has indeed suffered years of discrimination, directly contradicting the American creed of equality for all, . . . his emotions make him feel uneasy at the prospect of such equality for the Negro."[26] On the one hand, 88 percent of those polled endorsed the demand of blacks for equal job opportunities, and 82 percent recognized their right to decent housing. On the other hand, endorsement of rights expressed in such abstract, distant terms left unresolved nagging questions of definition. What constituted equal access to employment and housing? And was there even a problem outside of the South? When respondents were asked to consider questions that involved personal contact with blacks, the Harris findings were less encouraging. Although only 23 percent objected to their "own children going to school with Negroes," 51 percent said they would object to "having a Negro family as next-door neighbors," and as many as 84 percent said they would oppose "a close friend or relative marrying a Negro."[27]

In the light of the subsequent racial explosion in the North—one that mocked the doctrines of postwar liberalism and inspired a white backlash of immensely destructive proportions—the position on race that liberal legislators adopted in 1964 appears misguided and doomed to failure. Yet at the time, an outspoken commitment to the Civil Rights Bill, combined with a hopeful prognosis for race relations in the North and support for a War on Poverty that, though colorblind, would nevertheless benefit blacks disproportionately, represented the optimal strategy.

ABANDONMENT OF THE COLORBLIND
ORTHODOXY, 1964–1965

In June 1965, President Johnson told the graduating class of Howard University that black poverty was after all unique. Why did he make this bold admission, in view of its political dangers? The answer to this question has two components that may initially appear to be incompatible. First, it was a decision that was increasingly hard to avoid, both on political and intellectual grounds. Second, it may not have appeared at the time to be politically perilous.

A number of events and trends combined during 1964–1965 to render implausible previously cherished beliefs about the economic condition of black America. The first was a serious race riot in New York City in July 1964 (the same month that the Senate filibuster on civil rights was finally broken), which served to dramatize degrees of disadvantage and to strengthen calls for a black Marshall Plan. The riot followed a period of mounting tension in New York. In the aftermath of the World's Fair protest by CORE, a much publicized crime wave in May and June had the *New York Times* raising the specter of anarchy in the streets.[28] In a succinct telegram to the White House, Whitney Young, Jr., reported: "New York City is [a] racial tinderbox. We face [a] most hazardous and difficult summer."[29] Although Senator Javits continued to blame the disorder on Southern intransigence on civil rights, elsewhere the sources of tension were seen as transparently indigenous. The New York City Commission of Human Rights identified a "spontaneous reflection of a widespread malaise that exists in a community where poverty, unemployment, poor housing and inadequate schooling build up to a hopeless frustration."[30]

In this combustible atmosphere, the specific trigger for violence in Harlem (it also encompassed the Bedford-Stuyvesant district of Brooklyn) was the shooting of a black teenager by a police officer. During several days of violence, captured in lurid detail in the national press and news magazines, one person died, more than 140 were seriously injured, and property damage was extensive.[31] Only days later, in the upstate city of Rochester, the violence was repeated when the National Guard intervened to quell two days of unrest that had been sparked by an attempted arrest for public drunkenness. Taken together, and in the still wider context provided by a series of summer riots elsewhere, the shock impact of the New York violence was substantial.[32] Black leaders used the opportunity to reiterate their existing demands for massive economic intervention on behalf of poor minorities. King feared that the violence was but a prelude to even more substantial unrest throughout the nation:

> America will be faced with the ever-present threat of violence, rioting and sense-less crime as long as Negroes by the hundreds of thousands are packed into mal-odorous, rat-plagued ghettos; as long as Negroes remain smothered by poverty in the midst of an affluent society; as long as Negroes see their freedom endlessly delayed and diminished by the head winds of tokenism and small handouts from the white power structure.[33]

In place of "tokenism," King again commended his G.I. Bill of Rights. Even in the aftermath of the Harlem riot, he remained attached to the contemporary belief that "this country has the resources to solve any problem once that problem is accepted as national policy."[34] But elsewhere, both within the Southern civil rights movement and in Northern bodies, such as the Brooklyn chapter of CORE, disillusionment with the politics of accommodation was mounting.[35] A month after the riot, at the Democratic Party convention in Atlantic City, the philosophical divide deepened as King and Rustin, among others, were accused of having sold out the Mississippi Freedom Democratic Party by acceding in negotiations to the seating of the state's official, all-white delegation at the expense of the insurgents.[36]

Still more alarming was the mood of inchoate rage and militancy in the ghetto, and the prominence of those radicals who sought to marshal it. In April of 1964, at the time of the World's Fair episode, A. Philip Randolph told the principal leaders of the civil rights movement of his fear that they were losing authority. Among other sources for concern, Randolph referred his colleagues to "the declared intention of Malcolm X to project a social and political program, and his advocacy of rifle clubs." The veteran labor leader further noted that "his 'ballot or bullets' speech before a 1,000 [sic] people several days ago in Harlem requires of us the most careful analysis." More generally, Randolph expressed concern at "the rise of demagogic Negro leadership in a number of cities and their determined effort to sow confusion and compound frustration while offering the Negro masses no concrete alternative."[37] For all the unifying effect that the effort to defeat Jim Crow continued to have within the civil rights movement, evidence abounded of the growing strength of a new black agenda whose adherents found little appeal in either Gandhian nonviolence or liberal individualism.

The problem of how to reach alienated urban constituencies attracted to nationalism, separatism, and mob violence would soon preoccupy both black and white establishments.

Further evidence of disillusionment with the status of the black struggle for equality came from within the intellectual community and gained fresh intensity in the aftermath of the Harlem riot. In 1963, James Baldwin had arranged a meeting between Robert F. Kennedy and a diverse group of black associates; the attorney general was left shaken by the scale of their alienation.[38] Baldwin's *The Fire Next Time,* published that same year, issued a bleak warning of incipient racial turmoil. The novelist's response to the Harlem riot anticipated the future course of black activism. Predicting that whites would never accede voluntarily to black demands for "freedom now," he posited that "the Negro situation in North and South" could "only be changed by power."[39]

The prominent social psychologist Kenneth Clark was equally angry and distressed. Famous for his decisive testimony in *Brown v. Board of Education* on the harmful effects of separate schooling, Clark had more recently been involved in an innovative community action project in Harlem.[40] In the wake of the riot, he professed disgust at "the pretence of shock, surprise, horror" that greeted the violence:

> The horrible living conditions, the sanitation, pushing people around—apparently nobody gives a damn about it. They send hundreds and thousands of cops. They would do better to send one-third as many building inspectors or a thousand sanitation workers, or just an attempt at proper schooling. . . . But you know what I think we're going to get? "Quiet the natives, then go on with business as usual."[41]

Echoing Martin Luther King, Jr., Clark warned:

> [Riots] could occur in any other city with a large Negro population. . . . I've walked the streets of Harlem the last two days and I have heard Negroes saying, "We've got nothing to lose. What more can happen?" As a psychologist, I can't confuse my conscience with my profession, but I don't know whether the average Negro leader can ask his race to be moderate any longer.[42]

Whereas the authors of the G.I. Bill of Rights and the Marshall Plan were strongly critical of those in power who expressed noble ideals that were not observed in practice, their basic thrust was that blacks should fight for the opportunity to advance *within* the framework of such ideals. Clark, however, feared that the gap between promise and performance might be so ingrained, and so bound up in basic issues of economic and political power, that the ideals simply lacked practical relevance. He predicted an increase both in black militancy and white resistance and saw uncomfortable choices ahead for liberal policymakers:

> Action produces counteraction—a school boycott by civil rights groups stimulates a boycott by those who wish to preserve the status quo—and then the question becomes: to which group do the forces of actual power choose to respond? Will the actual power follow the direction of the verbal demands of Negroes for change or the verbal resistance of the majority of whites to change? The power to bring about a legislative consensus for change may not necessarily be the same power required to implement or enforce the consensus.[43]

Owing in part to the past operations of this pattern, and in part to what he characterized as a tendency to "assume . . . that the word *is* the deed," Clark viewed liberalism's record on race as "somewhat tainted." His conclusion was a somber one: "In those areas of life where liberals are powerful—labor unions, schools, and politics—one is forced to say that the plight of the Negro is not significantly better than in areas where liberals are not dominant."[44]

MAKINGS OF THE HOWARD UNIVERSITY ADDRESS

If liberal policymakers who pondered the lessons of the first "long, hot summer" were unable to endorse Clark's contention, then the riots of 1964 nonetheless produced a widespread distancing from some of the less sustainable claims of the War on Poverty. Platitudes about assimilation became somewhat less common, while growing numbers were prepared to acknowledge the unique nature of black poverty. And from these two trends came a third: a new willingness to confront the possibility that the "rising tide lifts all boats" doctrine did not apply to the ghetto poor. Between July 1964 and June of the following year, liberal perspectives on black disadvantage evolved to the point where Lyndon Johnson could embrace the possibility of racially targeted social policy.

With final passage of the Economic Opportunity Act a month away, the *New York Times* observed that "the antipoverty bill, in the new perspective given by the disturbances of this long, hot summer, is also an anti-riot bill."[45]

65

The same conviction and hope led one upstate New York mayor, Joseph P. Vaccarella, to tell Willard Wirtz: "We are all happy to see the anti-poverty bill passed and I hope that something can be done for the city of Mount Vernon as we have over 12,000 Negroes living here. Many of them are dropouts that I know would be greatly helped by the bill."[46]

In Congress, Hubert Humphrey made the same connection between the War on Poverty and racial tensions. While he viewed civil disorder as intolerable, he also argued that it was not enough simply to condemn the rioters and ignore the injustices that fomented unrest. Dispensing with the formulation that racial inequality was a sectional and essentially legalistic matter, the Minnesotan portrayed the Economic Opportunity Act as evidence of the nation's determination "to solve the problems of Harlem, Bedford-Stuyvesant, Chicago, Detroit, Mississippi, Minnesota, and wherever else in this great land difficulties arise."[47]

Within the executive branch of government, the cabinet department most alert to the economic plight of black America at this time appears to have been the Department of Labor. Throughout 1964, the department's *Weekly News Digests* were focused on the problem of black unemployment and its social consequences. One bulletin reported a speech by Secretary Wirtz that highlighted "the profound effects that the Negro's economic instability has on the rest of his circumstances." Particularly alarming was a pattern of family dislocation, evident since the 1940s and closely correlated with rates of male unemployment.[48]

Daniel Patrick Moynihan, Wirtz's assistant secretary for research and policy planning, was fascinated by these patterns, and by the relationship between indices of social disorganization and race. During the course of the February 1964 speech in which he had reportedly claimed that welfare "rotted" the poor, Moynihan made special reference to the poor blacks, warning a biracial audience that "the illegitimacy rate is destroying the Negro community."[49] In private, he developed this theme more fully, effectively endorsing Whitney Young's call for a black Marshall Plan at the very time that other administration officials were emphasizing the colorblind character of the nascent War on Poverty.

In April 1964, Moynihan told Secretary Wirtz that the response of policymakers to the concept of "unequal treatment for the Negro" had been "one of bewilderment and confusion at a wholly unfamiliar proposition." He continued: "But we cannot avoid it. The Negroes are asking for unequal treatment. More seriously, it may be that without unequal treatment in the immediate future there is no way for them to achieve anything like equal status in the long run." Alerting Wirtz to the proposal for a black Marshall Plan, Moynihan found the title unappealing but the logic of Whitney Young's case remorseless. He concluded in a fashion that summed up the troubling gap between political interest and problem solving: "Do you think the President might, under any circumstances, come out for some form of special treatment—as part of your plans for the coming Summer? Obviously this is filled with political peril, but I suspect we may have to face it anyway."[50]

A few weeks later, Moynihan warned again of "the major and sometimes wrenching changes in our way of doing things that will be required if we are going to bring [blacks] in as full-fledged members of the larger community." Rather than confront these changes, there existed the danger that government would simply "pension the Negroes off" through welfare:

> Nothing would be more terrible, if it should come to pass. We will have created an entire subculture of dependency, alienation, and despair. We have already done as much to whole sections of Appalachia, as I understand it, as also to the Indian reservations. It is in truth the way we cope with this kind of problem. As against giving the men proper jobs and a respectable place in their community and family.[51]

In Moynihan's view, the secretary of labor was "precisely the person to sound this warning." His foreboding suggests that he was not overly impressed with President Johnson's recent declaration of war on dependency, and indeed the maverick assistant secretary was already on record for his view that the program would "not be very startling."[52] In addition to his personal view, Moynihan was articulating a perspective consistent with the institutional interest of the Department of Labor, which preferred large-scale employment programs.[53]

Moynihan's warning about the dangers of a black "subculture of dependency" was anything but new. In general terms, the effect of doles on the human personality had preoccupied reform-minded Americans since the dawn of the republic, while the past decade had seen growing concern about family instability as an outcome of the ADC/AFDC program. Moreover, this preoccupation had long possessed a racial context: since the turn of the century, black intellectuals had been concerned with the distinctive structure of the black family—an interest they shared with white academics.[54] The National Urban League viewed family stability as a key goal of the black Marshall Plan.[55] Similarly, King's G.I. Bill directly addressed such "social evils" as "illegitimacy [and] swollen relief rolls."[56] And in terms of national politics, welfare reform during the Kennedy presidency was in part shaped by the black dependency issue, which gained prominence after the "Battle of Newburgh."

Moynihan's concerns, therefore, were no more "startling" than were those of the War on Poverty. What *was* dramatic, however, was the immediate political context: the assistant secretary of labor had articulated a viewpoint quite inimical to the War on Poverty, in which issues of economic and racial disadvantage were studiously separated. His memoranda would have had little political relevance were it not for the fact that by the late summer of 1964 the course of the civil rights struggle had generated a new receptiveness to broad conceptions of black economic rights.

In the autumn of 1964, as he embarked on a study of black unemployment and welfare dependency, Moynihan's conviction that government must acknowledge the peculiar magnitude of black poverty strengthened. His findings and interpretations, soon to acquire fame and notoriety, were contained in a March 1965 internal report entitled *The Negro Family: The Case for National Action.*[57] The purpose of the Moynihan Report was to discredit colorblind approaches to poverty by demonstrating that black poverty was uniquely intractable, and therefore required a different set of public policies than those associated with the War on Poverty. At the heart of the difference lay white racism (past and present), chronic joblessness, and the matriarchal structure of the black family. In combination, these forces created a "tangle of pathology" that was starting "to feed on itself." Unless the government provided jobs for the ghetto, and incentives to black family stability, African Americans would be unable to take full advantages of recent legal gains and the provisions of the Economic Opportunity Act.[58]

The Moynihan Report is remembered primarily for the storm of controversy that greeted its public release (in the aftermath of the Watts riot); however, its importance also derives from the fact that it informed President Johnson's Howard University address and, for a while, seemed destined to presage a fundamental redirection in public policy.

THE HOWARD UNIVERSITY ADDRESS

Lyndon Johnson's decision to embrace the politically dangerous notion of compensatory social programs for black America might be interpreted as a response to the dangers of black radicalism and ghetto unrest. Alternatively, it might be argued that intellectual conversion lay at the heart of his administration's departure from tradition. There is an element of truth in both versions, yet neither does justice to the "can-do" spirit that infused so many of the president's addresses during this period. In speeches concerned with the environment, education, health care, voting rights and, not least, the nation's mission in Vietnam (see especially the famous April 1965 speech at Johns Hopkins University), the presence of this spirit owed more to the *general* sense that every problem had a solution than to the existence of a practical blueprint for action.

Thus it was that President Johnson declared war on black poverty in June 1965, confident in his faith that, even if the administration's weapons had yet to be invented, the enemy could still be defeated with dispatch. In addition to its optimism about problem solving, this faith had a critical second element: the president, exploiting the spirit of his age and deploying his formidable political skills, had the power to build a nationwide consensus around any crusade he chose to wage. This was a new age, and old constraints, whether political or intellectual, need no longer arrest the triumphant advance of liberalism and the American way.

Despite the intense sense of foreboding generated by the 1964 riots, by the spring of the following year such anxiety was remarkably absent from liberal rhetoric. With the Selma protest and the campaign for voting rights, the civil rights movement assumed once more that sharpness of focus and moral clarity that had seemed imperiled at the time of the Harlem riot. Then, talk of a white backlash had been widespread, and the polarization of public opinion had been embodied in President Johnson's reelection campaign against Barry Goldwater. Now, liberalism had emerged triumphant, enjoying a reliable working majority on Capitol Hill for the first time in over twenty-five years. Moreover, having recently won the largest margin of victory in presidential history, Lyndon Johnson possessed a degree of political authority and legitimacy that, for all his successes in 1964, had previously been absent. Opinion polls taken in June 1965 revealed that President Johnson's personal popularity stood at 69 percent, while 63 percent approved of his handling of "domestic problems."[59]

The anxiety stirred by ghetto unrest had diminished, albeit not for long. In a political environment that permitted liberals to abandon the shibboleth that the War on Poverty could plausibly be fought on a color-blind basis, a new consciousness developed about the peculiar dynamics of black poverty. Black family structure was understood to be a sensitive political issue: conservatives and racists could be trusted to use it as justification for a renewed emphasis on self-help. But the report on *The Negro Family* was, after all, subtitled *The Case for National Action,* and it was this aspect that excited the White House aides who brought Moynihan's thesis to the attention of the president.

Their enthusiasm owed much to the report's timing, in terms of the overall standing of the president's Great Society agenda, and the status of the civil rights revolution. Johnson's initial legislative program was about to be enacted, yet his thirst for bold new commitments remained unquenched. It seems reasonable to suggest that he had an inherent preference for initiating grand designs over seeking to implement them; certainly this was too early in his presidency to get bogged down in the frustrating business of administration. Having already declared "unconditional" War on Poverty, Johnson would now go further and assault the evils of race hatred that consigned black Americans to the bottom rung of the economic ladder. In his Howard University speech, the president referred to "the glorious opportunity of this generation to end the one huge wrong of the American nation, and, in so doing, to find America for ourselves, with the same immense thrill of discovery which gripped those who first came to realize that here, at last, was a home for freedom."[60]

The status of the civil rights struggle fit well into this grand design. The established black leadership was, to a degree, confused and disoriented by the imminent attainment of its longstanding legislative objectives, and uncertain how to retain its primacy as the intractable problems of urban blacks moved center stage. The principal author of the Howard University speech, Richard N. Goodwin, confirms that Johnson relished the prospect of *initiating* the next stage of the black struggle for equality, rather than simply responding to events.[61] The Moynihan Report arrived on his desk at a propitious time.

At Howard University, Johnson endorsed a conception of equality notably similar to that which Martin Luther King, Jr., and Whitney Young, Jr., had embraced two years earlier. (King, Young, and Roy Wilkins, of the NAACP, had in fact reviewed and endorsed the president's address before its delivery.) He stated:

> Freedom is not enough. You do not wipe away the scars of centuries by saying: now you are free to go where you want, and do as you desire, and choose the leaders you please.
>
> You do not take a person who, for years, has been hobbled by chains and liberate him, bring him up to the starting line of a race and then say, "you are free to

compete with all the others," and still justly believe that you have been completely fair.

America would soon open the gates of equal legal opportunity. Johnson observed that the "next and the more profound stage of the battle for civil rights" was to ensure that all could "walk through those gates." He explained, "We seek not just freedom but opportunity. We seek not just legal equity but human ability, not just equality as a right and a theory but equality as a fact and equality as a result. . . . To this end equal opportunity is essential, but not enough."

Drawing heavily on the Moynihan Report, Johnson examined the roots of inequality of opportunity in some detail, referring to the poisonous legacy of slavery and the continuing blight of racism, "a feeling whose dark intensity is matched by no other prejudice in our society." America, he said, must recognize that black poverty was different from its white counterpart:

> Many of its causes and many of its cures are the same. But there are differences—deep, corrosive, obstinate differences—radiating painful roots into the community, and into the family, and the nature of the individual. These differences are not racial differences. They are solely and simply the consequence of ancient brutality, past injustice, and present prejudice.[62]

The declaration that "Negro poverty is not white poverty" represented a consequential departure from an orthodoxy that had seemed entrenched just months earlier. But the precise implications of this judgment for public policy were by no means clear. With this in mind, Johnson announced a forthcoming White House conference, "To Fulfill These Rights," at which administration officials, academics, and black leaders were to produce a blueprint for peaceful and equitable progress.

Johnson's remarkable speech would ring increasingly hollow in the years to come, as racial attitudes polarized in ways that mocked his quest for a consensus among idealists. Moreover, its radical implications for group entitlement and societal obligation were at odds with cherished values of individualism, to which he continued to adhere. Never again would he issue so blunt a challenge to the faith of that Middle American constituency whose allegiance he had always sought. Indeed, it is possible to see the final three years of his presidency as an increasingly desperate salvage operation aimed at keeping afloat a liberal creed transformed by the politics of race and imperiled by the unpopularity of its new principles.

It is tempting to view the Howard University address as an aberration: carried away by the euphoria of the times, attracted by the emotional charge of his speechwriter's magnificent words, Johnson expressed sentiments whose challenge to the American political tradition and social philosophy were only partially intended. Remarks made two months later, at the signing of the Voting Rights Act, represent a classic restatement of the *old* liberalism. Visionary in tone, his rhetoric was less so in substance: black Americans rather than the white majority were challenged to make equality a reality:

> Presidents and Congresses, laws and lawsuits, can open the doors to the polling places and open the doors to the wondrous rewards which await the wise use of the ballot. But only the individual Negro, and all others who have been denied the right to vote, can really walk through those doors, and can use that right, and can transform the vote into an instrument of justice and fulfillment.

Johnson further admonished the new black voter: "You must vote. You must learn, so your choice advances your interest and the interest of our beloved Nation." The Voting Rights Act placed particular responsibility on the civil rights leadership:

> Dedicated leaders must work around the clock to teach people their rights and their responsibilities and to lead them to exercise those rights and to fulfill those responsibilities and those duties to their country.
> If you do this, then you will find, as others have found before you, that the vote is the most powerful instrument ever devised by man for breaking down injustice and destroying the terrible walls which imprison men because they are different from other men.[63]

CONCLUSION

In acknowledging that black poverty was more than simply an individual condition, Johnson conceded that blacks, as a group, confronted obstacles that precluded their advance as individuals. This admission posed a serious challenge to the assumption that American society and values were essentially just and virtuous. If Johnson and other liberals tended still to view racism as "the one huge wrong" that Americans must overcome, the initial breach opened the door to subsequent and more wide-ranging critiques of the nation's underlying principles. Moreover, an additional breach would soon open within the ranks of American liberalism. While the president drew back from the more radical implications of the Howard University address, others—on Capitol Hill, in academe, and within his own administration—moved forward, defining ever broader rights for the disadvantaged American.

As the dominant strain of American liberalism distanced itself from an individualist tradition whose relevance to poor black Americans seemed increasingly uncertain, political interest acted as a restraining force. Advocacy of preferential treatment and group entitlement coexisted, albeit awkwardly, with the claim that all needy Americans would benefit from social programs designed for poor blacks. In their respective prescriptions for special treatment, Whitney Young, Jr., and Martin Luther King, Jr., had made just such a claim. Similarly, Daniel Patrick Moynihan recognized that programs to combat black poverty must be targeted at the entire deprived population, despite the unique problems faced by members of minority groups. In an address to the American Academy of Political and Social Science in the spring of 1965, Moynihan delivered a bald statement of this political truth: "In order to do anything about Negro Americans on the scale that our data would indicate, we have to declare that we are doing it for *everybody*. I think, however, that the problem of the Negro American *is* now a special one, and is not just an intense case of the problem of all poor people."[64] Moynihan reminded his academic colleagues that "Congressmen vote for everyone more readily than they vote for any one. Because the poverty program is a color-blind program, we can do what we could not have done otherwise." Yet, policymakers had to devise and implement social programs in the knowledge that black poverty was more grave than its white counterpart, both in terms of its severity and its implications for social stability. The fact that the colorblind illusion had to be publicly sustained had important consequences; in subsequent years, enhanced definitions of black entitlement would be extended to the entire disadvantaged population.

It should be reiterated that, despite the new complexity of their task, antipoverty warriors were still committed to the individualist ideals of the Economic Opportunity Act. By the middle of 1965, the tools by which self-help was to be facilitated and equality of opportunity secured were open to debate, but the primacy of those ends was undisputed. But these tools, which contributors to academic conferences and government task forces were now debating, could serve more than one master. Once the language of group rights and racial justice had entered antipoverty discourse, the language of mutual obligation tended to be relegated, if not abandoned altogether. This had powerful implications for income-maintenance policy, which was beginning to attract scholarly, bureaucratic, and activist attention. A 1964 public assistance task force emphasized the active role that cash support programs must play in equalizing economic opportunity, while Moynihan viewed the family allowance schemes of Canada and Western Europe as a useful mechanism for encouraging middle-class values and habits in the ghetto.

But shortly, such income-maintenance strategies would be propounded not as means to ends but as ends in themselves. Within the economics profession, considerations of efficiency had already lent a certain bipartisan momentum to the income strategy. The right-wing Chicago theoretician, Milton Friedman—suspicious of the knowledge revolution and hostile to large bureaucracies—was on record as favoring direct cash subsidies to the poor over expensive rehabilitative services.[65] By the end of 1965 a quite different rationale for the income strategy would gain ground: the victims of American capitalism and racism had an unqualified entitlement to generous cash support.

For now, however, the entitlement argument was rarely heard, while the efficiency rationale had little appeal. At the American Academy conference in May, the liberal economist James Tobin found that colleagues had little interest in his ideas for income redistribution. The distinguished immigration historian Oscar Handlin pontificated that "sometimes an increase in income increases the incidence of disorder in family life," while James Q. Wilson, a political scientist, averred that "there are those who are simply pathologically poor, who would not benefit either from welfare programs or from a gross increase in income." Edwin C. Berry, of the National Urban League, emphasized the importance of determining "whether we are concerned with improving the *condition* of the poor or their *status*." In his view, "emotional destruction" is "probably more devastating than whether a guy misses a meal or not." Finally, the anthropologist Clifford Geertz agreed that "just having more money would not necessarily strengthen the family."[66]

Evolving conceptions of black disadvantage had refined but not dispelled the buoyant optimism of 1964. The following chapters will examine how the basic tenets of liberal individualism were eroded during the last three and a half years of the Johnson presidency.

CHAPTER 4

Watts and Its Aftermath:
Rise of the Income Strategy

The summer of 1965 represented the zenith of Great Society liberalism. President Johnson's willingness to acknowledge the intractability of black poverty, as evidenced by his Howard University speech, stemmed from the remarkable strength of his political position. The naïveté of the War on Poverty's colorblind formulation might have been exposed, but legislative success and economic prosperity continued to sustain a crusading optimism that welcomed new challenges and assumed the existence of practicable solutions to the nation's problems. During the remainder of the year, however, the early promise of the Johnson presidency started to unravel. Associated initially with the Watts riot, but more generally with the inherently shallow foundations upon which earlier liberal optimism had been constructed, this process of unraveling gathered momentum during the next three years. Its casualties included both Johnson and the political tradition he represented.

The impending crisis of Great Society liberalism was not generally foreseen in mid-1965. During the previous eighteen months, President Johnson's celebrated legislative skills had produced a domestic record comparable to those of Woodrow Wilson and Franklin Roosevelt. What is more, his most important proposals, including the education and voting rights measures of 1965, were grounded in central elements of the dominant American credo, further complicating the Republican Party's attempt to recover from its recent electoral debacle.

Many of the principles of the Elementary and Secondary Education Act bore a striking resemblance to those of the War on Poverty. Members of the 1964 task force on education had cast a critical eye on contemporary America and cataloged reasons to support the importance of their mission, including "the crucial role of educated talent in modern society, the rise of automation, increased leisure, the unemployability of untrained men, and the knowledge explosion." In a global context, they believed that every American had an obligation to "be sufficiently educated to discharge his duties as a citizen and to exercise the responsibilities that go with freedom."[1]

In theory, they observed, the respective responsibilities of the citizen and the state should be attainable: "[A] child in rags should be as teachable as a child in tweeds." But in practice, equal access to the promise of education had been absent: "For too many of the poor, educational experience has been a series of failures, each failure reinforcing the lesson of failure so that education is for them an habituation to despair, to lack of self-confidence and self-respect, and to a sense of barriers not to be passed." The academics, bureaucrats, and representatives of miscellaneous interest groups who designed the 1965 education bill were convinced that such fatalism could be overcome. When the unmotivated child was shown "the marvelous equipment that nature gave him," he would discover "new worlds."[2] Congress agreed, and in April, during an emotional signing ceremony at Lyndon Johnson's first school in Stonewall, Texas, the president hammered home the message that "education is the only valid passport from poverty."[3]

Amid the general optimism generated by existing accomplishments and the expectation of more triumphs to come, problems associated with the War on Poverty cast something of a shadow. Sargent Shriver's choice for deputy director of the Office of Economic Opportunity, Adam Yarmolinsky, had been jettisoned by Johnson at the insistence of the South Carolina congressional delegation, and this loss, together with Shriver's continuing part-time role in the Peace Corps, reduced the effectiveness of the fledgling agency. Meanwhile, the two largest antipoverty initiatives were each experiencing difficulties. Robert A. Levine, deputy director of the research and evaluation unit of the Office of Economic Opportunity (OEO), later recalled that the effort to get the Job Corps off the ground was a "chaotic nightmare," while important mayors and governors were already complaining about the Community Action Program.[4]

However, Levine also recalls this period as a time of hope, energy, and idealism. The Economic Opportunity Act negotiated the congressional hearings of 1965 with ease, opinion surveys revealed widespread support for the Great Society agenda, and the high profile and popularity of the Head

Start program helped counteract the problems of other initiatives.[5] By July, Sargent Shriver was telling Johnson that "we may be over the hill in our continuing struggle to have this program properly understood by the newspapers."[6] Whether he shared this view or not, Johnson remained committed to the program and was optimistic regarding its prospects: at one particularly buoyant cabinet meeting, the president enthusiastically ordered each officer in turn, "You save money on your programs" and—pointing at Shriver—"You-all give it to him."[7]

Historians remembered the final week in July as the period when Johnson made the fateful decision to send 50,000 additional combat troops to Vietnam, but at the time the president liked to think of it as "the most productive and most historic legislative week in Washington during this century."[8] The voting rights bill was in conference, Medicare and Medicaid had secured enactment, social security benefits had just won a 7 percent increase, and the Housing and Urban Development Act (creating a new cabinet department and a pioneering rent supplements plan) was assured of passage. The president's stock had never been higher: Tom Wicker observed that "the list of achievements is so long that it reads better than the legislative achievements of most two-term Presidents."[9]

Senator Mike Mansfield (D-Mont.) went even further, telling a skeptical William E. Leuchtenburg in September that "Johnson has outstripped Roosevelt, no doubt about that. He has done more than FDR ever did or ever thought of doing."[10] Indeed, the Senate majority leader found the never-ending avalanche of reform measures somewhat overwhelming. When the administration introduced the Teacher Corps bill (relatively late in the session for major legislation), Mansfield pleaded publicly for a breathing space. Harry McPherson, a key Johnson adviser ever since the president's own days as majority leader, referred to "Mansfield's outstanding, if painfully typical statement" but urged Johnson to treat it with "understanding and amusement."[11]

Three weeks later, and just five days after the conclusion of the struggle for voting rights, riots on a scale unmatched since the Detroit outbreak of 1943 erupted in Watts, a poor, black suburb of Los Angeles. As with the Rochester, New York, disturbance a year earlier, the precipitating incident was the arrest of a black man on suspicion of drunk driving. This time, however, the ensuing disturbance was both more protracted and more costly. The official state investigation into the riot described how rioters "looted stores, set fires, beat up white passersby whom they hauled from stopped cars, many of which were turned upside down and burned, exchanged shots with law enforcement officers, and stoned and shot at firemen." As many as 10,000 rioters participated, 34 persons were left dead, and more than 1,000 were injured. Property damage amounted to $40 million.[12] But even that was hardly the full measure of the cost. At a stroke, the context for domestic policymaking had been transformed in a way that discredited the Great Society's ideology and seriously undermined its electoral coalition. As the fragility of President Johnson's cherished consensus became apparent, the ideals upon which it was based came under assault from both the right and the left; the former was increasingly certain that the poor did not deserve the War on Poverty's largesse, and the latter was equally adamant that they were entitled to far more.

POLITICAL CONSEQUENCES OF WATTS

In recent civil rights addresses, President Johnson had enunciated two distinct perspectives on the status of the struggle for black equality, but in the aftermath of Watts, both were in some measure discredited. On the one hand, the president's confidence that the nation would unite around the radical objectives of the Howard University speech was challenged by its hostile response to black violence. And on the other hand, the more traditional faith in America, the land of opportunity, as outlined in the address, was undercut by the conditions that had spawned the subsequent violence.

Johnson's initial response to the riot appears to have been withdrawal and denial. Joseph A. Califano, his top domestic adviser, later recalled the president's inability to acknowledge that such a catastrophe could even have taken place: "He just couldn't accept it. He refused to look at the cable from Los Angeles describing the situation. . . . He refused to take the calls from the generals who were requesting government planes to fly in the National Guard. I tried to reach him a dozen times. We needed decisions from him. But he simply wouldn't respond."[13]

Johnson's reaction reflected the numbing certainty that the spirit of reform, so buoyant for eighteen months, had suffered a grievous blow. George Reedy, a longstanding adviser to the president, warned him of the danger that "the rioters will become identified with the civil rights movement and thereby compound the difficulties of those seeking long-range solutions in the U.S."[14] Of particular concern to Johnson was the political climate in California, where Edmund G. Brown, the Democratic governor, faced a tough battle for reelection in 1966. Even before Watts, the success of a referendum that repealed the state's fair housing ordinance had suggested the existence of a mounting racial backlash. In the aftermath of the riots, Johnson was apparently worried that the Republican's most likely gubernatorial candidate, Ronald Reagan, might prove adept at exploiting racial antagonisms.[15]

Evidence that the riot had indeed damaged the liberal cause in California came in September, with the completion of the Justice Department's investigation into Watts. According to its report, the white population of California was now "far less sympathetic to and has greater difficulty trying to understand the needs of the poverty areas than before the riots."[16] Two adverse public opinion developments had been the demand for greater law and order, and strong support for a crackdown on welfare relief. Many whites saw "a close connection between peaceful demonstrations for civil rights and the rioting," while a widespread determination existed "not to yield to demands related to violence." In responding to the unrest, Johnson would have to recognize the widespread feeling "that assistance to the riot areas rewards lawlessness."[17]

Yet in public, Johnson's response to Watts was both sensitive and courageous. Even as he sought to limit political fallout with strong law and order rhetoric, he reiterated his pledge that "we shall overcome." Insisting that he was "enlisted for the duration," Johnson asked the nation for patience and cooperation:

> The brave story of the American Negro is . . . a compound of brilliant promise and stunning reverses. Sometimes, as in the past week—as the two are mixed on the same page of our newspapers and television screens—the result is baffling to all the world. And it is baffling to me, to you, to all of us. . . . Always there is the danger that hours of disorder may erase the accumulated goodwill of many months and years. I warn and plead with all thinking Americans to contemplate this for a due period.[18]

A few days later, Johnson raised conservative hackles by warning that the Los Angeles pattern might well be repeated anywhere where people "feel they don't get a fair shake . . . [and that] justice is not open to them." In the face of detractors, such as controversial Los Angeles Police Department Chief William Parker, who ascribed the violence to those liberals who "keep telling people they are unfairly treated," the president went out of his way to press for accelerated action on the Great Society agenda.[19] Uppermost in his thoughts was the perennial issue of home rule for the District of Columbia, currently stalled in Congress: "Those of you here in the District of Columbia, I want to warn you this morning that the clock is ticking, time is moving, that we should and we must ask ourselves every night when we go home, are we doing all that we should in our nation's capital, in all the other big cities of the country where 80 percent of the population of this country is going to be living in the year 2000." For Gerald Ford, the House minority leader, such remarks represented a bid by Johnson to use the "tragic memory" of Watts in a bid to subvert the "independent will" of Congress. It was "a tragic day for responsible civil rights champions and the entire nation" when the president risked "tempt[ing] those who generate rioting and plundering."[20] The respective critiques of Parker and Ford were to become increasingly common after 1965, and ever more damaging, as the cycle of violence combined with other problems to destroy public enthusiasm for the Great Society.

In terms of public policy, the administration's immediate response to Watts was what Johnson presented as "a combined program to restore and rehabilitate the damaged areas of Los Angeles."[21] But other evidence tends to support Robert Levine's recollection of a more unwieldy mélange of measures: "Program monies were poured in by OEO and other agencies on a not very organized basis."[22] The daunting long-term challenge facing Johnson was to design a combined civil rights–antipoverty strategy that would redeem the promises made in the Howard University address and defuse the anger of the ghetto, and, at the same time, remain faithful to the values of an increasingly skeptical Middle America. The inherent conceptual complexity of the task was made still more difficult by the crisis that confronted the civil rights establishment in the aftermath of the Watts riot.

WATTS AND THE CIVIL RIGHTS MOVEMENT

Watts dramatized both the alienation and militancy of the ghetto, and the continued inability of the established black leadership to establish its legitimacy among young, poor Northern blacks. Despite recent efforts to focus the nation's attention on the economic crisis of black America, neither marches nor programs could penetrate a world many times removed from the religious, disciplined, middle-class spirit of the Southern civil rights movement. One black leader in Watts, California State Assemblyman

Mervyn Dymally, was convinced that the riot represented not simply a warning to white America but "a revolt against the Negro leadership," including himself.[23] His sense of failure was shared by such national leaders as James Farmer of CORE, who concluded that "civil rights organizations have failed. No one had any roots in the ghetto." Bayard Rustin, too, feared that "we must hold ourselves responsible for not reaching them. . . . Roy [Wilkins], Martin and I haven't done a damn thing about it. We've done plenty to get votes in the South and seats in the lunchrooms, but we've had no program for these youngsters."[24]

Such self-criticism was accompanied by the sense that this alienated constituency was the one to which they must appeal, were they to retain their influence as the focus of the struggle for black equality shifted. Roger Wilkins, nephew of the NAACP leader and head of President Johnson's Community Relations Service, identified "some pride among Negroes about Watts."[25] This he ascribed to a recent mood change that had profound implications for those civil rights leaders accustomed to a close relationship with the liberal establishment:

> In earlier decades, the overwhelming majority of Negroes retained a profound faith in America, her institutions, her ideals, and her ability to achieve someday a society reflecting those ideals. The flaws were in the white people—their meanness, their funny stupidity or their inconsistency—but not in the institutions. Now, however, there is a growing and seriously held view among some young militant Negroes that white people have imbedded their own personal flaws so deeply in the institutions that those institutions are beyond redemption.[26]

The waning influence of the established black leadership created an additional dilemma for the Johnson administration as it sought to defuse ghetto anger without offending white Democrats: simply stated, the president had to decide which black constituency to court, the moderate leadership or the militants. He received quite different counsel from George Reedy and Ramsey Clark, respectively. Reedy's advice proceeded from two problematic premises. First, he drew a distinction between the "militant" Martin Luther King, Jr., John Lewis, and James Farmer, and the "older Negro leadership" represented by A. Philip Randolph, Roy Wilkins, and Whitney Young, Jr. Although the two groups had indeed been associated with different brands of activity during the struggle for legal equality, Reedy's dichotomy led him to neglect a more politically important divide that was now opening up: all six of these leaders were now banded together in opposition to the fiery black nationalism of Floyd McKissick and Stokely Carmichael. Second, he adjudged that "the basic problem now is less one of fighting for gains and more one of consolidating the gains already made."[27] Whatever its possible merits, this argument ran directly counter to the spirit of the Howard University address and seemed to ignore the lessons that Johnson had already publicly drawn from Watts.

Based on these doubtful propositions, Reedy believed that Johnson must act to shore up the position of "the older Negro leadership." If the president emphasized the importance that he attached to the counsel of Randolph and Wilkins, then their ranks would be swollen by "other men who are younger but possessed of similar temperaments and capabilities." He urged:

> The Federal Government would be well advised to make a public point of consulting Randolph, Wilkins, and Young *(particularly Wilkins)* in the period ahead. Frequent invitations to the White House would be in order, and anything that could be done to increase his prestige would help to shift the focus from demonstrations in the streets to the type of constructive work that now is so badly needed.[28]

Such counsel was undoubtedly congenial to the president. But given that these elder statesmen had—as Reedy himself observed—become "somewhat suspect as soft on whites and . . . forced into ludicrous postures to maintain any standing at all," associating them more closely with the White House would not necessarily help their cause. Ramsey Clark's contrary advice was based on a harrowing survey of Watts following the riot, which he had undertaken as deputy attorney general. Clark urged the president to acknowledge that militancy was here to stay, and act accordingly. The firebrand, indigenous leaders of the ghetto "may not be well trained or particularly skilled in the techniques of communication and the management of social change," he said, but they did "seem to enjoy the trust and confidence of the masses in whose name they speak. It is a matter of the greatest importance that these new leaders be understood, because increasingly it is through them that the restive minorities in our major cities will be reached."[29]

Black leaders had compelling reasons for distancing themselves from the politics of liberal gradualism, politics that the White House had no choice but to pursue. During the struggle for civil rights, the impatience among even the moderate black leaders with the temporizing world of

Washington politics had been balanced by legislative self-interest, allied to an authentic commitment to the ideals of American society. Now, self-interest dictated responsiveness to a constituency that, according to Roger Wilkins, rejected those ideals. As liberals sought politically practicable ways of reaffirming their commitment to black advancement, black leaders felt both a moral and a tactical need to distance themselves from their erstwhile allies and to embrace wider-ranging critiques of American society. During the autumn of 1965, both of these patterns were manifested. First, the release of the Moynihan Report produced a furor in which the alleged liberal obsession with black morality was dubbed irrelevant and racist. Second, a White House planning conference designed to produce a blueprint for racial equality instead turned into a sustained assault on the politics and principles of liberalism.

THE BLACK FAMILY CONTROVERSY

The post-Watts environment of confusion and disaffection had a profound impact on the reception Moynihan's *Negro Family* report received when it was publicly released in the late summer of 1965. That Moynihan's focus was controversial had been apparent back in March. When Willard Wirtz forwarded the report to Bill Moyers, he emphasized its confidentiality, noting that "there are *no* other copies in circulation." But the secretary of labor was excited by Moynihan's dramatic findings and believed that the document "warrants *very serious* consideration."[30] Johnson's awareness of the inherent delicacy of the black family issue is reflected in the care with which the authors of the Howard University speech emphasized white society's culpability. Reflecting on the speech's reception in July, the president conceded to one correspondent that "there was, of course, some apprehension that so frank a discussion of a somewhat sensitive issue might be misunderstood"; however, he was "pleased to report to you that the reception has been uniformly positive."[31] His pleasure was not misplaced; the speech had indeed been praised for displaying "an amazing comprehension of the barriers that are present in our society to the Negro's progress and . . . the debilitation that results from slum living."[32] Just one week before the Watts riot, Johnson sought to capitalize further on the success of his message by having 4,500 complementary presentation copies of his remarks distributed to selected worthies.[33]

83

At this stage, the source document for this heralded speech had not yet been published, but leaked portions from the Moynihan Report were beginning to appear in the press, causing some anxiety to the administration. One Department of Labor official, John W. Leslie, expressed concern that the report might damage the black cause, if used out of context. But if the report's apocalyptic tone was warranted, he felt that it was surely "incumbent upon us to make some effort to forestall the crisis and to correct the conditions which are fomenting it."[34] Lee White, the president's leading civil rights adviser, was particularly worried that it would "be picked up by the segregationists and used against the Negro and as a political document."[35]

Administration officials who worried that the Moynihan Report could be exploited by the right as representing the case for inaction did not seem to consider that liberals might be accused of a similar design. As it turned out, conservatives' exploitation of the report was negligible compared to the storm of criticism from the left that beset Moynihan and the administration in the aftermath of the report's final release at the end of August.

The negative reaction was intense and sustained. Moynihan was condemned variously for a naive and statistically inadequate rehashing of outdated research, and for producing a racist polemic intended to demonstrate the superior virtue of the white middle-class family. According to Floyd McKissick, James Farmer's radical replacement at CORE, "Moynihan thinks everyone should have a family structure like his own. . . . Moynihan also emphasizes negative aspects of the Negroes and then seems to say that it's the individual's fault when it's the damn system that really needs changing."[36] Various church groups (most notably the National Council of Churches at its New York convention) passed resolutions denouncing Moynihan's "racism," while one Detroit group voiced objections to the report's supposed contention "that the American Negro was . . . somewhat less than human."[37] William Ryan, a Boston psychiatrist and subsequently author of the 1971 book *Blaming the Victim*, accused Moynihan of "irresponsible nonsense" for drawing "inexact conclusions from weak and insufficient data" and criticized the report for unintentionally encouraging "a new form of subtle racism" that "seduces the reader into believing it is not racism and discrimination but the weaknesses and defects of the Negro himself that account for . . . inequality."[38]

So visceral and hostile a response may seem puzzling, given Moynihan's commitment to accelerated federal action on behalf of the black poor. Moynihan was an early advocate of affirmative action, a proponent of public works, and a critic of the opportunity approach of the War on Poverty. Writing to Secretary Wirtz, Moynihan observed that European countries less affluent than the United States had "solved" poverty by the simple expedient of focusing on redistributing income rather than on equalizing opportunity. America had chosen the latter strategy, but Moynihan pointed out that "the two are not opposite sides of the same coin."[39]

Moynihan's preference for the European approach was evident from his contribution to a February 1965 conference on poverty held at the University of California at Berkeley. In a coded criticism of the community action concept and its "effort to change the poor," he suggested that "the relation between poverty and affluence in the United States" was in fact "not paradoxical, but in some aspects causal." His preferred solution for poverty centered not on reforming individual behavior but rather on creating an economic environment in which desired traits would naturally flourish. At the heart of social policy must be "the question of how to insure a decent family income and a decent family setting for the working people of America."[40]

An intriguing insight into Moynihan's view of how the commitment to a national family policy should be implemented can be gained from a letter he wrote in September to his friend Harry McPherson. Revealing once more his interest in European antipoverty strategies, he told the White House aide that "if I had my way, I would press ahead with the most obvious and powerful of all family welfare policies: a family allowance." But he also recognized that this might be regarded as "too much, too soon," both for political reasons and because "it is not all that clear what ought to be done." In place of an immediate federal program, therefore, he suggested the possibility of a general "declaration of policy with the thought that programs will come along in time."

Moynihan's key recommendation was to legislate a Family Welfare Act of 1966, whose principal creation would be a Family Welfare Administration within HEW. Each year the new agency would prepare a Report on the American Family and, presumably, generate insights from which an integrated strategy would emerge. Commending his proposal to McPherson, Moynihan anticipated that it would have "profound effects on the Negro community without singling them [sic] out for special treatment." His plan would circumvent "what I assume would be the agonies of starting a Negro Marshall Plan." He suggested a rubric for the Family Welfare Act:

It is the policy of the United States to foster the welfare, stability and quality of family life to the end that the greatest possible number of American children may pass their childhood in a normal family environment.

Family income sufficient to provide for the normal needs of the entire family is essential to this end.

As far as possible, mothers of minor children ought not to be forced to work in order to supplement family income.

Programs and policies of the federal government which affect or influence family life ought to be carried out so as to enhance the welfare, stability and resources of the family unit.[41]

It is unfortunate that Moynihan should have been consigned by black activists and their white allies to that rogues' gallery reserved for racist apologists for societal injustice. It is not enough to say that his preoccupation with black family structure was inherently offensive and bound to provoke an angry response; Moynihan's thesis was a familiar one and had been widely applauded when outlined by President Johnson in his speech at Howard University. Neither is it sufficient to argue that his critics correctly exposed a nefarious liberal plot to excuse federal inaction regarding black poverty; rather, they *exposed* a dramatic plea for the commitment of far greater resources. How then can the assault on Moynihan be explained? Three general points warrant particular attention.

First, it is undoubtedly the case that *The Negro Family* left itself acutely vulnerable to criticism. It moves uneasily between the academic and political worlds, claiming for itself scientific justification, yet adopting the incautious tone of a polemicist's brief. In their valuable 1967 book, *The Politics of Controversy*, Lee Rainwater and William Yancey demonstrate that Moynihan's melodramatic prose actually served to distort his own argument, thereby paving the way for further distortion by others, especially those who had only read leaked highlights or had no patience for complexity. One notorious passage, widely reported, stated that "the very essence of the male animal, from the bantam rooster to the four-star general, is to strut."[42] Selective quotation and willful misrepresentation transformed this foolish but unimportant analogy into compelling "evidence" of the author's racism and mendacity. Elsewhere, Moynihan produced the bald statement that "Negro children without fathers flounder—and fail." The next sentence but one qualified this dramatic claim by observing that "the Negro community produces its share, very possibly more than its share, of young people who have the something extra that carries them over the worst obstacles."[43] Yet the previous, unqualified statement was the one most likely to remain in the mind of the reader.

Of greater substantive importance, the quest for sensation led Moynihan to attach fundamental causal significance to *all manner of factors*. Seeking to explain the "social pathology" of the ghetto, for example, he declared at one point that "the fundamental, overwhelming fact is that Negro unemployment . . . has continued at disaster levels for 35 years."[44] Referring to a 1940 study of white unemployed families, Moynihan effectively demonstrated that race was *not* the source of family breakups.[45] Yet elsewhere, he ascribed instability to "the matriarchal pattern of so many Negro families," explaining that "a fundamental fact of Negro American family life is the often reversed roles of husband and wife."[46]

The absence of recommendations, if defensible given the problem-dramatizing mission of the report, was also damaging. It is apparent that Moynihan's preference was for an integrated employment and family allowance program. Had this recommendation been straightforwardly stated in the report's conclusion (it is implicit within much of its main body), the author would have been less vulnerable to charges of blaming the victim.

In addition to its substantive content, *The Negro Family* was damaged by the circumstances of its release. The partial leaking of the document between June and August 1965 was probably more damaging to the administration's cause, encouraging distorted impressions of its thesis, which persisted even after the full version had been released. Rainwater and Yancey believe that the leaking was orchestrated by elements within the administration who disliked both Moynihan and his argument, and who sought to discredit the report. More recently, Nicholas Lemann has contended that the principal force behind the release of the report was Moynihan himself, acting from "a pride of authorship and of intellectual discovery that would have made it painful for him to know that he was not getting full credit for an important breakthrough."[47]

MOYNIHAN AND THE CHANGING POLITICS
OF RACE

Despite the Moynihan Report's inherent vulnerability to criticism, on grounds both presentational and substantive, it seems increasingly clear that the avalanche of opprobrium that engulfed Moynihan in the late summer and autumn of 1965 owed more to a third factor, namely the political environment in which it emerged. In the aftermath of Watts, both the politics and philosophy of Great Society liberalism were under assault. Intended as an imaginative break with the conventional wisdom, Moynihan's thesis instead became a symbol of everything that was found wanting in Great Society conceptions of justice and morality. Additionally, black leaders had a *tactical* interest in distancing themselves from the Johnson administration.

Moynihan himself appears to have shared the sense that he was the unjust victim of both tactical exigencies and a burgeoning assault on liberal values. In a 1966 letter to Harry McPherson, he reflected upon the optimistic mood of early 1965, recalling that "we had the money and the votes" to initiate a national family policy. Yet as events unfolded, it had become clear that two very different interests had a stake in discrediting the proposal: "we underestimated . . . the savage reaction of the Federal bureaucracy in HEW, and Labor, and to some extent OEO, and the even wilder resentment on the part of what might be called the Civil Rights left." He believed that bureaucrats whose programs were imperiled by any incipient redirection of policy had gone "outside the government to tell persons in the civil rights movement that the report was inaccurate, insulting, misleading and dangerous to the interests of the movement." At the time that the controversy broke, "the older civil rights leaders" had been "willing enough and in some cases even anxious to pursue the Howard thesis," but they "could not take the heat from the younger militants who are, after all, rivals as well as colleagues."[48]

In addition to such maneuverings, there is also the sense of a more general assault on liberal values. Two charges that critics of the report leveled against Moynihan were shortly to become standard indictments of the Great Society. First, critics detected, both in the report and within the entire Johnson agenda, the insupportable yet archetypal liberal conviction that American society was fundamentally sound. (This was, of course, a breathtakingly inaccurate reading of Moynihan's argument.) Second, they found distasteful Moynihan's implication that there was one ideal middle-class mold for the American family, and that deviations from that norm generated poverty.

Moynihan's enemies produced two alternative formulations that attested to their broader alienation from the tradition of liberal individualism within which the War on Poverty was located. They argued that the poor were victims not of their own immorality but of society's imperfection. With respect to the second point, they insisted that middle-class Americans had no authority to make the rights of the poor contingent upon the acceptability of their behavior. Both propositions gained strength when placed in a racial context, yet increasingly the doctrine that victims have unconditional rights while society has only obligations would inform broader perspectives on public policy.

Representing an attack on Great Society notions of reciprocal obligation and morality, these broad definitions of entitlement did nevertheless gain some support from attitudes that existed *within* the Johnson administration. Despite the War on Poverty's emphasis on "turning tax-eaters into taxpayers," the idea that income-maintenance strategies were philosophically inimical to self-help had been deprecated by the president's own 1964 task force on income maintenance. It may be true that task force members who demanded a more generous and equitable welfare system were animated by a distinctly traditional purpose, namely equalizing opportunity such that self-help became practicable. Yet once income maintenance as a strategy in the War on Poverty had emerged as a fit subject for intra-administration discussion, its advocacy on grounds of universal entitlement became less far-fetched, while the notion that poverty could be blamed on the individual lost ground.

It may also be possible to find the ethos that subsequently legitimized the guaranteed-income approach within the War on Poverty's espousal of the doctrine of maximum feasible participation. Partisans of maximum feasible participation by the poor tended at first to be the strongest advocates of the opportunity theory; they rejected doles and believed in the empowering potential of involvement. Doles were a palliative; participation was a means of access to a political system from which the poor were presently excluded. Insofar as this doctrine emphasized changing the individual and finding alternatives to anaesthetized dependency, its focus was traditional and congenial to those who boasted the virtues of American values.

But maximum feasible participation was also about confrontation. For Richard Boone, who left the OEO in 1965 to work for the newly founded Citizen's Crusade Against Poverty, empowerment resulted from a once voiceless and passive poor confronting unsympathetic political and social welfare institutions. And to the extent that the OEO interpreted maximum feasible participation in this way, it recognized the poor's right to define aims and ideals at odds with the traditional assumptions of city politics, federal bureaucracies, and the Economic Opportunity Act itself. In the winter of 1965–1966, poor Americans sponsored by the OEO began agitating for a guaranteed income.

TRYING TO KEEP THE GREAT SOCIETY AFLOAT

President Johnson's standing in the country remained impressive throughout this period. A Gallup poll taken at the beginning of November indicated that 66 percent of Americans approved of his performance in office, while only 21 percent expressed disapproval.[49] Yet judging by a number of political decisions made during the autumn of 1965, it also seems apparent that he was having to struggle to preserve a New Deal Democratic coalition threatened by the divisive politics of poverty and race.

Kenneth Clark had responded to the Harlem riot of 1964 with a general observation regarding the reformist impulse: "Action produces counteraction, . . . and then the question becomes: to which group do the forces of actual power choose to respond?" President Johnson was confronted with a number of such dilemmas during this period. But his response to each reflected a characteristic unwillingness to make the kind of choice that Clark's remark anticipated. On the one hand, Johnson's response to conflicts engendered by the antipoverty program, school desegregation, and the black family question revealed familiar centrist instincts and a distaste for controversy. But on the other hand, in each instance Johnson endeavored to persuade impatient activists that their objectives could still be achieved through his policies. Both from his decisions, and from those decisions that he failed to take, one can perceive a still strong but increasingly embattled president hoping to shore up a cherished consensus.

In each case, the president's balancing act was rendered still more delicate by the fact that he was forced to dampen a conflict for which he had in a sense been responsible. The political problems associated with the War on Poverty provide a case in point. Within months of the program's inception, the OEO's two major programs had become enmeshed in divisive controversy. Throughout 1965, the intensity of the conflict increased to the point where the president felt compelled to intervene.

As is familiar from the copious literature on the subject, the issue of maximum feasible participation by the poor in Community Action Programs (CAPs) generated particular acrimony. Johnson and the Council of Economic Advisors, insofar as they even considered such matters of detail, had envisioned the community action agency as a coordinating mechanism for disparate federal programs. Little concerned with the precise wording of Title II of the Act, neither they nor the Congress attached much significance to the commitment to participation. Yet, as has been seen, many antipoverty warriors viewed the maximum feasible participation clause as the program's most exciting and important provision, finding within it the authority for a confrontational relationship between the OEO and intransigent local establishments. This emphasis could scarcely have been more removed from the ethos of Johnson's liberalism.

As early as January 1965, Theodore McKeldin, Republican mayor of Baltimore, had warned Johnson of the "extremely strong and almost unanimous feeling" of the U.S. Conference of Mayors that "your plans are being hindered at the Federal level by individuals . . . who do not understand the problems and operations of local governments." He was worried that unless the early problems were resolved, the "important anti-poverty program might well obtain an unfavorable image which could hurt it immensely."[50] Hubert Humphrey, who was asked by Johnson to liaise between Sargent Shriver and the mayors to resolve the conflict, reiterated the warning two months later, reporting that "there are numerous problems . . . developing."[51]

By June, the publicity accorded two such problems had prompted James Rowe, a Washington lawyer and longstanding political ally, to alert the president. First, the veteran New Dealer directed Johnson's attention to a *New York Times* story that featured a Syracuse CAP whose $300,000 OEO grant was financing protests by the poor against the city's Housing Authority.[52] Second, he warned of a potentially troublesome initiative in the nation's capital, where "high-minded . . . innocents" at the OEO's national headquarters were "giving instructions and grants to local private groups for the purpose of training the Negro poor on how to conduct sit-ins and protest meetings against government agencies, federal, state and local." He further warned that a Republican congressman from New Jersey was investigating the case, and suggested that "the *political implications* of using public funds . . . to *instruct* people how to protest are quite obvious." An agitated president evidently agreed: in a scribbled note, he ordered Moyers, "Bill—for God's sake get on top of this and just put a stop to it at once."[53]

The predictable outcome of this series of embarrassments came in September 1965, when Johnson endorsed Charles Schultze's observation that "we ought not to be in the business of organizing the poor politically." Schultze, director of the president's Budget Bureau, averred that the proper role for the poor lay not in strategic planning or political protest but rather in working for professionally constructed local agencies. Whereas existing social welfare programs served to "destroy self-reliance among the poor and perpetuate the dole," successful CAPs would "talk . . .

to poor people to find out what their problems are."[54] Sharing the director's desire to minimize the "inevitable tension between CAP and local political officials," Johnson ordered Schultze to ensure that the OEO curtail its confrontational activities.

Yet Johnson's deference to local political establishments was matched by a desire to retain the allegiance, or at least limit the dissent, of the Great Society coalition's more radical wing. In this instance, the balancing act led him to reject calls for the OEO's disbandment. At the end of 1965, Joseph Califano and a task force on urban problems had each recommended that the troublemaking agency be disbanded and its functions transferred to older agencies and the new Department of Housing and Urban Development. Johnson's demurral stemmed from a familiar reluctance to expend political capital unnecessarily. The OEO's defenders, as well as its assailants, represented a critical component of his political coalition.

The same political equation guided Johnson's response to the unwelcome Chicago school desegregation controversy that materialized in the autumn of 1965. According to the Civil Rights Act of 1964, states and municipalities that refused to integrate public facilities, such as schools and hospitals, could be barred from receiving federal funding. Clearly the principal target was the recalcitrant South, but the mounting debate over de facto segregation in housing and education lent nationwide significance to the provision. In the wake of the Elementary and Secondary Education Act of 1965, Commissioner of Education Francis Keppel was under pressure to use the federal government's new leverage to insist on an end to racial discrimination in Northern school systems. To Keppel, Chicago must have appeared a logical target: at recent congressional hearings, the allegedly racist policies of the Daley administration had come under sharp attack, while CORE, the NUL, and the NAACP had all made the city a principal focus for their activism on the schools question.[55]

Yet in seeking to palliate one constituency, the commissioner antagonized another—one whose importance to the Johnson coalition was also considerable. As Joseph Califano explains, "Daley was critical to the success of the Great Society. A call to Daley was all that was necessary to deliver the fourteen votes of the Illinois Democratic congressional delegation. Johnson and others of us had made many calls to the Mayor and Daley had always come through."[56] Accordingly, the Keppel decision, already vulnerable on procedural grounds, was reversed, and its author demoted. On the surface, this episode is another example of the administration's retreat from the battle when confronted with the forces of conservatism; but again, such a version is too simple. Rather than retreating from reform, Johnson was intent on preserving the broad coalition that would allow his ambitious agenda to survive. Accordingly, on 17 November 1965, Johnson sought to protect his other flank by asking the Civil Rights Commission to launch an investigation into the general problem of de facto segregation in Northern schools. Significantly, this was also the day that the White House planning conference "To Fulfill These Rights" was launched.

WHITE HOUSE PLANNING CONFERENCE

During the preparations for the White House planning conference, President Johnson was compelled to respond to a backlash against liberal gradualism still more serious than those that had occurred before. Here, a transformation in the Johnson administration's relationship with the cause of reform was apparent. Hitherto, it had been plausible to argue that the Great Society program represented the cutting edge of reform, with the Economic Opportunity Act and the Howard University address the autonomous products of liberal brio. From now on, Johnson's domestic program had an increasingly *reactive* character, responding to powerful forces of disruption (riots, backlashes, budgetary constraints) over which he had little control. In the case of the civil rights conference, the defensive character of Johnson's actions is so strong that it becomes harder to find in them any strategy for advancing the Great Society.

Indeed, Lee Rainwater and William Yancey have argued that post-Watts racial polarization, together with budgetary constraints associated with the expanding commitment in Vietnam, led Johnson to retreat from the battle for racial equality during the autumn of 1965, and to make the Moynihan controversy his excuse for doing so. A number of pieces of evidence seem to substantiate this charge. During this period, for example, Johnson chose to reorganize his civil rights agencies, removing his activist vice president from overall command of their operations. It should be noted, however, that Johnson's top domestic adviser believes this change to have been inspired by the president's desire for a *stronger* personal identification with the cause of civil rights.[57] More persuasive evidence in support of the Rainwater and Yancey thesis is provided by Johnson's apparent lack of interest in the civil rights conference as the problems associated with it mounted.

At his Howard University address in June, Johnson had promised an autumn conference whose particular task would be to draw up a strategy for promoting black family stability. In the warm afterglow of the president's remarks, planning for the conference had proceeded apace, with experts being invited to the White House for consultation and with administration officials anticipating an early October date for the meeting.[58] In the wake of Watts and the Moynihan controversy, however, the conference was delayed and reoriented, while the author of the *Negro Family* report (who had resigned to seek elective office in New York) became persona non grata. (A year or so later, when Moynihan was appointed chairman of an HEW traffic safety committee without the president's knowledge, Johnson penned a furious note demanding, "Ask Cater who the Hell appointed Moynihan and get him out now —L.")[59]

More generally, the president's transparent lack of enthusiasm for the reconceived White House conference seems to bolster the Rainwater and Yancey argument. Anxious lest it degenerate into a damaging attack on administration policies, White House advisers sought to exclude supposed troublemakers within the civil rights community from participating. Among those whom the president hoped to marginalize was Bayard Rustin. In the view of Lee White, it was "essential that Bayard Rustin be invited to attend," partly because he was the personal representative of A. Philip Randolph, the conference chairman, and partly because he was regarded by the civil rights leadership "as one of the creative intellectual leaders in the Negro community." Johnson, however, was bothered by stories about Rustin's private life, and by the FBI's foolish concern that he was "a confirmed Marxist," causing White to emphasize that Rustin "would not play a leading role."[60]

Beyond his concern for minimizing dissension, Johnson appeared little interested in the activities of those whom he had charged with designing the conference agenda. One vexed organizer, Berl Bernhard, warned Johnson aides that "if any modicum of success is to be achieved, it is essential that we have the unequivocal backing of the White House."[61] Meanwhile, Joseph Califano warned that "almost everyone raises the issue," and conference co-organizer Morris Abrams complained that he remained "essentially in the dark."[62] But only at the last minute, and then after repeated prodding, did Johnson give the go-ahead for a November planning conference designed to come up with a program for the full meeting to be held in the spring of 1966. Rustin complained of "the haphazard manner with which things have occurred to date," and told civil rights colleagues that in the absence of

White House leadership *they* would have the principal responsibility for making the conference meaningful."[63]

The evidence in support of the Rainwater and Yancey view thus far seems persuasive. Closer investigation, however, casts doubt on its merit. Moynihan himself discounted the idea that Johnson "was using the umbrage of the militants as an excuse for backing down from the genuinely radical position he took at Howard." Writing to Harry McPherson in 1966, he remarked, "I don't have to tell you I believe life is more complicated than that."[64] In his view, the administration's abandonment of the black family issue stemmed from naïveté rather than cynicism; it had endeavored to appease militants whose approval was still deemed valuable. This courting of the report's critics had been, in Moynihan's view, the misguided product of the fact that "you fellows, being Southern populist types, do not really understand the Northern left." In truth, "these people do not intend any good toward the President, nor any of us." To the contrary, he felt that the *Negro Family* controversy had been part of a broader and coordinated attempt to wound the administration.[65]

Moynihan's account highlights the biggest single weakness of the Rainwater and Yancey thesis: it is by no means clear that the Johnson administration gave up on the Great Society during the autumn of 1965. Indeed it has commonly been argued that it was precisely his *unwillingness* to downgrade the Great Society as the Vietnam War escalated that grievously wounded both Johnson's presidency and the national economy. By the time that *The Politics of Controversy* was published in 1967, the full impact of racial polarization and war on the administration's early hopes was obvious, and understandably it encouraged the kind of interpretation that the two sociologists produced. Yet in the autumn of 1965, the administration and its programs remained popular, the future course of the war in Vietnam was not foreseen, and the economic problems of 1966–1968 had yet to materialize. Rainwater and Yancey provide an instructive insight into the mounting problems that beset the liberal reformist impulse in the autumn of 1965. But they misread the administration's political equation, and neglect to consider Johnson's stubborn belief that his mastery of the game of politics would allow him to continue to build a Great Society in the face of competing pressures.

Nevertheless, the course of the White House planning conference "To Fulfill These Rights" did go some way toward demonstrating the futility of the presidential balancing act, the quest for consensus. At the conference, assembled black leaders, antipoverty activists, and academics subjected the

philosophy as well as the politics of Great Society liberalism to all but continuous attack. And as the various sessions proceeded, arguments that had
emerged in opposition to the Moynihan Report appeared once more, this
time as part of a philosophy of entitlement quite divorced from opportunity-based liberalism. At the time, the appeal of this nascent creed was limited, and its principles were not fully articulated, but within two years an
important strain of American liberalism would find merit in its radical
propositions. Three themes of the conference seem particularly relevant to
subsequent developments.

The first of these pervasive themes is well summarized by the conclusions of the solitary panel concerned with the family question: "All families
should have the right to evolve in directions of their own choosing . . .
[and] should have the supports—economic and non-economic—to exercise that right."[66] Martin Luther King, Jr.'s representative, Andrew Young,
expressed the dominant view that "there probably isn't anything wrong with
the Negro family as it exists," while other contributors protested the persistent moralism of federal policy.[67]

A second striking feature of the gathering was the frequency with which
delegates argued that liberal values were an impediment to social and racial
justice. The view that traditional liberalism and the nation's individualist tradition were obstacles to effective antipoverty policy pervaded conference
discussions on the structural basis for deprivation. Given that the same suspicion had begun to find voice *within* liberal ranks, this much was unsurprising. More radical, however, was the claim by some speakers that the federal
government was an agent of repression that friends of the poor must necessarily confront in the name of equality. The academic and activist Richard
A. Cloward, for example, bemoaned the traditional liberal "tendency to
convert social problems into personal inadequacies, rather than institutional inadequacies." But the conclusions he drew from this insight were
quite different from those of Bayard Rustin or Daniel Patrick Moynihan.
Cloward asked:

> When does a society begin to . . . turn to a searching appraisal of its own institu-
> tions? Only, I would suggest . . . when enough power is generated on the part of
> those who are implicated in the problem, or other allies, like those of us who are
> neither Negro nor poor who do care about this problem. . . . I do not think we
> will come out of this conference with anything useful if all we do is recommend
> that the Federal Government do this, this and that. They are not going to do
> it. . . . They are only going to move if we can somehow or another grapple with
> the question of how communities organize to force the Federal Government to

move in areas that we know action has to be taken in. . . . The only relevant subject for us to discuss here is how we mobilize power.[68]

The seeming logic of this position was that OEO programs might most
effectively be used *against* the institution that had brought them into being.
Chicago activist Lawrence Landry, whose powerbase was funded by the
OEO, wholeheartedly endorsed Cloward's thesis but was troubled by the
vexing problem of how to "con the Federal Government into loosening up
some power." Every time he tried to radicalize the local black community
against the white power structure, he "ran into these stupid Federal bureaucrats."[69] Responding to Landry's suggestion that "the foundations, the
mayor's committees, the Federal Government are the enemies," Cloward—
apparently not discomforted by the fact that his own research into juvenile
delinquency had been supported by just such sources—issued a laconic, "So
what else is new?"[70]

A final theme of the conference, one that would be heard with ever
greater frequency during the remainder of the decade, was the notion that
the rights of disadvantaged groups are unconditional. References to self-
help, equality of opportunity, and reciprocal obligation were conspicuous by
their absence at a conference that seemed preoccupied with the two distinct
tasks of defining rights for the poor and responsibilities for the federal government. This emphasis on entitlement may be attributed in part to the fact
that this was ostensibly a racially oriented gathering, at which references to
reciprocity could easily seem inappropriate. The notion that rights owed
black Americans on account of historical racism could not properly be
made conditional was unremarkable.

More noteworthy at this gathering was the extent to which the rights-ori-
entation of the discussions persisted, even when the rhetoric of race disappeared. Conferees frequently stressed the similar dynamics of black and
white poverty, partly because notions that the black problem was unique
recalled the Moynihan thesis, and partly because an ostensibly colorblind
public policy was easier to sell. Far from being devoted to a distinctly black
problem, the White House conference was told that it must consider problems common to all poor Americans, irrespective of their color.[71] Income
deficiency was clearly the most basic problem, and in considering the merits
of the guaranteed income concept, the welfare panel paid relatively little
attention to race.

One discussant, Professor Edward E. Schwartz, favored abolishing the
current welfare system and replacing it with a negative income tax (NIT)

dispensed purely on the basis of need. This new antipoverty strategy would be achieved through the attractively straightforward expedient of continuing the income tax sliding scale below the threshold so that the Internal Revenue Service paid the poor rather than vice versa. Rapidly winning new converts among social scientists and bureaucrats, the NIT concept as yet failed to excite many activists. Reflecting on the welfare session a week later, Elizabeth Wickenden observed that income-maintenance options had "provoked extensive debate among the professionals with relatively little interest or support from the grass-roots participants." She noted that Schwartz had failed to receive the hoped-for endorsement for the NIT, in part because "the grass-roots people seemed far more interested in *jobs* than any fancied-up form of assistance payments."[72]

Not surprisingly, the Johnson administration and its allies found the tenor of the November planning conference distressing. No longer could Great Society liberalism claim to embody some kind of consensual approach to the challenge of affluence. The rancor and radicalism of the meeting suggested that the administration's existing accomplishments had been forgotten and its programs marginalized. Moreover, the ethos of entitlements for victims and obligations for government was deeply dispiriting, in political terms. As Monroe E. Price, a Labor Department official, observed to Secretary Wirtz, "Washington is looked to as the great answer. There was very little attention given to the responsibility of institutions and individuals outside the federal government."[73] Harry McPherson recalls his disquiet concerning the political implications of the emerging judgment that personal morality was of no relevance to public policy:

> No doubt there were beneficent values in Negro lower-class life. . . . But there was also an abundance of crime, brutality, idleness and poverty, and not much hope of better. The adoption of at least some middle-class values seemed indispensable to changing that. Anyway, it was certain that middle-class taxpayers, black or white, would not wish to pay for the preservation of a "value system" that tolerated illegitimacy and male irresponsibility.[74]

Wickenden, a veteran of the New Deal, social work consultant, and longtime personal friend of the Johnsons, was vexed by the administration's attempts to present the November planning sessions as a success:

> Without understanding the precise purpose of this conference it is extremely difficult to assess the extent of its success or failure. It certainly did *not* produce: (1) a plan for the full conference, (2) a consensus on needed programs

or policies, or (3) a consolidation of support behind the existing programs of the administration. It seemed rather to consolidate and intensify the dissatisfaction, frustrations and militancy of the Negro leadership. . . . I heard nothing that reflected either on the President's speech or on his sincerity in calling the conference.[75]

TOWARD AN OPPORTUNITY-ORIENTED INCOME STRATEGY

If American liberals felt compelled to modify the traditionalist message of 1964 in response to black anger, then their approach to problems of poverty and race had also to recognize the electorate's continued resistance to more expansive definitions of income entitlement. When the Gallup organization asked Americans to pass judgment on the idea of a guaranteed income for all, only 19 percent expressed approval.[76] Political exigencies and personal preference alike suggested the need for a revised theory of economic opportunity, one which respected popular individualism but also abandoned the assumption that existing rehabilitative strategies could adequately address America's escalating social crisis.

This was not the first generation of reformers in American history that was forced to confront the conceptual limitations of an inherited individualist tradition. In the Progressive Era and the New Deal period, the reformist spirit had confronted profoundly dislocating forces of modernity and economic depression, respectively. Yet in each case, reformers had managed to fuse new insights with old values that retained popular appeal. During the autumn of 1965, it appeared that American liberalism's adaptive capacity might be demonstrated once again, this time in response to racial conflict and the obvious inability of the Economic Opportunity Act to ameliorate economic disadvantage or stave off social disorder. As had Moynihan before them, Ramsey Clark, Wilbur Cohen, and Sargent Shriver each sought more plausible means (plausible, that is, in both political and conceptual terms) of attaining President Johnson's traditional ends.

One product of the administration's bid to rethink the Great Society was Ramsey Clark's investigation into the Watts riot. Although his report was careful to emphasize the importance of existing Great Society initiatives in building individual competence and facilitating self-advancement,

Clark also urged a massive public jobs program—a strategy that had been explicitly rejected in 1964 as both costly and unnecessary. Simply providing vocational training, such as that offered by the Job Corps or the Manpower Development and Training Act, would not create opportunity where private sector job vacancies did not exist. OEO programs would only contribute to unrest, unless jobs commensurate with acquired skills could be created in black communities:

> The most important and immediate task is to put people to work and to make sure that opportunities are provided for people with ability to be promoted on their merits. The high unemployment statistics and low income figures in the Watts and South Los Angeles areas tell only part of the story. They do not tell of the frustration [of continual rejection or] . . . the humiliation felt by men who stay at home with their children while their wives support them. . . . And they do not tell of the social dynamite locked inside the clusters of angry unemployed men seen on the streets of the slum, day after day and night after night. These are the raw materials of riots.[77]

Clark's recommendations reflected the new urgency of the War on Poverty and the need to demonstrate the relevance of mainstream politics to angry black youths by producing immediate results. For this purpose, the OEO's programs were clearly inappropriate. Their projected gains were uncertain, indirect, and long-term; their scale, hopelessly inadequate. If future riots were to be averted, then the federal government must assume responsibilities that the Economic Opportunity Act reserved for the individual.

Another challenge to the orientation of the Economic Opportunity Act, or at least to the conviction that welfarism should be conceived as a principal adversary, came with the findings of the 1965 Inter-Agency Task Force on Public Assistance. Chaired by Wilbur J. Cohen, undersecretary at HEW, the report went further than its 1964 predecessor in seeking to convert welfare from villain to weapon in the War on Poverty:

> The largest problem in the public assistance program is that under present arrangements most persons receiving assistance do not receive enough money to make it possible for them to live at even a minimum level of decency and dignity. . . . Without adequate income support for those needing such support, programs aimed at providing the tools for poor people to move from poverty may have limited success, since the prior meeting of basic needs is essential for individual development in the majority of cases.[78]

Cohen was convinced that the grudging terms upon which relief was dispensed stigmatized welfare and humiliated recipients without providing opportunities for self-advancement. But the task force report did not go so far as to suggest that the behavior of the dependent poor was an improper subject for debate, a contention that accompanied guaranteed income advocacy in subsequent years. Instead, it remarked that "rewards are more effective than penalties as an incentive to acceptable behavior. . . . The way to convince people they want to be part of the majority social and cultural life of the Nation is not to isolate them further but to help them into that life, at least at a minimally adequate level."[79]

The report's preferred solution was a radical one: "If public assistance programs are to be an effective source of help in eliminating poverty, they must be defined and designed to reach all the poor."[80] However, the task force proposed to achieve this end by amending the existing welfare system rather than by substituting the "broad income maintenance approach." The latter option was rejected as inefficient, expensive, and lacking in social service provision. Furthermore, the task force was highly conscious that America's existing welfare system was "held in disrepute" because of the "widespread impression . . . that public welfare administers a static, dole type of program."[81] As a result, it sought reforms "consistent with— and seeking to reinforce—two cherished American values: 1) The importance and morality of working for a living, and 2) family responsibility."[82]

While the public assistance task force struggled to develop income-maintenance proposals that would relieve poverty without offending popular sensitivities, Sargent Shriver's Office of Economic Opportunity moved aggressively in favor of a more sweeping departure, namely the negative income tax (NIT). At first glance, it might seem strange that the War on Poverty's coordinating agency should have become enthusiastic about a concept that proposed to attack deprivation by dispensing income rather than services, but at this stage the NIT was viewed neither as an admission of failure by the OEO nor as a permanent addition to the welfare state. Fired by an optimism that would soon seem naive in the extreme, one agency official, Joseph Kershaw, enthusiastically noted that "one of the attractive features of the Negative Income Tax is that it would automatically go away as the [poverty] problem is cured."[83]

The OEO's interest in the NIT, and its conviction that income support was essential rather than antithetical to any comprehensive war on poverty, were reflected in the antipoverty budget presented by Sargent Shriver to President Johnson on October 20, 1965. In its preliminary deliberations, the agency had anticipated the income strategy's philosophical problems:

> The main arguments that will be offered against a negative income tax are that it will:
>
> • fight poverty by income maintenance rather than direct human investment—a change in strategy (but we know both are necessary);
>
> • give public money to people who could earn their own way . . . ;
>
> • provide money to undesirables such as drug addicts, alcoholics and beatniks who may be able to survive without working if given this handout.[84]

Shriver faced an uphill task in seeking to convert Johnson to the NIT principle, and to a proposed antipoverty budget of some $9 billion for 1967, as compared to $1.5 billion in fiscal year 1966. With these ambitions in mind, the OEO director promised domestic tranquillity as the prize and allied his purpose to Johnson's cherished vision of American pluralism: "Racial and economic integration are basic to each other and can only be achieved together. . . . The integration of the poor into American society will assist in perfecting the democratic process so that every citizen may share in national decisions."[85] Having reminded Johnson of the stakes, Shriver reassured him that OEO's commitment to self-help remained undimmed:

> Given the goals of the Great Society and the language of the Economic Opportunity Act, it is not permissible to view the war on poverty merely as a program to provide money to the poor. Rather, we emphasize altering society so poor people are able to raise *themselves* above the poverty level through their *own* efforts. . . . Although an annual injection of $12 billion could end poverty as currently defined in the United States, this improvement would not last. . . . Thus, in comparing various poverty programs, we define cost-effectiveness primarily in terms of a *permanent* increase in opportunity and productivity.[86]

Shriver presented the president with a revised "total antipoverty plan" that had three inseparable elements: jobs, social programs, and transfer payments. In immediate budgetary terms, this required an increase of $2.5 billion in the OEO's budget, $4.7 billion in appropriations for the negative income tax, and $5.3 billion more for social security. Shriver's proposed public employment program was remarkably bold, projecting a "growth of Public Sector jobs from 200,000 in 1967 to 800,000 in 1970."

The OEO echoed Ramsey Clark in contending that "it would be meaningless to prepare people unless there are jobs in which [trainees] can fulfill their capabilities." Jobs alone, however, were not enough; hence the continued importance of community action and other initiatives "designed to counteract or avoid the destructive effects of poverty on poor people." Shriver stressed the reciprocal relationship between social and economic programs:

> It is necessary to provide the job skills that people need and to change the environment which prevents them from improving themselves. This is fundamental. Were we to try to cure poverty purely by creating jobs, we could cause inflation before creating enough of the type of jobs to support those poor whose capabilities have not been improved. Conversely, the job program is necessary to the success of social programs. Without jobs, programs to increase capabilities would create hopes without creating a chance for their fulfillment.

Finally, transfer payments, including a negative income tax, would provide "temporary help for those who will ultimately be helped by the job and social programs, but, in the interim, require some minimal standard of decency." If Johnson and subsequent presidents were to adopt the OEO's new blueprint, then poverty might be eliminated in about two decades. At that point, the federal government should consider guaranteeing an income to all low-income Americans, for "those capable of raising themselves above poverty will already have income above this guaranteed minimum."

CONCLUSION

In the aftermath of the Watts riot, leading figures within the Johnson administration—Ramsey Clark, Wilbur Cohen, and Sargent Shriver, to name but three—developed and promoted antipoverty initiatives that implied a significant departure from the modest service strategy of 1964. The OEO's programs could still be represented as a war on dependency, but—largely as a result of racial imperatives—the elimination of poverty had acquired new urgency. Previously an expression of Great Society liberalism's faith in the virtue and vitality of American values and institutions, the Economic Opportunity Act now seemed compelled to challenge a host of cherished popular assumptions in order to convince an alienated minority that American pluralism could incorporate their interests and aspirations.

Sargent Shriver presented his grand design to Johnson in October 1965, telling the president that it was predicated on the assumption that there would be "little or no increase in the defense budget." Just three months later his expectations, along with those of Clark and Cohen, were to be deflated as the escalating cost of the Vietnam War forced domestic retrenchment. With the introduction of the fiscal year 1967 budget in January 1966 came President Johnson's response to these proposals, and the beginnings of serious liberal dissension.

CHAPTER 5

Vietnam, Black Power, and the Decline of the Great Society

In his 1966 State of the Union Address, Lyndon Johnson reassured his countrymen that America was "strong enough to pursue our goals in the rest of the world while still building a Great Society at home."[1] But this was to be the year when the Vietnam War's economic and budgetary effects started to place a severe strain on the president's relationship with the liberal community. The first session of the 89th Congress had compiled a remarkable record of social reform; its successor was to be more concerned with the successful implementation and funding of existing programs than with further legislative accomplishment. In the aftermath of the Watts riot, congressional liberals had shared their president's shock and confusion, and at the end of 1965 they continued to view him as the tribune of their values, despite growing black disaffection.[2] If they shared Sargent Shriver's conviction that the War on Poverty must assume an altogether bolder character in response to America's disturbing social crisis, then there seemed no reason to doubt the president's similar commitment and every reason to believe that their common concerns would be embodied in the FY 1967 budget.

This chapter examines the consequences of Johnson's failure to honor his guns-and-butter rhetoric during the first eight months of 1966. Liberals who already viewed the Vietnam War with disfavor were uniformly shocked by the modest domestic funding requests that military commitments impelled. And as the president's popularity collapsed (from 62 percent in December 1965 to 46 percent in May 1966),[3] they became increasingly willing to distance themselves from the White House. Meanwhile, to their left, a radical welfare rights movement was emerging, one whose objective went far beyond that of Sargent Shriver's "total antipoverty program." Liberals and their radical critics were now to some extent enmeshed in a recurring bidding cycle whose momentum increasingly led members of the Great Society coalition to question their individualist precepts.

THE ECONOMICS OF VIETNAM

It is in retrospect ironic that the Council of Economic Advisors (CEA) was initially inclined to view the escalation in Vietnam as a useful economic stimulus. Writing in July 1965, Council Chairman Gardner Ackley assured President Johnson that "it means extra insurance against slow-down or recession, . . . not a threat of overheating. . . . On a coldly objective analysis, the overall effects are most likely to be favorable to our prosperity.[4] Slightly more than four months later, however, the administration was forced to conduct its FY 1967 budget negotiations under very different conditions. As Sargent Shriver, Wilbur Cohen, and Ramsay Clark were submitting ambitious recommendations for massive federal expenditure, the threat of an uncontrolled explosion in economic demand called out for cutbacks in nondefense expenditure. Arthur Okun, a member of the CEA, identified "a straightforward recipe for dealing with the problem of war finance. Take a substantial rise in taxes and a small cutback in federal nondefense outlays so that, in combination, overall fiscal policy remains about as stimulative as it would have been in the absence of the additional defense spending."[5] Ackley warned that if the budget for 1967 were $115 billion (i.e., an increase of almost 15 percent), a tax increase would be the only way to avoid severe inflation. Even a $110 billion budget would probably require such a move.

But Johnson felt politically unable to accept such counsel. For one thing, he had piloted a large tax cut through Congress less than two years earlier, and House Ways and Means Chairman Wilbur Mills warned that legislators were in no mood to acquiesce to an increase now. The only way he could secure a rise was by citing war escalation as the cause, but this would generate conservative calls for severe domestic cutbacks and embolden the hawks, who at this time provided the most serious opposition to Johnson's Vietnam policies.[6] Additionally, Johnson had very little idea of what the war was likely to cost during FY 1967, and hence how much strain defense expenditures would put on the budget and the economy.[7] As Okun later recalled, "to the untrained eye, the economy seemed to be doing remarkably well. Anybody who wanted to slow things down was a killjoy. . . . All [the] unfavorable consequences of the boom were still forecasts rather than facts."[8]

At this critical moment in December 1965, social, political, and economic exigencies were all pulling in different directions, and the administration was confronted with a singularly difficult balancing act. By approving only a modest "bits and pieces" revenue package, keeping his war options open, and limiting increases in nondefense expenditure to a distinctly modest $600 million, the president hoped to protect his fledgling Great Society until such time as desired expansion could responsibly be financed. Nevertheless, with hindsight it can be seen that Johnson's decision not to seek a tax increase at this time was a fateful one, whose consequences would include economic dislocation (inflation), political division (the growing resistance of liberal legislators to Johnson's alleged parsimony), and social polarization (the strengthening of radical alternatives to orthodox liberalism). The two latter trends developed increasing force during the remainder of 1966 and, in 1967–1968, combined to lend respectability to a bold social philosophy whose conception of income entitlement represented a stunning repudiation of the New Deal tradition.[9]

THE POLITICS OF THE FISCAL YEAR 1967 BUDGET

If the CEA warned of "less rapid progress toward the Great Society" and the Budget Bureau predicted "conditions of great uncertainty,"[10] then the liberal community was more inclined to adopt President Johnson's guns-and-butter message. Jacob Javits was upbeat in his assessment of the economic and budgetary situation. Rejecting "the idea that the relevant choice is between guns and butter," he was confident that "our private enterprise system is flexible and inventive enough to provide both in an atmosphere of confidence fostered by wise and creative government policy."[11] House Speaker John McCormack was similarly sanguine, noting that "President Johnson has harmonized the situation where we now protect effectively freedom's interests in the world and yet go ahead with a progressive America."[12] Labor leader Walter Reuther assured the Economic Club of Detroit that "the American economy is equal to meeting both of these challenges."[13] Opinion samples suggested that the public shared contemporary liberalism's optimism. One Harris poll indicated that as many as 72 percent of Americans dissented from the proposition that domestic programs should be curtailed as Vietnam expenditures increased.[14]

Given the absence of any signals from the administration as to the likely duration of the Vietnam War, and widespread support for the guns-and-butter formulation, it is scarcely surprising that liberal legislators responded with dismay to a series of surprisingly low domestic budget requests. Time and again during subsequent weeks—in response to the new Model Cities initiative, the rent supplement program, the Economic Opportunity Act, and the Teacher Corps bill—the administration was assailed for failing to honor program commitments made during the previous two years. As Congressman James Scheuer of New York, head of the influential Democratic Study Group, remarked in March, "We do not support the President's request for added military procurement authorization with the idea that the poor or any other disadvantaged group in our Great Society will pay that bill."[15]

Since the power of education to redistribute opportunity lay at the heart of the Great Society's mission, the congressional debate surrounding renewal of the Elementary and Secondary Education Act provides a particularly instructive insight into the increased fragility of the liberal coalition. To both Johnson and liberals generally, the 1965 Act represented the very embodiment of America's commitment to self-advancement. Congressional dismay at 1966 cutbacks confirms that liberals were first alienated from the White House by the scale rather than the orientation of the Johnson program.

The Act's many enthusiasts were particularly vexed by the administration's refusal to request more than $1 billion for Title I (which provided assistance to children in disadvantaged school districts). John Brademas (D-Ind.) told HEW Secretary John W. Gardner that talk of increased spending over FY 1966 masked cutbacks below previously anticipated expansion. John Ford (D-Mich.) concurred:

> Great expectations were raised throughout the country last year when we presented this bill on the floor. The administration . . . said that a matter of first priority in the coming year would be the pressing problem of unhoused schoolchildren. . . . Isn't the risk of losing an additional year or two years or three years of full-time education to a substantial number of children . . . something that threatens the future security of this country?[16]

Gardner could only concede the "cogency" of Ford's argument and cite overall budgetary constraints as precluding expansion, but Hugh Carey, a congressman from New York City, found such reasoning unacceptable. In his view, "We are being forced to make a choice here between books and bullets." Recalling that passage of the original bill had been accompanied by "assurances from the highest possible sources that there would be more money next year," Carey observed that the need for adequate federal aid to education was greater now than ever. At a time when the nation's cities were "at their very wits end trying to find sources of taxation to cure the great cities' problems in education," legislators were "being shortchanged."[17]

James Scheuer was one of a number of Democrats who attributed the administration's rough ride to the intoxicating optimism of Great Society rhetoric during the previous two years: "The frustration and disappointment that you heard today is in a sense due to your own eloquence and your own creativity in whetting our appetites. . . . The scope of the proposal which you have made and the increasing authorization which you have requested over the last year's program are immoderately moderate."[18] In 1965, northern Democrats had striven to associate themselves with the programs and pronouncements of a popular president, but as the magic faded, some sought to insulate themselves from Vietnam-impelled restrictions by stressing the independence of Congress. Scheuer reminded Gardner that "we have a separate and distinct role to play."[19] And Brademas asserted that "some of us in Congress feel constrained at times to take a sober second look, and not to regard as divine ordinance anything, simply because it bears a label stamped made in the executive branch." He continued:

> There has been a lot of conversation in this town in the last few years on whether or not Congress can have any creative or initiative role in making policy, or whether we are simply going to be confined to amending or ratifying proposals for legislation presented by the administration. . . . We have a right, and indeed an obligation, to make our own judgment on what wise public policy is, because we are the ones who have to go back home every two years and defend it. Members of the cabinet don't.[20]

Despite their genuine dismay, such remarks probably gave a certain satisfaction to liberal legislators whose endeavors had been overshadowed by Johnson's leadership during the past two years. As early as July 1965, one anonymous legislator told *U.S. News and World Report* that many colleagues, ostensible friends of the administration, welcomed the growing Vietnam controversy as "an excuse to assert some independence."[21] Recalling this period in their book *Lyndon B. Johnson: The Exercise of Power,* Rowland Evans and Robert Novak suggest that "sensitized . . . liberals" were "ready to explode at the first major grievance that came along. . . . Their honeymoon with Johnson had about run its course. They had lived with consensus long enough and were not only prepared but were eager to make the break with Johnson."[22] When the journalist Jack Newfield accused the Americans for Democratic Action—self-appointed guardian of the liberal spirit—of belonging to a consensual "Liberal Establishment," an aggrieved founding member emphasized the organization's dissension on key foreign policy questions.[23]

This combination of factors ensured that when the administration's education proposals reached the Senate, they encountered a response as hostile as the one they had received in the House. If anything, liberal unhappiness was greater, partly because Senate committee deliberations coincided with the body's approval of a $13.1 billion Vietnam supplemental appropriation. When Secretary Gardner appeared before the Labor and Public Welfare Committee, Senator Robert Kennedy (D-N.Y.) balanced support for the appropriation with a strong attack on the concomitant education cutbacks. The senator pointed out that "much of this money is being used for the deprived [and] in areas where there are minority groups, including the Negroes." In view of high black casualty rates in Vietnam, it seemed doubly unfortunate that they were suffering disproportionately from domestic cutbacks. "When we think that probably the . . . $200 million that is being cut is what it costs to send the B-52's over Vietnam for perhaps a week, it is a matter of great concern to me."[24]

For the Johnson administration, Senator Kennedy's attempt to meld education, civil rights, and military issues into an overall critique of White House policy was peculiarly significant, given the long-standing assumption that the former attorney general would use any sign of vulnerability to promote his own leadership credentials. The intensity of the rift between the Johnson and Kennedy camps is too familiar to require much elaboration here. But it is revealing that within a month of President Kennedy's assassination, Arthur M. Schlesinger, Jr., complained to Robert Kennedy about the "hard fact" that "Johnson has won the first round." If liberal Democrats in general were by 1965–1966 looking for reasons for revolt, it seems still more clear that some New Frontiersmen viewed themselves as a government-in-exile, headed by the junior senator from New York. The specific source of Schlesinger's disquiet in December 1963 was the controversial appointment of Thomas C. Mann to the State Department, an appointment the Kennedy camp found obnoxious. As Schlesinger observed, "We have supposed that Johnson so badly needed the Kennedy people for the election that we would retain a measure of power for eleven months." This fact was, however, no longer clear and "so long as he maintains an ostensibly liberal position on issues, it will be very difficult to do anything about it." A glum Schlesinger—like Kennedy, still ostensibly working for the administration—concluded that "the only sanctions we have are resignation and/or revolt," but in truth, "both sanctions are meaningless, and will seem sour grapes, unless they are provoked by a readily understandable issue—and this LBJ will do his best to deny us. . . . As you say, it promises to be a long, hard winter."[25]

Eighteen months later, Harry McPherson sent Johnson a lengthy memorandum on the emerging political challenge:

> [Kennedy] is trying to put himself into a position of leadership among liberal Senators, newspapermen, foundation executives, and the like. Most of these people have mistrusted him in the past, believing him (rightly) to be a man of narrow sensibilities and totalitarian instincts. A number of brave votes for pure liberalism [however] . . . and he will seem to these liberals [to be] St. George slaying the conservative dragon. . . . He will not care whether he ever becomes *of* the Senate. It will be enough that he is *in* the Senate and can use it as a platform in his search for power.[26]

The president's liberal record, together with Kennedy's inconveniently hawkish Vietnam stance during the previous administration, initially limited the possibilities for effective dissension. As dissatisfaction with Johnson mounted, however, Kennedy's sensitive political antennae detected a valuable opportunity to further his ambitions. Many of the president's domestic allies had nourished gnawing doubts about his aptitude for international relations since the escalation of bombing in Vietnam in February 1965, and the invasion of the Dominican Republic two months later.[27] As the crisis in Southeast Asia deepened, their anxiety increased, although ambivalence and uncertainty regarding America's role were more characteristic than outright opposition. By the start of 1966, deep unhappiness about military escalation was apparent from the results of Senator Mike Mansfield's fact-finding mission to Vietnam, and from the so-called Hartke note, in which fifteen Democratic senators unavailingly urged the president to extend a month-long bombing halt.[28]

But Senator Robert Kennedy's political equation during the first half of 1966 remained a difficult one, as is apparent from the counsel he received from such friends and advisers as Schlesinger, Richard Goodwin, and Frederick Dutton. Dutton, contemplating "the long haul ahead" in July 1965, was impressed by the importance of "communicating a few well-discerned qualities." The senator was "an obviously complex individual, with some qualities that many people admire greatly, but also some that cause antagonism, and are negative with many who never knew you." Kennedy was advised to find issues with which the public would identify (nuclear proliferation and education were suggested) while also evidencing his "personal growth."[29] Writing again in November, Dutton argued that "since you still remain suspect to much of the Jewish community and liberal wing of the Democratic party ('too much zeal' . . . 'too much latent hostility' . . . 'a cop' . . . 'he was soft on McCarthyism' . . . , etc.), I urge that you undertake on a long-range basis to push an important civil liberties proposal of real substance."[30] Schlesinger also stressed the importance of reaching out to the left, urging Kennedy to "let the professional liberals see that you do not always wear horns and a tail."[31]

But the costs of too close an association with the liberals were also apparent. Goodwin, who had left the Johnson administration late in 1965, identified "some danger of your developing a rather hard 'ideological image' as a liberal—anti-business, against conservative sentiment across the board." He added, "It is not good national politics to be regarded as an ideological liberal—or an ideological anything. It is much better if there is a large area of uncertainty, leaving room for wishful thinking on the parts of many groups that you may be the man for them."[32]

As Vietnam moved to the center of the nation's political consciousness, the route to career advancement became increasingly clear. In essence, Kennedy sought to use the guns-and-butter issue as a way of encouraging opposition, without explicitly attacking the legitimacy of the United States' role in Southeast Asia. As Dutton observed in February 1966, cautious dissension from administration positions meant that "the really significant base you are developing throughout the nation to augment the hard-core Kennedy following you already have is slightly to the left of Johnson philosophically and politically." Yet, like Goodwin, he also felt that Kennedy should not appear to be an ideologue: "To the extent you are a critic of present Viet Nam policies, you can do more good by letting Mansfield, Aiken, Fulbright and others continue their present public illumination of the problem, then step in as a thoughtful supporter of their policies."[33]

THE INCOME STRATEGY ADVANCES

While the first serious liberal opposition to Lyndon Johnson's domestic policies resulted from their scale rather than their underlying philosophy, the opening months of 1966 also saw the introduction of two sets of policy recommendations that gave a public profile—and a modicum of political respectability—to the concept of a guaranteed income. The first came from the House of Representatives' Democratic Study Group (DSG); the second, from the President's Commission on Technology, Automation and Economic Progress.

The DSG's Action Program for Full Employment was presented to the House by Congressman Scheuer on January 6, and brought many of the private recommendations of Sargent Shriver, Ramsay Clark, and Wilbur Cohen into public debate. Once again, however, a bold philosophical departure was presented as a rededication to age-old American values:

> The time has come when we must begin to provide a minimum income for everyone. Although we cannot hope to return to the early American frontier society of individual, independent, family farms, we can re-create in our modern industrial urban environment the economic conditions for that cherished independence and individualism. We can assure everyone an adequate minimum income.[34]

Although the Action Program for Full Employment clearly did not view welfare as the principal vehicle for assuring able-bodied Americans an adequate income, its emphasis on the importance of work could not disguise a basic philosophical departure. The willingness of the DSG to guarantee income through employment challenged implicitly the War on Poverty's assumption that barriers to self-advancement were to a great extent internal rather than societal.[35] Throughout this period, liberal assumptions about culpability were undergoing a rapid shift, and as legislators and other policymakers felt impelled to accept society's role in determining life chances, it became correspondingly easier (although by no means inevitable) to conclude that the poor were entitled to an income, whatever their behavior or status.

At this stage, however—and irrespective of any philosophical legitimacy which it might possess—the unconditional guarantee would have seemed an unaccountably fatalistic response to poverty. Scheuer believed that the DSG's proposal "should produce its own demise, out of its very success in reducing poverty." Illustrating the tenacity of traditional notions of recipro-

113

cal responsibility, he noted that the Action Program for Full Employment would "assist the vast majority of the poor in finding a new sense of personal dignity and worth by making a substantial contribution to themselves and our society."[36] And even if one dismisses such rhetoric as mere political opportunism (which one should not), the very fact that liberal politicians understood the political advantages conferred by their association with the self-help tradition is itself significant. The way in which the DSG program was packaged confirms what the Cohen, Clark, and Shriver initiatives had already hinted at: namely, that there was nothing inherently un-American about the income strategy. What made the guaranteed income movement of later years so unique was its notion that economic security should be divorced from work, and could be *sold* politically on that basis.

If the Democratic Study Group report is historically noteworthy as one marker on the way to guaranteed income advocacy, its immediate impact was limited when compared to that of the Automation Report. Discounting the view that technological change precluded full employment, the authors of the report insisted, "If unemployment does creep upward in the future, it will be the fault of public policy, not the fault of technological change."[37] But they also believed that sound public policy must include a massive job program of the kind suggested by Shriver and Ramsey Clark in the autumn of 1965 but rejected during the subsequent budget negotiations. To facilitate adjustment to economic change, the report proposed a threefold approach. First, sound economic management would ensure that workers with "reasonably attractive skills" found suitable employment. Second, public sector jobs should be provided to those who lacked such skills. Third, there should be a more comprehensive system of income maintenance: "Under the best of circumstances there will be some who cannot or should not participate in the job economy. For them, we believe there should be an adequate system of income maintenance, guaranteeing a floor of income at an acceptable level."[38]

Like Wilbur Cohen's 1965 task force, and the DSG's Action Plan, the National Commission on Technology, Automation and Economic Change was convinced that niggardly welfare provision only exacerbated the long-term problem of dependency. Denouncing the existing system of categorical relief as "absurd," it found it "hard to imagine a system less consistent with our society's high valuation of work and self-help"; nevertheless, it stated that "nearly all [citizens] should and do wish to earn their own support, for the dignity and self-respect that come from earning one's own living can hardly be achieved otherwise."[39]

Demonstrating still further how far American liberalism still had to go before it moved to advocate unconditional welfare, the commission emphasized both the philosophical and the practical obstacles to such a system:

> It is not likely that society will decide in the foreseeable future to allocate the resources needed to win total victory over poverty, nor would excessive reliance upon transfer payments appear to constitute sound public policy. While allocation of additional income for the poor is an essential element in the war on poverty, simply raising income to fill even their minimum requirements would result in economic dislocations by eroding incentives to work. It may also be preferable in many cases to stress income in kind rather than in cash. This might apply to alcoholics and others afflicted with diverse maladjustments. . . .
>
> Whatever may be the merits of the various income maintenance programs discussed [in the report], there does not appear to be any wide consensus supporting their adoption. Although such a plan [as a negative income tax or family allowance] might receive serious consideration at some indeterminate future time, to improve the lot of the poor in the short term we must realistically turn to more modest programs.[40]

If racial disorder and the early lessons of the War on Poverty had produced more refined expressions of the individualist tradition than those encountered in 1964, then the perceived philosophical validity and political vigor of that tradition continued to present seemingly insurmountable obstacles to the guaranteed income. For those whose views placed them outside the arena of mainstream politics, however, such constraints were irrelevant—and not necessarily permanent. As America's interlocking racial and social crises forced erstwhile traditionalists to rank social stability above consensual politics, might they not be compelled to abandon some of the more cherished tenets of their liberal ideology? During 1966, the War on Poverty's emphasis on empowerment contributed to the emboldening of a radicalized poor who asserted welfare rights wholly at odds with the mission of the Economic Opportunity Act.

MOBILIZATION OF THE POOR: BIRTH OF THE WELFARE RIGHTS MOVEMENT

For many of those professionals who had designed the community action concept under the auspices of the Ford Foundation and President Kennedy's juvenile delinquency committee, the mere act of confronting local political establishments was therapeutic. For all the ostensible threat it posed to traditional structures, and for all its wild demands, this was essentially a vehicle for personal growth and individual transformation. For Norman Hill of the NAACP, this view represented "a remarkable intellectual feat accomplished by members of the middle class." According to Hill:

> In a classic case of elitist condescension and the perversion of democracy by some of its most vocal advocates, the middle class decided that what the lower class needed was participation, and the maximum feasible amount of it to boot. They needed not money, but identity; not jobs, but self-respect; not decent homes, but a sense of community; and finally not better schools with more funds to make education effective, but control over their destiny.[41]

Yet little more than a year after the program's inception, it was becoming clear that many practitioners of maximum feasible participation *did* want money. During the winter of 1965–1966, supporters of a war on dependency witnessed the sight of federally funded activists agitating for welfare rights and the guaranteed income. An early instance of the OEO financing welfare rights activity was the establishment of the Committee of Welfare Families in Manhattan's Lower East Side. The local community action program, called Mobilization for Youth, encouraged its formation, seeing it as a way in which traditionally submissive welfare mothers could claim their full entitlements from an unhelpful welfare department. According to Rabagliati and Birnbaum, some staff members went further, characterizing it as the start of "a large social movement whose aim would be to bring about basic changes in the welfare system throughout the country."[42] A winter clothing campaign served as a confidence-building exercise, and between January and April 1966 a series of training sessions were held, at which sympathetic welfare workers and Columbia University professors encouraged recipients to put pressure on the Department of Welfare.[43]

Professional organizers encouraged emotionalism and a sense of grievance on the part of newly assertive claimants. As one organizer recalls, the choice of target was not so important as the new mood:

> In dealing with low-income people who rarely have the experience or the education of thinking in conceptual terms, in terms of where the system is at fault, it's the immediate thing like the Jewish landlord, the Irish cop on the beat, the Italian grocery-store owner, the lousy teachers, or the welfare investigator, and it's important to maintain this immediate close-at-hand-target and let the chips fall where they may. . . . If you try to tone this down at the very beginning, you're

116

running the danger, through your own intellectual and professional goal-setting methods, of alienating yourself from the people you want to organize.[44]

Encouraged by such techniques, militancy among the local black and Puerto Rican communities increased dramatically. At some Committee for Welfare Families meetings, "the emotional atmosphere was such that any proposed action was immediately cheered and approved."[45] The formation of George Wiley's Poverty/Rights Action Committee (soon renamed the National Welfare Rights Organization) gave such protests a nationwide profile and, by popularizing the guaranteed income demand, gave them a tighter focus.

The new organization was the product of a meeting between Wiley and Richard Cloward in January 1966. Wiley had just been defeated by Floyd McKissick in his bid to succeed James Farmer as national director of CORE. Disenchanted with the Northern civil rights movement's inability to achieve the clarity of purpose and tangible success of its Southern counterpart, he sought new ways of forcing President Johnson to implement his Howard University promises. Cloward, whose contribution to the November planning conference was described in the last chapter, was one of a number of intellectuals who shared his impatience. In Moynihan's words, they "grew steadily more radicalized in their demands for the transformation of American society. The initial desire to facilitate entry into that system by outsiders . . . was supplanted by a near detestation of the system itself."[46]

Cloward and his research assistant, Frances Fox Piven, were struck by the fact that only about half of those eligible for public assistance under the existing terms of the Social Security Act actually received relief. Despite the existence of mass poverty and the impracticability of self-advancement, American society remained "wholly and self-righteously oriented toward getting people off the welfare rolls." They believed that the archaic self-serving individualism of the political establishment would, perforce, be supplanted by more humane and appropriate values if the poor, the civil rights movement, and labor activists would cooperate in "a massive drive to recruit the poor *onto* the welfare rolls."[47]

Cloward and Piven observed that if all poor Americans claimed the relief to which they were currently entitled, then the Social Security Act's system of matching state and federal grants would be unable to cope. By disrupting local fiscal policy and choking welfare bureaucracies, this putative alliance would endanger the "big city Democratic coalition" so as to "impel action on a new federal program to distribute income, eliminating the present public welfare system, and alleviating the abject poverty which it perpetuates." The true solution to deprivation lay not in social engineering but in basic economic restructuring:

> The ultimate objective of this strategy—to wipe out poverty by establishing a guaranteed annual income—will be questioned by some. Because the ideal of individual social and economic mobility has deep roots, even activists seem reluctant to call for national programs to eliminate poverty by the outright redistribution of income. Instead, programs are demanded to enable people to become economically competitive. But such programs are of no use to millions of today's poor. . . . Individual mobility is no answer to the question of how to abolish the massive problem of poverty now.[48]

Such a question ("how to abolish . . . poverty now") had of course not even been on the agenda when the Economic Opportunity Act entered the statute book, and the fact that it was being asked now provides an insight into the dramatic changes of the intervening months. Nevertheless, Cloward and Piven were clearly frustrated by the tenacity and all-pervasiveness of the individualist tradition. Piven later recalled the hostility of the civil rights leadership to the idea of mobilizing around the guaranteed-income concept:

> Nobody knew anything about welfare, and nobody wanted to know anything about it. Even among radicals and organizers, the American values toward welfare prevailed, so that everywhere we turned, we got no help. We met with Whitney Young . . . and he gave us a long speech about how it was more important to get one black woman into a job as an airline stewardess than it was to get fifty poor families onto welfare. We went to Bayard Rustin, but he said, "if you have an idea that takes two hours to explain, then you don't have an idea."[49]

George Wiley, by contrast, was immediately enthusiastic about the possibilities of the Piven-Cloward strategy and attempted to enlist the support of the Citizen's Crusade Against Poverty (CCAP), with which he had recently become affiliated. The crusade's membership included a number of the empowerment concept's most fervent disciples, including Richard Boone and Jack Conway, both of whom had recently departed the OEO in protest at Sargent Shriver's alleged retreat from maximum feasible participation. Funded in large part by the United Auto Workers, the CCAP appeared to regard itself as the conscience of the antipoverty program.

For all its disaffection with the Johnson administration, the crusade remained wedded to the War on Poverty's original purpose. In November 1965, when the CCAP had met to consider its legislative priorities for the following year, Boone had betrayed no concern at all about any flaws in the nation's welfare system.[50] Although initially intrigued by the Piven-Cloward welfare crisis strategy, his organization proved unwilling to spearhead the campaign.[51] In April, Wiley quit the crusade. Just before his departure, he wrote to Boone that he felt his "true constituents" were "that great mass of deprived Negroes at the bottom of the social and economic ladder" and explained his reasons for leaving:

> From my years in CORE, I had gotten used to being part of a militant, action-oriented organization, which was prepared to move swiftly into situations as they developed, with relatively little concern about whose toes got stepped on in the process. I am therefore more disposed toward being part of an energetic little phalanx, pressing for radical change, than always having to tone down statements to keep from offending divergent elements of a tenuous coalition.[52]

The temperamental and philosophical gulf between the CCAP and the incipient welfare rights campaign was clearly displayed at the crusade's annual convention, which took place in the same month as Wiley's departure. Sargent Shriver chose this as the occasion for a relentlessly upbeat assessment of the antipoverty program, but his message was drowned out by uninvited "delegates" led by welfare mothers, grass-roots activists, and student protesters. Conference organizers may have felt little warmth toward Shriver, but on this occasion their spleen was vented against the agitators, whom Boone feared had "misunderstood the nature of the conference." Jack Conway of the UAW told the *New York Times,* "I don't know where we go from here. They're wrecking the meeting. They have turned on the people who wanted to help them." An equally disturbed Eugene Carson Blake, representing the National Council of Churches, scolded protesters, telling them that "there won't be anything to take over after you've taken over."[53]

Liberal idealists who expected to direct the welcome anger of the poor in constructive directions misunderstood the nature of the social forces that they had helped to unleash. One observer of the April gathering believed that it had been conceived as "a weak attempt by the liberal establishment to carve out a new role for itself in the face of a shift in focus of the civil rights movement." Yet far from being a poor people's convention, the poor had simply been on "display."[54] For all their bold opposition to the Johnson administration's "conservatism," even disaffected Great Society liberals remained firmly wedded to orthodox antipoverty objectives. Meanwhile, George Wiley had abandoned the CCAP and embarked on a campaign to bankrupt the nation's welfare system and thereby force the federal government to institute a guaranteed income.

WELFARE RIGHTS AND THE SOCIAL WELFARE COMMUNITY

The spirit of militant disaffection apparent from the activities of the Poverty/Rights Action Committee exerted a powerful impact on the social welfare community. As with the uproar at the CCAP convention, it appeared that the poor had elected to "turn . . . on the people who wanted to help them," in this case social workers. The welfare crisis strategy had in fact been launched at a singularly propitious time, for in June 1966, the Johnson administration's Advisory Council on Public Welfare was due to report on the status and prospects of the American welfare system. Its verdict, contained in a report entitled *Having the Power, We Have the Duty*, amounted to the most significant challenge yet to the self-help tradition to come from *within* the liberal community.[55]

That this challenge should have emerged from this source and at this time was no coincidence. Social welfare professionals, after all, were the group most immediately affected by the Poverty/Rights Action Committee's bid to flood the benefit system with new claims. Already suffering from excessive caseloads, social workers now found themselves the subjects of concerted campaigns to make their task unmanageable. Moreover, the intrusive investigations that caseworkers were obliged to undertake in determining eligibility for AFDC and other benefits made them obvious targets for the ire of the guaranteed income lobby. Finally, the social welfare lobby were able to draw radical lessons from America's current condition because its members were not obliged to satisfy a heterogeneous electoral constituency. Loula Dunn, director of the American Public Welfare Association, felt that this fact liberated members from political constraints: "If the American Public Welfare Association is of any use . . . it has always to point to the Congressional committees, the key state and local leaders and the federal departments the needs of people, not whether this is politically sound but to keep the needs of people before these policy-making groups."[56]

Guaranteed income advocates, such as George Wiley and Robert Theobald (the economist who had conceived the 1964 Ad Hoc Committee on the Triple Revolution), appear to have recognized that the welfare establishment constituted the liberal grouping most susceptible to their arguments. When, for example, Theobald organized the first major conference on the guaranteed income, he chose to hold it in Chicago to coincide with the May 1966 conventions of both the National Association of Social Workers and the National Conference on Social Welfare.[57]

Speaking before the latter organization, Elizabeth Wickenden declared her support for "the legal right to a minimum but adequate level of living." Simultaneously, however, she distinguished her position from that of the guaranteed income movement in three ways. First, she questioned the movement's tendency to attack "the one governmental agency which has as its assigned legal task the assurance of minimum income—the public welfare machinery of federal, state and local government." Second, she feared that the campaign might put at risk the existing "legal rights of the poor." Third, she cited President Johnson's hope that "the days of the dole are numbered," and suggested the inconguity of urging "that 30 million Americans be placed on a dole rechristened under happier terminology."[58]

As with most advocates of increased income maintenance programs, Wickenden continued to view welfare as a necessary means to a more noble end, rather than as an adequate goal in itself. While she praised advocates of the guaranteed income for recognizing that "inadequate cash income" was the principal problem of the poor, she found their goal distressingly unambitious:

> The principal difficulty with the guaranteed *minimum* income advocacy is that it puts the cart before the horse; it assumes that poverty must become an accepted and hence subsidized way of life for a large proportion of the American population rather than a reducible evil. It is defeatist about our ability to prevent rather than alleviate most forms of poverty. . . . Of course so long as we tolerate the evil, the alleviative remedies will be necessary and should be improved. But we should set our *sights* on preventing poverty before it occurs.[59]

Still, the fact remains that Wickenden's traditional ends coincided with her endorsement of a comprehensive package of legal guarantees for the poor. A member of the Advisory Council on Public Welfare, she appears to have been its principal advocate for a break with the convention of anodyne rededications to tired old objectives. The impact of the new militancy on the council's thinking is clear from a succession of draft reports that emerged between October 1965 and June 1966. The substantive recommendations of successive versions changed little, but their progressively more militant tone attested to mounting political pressures from the left.

The first draft echoed earlier task force reports, making the by now familiar demand for a "single, comprehensive, public assistance program . . . available equitably to all needy persons." The assumption that the success of the War on Poverty would reduce need pervaded this early version, as did the judgment that "assistance is, of course, no substitute for self-reliance and self-support."[60] Three months later, after the White House planning conference "To Fulfill These Rights," a much more angry tone was deployed in support of much the same recommendation. In place of the colorless wording of the first version, this draft protested that "for the federal government to continue to collaborate in a nationwide program of public assistance payments that are grossly inadequate perpetuates destitution, exacerbates poverty-related problems, and makes a mockery of the nation's commitment to its poor."[61] By April—that is, after the welfare crisis strategy had first been outlined—the Advisory Council was questioning the continued utility of the liberal individualist tradition and emphasizing the need for dramatic action at "a time of unprecedented national concern about the causes and consequences of poverty, dependency, and social dislocation."[62]

As late as May, and within two months of the publication of *Having the Power, We Have the Duty,* Wickenden remained unhappy with the main body of the report. In an anxious letter to Fedele Fauri, dean of the School of Social Work at the University of Michigan and chairman of the Advisory Council, she expressed "profound uneasiness about the adequacy of our report to the challenges of the moment." In her view, "We are vulnerable to a degree of challenge from both the right and left which seems to me unprecedented in my whole experience with the field of public welfare." Wickenden complained that the right was questioning HEW's 1967 appropriation, while "advocacy for the negative income tax . . . is running riot in every direction," yet the proposed report lacked style and direction:

> It is bland, discursive, lacking in focus, and obscures our really drastic recommendations in a forest of verbiage, banalities, generalities and relatively secondary recommendations. Unless a miracle occurs it will, I fear, be written off as just another rear-guard action in behalf of the "welfare establishment." I myself

am fighting this battle on so many fronts, at such hazard to my reputation as a crusader for the underdog, that I cannot risk being put in this position.[63]

Wickenden went on to refer to serious conflicts within the council, telling Fauri that her unease was shared by other members. One option would be for her to "simply settle for a supplementary statement of my own viewpoint." As it was, she would wait for the next draft, albeit without much "faith in the results."[64] Meanwhile, she would rewrite the introduction to the report, for which she was already responsible.

The published version, released on 30 June 1966, was important for both its tone and substance. In it, council members proclaimed that the government was "a major source of the poverty on which it has declared unconditional war." They felt certain that "neither the war on poverty nor achievement of the long-range goals implicit in a Great Society concept can succeed so long as the basic guarantees of a practical minimum level of income and social protection are not assured for all."[65] Proposing a "new nationwide program of basic guarantees," the council favored abandonment of the New Deal welfare system. In place of the existing system of categorical public assistance, the federal government should introduce general assistance, dispensed purely on the basis of need. Responsibility for the new system should still be shared between the federal government and the states, but the financial burden on poorer states should be reduced.

These recommendations were not new, although they had not previously appeared in an official published document. More striking than the substance of *Having the Power, We Have the Duty* was its overall purpose, which was to disengage policymakers from the platitudes of the past. However appealing such platitudes might be, there was "little value in closing one's eyes to the practical needs of the day or mourning for the different conditions of an earlier time."[66] The Advisory Council used heightened public and political consciousness about poverty and racial inequality to destroy a series of alleged myths about social mobility. In bluntly asserting, for example, that "most public welfare recipients . . . cannot realistically be expected to become self-sustaining," the ethos and purpose of the War on Poverty were boldly contradicted.[67] (This was poignant, given that the report's title had been taken from President Johnson's 1964 antipoverty address.) The elimination of poverty could only be achieved if policymakers abandoned the "melting away" myth. Folksy Emersonian homilies about self-help must be replaced by direct government intervention in an inherently inequitable socioeconomic system. Meanwhile, the "long-ingrained habit patterns of sentimental pity or thinly disguised contempt for those who cannot, un-aided, achieve a reasonable standard of living must be supplanted by national action firmly based upon principles of social justice."[68]

Conservatives were predictably grateful for such heretical pronounce-ments. Congressman O. C. Fisher (R-Texas) conjured up a distressing image of the Advisory Council's brave new world, asking "Can it be that this proud nation is on the threshold of surrendering to the apostles of total welfarism?"[69] But more significant than the substance of this line of attack was its sheer implausibility. It is hard to find any reaction to *Having the Power, We Have the Duty* from those politicians who by the end of the decade would be most strongly associated with the guaranteed income movement. In the same month as the Advisory Council on Public Welfare released its report, George McGovern—later to be one of the guaranteed income's most fervent advocates—praised the Johnson approach as a spir-ited attempt "to overcome the handout approach to the problems of the poor. . . . The Economic Opportunity Act of 1964 is not a blueprint for handouts, but an aid to human development that enables the poor and indolent to contribute to society rather than surviving as a drag on soci-ety."[70] Such rhetoric reflected a combination of philosophical conviction and political acuity: the nation's social and racial crises would have to deepen considerably before liberal legislators could entertain the concept of unconditional income support.

VIETNAM AND THE INCIPIENT COLLAPSE OF THE LIBERAL COALITION

Both Johnson's perceived withdrawal from domestic affairs and the rising tide of liberal disaffection with his administration owed much to the escalat-ing course and consequences of the war in Vietnam. Even at the start of 1966, the Hartke note, the Mansfield Report, and Senator Fulbright's dra-matic televised hearings had attested to growing unease within the Demo-cratic party. During the course of the year, the costs of the war piled up and could be gauged in a number of ways. Most obviously, $21 billion was expended and over 5,000 lives lost. These statistics dwarfed those of previ-ous years and undercut Johnson's standing with doves as well as hawks (who believed that such sacrifices were wasted without a massive further commit-ment that alone could bring military victory).

But the price of war could also be measured in terms of domestic casualties. In addition to the curtailment of Great Society programs, war exacted what Senator Fulbright termed a "mental and spiritual" cost:

> A year ago . . . we vigorously reasserted our preference for life and peace; it seemed that the United States might be about to undergo something of a social revolution. But for the present at least, the inspiration and commitment of a year ago have disappeared. They have disappeared in the face of deepening involvement in an Asian war, and although it may be contended that the United States has the material resources to rebuild its society at home while waging war abroad, it is already being demonstrated that we do not have the mental and spiritual resources for such a double effort.[71]

Senator William Proxmire (D-Wisc.) concurred, regretting that "Vietnam has yanked public attention away from almost every other subject and monopolized so much of public and government concern" that America's continuing racial crisis had acquired a lower profile.[72] Increasingly during these months, Vietnam was presented as being Johnson's war, and as public satisfaction with his military leadership declined (from 63 percent in January to 49 percent in March according to one Harris poll),[73] his image and credibility—and consequently his political strength—suffered accordingly. With the media starting to report the president's apparent lack of candor and rising liberal discontent, the president widened the credibility gap by abandoning regular press conferences and substituting informal gatherings with favored newsmen. One liberal columnist, who had spent the past two years eulogizing the administration's domestic achievements, sorrowfully recorded that "there is something petty and pettish about this in a great man."[74]

Presidential assistant Robert Kintner, a former television newsman himself, warned Johnson that while he understood that "all presidents have trouble with reporters and columnists," he had nevertheless been "startled by direct and indirect gripes" at a recent function.[75] Writing confidentially to Bill Moyers (himself about to resign from the administration because of the war), Kintner worried that "everyone remarks on the president's sensitivity to what is printed about him. While I understand this sensitivity, which is human, I don't like implications that he will not be able to work most effectively as president because of this concern."[76]

During the spring of 1966, liberal criticism of Johnson's conduct of the war became increasingly routine. Senate Majority Leader Mike Mansfield demanded a more serious search for peace, and in the same week Senator

Fulbright presented his famous "arrogance of power" thesis at Johns Hopkins University. Simultaneously, the president actually fueled discontent by accusing his detractors of being "nervous Nellies" and ordering the bombing of petroleum facilities within two miles of Hanoi.[77] While the administration sought to strengthen its position in the Senate by recruiting younger members, Johnson's foremost adversary was moving into open opposition.[78]

Three weeks before the full White House conference "To Fulfill These Rights" was to convene, Senator Robert Kennedy made his most explicit bid yet to associate diverse liberal and black sources of discontent in a unified critique of Johnson's leadership. Harry McPherson warned Johnson of the danger the day after the "nervous Nellies" speech:

> There is trouble on the horizon on the civil rights conference, and it is related to Viet Nam. [New York Mayor John V.] Lindsay, Kennedy, and some of the far-out Negro leaders such as Rustin are talking the same game—as Lindsay put it last night, "Vietnam or Brownsville." They are using the money-for-the-ghetto argument to capitalize on our Viet Nam problem without explicitly condemning our policies there, for which they have no viable alternatives.[79]

BLACK POWER

Far from dominating civil rights activity during the summer of 1966, the June White House conference "To Fulfill These Rights" was overshadowed by the emergence of the Black Power slogan. The troubled course of the administration's civil rights bill (contentious on account of its controversial open housing provision), and the failure of the White House conference to produce anything other than ritual demands for massive federal spending, indicated the declining force of traditional modes of organization and protest, allowing extremists to fill the leadership vacuum.

The slogan itself was less significant than the spirit of assertiveness and rebellion it represented, a spirit that struck fear into the hearts of white liberals, making them ever more receptive to wide-ranging critiques of American society. Black Power posed a particular threat to the moderate civil rights leaders with whom the liberal establishment had traditionally felt most comfortable. Responding to the incipient defeat of the 1966 civil rights bill, an anguished Roy Wilkins warned that "words are not adequate to translate to you our mood on this matter." The weakening or defeat of open housing, he said, would cause the ghettos to "become poorer, blacker and more desperate than at present." Were the bill to fall, "individuals will believe that questions of social justice can be settled by private guerilla warfare," for "a large segment of Negro and white America already is jeering the legislative approach to civil rights." In the light of Black Power, defeat would "increase skepticism among more sober citizens as well."[80]

Such skepticism can only have been enhanced by the violent conclusion to the Southern Christian Leadership Conference's (SCLC) much vaunted open housing campaign in Chicago. Attacked by white counter-demonstrators sporting Confederate flags and chanting "Wallace for President," a shaken Martin Luther King, Jr., admitted he had "never seen anything like it in my life." In his view, "the people from Mississippi ought to come to Chicago to learn how to hate."[81] Although the SCLC claimed that the eventual housing agreement with city hall and local real estate interests was a victory for traditional methods, it was condemned by more radical blacks as a sell-out.[82] The troubled course of this campaign presumably contributed to the SCLC's subsequent change of strategy. King was one of a number of established black leaders (Bayard Rustin and Whitney Young, Jr., being two others) who responded to the plight of the movement by adopting the guaranteed income as a central demand. (Robert Theobald had anticipated this development back in April.)[83] On August 8, King announced that, for the "foreseeable future," economic demands would eclipse civil rights legislation in the SCLC's activities: "If society does not provide a job for a man, then it must not strip him of an income. I would prefer getting to an annual income through providing jobs—massive public works and job training programs—but if this is not done, the society should provide people with enough money to live."[84]

In mid-1966, as congressional liberals surveyed the fading promise of the Great Society, they identified the Vietnam War as a principal source of domestic retrenchment and, by extension, racial unrest. Their willingness to challenge the White House by endorsing black claims for massive federal spending increased accordingly. To cite just two examples, Senator Javits demanded a $35 billion "Marshall Plan for the American Negro,"[85] while Edward Kennedy suggested that a nation that could afford to spend "$2 billion a month to defend the freedom of 14 million people in South Vietnam" could surely "make the same kind of efforts for the 20 million people of the Negro race right here in America."[86]

Such schemes represented an aggressive attempt by shaken liberals to win back the support and trust of former allies, and President Johnson was urged by a number of administration figures to attempt to regain the initiative by similar methods. Roger Wilkins, of the Community Relations Service, had demanded back in March that the president use his office to create a coalition for change rather than simply wait for an illusory consensus to appear. In an angry and deeply pessimistic memorandum, Wilkins characterized existing administration policy as "a tiny drib here and a tiny drab there and not very much for anybody." He believed that the anger of the November 1965 planning conference had accurately reflected the dominant mood of black America:

> If the government was committed to doing this job as it has been committed in doing other things, the condition of the lives of impoverished Negroes could be improved dramatically. . . . But I doubt that we will move rapidly enough, and I suspect the Negro anger will manifest itself in some very ugly form in some city or cities this summer no matter what we do, because the resources we are talking about mobilizing for this summer just aren't enough. . . . It is absolutely clear to me that the target should not be riots but rather the conditions of the lives of American citizens who have been kicked around and locked out for centuries.[87]

A DISAPPEARING CENTER

Concerned by the widespread perception that Johnson's leadership had lost vigor and direction as military and domestic problems mounted, Milton Semer, one of the president's assistants, undertook a survey of liberal sentiment both in and out of the administration. Struck by the universal "sense of urgency," he reported to the president:

> Some of them think that my call was the prologue to your moving in and taking charge of programs that they want administered more expeditiously. In fact, it was hard to get some of them off the phone, they are so eager to help you make these programs work.
> We don't need any more White House conferences. What's needed is to get the impression across, through small meetings with key people—mayors, governors, and other leaders and opinion-makers—that you are taking charge, that this is the "old LBJ" as some of them referred to you, who has sized up the situation, knows what needs to be done, and is moving in to get results.[88]

While Lyndon Johnson continued to declare his dedication to the Great Society in speeches to the United Auto Workers and the civil rights conference among others, his response to the perceived "crisis of leadership" was scarcely likely to appease his critics. Alarmed by the growing assumption that Washington alone could solve America's domestic problems, Johnson continued to maintain a determinedly individualist tone. In the spring, Robert Theobald had observed that "regrettably, many Americans are still not even aware of the [guaranteed income] issue," while "most others are confused."[89] Yet Johnson's response to entitlements advocacy suggests that he had little doubt what the response of his national constituency would be to the idea of a guaranteed income. He viewed the June civil rights conference as a consciousness-raising exercise that must convince business, labor, the civil rights fraternity, and the public at large that they, too, should share the burden of creating social justice:

> Some believe that the federal government can assume their personal responsibilities for justice to the Negro American. They contend, even when they refuse to admit it, that the mere existence of federal funds and programs and civil rights laws makes private action unnecessary.
>
> Yet we know that no national government, however enlightened, can by itself change the conditions of Negro life in America. . . . So do not expect from me, or from any man, a miracle.[90]

At a time when the attachment of many reformers to the concept of reciprocal obligations was perceptibly weakening, as society's culpability for the crisis of the ghetto became increasingly unavoidable, the president ordered cabinet members to draft a "Bill of Rights and Responsibilities" in defense of the proposition that entitlement was a contingent concept. Johnson hoped for a pithy statement of basic philosophy comparable to Roosevelt's "Four Freedoms."[91] Although this project never came to full fruition, he addressed the basic theme in what he hoped was a "Gettysburg-type address," delivered in August at the University of Rhode Island.[92] Johnson reiterated his conviction that "the American system seems to work" and that the keys to both civil peace and social justice depended "upon a fabric of responsibility woven between man and man." He stated:

> The causes and the conditions of poverty are too deep, too various, too subtle, and too firmly interlocked for simple remedies. We deceive ourselves and we deceive the poor as well, if we imagine there is some magic sword, some system of federal funds that can cut this chain and cut it with just one strike. . . . Civil

peace can exist only when all men, Negro and white alike, are as dedicated to satisfying their responsibilities as they are dedicated to securing their rights.[93]

Rhetoric such as this represented not a retreat from activism, but a simple restatement of a philosophical creed which had long attracted American liberals. Against a background of social and racial unrest coupled with domestic retrenchment, however, it is not surprising that many erstwhile allies viewed such traditionalist sentiments as both inappropriate and an excuse for inaction.

CHAPTER 6

Political Polarization and the Search for a New Liberalism

Gauging by the changing patterns of public opinion, July 1966 and the months that followed were a critical juncture for Great Society liberalism. For President Johnson, it was a disastrous period, during which his personal popularity—after a brief revival—collapsed from 56 percent to 39 percent.[1] Revealingly, during the same period, confidence in his handling of the Vietnam War declined, from 49 percent to 33 percent,[2] while perspectives on the wisdom of America's engagement underwent a parallel shift. In September 1966, Americans approved of the initial intervention by 49 percent to 35 percent; a year later, they disapproved by 46 percent to 44 percent.[3]

It is hard to imagine that the concept of a guaranteed income could have gained the support it enjoyed among American liberals by the end of the decade in the absence of the Vietnam War. Admittedly it was the radicalization and redirection of black protest during the mid- and late-1960s that helped most to discredit the *principles* of Great Society liberalism; yet the war in Southeast Asia did more to disrupt the *politics* of liberalism, destroying the president's authority and domestic vigor, thereby persuading erstwhile supporters that their interests were better served by distancing themselves from Johnson than by continued association. The two sources of dislocation were closely related: Vietnam deflected the administration from cherished domestic commitments at the very time when the racial crisis at home was lending new urgency to those same commitments. The two sources of liberal disaffection would reinforce one another throughout the remainder of Johnson's presidency.

As the unpopularity of the administration mounted, disaffected liberals in

Congress actively sought opportunities to demonstrate that they were not morally implicated in the president's failure. During the latter half of 1966, three of their leading representatives—two of them Democrats, one a Republican—used Senate hearings on the urban crisis for just this purpose. Abraham Ribicoff, Robert Kennedy, and Jacob Javits each had an obvious stake in high-level dissension from failed orthodoxy, and each exploited it to the full.

This chapter explores their deliberations and strategic gambits, concluding that the hearings revealed American liberalism at the crossroads. Although these congressional critics were as yet unwilling to embrace radical new definitions of income entitlement, they did evidence great dissatisfaction with existing policies and were now starting to question the underlying philosophy of Great Society programs, as well as their scale. This new receptivity to philosophical redirection, together with the growing sensitivity of these same senators to a phenomenon that would soon be labeled the New Politics, was an essential precondition for guaranteed income advocacy.

Equally critical to the prospect for American liberalism, its incipient radicalization developed as the mood of the country was becoming increasingly conservative. This constitutes the second major theme of this chapter: the growing assault on liberalism from the right, as revealed by the midterm elections of November 1966. Politicians who came to be associated with notions of unconditional income entitlement between 1967 and the early 1970s did so at a time when growing popular conservatism seemed to imperil even more orthodox brands of liberalism. Centrist liberalism—a creed whose appeal had appeared almost consensual during 1964–1965—was now under assault from both sides, and as the future of the New Deal Democratic coalition came into question, it was this twin attack that did most to legitimize once improbable ideologies.

THE ECONOMICS OF WAR

At a time when Edward Kennedy and Jacob Javits were demanding vast "Marshall Plans" to assuage the discontent of the ghetto, and when A. Philip Randolph was promoting a $100 billion Freedom Budget, the highly traditional message of President Johnson's speeches in Rhode Island and at the civil rights conference had a somewhat dissonant ring. Moreover, its optimism about the continuing promise of American values seemed misplaced, given the rising tide of urban unrest. But in terms of his political strength, identification with a center that appeared to be shifting to the right was essential. Economic constraints, as well as philosophical preference and popular sentiment, provided compelling rationales for Johnson's stubbornly traditional rhetoric. Together with the administration's continuing efforts to restore its fading identification with the nation's dominant values, the budgetary and economic implications of America's engagement in Vietnam must represent a recurrent and dominant theme in any explanation of the fracturing of the New Deal coalition during the Johnson presidency.

Having counseled a tax increase in January 1966, the president's economic advisers saw their projections of uncontrolled, inflationary growth amply fulfilled during the remainder of the year. Consumer prices rose by 5 percent—a sharp and portentous departure from the remarkable price stability of the previous five years.[4] By the middle of 1966, economic expansion was running at an annualized rate of 8.1 percent, a boom that was accompanied by spiraling wage settlements and acute labor shortages.[5] The federal government sought to use its powers of suasion to slow price increases and excessive wage increases in the private sector but, as Arthur Okun (a member of the President's Council of Economic Advisors) later acknowledged, "within the administration, there were no illusions: it was clearly recognized that the public budget and not private action was the engine of inflation."[6]

But if such recognition came early, it remained difficult to develop economically appropriate responses that could surmount political obstacles. For, at the root of both the economic problem and federal attempts to resolve it lay America's dramatically escalating commitment in Vietnam. The 1967 budget underestimated overall defense spending by 16 percent and Vietnam expenditures by $10 billion. The latter figure increased from just $6 billion in fiscal year 1966 to $20.6 billion the following year, necessitating two substantial supplemental appropriations.[7]

From a low of 7.2 percent of federal spending during the third quarter of 1965, defense purchases swelled to 8.4 percent a year later, with half of the increase coming in the third quarter of 1966.[8] Such spending was still small when compared to the levels associated with the Korean War, and a frank statement of the administration's military needs might have made a tax increase politically viable. But Johnson was not prepared to furnish the Congress with revisions to the clearly understated budgetary estimates of January, although private revisions were being produced by the administration on a monthly basis.[9] Charles Schultze later recalled as "difficult and embarrassing" his enforced refusal to discuss war costs with congressional committees.[10]

One can only speculate whether Johnson could have secured a tax increase early in 1966 had accurate Vietnam estimates been made available, but in the absence of this information, such a proposal was clearly doomed. In his memoirs, Johnson detailed meetings with business, labor, and congressional leaders, in the spring of 1966, at which uniform opposition was expressed. The sentiments of the business community (whose support was an essential prerequisite for congressional action) were particularly striking: "I outlined our economic situation and asked them: 'How many of you would recommend tomorrow a tax increase to the Congress for the purpose of restraining our economy . . . ?' Not a single hand went up."[11] Given the impracticability of a tax increase, the burden for economic restraint had to fall on monetary policy and nondefense expenditure. The latter became a principal concern of President Johnson (and more reluctantly, of the Budget Bureau) at an early stage in 1966, and created a critical predisposition toward any call, be it from federal agencies or congressional liberals, for new Great Society programs. When Joseph Califano told Johnson of Whitney Young, Jr.'s recommendation that the White House privately assure civil rights leaders of his determination to "fight any cutbacks in funds for the War on Poverty in a forcible way," the president flatly refused to oblige.[12]

At cabinet meetings held between March and June, Johnson continually emphasized the need to cut spending, both for the substantive impact that such action would have on the economy, and for the signal it would send to Congress and the nation.[13] However, since federal departments and agencies had an instinctive tendency to seek to exempt their own programs from overall policies of restraint, such exhortations had only meager results. Robert Kintner, special assistant to the president, regretted that the cabinet's thinking except "in a few cases is not very responsive" and must become "more aggressive and affirmative."[14] Califano urged Johnson to demand a $3 billion reduction, noting that it was "of paramount importance . . . to reduce the inflationary impact of the federal budget." Citing Gardner Ackley's contention that "every dollar of expenditures that we can avoid has at least the same economic effect as a dollar in additional taxes," he went on to echo Kintner's complaint, bemoaning a common departmental tendency "to recommend reductions in programs and expenditures in areas where they know the Congress will put on sufficient heat to get them restored."[15]

But by the end of the summer, the harmful effects of a credit crunch and the most serious breach yet of the administration's wage guideposts (the airline settlement) effectively compelled the tax package that Johnson had hitherto resisted. In a September 8 message to Congress, Johnson suspended the 7 percent investment tax credit (which was felt to have fueled the uncontrolled investment boom of the previous year), castigated Congress for adding its pet projects to requested authorizations, and announced $3 billion in nondefense cuts. Despite their earlier qualms, cabinet and agency heads were almost unanimous in endorsing this action as an unavoidable response to inflationary pressures. According to Califano, the sole dissenter was Willard Wirtz, who was "concerned about slowing down any of the Great Society–type programs at this time, both on philosophical grounds and also because of the congressional opposition he feels it will generate."[16]

POLITICAL CONTEXT OF THE CITY HEARINGS

The Senate Government Operations Committee's Subcommittee on Executive Reorganization began its hearings on the "Federal Role in Urban Affairs" (known as the City Hearings) in August, three weeks before the president's tax message. But Chairman Abraham Ribicoff and his colleagues could hardly claim ignorance of the government's budgetary constraints, despite the administration's continued lack of candor regarding the cost of the Vietnam War. The economic pressures that overcame Johnson's reluctance to end the investment tax credit were there for all to see, as can be gauged from the results of a congressional poll undertaken by Fred Panzer (a White House staffer) in June. Asked to name the five most important political issues among their constituencies, respondents placed inflation second only to Vietnam, and well ahead of civil rights and the War on Poverty:[17]

House		*Senate*	
1. Vietnam	82%	Vietnam	76%
2. Inflation	61	Inflation	56
3. War on Poverty	34	Agriculture	40
4. Civil Rights	29	Civil Rights	28
5. Education	19	Education	20

Throughout the summer, statistical evidence of economic dislocation mounted amid pervasive rumors that the administration was about to impose mandatory price and wage controls.[18] The prospects for passage of any Freedom Budget or Marshall Plan introduced to Congress in this context were negligible. So why did Abraham Ribicoff choose so seemingly unpropitious a time to launch high-profile congressional hearings on urban crisis—hearings that were certain to spawn massive new spending proposals? The answer to this question reveals much about the changing politics of liberalism during 1966.

The heightened apprehension with which liberal legislators viewed racial tension in the aftermath of the advent of Black Power and the summer riots of 1966 provides the most obvious answer to this question. As the Kerner Report observes, "The events of 1966 made it appear that domestic turmoil had become part of the American scene." Black activists with a gift for exploiting the fear and guilt of white liberals gained new prominence during this period.[19] If opposition to the Great Society programs was coming overwhelmingly from the right, then the most vocal hostility to administration policies came from the left, that is, from civil rights and antipoverty activists who were facing their own challenge from Black Power and welfare rights movements. Many liberals were no doubt genuinely uncomfortable about being rebuked by their most natural constituents, particularly after investing so much rhetorical energy in civil rights and social welfare legislation.

In their contributions to the city hearings, Senators Ribicoff, Kennedy, and Javits voiced acute alarm about the socioeconomic crisis of the ghetto and, more particularly, about the current failure of the nation to face up to its responsibilities. Robert Kennedy warned his colleagues on the Ribicoff committee "that we are . . . on sort of a razor's edge in the direction that we are going to ultimately be headed, as to whether we are going to fall off into this chasm of lack of hope versus the other side which gives us some opportunity for the future."[20] Jacob Javits echoed this foreboding, anticipating "only danger and dreariness ahead, if we don't do very much more than we are doing now." The New Yorker was "deeply disturbed" by the juxtaposition of "bitter and depressing ghettos, surrounded . . . by relatively well-off, and often disinterested and disengaged, suburbs." The persistence of this pattern, he said, seemed to "be creating a base for a real explosion in the United States."[21]

Admitting to similar anxieties, Abraham Ribicoff insisted that politicians could not afford the luxury of passively bowing to popular conservatism. Moreover, he felt that such fatalism was not even politically warranted. In the long term, advocacy of redirected and reinvigorated social activism would pay greater dividends than acceptance of the status quo. Ribicoff believed that America was "in the midst of a revolution," and once that fact was recognized, the political landscape would be transformed.[22] The purpose of the city hearings was to identify fresh activist approaches whose wider societal benefits would soon be more widely understood.

It seems, therefore, that Ribicoff's willingness to ignore the nation's growing conservatism, far from being irrational, was the product of a long-term calculation regarding the prospects for liberalism. That calculation may have been misguided, but the sense that the old liberalism was dying and that a new creed more responsive to current strains must emerge from its ashes was becoming increasingly widespread at this time. This judgment lay at the heart of a more general liberal receptiveness during the later 1960s to the spirit and philosophy represented by the New Politics agenda: once the bankruptcy of existing creeds became manifest and social disturbances increasingly intruded on the lives of mainstream Americans, their conservatism would give way to support of a radical redirection.

In the short term, moreover, two factors made it easy for Senators Ribicoff, Kennedy, and Javits to challenge the nation's growing conservatism. First, all three represented the section of the nation that was proving most resistant to the rightward swing. Asked whether they had a "favorable" or an "unfavorable" impression of the Great Society, Americans gave the following responses:[23]

	All	*East*	*Midwest*	*South*	*West*
Favorable	32	39	32	20	40
Unfavorable	44	34	46	54	38
No opinion	24	27	22	26	22
Plurality in favor	−12	+5	−14	−32	+2

Second, none of these three senators faced reelection in the nationally adverse climate of 1966. Those liberals and moderates in the Senate who did face strong challenges in November were compelled to downplay their earlier enthusiasm for the legislative achievements of the 89th Congress. Senator Fred Harris (D-Ok.), for example, would become a passionate advocate of social spending in the aftermath of his successful 1966 campaign; yet in the latter stages of that year's congressional session, such potential was rarely on display. Harris was even reluctant to support the Model Cities bill. A response to the political problems of community action, this proposal sought to inject capital for long-term urban regeneration projects in ever more tense inner-city ghettos. Mike Manatos, head of the president's Senate liaison team, reported that Harris, while "for it in principle," was receiving "much negative mail on [the] economic situation" from voters who believed that "Congress [is] spending too much money."[24] Senator John Sherman Cooper (R-Ky.) was similarly constrained, despite being "reported enthusiastic" about the bill.[25] On a separate issue, Senator Lee Metcalf (D-Mont.), also up for reelection that autumn, warned the administration that he would only support the contentious rent supplements program in an emergency, citing "campaign problems at home and right-wing attacks."[26]

Absent such immediate pressures, Ribicoff, Kennedy, and Javits felt freer to pursue an activist line to which they were already disposed, and which they viewed as the wave of the future. Yet Ribicoff's decision to embarrass the Johnson administration by embarking on his city hearings still seems somewhat surprising. Superficially, he was an unlikely source for a high-profile assault on the ethos of the War on Poverty. As President Kennedy's secretary for health, education, and welfare, he had self-consciously aligned the administration with antiwelfare sentiment, loyally incanting the trusty individualistic precepts from which the Economic Opportunity Act subsequently emerged. And more recently, he had been closely associated with the Johnson administration through his membership on the 1965 task force that produced the Model Cities program and the Department of Housing and Urban Development.

However, Ribicoff was also reputed to be a singularly opportunistic operator, even by the standards of his profession. Wilbur Cohen described Ribicoff's record at HEW in unflattering terms: "He was never interested in management, and he didn't have that capability; he didn't have the interest in HEW as an institution. He was more interested in politics [and] becoming Senator. . . . I don't think he really understood the Department or many of its programs or its objectives. . . . [I] believe that Ribicoff was a politician through and through."[27]

In 1965, the principles and politics of traditional liberalism had retained an appeal that made association with Johnson both comfortable and opportune. As 1966 progressed, this appeal disappeared, and so did Ribicoff's desire to be associated with the White House. Both Hubert Humphrey and Lyndon Johnson sought to dissuade the senator from embarrassing the administration by further undermining its already embattled domestic program, Johnson warning, "Abe, if you want to eat from the cake, don't piss on it."[28] Yet how could even so pungently stated an injunction have the desired effect, when the president's patronage had so little value?

Further evidence that Senator Ribicoff conceived of the hearings as a means of insulating himself from the problems of the domestic agenda comes from the reminiscences of his legislative aide, Wayne Granquist, who believes that his boss "didn't give a damn" about Johnson's anger:

> I suspect it was as much to do with Johnson's plunging popularity as it was any-thing that Johnson was or was not doing in terms of substance. . . . Ribicoff, basically, is a politician from Connecticut whose job it is to represent the peo-ple of Connecticut, and be a responsible national leader. And so as Johnson plummeted, there was little, if any, support from Ribicoff.[29]

In this context, Granquist remarks, "the cities issue was a good way to distin-guish yourself from those who wanted to pursue the Vietnam war without taking a strong position against the urban problem." Discontented liberals, not to mention assorted activists, were increasingly accusing Johnson of just such a combination. As Vietnam began to destroy the Johnson presidency, Ribicoff's aides sought to "give him a way to get away from total unity with Lyndon Johnson . . . without being associated in the minds of the hawks with the doves."[30]

A final source of Ribicoff's enthusiasm for the hearings is to be located in his anger at Robert Kennedy's easy command of the airwaves. Joseph Cal-ifano told Johnson of the rivalry, seeking to explain Ribicoff's seeming will-ingness to jeopardize a Model Cities proposal which he had himself helped to construct:

> I talked to Abe Ribicoff today about the cities hearings. I expressed our concern that having Schultze and others up there would create problems on the House floor for the [model] cities bill, which is already in trouble. Ribicoff said he thought the cities bill was the most imaginative proposal in the whole area and he did not want to do anything to injure it. . . . I think Ribicoff might like to cooperate with us, but that he is plagued with Bobby Kennedy getting out in front of him in terms of publicity.[31]

Ribicoff heatedly denied that this was his motive for launching the city hearings.[32] Either way, Robert Kennedy derived considerably greater pub-licity from them than did the chairman. At one stage, a nettled Ribicoff bemoaned the fact that journalists "often think the only story involved in these hearings is a man by the name of Senator Robert Kennedy."[33]

If some of Ribicoff's willingness to defy the growing conservatism of white America reflected his belief that a new social order must inevitably emerge from these "revolutionary" times, then Kennedy was also in a good position to take the long-term view. Like his Democratic colleague, Kennedy's presidential ambitions were concentrated on 1972; Johnson was not yet sufficiently vulnerable to make a 1968 challenge seem feasible. An additional factor for Kennedy, as he endeavored to acquire a loyal, personal constituency, was his growing identification with youthful protest and idealism. In April, Frederick Dutton had alerted the senator to the most distinctive source of his appeal:

> You need to allow dramatic insights into your own life and interests occasionally, especially for the younger people for whom you are almost a personal model. This outlet also moves you into the "existential" politics that I believe will be more and more important in the years ahead; and it allows you to show the verve and vitality that are so attractive and authentic about you, among all the public figures of our time and especially in contrast to the dull middle-aged tone that President Johnson and Hubert have hanging like a pall over the country.[34]

In Dutton's view, Kennedy would benefit politically from "at least one major, exciting personal adventure or activity every six months or so, [such] as mountain climbing, river boating, etc." One idea might be "that you live for four or five days in a kibbutz in Israel," a move which would be "useful in New York." Alternatively, an "archaeological expedition in Peru or a non-shooting safari in Africa" would fit the bill.[35]

Adam Walinsky, considering the senator's options for the forthcoming midterm elections, insisted that he must exploit the opportunity presented by youthful support in a time of dislocation and change: "Are you ready—now—for the politics of the future, remembering not only that before you again face the voters life will be very different than it is today, but also that probably two-thirds of the nation (if you count the kids who do not yet vote) look to you for the only clear and honest and courageous leadership it can hope to find?"[36] During the autumn of 1966, Kennedy campaigned extensively on behalf of Democratic candidates throughout the nation, everywhere pursued by an entourage of admiring teenagers. When prospective voters were asked to choose their favorite Democratic Party candidate for 1968, age had a dramatic bearing on their preference.[37]

	Total	*Age 21–29*	*Age 50+*	*Democrats*
Kennedy	41	56	31	48
Johnson	45	33	51	44
Undecided	14	11	18	8

Kennedy, in turn, was quick to capitalize on his popularity with young and future voters. The Ribicoff hearings, conceived all along as a publicity vehicle, presented the perfect opportunity for him to convey passion, commitment, idealism, and detachment from the old politics. Throughout the Ribicoff hearings, he would return to the theme of youth alienation. In early 1967, following the conclusion of the hearings, he addressed the Americans for Democratic Action (ADA), titling his talk, "What Can the Young Believe?" His courting of the college generation was obvious:

> They see us spend billions on armaments while poverty and ignorance continue at home; they see us willing to fight a war for freedom in Vietnam, but unwilling to fight with one-hundredth the money or force or effort to secure freedom in Mississippi or Alabama or the ghettos of the North. And they see, perhaps most disturbing of all, that they are remote from the decisions of policy, that they themselves frequently do not, by the nature of our political system, share in the power of choice or great questions shaping their lives. . . . The words which submerge us, all too often, speak the language of a day irrelevant to our young. And the language of politics is too often insincerity.[38]

Kennedy's decision to address the ADA was a politically significant one, for he had previously resisted such a move. Increasingly, however, the activist character of his natural constituency was becoming clear. As centrist liberalism declined, it lent new appeal to the *true believer* brand represented by the ADA. Arthur Schlesinger presented the case for addressing the organization: "I think it might be a good chance to consolidate a position among organized liberals, some of whom may still have a lingering mistrust while others will be red hot."[39] That Kennedy's visceral reaction to the ADA was still unenthusiastic is apparent from his initial rejection of Schlesinger's advice, and from the fact that he underlined the words "lingering mistrust," appending the comment, "I have some for them too." But pragmatic exigencies suggested that he bite the bullet, and his February 1967 keynote address embodied the unmistakable tones of the fervent convert, incorporating three of the most powerful sources of restiveness among ADA liberals: Vietnam, youth alienation, and the plight of poor blacks.

Kennedy's success in disengaging himself from the old liberalism of Johnson and Humphrey was apparent from the testimony of a group of poor residents of Washington before the Ribicoff committee. One, Mrs. Katie Ridley, asked Kennedy to help "save" the War on Poverty, eliciting from Ribicoff the careworn observation that "Senator Kennedy is one senator. I am another senator. There are ninety-eight others." Mrs. Ridley, however, remained powerfully impressed by Robert Kennedy's personal capacity: "Of all the speeches I have heard from Mr. Kennedy, and I will say kind of quietly Mr. Johnson, I feel that Mr. Kennedy [applause]—I feel that Mr. Kennedy is one of the poor man's friends. I do not think this of our President [applause]."[40] Not surprisingly, Senator Kennedy told his admirer that her testimony had been "very valuable." No doubt he also gained a certain amount of satisfaction from the remarks of the next speaker, Mrs. Etta Horn, of the Barry Farms Welfare Movement, who proclaimed that "it is a sad day when the poor people find out that the president of the United States is a rich man's president."[41]

The third in this trio of senators, Jacob Javits, was a long-standing and consistent devotee of liberal causes, popular with civil rights and labor groups and endorsed by the New York Liberal Party. Earlier in the year, he had hoped to move to Albany and succeed the increasingly unpopular New York governor, Nelson Rockefeller. Ultimately, he had chosen the reflected glory of running the incumbent's successful reelection campaign. Robert Kintner told President Johnson that Javits's ambitions now extended beyond the governor's mansion: "He and Mrs. Javits have indicated to me that he is shooting for the V.P. nomination in 1968, at the least, and I have a justified suspicion that he is really longing for the presidential nomination."[42]

Javits, like Ribicoff, was clearly jealous of Robert Kennedy's media appeal and, during the course of the hearings, implied more than once that his junior colleague had stolen *his* ideas (such as private sector involvement in the War on Poverty, and a domestic Marshall Plan). More specifically, he was irritated that both Kennedy and Ribicoff could spare so much time for such a valuable media event:

> I might state for the record . . . that my problem has been the fact that while we have been holding these hearings, [hearings] on the very things that we need to do in order to meet these conditions are going on in all the executive chambers of the Senate. We are marking up the poverty bill, we are marking up the civil rights bill, which is what I am called to now, and it is very difficult for a senator and I am so delighted that at least two of my colleagues have been able to concentrate on these hearings.[43]

THE CITY HEARINGS: EARLY SESSIONS

It would be a mistake, therefore, to view the Ribicoff hearings as simply the response of concerned idealists to a burgeoning urban crisis whose intensity had defeated traditional approaches. They were, rather, the product of the political aspirations of their instigator, and their course was determined by the rival ambitions of a trio of mutually antagonistic legislators. The transparent grandstanding that consumed the earliest sessions detracted significantly from their substantive value. Accordingly, the politics of the hearings are more salient to the present analysis than their content.

During the first week of the committee's deliberations, a series of senior administration officials were subjected to a barrage of outspoken criticism from Ribicoff and Kennedy. The first witness, Secretary for Housing and Urban Development Robert Weaver, was prevented from completing a lengthy list of his administration's accomplishments by repeated interruptions from the chairman and Robert Kennedy. The latter complained that "it sounds on paper as if the problem had disappeared," adding, "I hope you will not go on talking about what you have done." In one melodramatic outburst, Kennedy announced that "if this is the answer, then we'd better get off the ship."[44] Ribicoff, who had played a significant role in the conception of Weaver's department, charged that "despite the programs, you are slipping further and further behind." The committee chairman found Weaver's praise for urban renewal projects particularly offensive: "You're talking about programs that helped suburbia in the past—not the ones that are needed for the cities in which we live. We're reaping a whirlwind of violence in our cities that indicates that these programs are not having the impact that they should."[45]

The following day, Nicholas Katzenbach, Kennedy's successor at the Justice Department, was subjected to a similar attack from his former superior, this time focused on the Model Cities program. Charging that existing programs represented nothing more than "a drop in the bucket," Kennedy proclaimed himself "just not satisfied." The attorney general replied that Kennedy's discontent was "quite clear," but went on to remind the senator that Model Cities was "just the kind of philosophy you've been asking for."[46] On the third full day of hearings, Ribicoff admonished John Gardner, his successor once removed at the Department of Health, Education and Welfare, that "I hope you will be frank,"[47] while Kennedy scolded his brother-in-law, Sargent Shriver, for defending spending priorities of which, "as a civilized nation," America should be ashamed. If the nation could afford to spend $24 billion in Vietnam, why could Head Start appropriations not be increased? Shriver responded with the administration line: "It isn't just a question of civilization. I think it is also a question of what happens to interest rates, what happens to the dollar in all these factors."[48] The final administration witness, Willard Wirtz, was less fulsome in praising Johnson's record. Accordingly, he earned praise from Ribicoff for "candid and refreshing testimony [of] the type . . . that I had hoped to have all week from members of the executive branch."[49]

In terms of the fate of liberal individualism, two aspects of these early sessions (concluding in September, they resumed after the midterm elections) appear particularly arresting. First, contributors tended to argue that existing policies, even were they greatly expanded, possessed intimidating conceptual flaws. This represented an important shift from the first half of the year, when Johnson's liberal critics had typically condemned the scale rather than the orientation of the Great Society. Senator Ribicoff, for example, echoed the spirit of *Having the Power, We Have the Duty* in observing that "we want to break away from the continuous repetition of old and worn-out ideas that still receive currency."[50] Particular respect was accorded the recent findings of James S. Coleman, whose damning investigation of the popular Head Start program found educational spending largely irrelevant to individual attainment, in the process undermining an important source of Johnson's faith in rehabilitation, and strengthening the case for an income strategy. Coleman concluded, "Family background differences account for much more variation in achievement than do school differences." His evidence revealed that "per pupil expenditures, books in the library and a host of other facilities and curricular measures show virtually no relation to the achievement of the social environment of the school, if the educational background of the students and teachers is held constant."[51]

Second, advocates of redirection remained suspicious of the income maintenance approach and sensitive to the political utility of the "jobs, not doles" formulation. Considering questions that Kennedy might like to put to John Gardner, Adam Walinsky suggested: "What is the trend of welfare payments in the last five years?" and "What, in your judgment, could we do to help more people get off welfare and become independent?"[52] During these early sessions, the issue of income maintenance attracted little attention. It appears that legislators were under less pressure than the welfare establishment to address so fraught an issue as the guaranteed income. When hearings resumed in November and December, the issue had penetrated the political consciousnesses of committee members, but their response remained strongly negative.

ATTACK FROM THE RIGHT: MIDTERM ELECTIONS OF 1966

Meanwhile, the midterm elections provided a critical measure of the strength of Great Society liberalism. In particular, the character of the fall campaign, together with its eventual outcome, offered important indicators regarding the political viability of the kind of renewed yet redirected liberal activism that Ribicoff's rhetoric demanded. The results indicated that Americans were "tired of being improved," and that a rejuvenated Republican Party had successfully shed its damaging identification with the reactionary conservatism of Barry Goldwater. The GOP gained a net eight governorships, three Senate seats, and—most significantly—forty-seven House seats. Given that the party in control of the presidency had suffered an average midterm loss of thirty-three House seats during the last eight such contests, significant Republican gains were to be expected in 1966, with the size of the 1964 Democratic advance increasing the likelihood still further.[53] Particularly at risk were the forty-five freshman Democrats in formerly Republican districts who had benefited from President Johnson's long coattails in 1964, and whose liberalism in turn had made possible the legislative achievements of the 89th Congress.

Three themes dominated the campaigning, but their individual impact on specific races was ultimately less powerful than the overall mood of national dissatisfaction to which each contributed. Vietnam, the state of the economy, and racial strife were all issues whose current character tended to emphasize just how swiftly the rich promise of 1964 had dissipated.

Two years earlier, Johnson had pledged his determination that "Asian boys" should do the fighting in Vietnam. Yet two years later, 500,000 Americans were engaged in a conflict whose only certain outcome was more bloodshed. On the economic front, the miraculous prosperity initially associated with the New Economics was suddenly threatened by inflation and rising interest rates. In terms of civil rights, the contrast was still more stark. The results of the 1964 elections had belied talk of a white backlash, while the first session of the 89th Congress had cheered the president's adoption of the slogan "We shall overcome" and subsequently passed his Voting Rights bill. A year later, the civil rights movement was tainted by its association with Black Power and racial violence, its aspirations further thwarted by white hostility to open housing and desegregated schooling.

Vietnam was an issue from which Republicans were able to profit without explicitly condemning administration policy. Indeed, overt criticism of existing strategy was a tactic fraught with peril, given the absence of obvious alternatives, the conflicting reasons for popular opposition, and the danger of appearing unpatriotic. Furthermore, attitudes toward the war did not divide neatly along party lines; prominent Republican victors in November included doves, such as Mark Hatfield, as well as hawks, such as Ronald Reagan.

While the specter of Vietnam overshadowed the administration's successes and emphasized its failures, its direct impact on individual races was limited. In Connecticut's sixth district, the entry of a peace candidate allowed the Republicans to defeat a liberal Democrat—one of relatively few GOP gains in New England—but elsewhere their impact was negligible. The principal effect of the war on domestic politics was to diminish the president's personal popularity. From a high of 56 percent in the summer, the result of the stepped-up bombing of North Vietnam, his popularity fell to 48 percent by election time. Even here, Johnson managed to minimize the political impact of the apparent stalemate by embarking on a timely Pacific tour.[54] According to the *Congressional Quarterly*, there was "little evidence to suggest that public anxiety over the war was directly reflected in the election results."[55]

The state of the economy, and especially inflationary pressures, provided more promising material for the Republican Party.[56] This was true both for conservatives preaching a return to small government—for example, Ronald Reagan and Harold LeVander in the California and Minnesota gubernatorial contests, respectively—and for liberals promising sound management—such as Charles Percy, whose opponent was his former economics professor, Paul Douglas. Senate Minority Leader Everett Dirksen, purported to be a capable judge of the public mood, told colleagues, "It is the nonessential expenditures and not Viet Nam that accounts for the inflationary fever that is in the country today."[57]

Changing attitudes toward race may be considered part of a broader cultural shift whose implications for Great Society liberalism were also deeply disturbing. If contact with Goldwaterite Republicanism had created a coalition for liberal reform in 1964, then it was easy to exaggerate both the depth and the permanency of this coalition. This was not a mistake the president made, as may be observed from his determination to enact the principal components of the Great Society during the first two years of his presidency. Yet correspondingly, the sheer pace of change undoubtedly served to hasten the inevitable counterreaction. Even more important, the first half of the Johnson presidency was accompanied by a number of events and trends that could not fairly be attributed to (or controlled by) the administration, but which seemed somehow to lend an unfavorable hue to Great Society liberalism.[58]

One example is particularly relevant to the present investigation. While the Economic Opportunity Act was presented by Johnson and his supporters as a war on dependency, and while the Civil Rights Act of 1964 explicitly opposed preferential treatment, both focused upon groups (the poor and blacks) whose aspirations and behavior seemed increasingly divorced from those of Middle America during 1965 and 1966. Despite the War on Poverty's impeccably orthodox rhetoric, and despite unparalleled prosperity, welfare rolls continued to rise during the mid-1960s, while academics and activists alike started to promote the concept of a guaranteed income. Such developments undercut the administration's claim that antipoverty warriors were proud heirs to the individualist tradition, and provided valuable ammunition for conservatives keen to exploit the nation's hostility to dependency.

Another strand in this elusive, yet pervasive, cultural reaction against liberalism may be detected in the judicial sphere. Two Supreme Court opinions that received prominent attention in 1966 set the forces of liberalism apart from mainstream sentiment. The decision banning prayer in public schools, *Engel v. Vitale,* was handed down in 1962, but in 1966—with 80 percent of public opinion in his favor—Everett Dirksen introduced a bill to amend the First Amendment to allow voluntary prayer. The sponsor sought to associate this particular crusade with a much wider campaign for the ideological initiative: "Now, the thing that entrances me about all this is that there is a godless mass. You cannot contemplate the gangs in our large cities, and the mass of atheistic Communism, and all of these other forces that are trying to destroy the religious traditions of this country, without coming to the conclusion that they have made a lot of progress in that direction."[59]

The second legal judgment to attract the attention of conservative politicians in 1966 was *Miranda v. Arizona,* which protected defendants in criminal trials against the use of statements obtained through violations of procedure. In his dissenting argument, Justice Byron White warned that the majority opinion would "have a corrosive effect on the criminal law as an effective device to prevent crime."[60] For conservatives, the verdict could scarcely have come at a more propitious time, given rising public concern about crime and the prevalence of racial disorder in the American city— one news magazine identified thirty-eight serious disturbances in 1966.[61] House Minority Leader Gerald Ford (R-Mich.), whose state experienced four such disturbances in 1966, drew maximum political benefit from the Democratic Party's uncomfortable position. He ungenerously characterized the Democrats as "the party with the big riots in the streets," adding, "The Democratic Party promised big but failed to deliver. That's why we are in trouble now. . . . How long are we going to abdicate law and order—the backbone of any civilization—in favor of a soft social theory that the man who heaves a brick through your window or tosses a firebomb into your car is simply the misunderstood and underprivileged product of a broken home?"[62]

In 1964, the Democrats had been able to profit from their identification with the fears and aspirations of the American people; two years later, the Republicans were in a position to do the same. Barry Goldwater had marginalized his party by assailing the social security system and pledging "extremism in the defense of liberty"; antiadministration liberals now threatened to do the same by appealing to a disparate coalition of minorities rather than to mainstream sentiment.

Nowhere was the nation's mood of unease and disaffection more apparent than in the area that had dominated the domestic politics of the 1960s and contributed so much to the activist zeal of Great Society liberals, namely race relations. As with Vietnam, Republicans could gain from voter anxiety without so much as taking a position. Such civil rights advocates as Charles Percy, Senator Clifford Case (R-N.J.) and Raymond Shafer, GOP gubernatorial candidate in Pennsylvania, were able to benefit from the backlash simply because of their opponents' party identification.

Even had it wished to, the Johnson administration could hardly have dissociated itself from the civil rights cause, despite the existence of a political climate in which, in Harry McPherson's words, "it would have been hard to pass the emancipation proclamation."[63] Poll data compiled by Tad Cantril for the Johnson administration indicated a dramatic shift in popular sentiment during the year since Watts. A majority of the respondents now believed that the administration was pushing integration too fast. The following table shows how the percentage endorsing this view increased:[64]

	Aug. 1965	*Sept. 1966*	*Shift*
National	40	52	+12
Democrats	35	44	+ 9
Republicans	46	61	+15
Independents	43	61	+18
East	28	38	+10
South	61	64	+ 3
Midwest	35	55	+20
West	35	51	+16
Professional/business	42	55	+13
Clerical/sales	45	49	+10
Farmers	32	66	+34
Manual labor	40	49	+ 9

The open housing issue did much to nationalize voter sentiment on questions of race. The conservative rhetoric of two Midwestern Democrats who had been reliable civil rights advocates before 1966 reflected acute anxiety about the white backlash in the region that had produced half of the Democratic freshmen in 1964. Congressman Wayne Hays, whose Ohio constituents had recently been shaken by serious rioting in Cleveland's Hough ghetto, recorded his opposition to open housing in a fiery oration to the House. He was particularly irritated by a *Washington Post* article that attributed urban unrest in Washington, D.C., to the squalor of its public housing and commented, "I would just like to say that when these houses were built they did not come furnished with roaches. I have public housing in my district, and the administrator sees to it that the tenants observe simple sanitation, and if they do not, they find themselves without a place to live. What are we to do now? Go out and clean houses for these people?"[65]

Congressman Roman Pucinski (D-Ill.) represented the white ethnic Chicago district where acrimonious confrontations had taken place between local residents and SCLC demonstrators throughout the summer of 1966. He had found, of late, that "people are not talking about Viet Nam or rising prices or prosperity. They are talking about Martin Luther King, Jr., and how the [blacks] are moving in on us and what's going to happen in our neighborhoods."[66] The *New York Times* reported that the incumbent and his Republican challenger were "debating who will do the most to preserve the character of the neighborhoods."[67] Some of the Democrats' arguments sounded remarkably similar to those that

149

Dixiecrats tended to employ in denouncing civil rights activities. Referring to King's activities in Chicago, Pucinski asked: "Can the organizers truly be nonviolent, knowing in their minds and hearts that their conduct will assuredly precipitate violence in others?"[68]

But if race proved to be a prominent campaign theme in some Northern contests, it is hard to identify races in which it was clearly decisive. Despite some hopeful signs, such as Winthrop Rockefeller's gubernatorial success in Arkansas and the virtual collapse of the Byrd machine in Virginia, it was in the South that the backlash had the greatest electoral significance. Congressman George Grider of Memphis, one of a small band of Southern moderates in the House, fell victim to white hostility to the 1966 civil rights bill. Nicholas Katzenbach warned Joseph Califano that Grider "believes the legislation dealing with State Juries and Housing is outrageous and will eliminate Congressmen like himself and Weltner. He said this legislation will defeat him whether he votes for it or against it."[69] This prediction proved accurate, although Charles Weltner, congressman from Atlanta, chose to resign his seat rather than face the electors, claiming that while the forces of Southern moderation had been marginally ascendant in the summer of 1966, they had been wiped out by Black Power and rioting.

Congressman Weltner's decision to withdraw seems to have been powerfully influenced by the astonishing success of Lester Maddox in capturing the Democratic gubernatorial nomination in his state. A segregationist to the point of caricature, Maddox had previously gained prominence by selling axe handles to white patrons, and brandishing revolvers at black would-be.patrons of his chicken grill. In 1966, he faced an uphill battle, initially in a seven-man Democratic primary and then in a runoff against Ellis Arnall, a racial moderate and former governor. Arnall attributed his shock defeat to the unwillingness of other candidates, such as state senator Jimmy Carter, to repudiate Maddox, as well as to a recent riot in Atlanta.

The border state of Maryland was the scene of a second defeat for racial moderation. Carlton Sickles, the early front-runner for the state governorship, fell victim to the sudden popularity of George Mahoney, a Baltimore County paving contractor. The victor had been a perennial candidate at Democratic state primaries since 1952, but 1966 brought him his first success. Baltimore had been designated CORE's "number one target city" for its resistance to residential and educational integration, and civil rights activism added appeal to a campaign that centered around the slogan "A Man's Home Is His Castle."[70] Unlike in Georgia, however, the backlash was not sufficiently powerful to propel the Democratic candidate to the governorship; enough Democrats defected to ensure the election of Spiro Agnew.

A third race in which the new South confronted the forces of reaction occurred in South Carolina, where Democrat Ernest Hollings's Senate bid faced strong competition from a right-wing Republican associated with Strom Thurmond. Forced onto the defensive by white hostility to the national Democratic Party and by a potentially troublesome Kennedy connection, Hollings assured voters that his disenchantment with Lyndon Johnson's leadership was so great that he was unlikely to support the president's reelection bid in 1968. Furthermore, he had not seen Bobby for two years![71]

AFTERMATH OF THE MIDTERM ELECTIONS

The results of the midterm elections of 1966 represented a repudiation not just of Great Society liberalism but also of Goldwater Republicanism. The latter fact constituted a powerful political challenge to the Johnson presidency, given the high caliber of the moderate Republicans whose standing gained most from the election. Governor George Romney of Michigan, viewed as the president's most likely GOP challenger in 1968, secured easy reelection, while his coattails helped elect a Republican senator and no fewer than five congressmen to formerly Democratic seats. Governor James A. Rhodes, similarly, was reelected with the largest majority in Ohio history and helped his party to pick up four House seats.

In other contests, the success of a new generation of attractive and ideologically moderate Republicans confirmed the return of the two-party system. Senators Mark Hatfield (Ore.), Charles Percy (Ill.), Edward Brooke (Mass.), and Howard Baker (Tenn.), along with Governors Raymond Shafer (Pa.) and Daniel Evans (Wash.), were among many GOP contestants who successfully articulated voter discontent without embracing rightist dogma. Henry Wilson, a congressional liaison aide, warned the president that his administration must reclaim the center field it had seemed to command so effortlessly in 1964:

> The Great Society has become associated in the public mind with eliminating ghettos and generally pouring vast sums into the renovation of the poor and the

Negro. The average American is tired of it. The swing vote in 1968 will be the suburban vote, and though the average suburbanite does not want to vote for a George Wallace, he is perfectly willing to accept a candidate who takes the stress off poverty, and civil rights, and expresses more concern about the problems of the suburbanite.[72]

Charles Schultze believed that even if voters had retained their enthusiasm for the ideals of the Great Society, they would have been alienated by the rhetorical excesses associated with the administration. A host of new social programs had been launched, yet economic and budgetary constraints precluded funding levels commensurate with their ambitious objectives. Schultze's memorandum, entitled "Great Expectations vs. Disappointment," summarized the difficulty:

> As I get deeper into the review of the 1968 budget, one major problem stands out above all others—a problem which could be very troublesome in the 1968 campaign. That problem is simply that *we are not able to fund adequately the new Great Society programs*. At the same time, states, cities, depressed areas and individuals have been led to expect immediate delivery of benefits from Great Society programs to a degree that is not realistic. . . . HEW, for example, is administering forty new health and education programs. As we add to these, we have to *hold down* financing of last year's new programs to finance this year's. . . . If this goes on long enough, and we do not make good, the Administration loses credibility. We risk losing the support of large groups, and we invite defections by members of our own party in the Congress.[73]

James Gaither, recently appointed as Joseph Califano's principal domestic aide, was disturbed that despite this pattern, agency and interagency task forces were continuing to produce a host of expensive new social welfare recommendations: "While I recognize the justice and efficacy of various proposals legislatively, I just don't believe that the political atmosphere is such that the program can be accomplished. . . . It should be pruned down so that more emphasis is placed on administering the government and less on new legislation."[74]

The administration's experience with the new Congress fully justified such cautious advice. *Congressional Quarterly* recorded a dramatic increase in the success rate of the so-called conservative coalition, particularly in the House:[75]

Year	House	Senate	Total
1964	67%	47%	51%
1965	25	39	33

| 1966 | 32 | 51 | 45 |
| 1967 | 73 | 54 | 62 |

Shaken by the scale of his repudiation, and impressed by the cautious counsel of Wilson, Schultze, and Gaither, Johnson sought to project a moderate and consensual image. In an early public response to the November elections, the president claimed to welcome the return of the two-party system and pledged, "we will be very careful in our preparation of our recommendations, and we will try to enlist the support of both parties." He added, "We are not overly optimistic. We will have difficulty in preparing the new programs we have. I anticipate that our big problem is to get good administration, get the programs we have already passed funded, and try to get them organized and executed in the proper manner."[76]

Reflecting the same preoccupations, the president's 1967 State of the Union Address attempted to capture the formula that had brought the moderate Republicans such success in November—the promise of capable economic and programmatic management at home, combined with principled, statesmanlike leadership abroad. Poverty and civil rights were less prominent than in previous years—the latter received only forty-five words, squeezed in between beautification of the environment and the revision of military draft procedure.[77]

As 1967 began, Great Society liberalism was clearly, and necessarily, on the defensive. Nevertheless, the president's continued commitment to its ideals is suggested by his enthusiastic response to Mike Manatos's recommendation that he redouble existing efforts to unify an embattled and fractious Democratic Party. The poor results of the 1966 House elections placed added responsibility on the president and Senate to provide the sort of leadership that would maintain forward momentum without fatally offending public opinion. Manatos suggested a White House summit "to infuse into our friends . . . the urgency of a team effort. They certainly need you, and Lord knows we need them." He continued:

> You will recall that the Second Session of the 89th [Congress] got off on the wrong foot early this year, and the belligerency that mood generated made matters more difficult for us as the legislative year unfolded. . . . This year's elections place on the Senate, in my view, added responsibility for bellwethering your domestic programs. The Senate is now forced to lead, and if we are to succeed it cannot enjoy the luxury of sitting back awaiting House action, except on matters involving revenue. You have the unique ability to persuade almost anyone, and you have not hesitated to use that talent whenever you believed it would not be wasted.[78]

Johnson's response was to ask Manatos to organize a White House meeting with the Senate's Democratic Policy Committee, together with additional committee chairmen and liberal leaders.[79] Parallel with such efforts, however, came the resumption of the Ribicoff hearings, whose deliberations contained little to encourage would-be architects of consensus.

CITY HEARINGS: LATE SESSIONS

Senator Ribicoff and his colleagues had earlier assailed administration policies without producing or even being exposed to clear alternatives. By December, however, the search for new directions had produced a daring possibility. In response to Ribicoff's demand for new directions, Daniel Patrick Moynihan, Martin Luther King, Jr., and Whitney Young, Jr., were among those who promoted the guaranteed income concept.

Moynihan used Senator Ribicoff's expressed interest in the Coleman Report on education to sell the virtues of the income strategy. He pronounced himself struck by the futility of Sargent Shriver's expressed intention to reduce pupil : teacher ratios from 25 to 15, a scheme that would cost no less than $340 per pupil each year, that is, over $1,000 for a family with three school-age children. Recalling Coleman's conclusions, Moynihan suggested that the money would be better spent on direct cash grants to poor families: "A fundamental issue . . . is to choose between a strategy of services, which Mr. Shriver's proposal would entail, as against a strategy of income. . . . To propose spending the money on services which such research as we have suggests will produce little or no effect is to risk being thought ridiculous or worse by members of the public, and we would delude ourselves if we did not see that this judgment has already been reached by large numbers."[80]

Rejecting the popular assumption that the able-bodied poor were shiftless chiselers, though not suggesting how such prejudices might be overcome, Moynihan informed a respectful audience that "it is a basic rule of social science that people by and large do their best. . . . People do not cheat. People do not abandon their responsibility. Some do on the margin. The overwhelming number of people do not."[81]

Whitney Young, Jr., of the National Urban League echoed this confidence, telling the committee that "we can trust people. . . . There will be no more chiselers among the poor than we have among the rich."[82] Martin

Luther King, Jr., concurred with both Moynihan and Young in promoting the guaranteed income as a just and effective alternative to the existing orthodoxy, as a prerequisite for self-advancement: "We are likely to find that the problems of housing and education, instead of preceding the elimination of poverty will themselves be affected if poverty is first abolished. . . . The dignity of the individual will flourish when he knows he has the means to seek self-improvement, and the assurance that his income is stable and certain."[83]

The Ribicoff hearings provided the guaranteed income's early converts with a first opportunity to propound their arguments on so public a political stage. Nevertheless, Johnson's emphasis on personal responsibility and self-advancement had commanded almost universal support until this time, and the individualist tradition was too firmly embedded to fall at the first challenge. Kenneth Clark told Ribicoff that "as to the matter of a guaranteed annual income, I am afraid my feelings are not quite as clear and definite as Pat Moynihan's." In his view, policymakers still had to acknowledge "that problems of self-worth, problems of self-respect, problems of respect of others for you, are as necessary for the human spirit as merely providing the material economic basis for living."[84] Rev. Leon Sullivan, founder of a highly successful antipoverty program in Philadelphia (the Opportunities Industrialization Center), lamented the notion that individual behavior was somehow irrelevant as a determinant of social policy. His experience had been that "no amount of money poured into a community to relieve poverty, squalor, and want can help out so much unless the people who live there are inspired and motivated to first help themselves."[85]

Presented with these two positions—the first questioning, the second reinforcing the validity of the philosophical propositions that underpinned the War on Poverty—Ribicoff shied away from the idea of a guaranteed income. Neither he nor Javits seemed particularly disturbed by its philosophical implications (indeed both professed themselves powerfully impressed by Moynihan's testimony), but the chairman pointed out that in political terms it was something of a nonstarter:

> As I foresee the political difficulties, and they would be grave, the person earning $100,000 a year wouldn't be worried very much about someone who would be getting $3,000 a year. But how about the man who works 40 hours a week and gets $3,500 a year seeing his neighbor get $3,000 a year for not working? This is something I think that the American people will just not be able to swallow.

155

The question comes back to finding jobs, because I still think you have got this attitude on work in this country. Getting something for nothing is not going to go down politically.[86]

If Ribicoff's response to the crisis of urban America revealed a determination to find policy directions more promising than those the Johnson administration had pursued to date, then he retained an appreciation of the continuing political potency of the work ethic. Similarly, Robert Kennedy, who had recently sponsored a high-profile community development project in the Bedford-Stuyvesant area of Brooklyn, was urged by a congressional aide to exploit the contrast between his ideas and the income maintenance approach:

Ask him [the witness] about the guaranteed income. . . . It seems to me that the guaranteed annual income has implications which run contrary to your community development corporation idea. Your premise has been that we should put people to work, that we should give all men who are willing and able to work a job, that a job brings dignity and contributes to family stability. . . . *Unless the guaranteed annual income is viewed as a guarantee only for those who are unable to work, I think it is a rather dangerous concept.*[87]

As 1967 dawned, disaffection with administration social policies had started to focus not simply on their scale, but also on their orientation. The fact that income maintenance must play a far larger role in efforts to relieve poverty had won widespread acceptance within the liberal and civil rights community. As yet, however, the principle of a right to income detached from any expectation of employment remained politically far-fetched. If an income strategy were to emerge, it seemed more likely that any new social contract between government and the individual would center on the right to a job. Such a development would have been grounded in the New Deal liberal tradition, albeit in an aspect of that tradition which had been muted since the 1940s. Ultimately, however, job-based income strategies were to gain remarkably little momentum during the late 1960s, while the principle of an unconditional right to welfare was to take the imagination of many liberal legislators. An inkling of what was to come could be gleaned from the course of the welfare reform debate of 1967.

CHAPTER 7

Welfare Reform and the Crisis of Liberalism: 1967

The escalating war in Vietnam, racial tensions, and economic constraints had already distanced numerous liberals from the perspectives they formerly embraced without question. In the summer of 1967, disaffection with the Johnson administration's handling of domestic and foreign policy reached a peak among both liberals and conservatives, contributing to a profound crisis of national direction which substantially weakened liberal attachment to traditional conceptions of mutual obligation and hastened the search for a New Politics. As the situation worsened, Lyndon Johnson again sought to regain the allegiance of disaffected components of the New Deal Democratic coalition.

Liberal dissidents in Congress remained, for the most part, uninterested in or wary of the guaranteed income "solution" to poverty. Nevertheless, their growing interest in the New Politics, and their parallel disdain for the sensibilities of traditional Democratic constituencies, represented important preconditions for a subsequent endorsement of radical new approaches to income maintenance. Meanwhile, within the Johnson administration the guaranteed income concept commanded ever greater support, despite the president's lack of enthusiasm. This chapter focuses on the welfare reform package introduced by the administration at the beginning of 1967, which fell spectacular victim to the polarized political climate in the summer of that year.

* * *

SOCIAL SECURITY AMENDMENTS OF 1967:
ADMINISTRATION PROPOSAL

President Johnson constructed his 1967 welfare package in the uneasy knowledge that the philosophical consensus of earlier years had largely disappeared. In 1964, liberals and conservatives debating the Economic Opportunity Act had, for all their differences on other issues, been able to agree that income dependency was an ignoble and undesirable condition whose obviation must lie at the heart of public policy. Three years later, both liberal and conservative perspectives on social welfare had polarized to a degree that signally complicated any administration attempt to reform the Social Security Act.

The most striking features of this polarization during 1966 had been the simultaneous emergence of a vocal welfare rights movement and an even stronger welfare backlash. Two factors contributed to the latter phenomenon. First, the cost of AFDC payments had increased by 35 percent since 1964, significantly undermining the credibility of the Economic Opportunity Act:[1]

	No. of Recipients (000s)	Cost of Payments ($000s)
1964	4,219	1,634
1965	4,396	1,809
1966	4,666	1,924
1967	5,309	2,280

If the War on Poverty could not reduce welfare rolls at a time of unparalleled prosperity and economic growth, how could it expect to retain conservative support? If anything, OEO programs appeared to have contributed to burgeoning rolls by encouraging the poor to mobilize in defense of their rights.

The second factor was a growing public tendency to associate dependency with negative racial stereotypes. This tendency was not new, but it did gain fresh momentum during the mid-1960s. In the wake of the Watts riot, for example, some commentators presented the Moynihan Report as an explanation for racial disorder, while the McCone Commission also traced a direct connection between welfare rolls and black violence.[2] And during the following year, militant black discontent came increasingly to be associated with welfare rights advocacy.

At a time when riots, the open housing issue, school desegregation, and the Black Power movement were already alienating white America from the aspirations of the minority poor, welfare chiseling provided an attractive campaigning theme for conservatives who were happy to exploit the backlash yet reluctant to adopt an explicitly race-based message. *America* magazine observed that "although in most cases the critics of welfare don't talk openly about race, most of them regard relief programs as the special preserve of shiftless and morally obtuse Negroes." It added that such resentment was prevalent among all classes, but that "lower-middle-class" Americans "reserve a special scorn for those who don't support themselves."[3] Finally, *America* reported the *Wall Street Journal*'s conclusion that "irritation about supposed welfare chiseling by Negroes" was hurting Democrats even more than the backlash against integrated housing.[4]

If rising welfare rolls made the rehabilitative rhetoric of 1964 appear somewhat naive, then liberals initially responded by adapting, rather than abandoning, the opportunity theory upon which the Economic Opportunity Act had been founded. In advocating a larger role for income maintenance in the fight against poverty, they remained attached to the ultimate goals of rehabilitation and prevention. By 1966, however, growing numbers of analysts—for example the authors of *Having the Power, We Have the Duty*[5]—were highlighting barriers to opportunity that demanded a permanent extension of the welfare state. A case in point is the 1966 Task Force on Income Maintenance, whose deliberations, together with those of the Advisory Council on Public Welfare, provided the basis for President Johnson's 1967 welfare reform package.

The most striking difference between the 1966 task force report and its 1965 counterpart concerns their respective treatment of the War on Poverty. The earlier report endorsed the lofty goals of the Office of Economic Opportunity, while warning that success would be contingent upon the liberalization of an archaic welfare system. In contrast, the 1966 report made not a single reference to the Economic Opportunity Act, preferring instead to justify welfare reform as a straightforward act of income redistribution. Robert A. Levine, who headed the OEO's research division from 1965 to 1969, has observed that the Johnson administration was initially torn between competing objectives, namely, eliminating poverty and extending opportunity.[6] The evidence of these two interagency reports suggests that a critical shift in favor of the former goal occurred during 1966, so much so in fact that task force members ceased to embody the nation's dominant commitment to work.

The 1965 body had accepted the need to adapt to long-standing popular prejudices about welfare entitlement, but its successor viewed these attitudes as fundamentally anachronistic and sought to change them: "Because of public attitudes regarding the 'deserving' and the 'non-deserving' poor, programs for the aged enjoy a degree of acceptance withheld from anti-poverty programs aimed at non-aged households with children. Any shift in emphasis will require public re-education which should begin now."[7]

If the growing desire of liberal policymakers to "educate" public opinion was eminently understandable, and if traditional approaches seemed of doubtful relevance to the problems of American society, then advocates of redirection faced a daunting political task. The 1966 task force came up with a number of ways in which an enlightened liberal elite might convince initially reluctant Americans of their social responsibilities. First, the Johnson administration could introduce modest welfare reforms whose intended but unstated effect would be to prepare the public for a more comprehensive overhaul. Second, it could appoint a presidential commission to investigate alternative income maintenance strategies, thereby stimulating public debate and presumably helping to dispel outmoded notions about self-reliance. Third, it could promote—either privately or openly—congressional hearings with the same purpose. Finally, experimental guaranteed income programs could be launched in selected locations, with the possibility of their wider deployment left open.

President Johnson's proposed Social Security Amendments of 1967 embodied a number of the more modest recommendations from the task force, albeit in limited fashion. In particular, the administration asked Congress to insist that states raise their AFDC payments to at least the level that the individual state had set as the minimum for subsistence. Since only twenty states at the time fulfilled this condition (while Mississippi provided only 23 percent of its already pitiful standard),[8] this reform represented a substantial liberalization. However, by continuing to allow states to produce their own definitions of need, the president backed away from any immediate assault on the federal-state system.

A second significant but similarly limited concession to the welfare system's liberal critics came with the permanent extension of the AFDC-Unemployed Parent (UP) program. Introduced as an experimental measure in 1961, AFDC-UP allowed states to provide relief to two-parent families where the father was "chronically unemployed." The program remained small in 1967 (only twenty-two states participated)[9] but its acceptance of the fact that there could be such a thing as a deserving, able-bodied male was important. As a corollary to the extension of the UP program, Johnson demanded that states provide opportunities for re-training under the little-used Community Work Training Program (which had been enacted with the Public Welfare Amendments of 1962).[10] Finally, the proposed reform package included enhanced earned-income exemp-tions of up to $50 per month per adult (that is, monthly welfare benefits would not be reduced on a dollar-for-dollar basis until the recipient had earned $50).

Collectively, Johnson's proposed amendments sought to address the principal grievances of both conservatives and liberals, removing some of AFDC's more restrictive characteristics, while simultaneously strengthening its rehabilitative potential. More important, however, than any of these rele-vant but piecemeal reforms was the president's announcement, in January 1967, of his intention to appoint an income maintenance commission. In his Economic Report, Johnson warned that such schemes "may not prove to be practicable at any time" and that "they are almost surely beyond our means at this time." Nevertheless, by pledging "to establish a commission of leading Americans" that would "examine any plan, however unconven-tional," he gave new political prominence to the guaranteed income con-cept.[11] Robert Levine, referring to Johnson's known resistance to such ideas, suggests that "the President must have immediately regretted this moment of weakness."[12]

Having made this announcement, however, Johnson revealed his per-sonal resistance to enhanced conceptions of income entitlement in two ways. First, he refused to establish the commission for a further twelve months, despite repeated entreaties from within the liberal and academic communities. Second, he strove, in a number of important addresses, to emphasize his continued devotion to the ideals of equal opportunity and self-advancement. His Manpower Report, for example, reassured doubters that "we will never lose sight of our goal—to guarantee to every man an opportunity to unlock his own potential; to earn the satisfaction of standing on his own two feet. Our goal, in short, is to offer to every citizen one of the greatest blessings: a sure sense of his own usefulness."[13] And in his March address to Congress on the problems and promise of the antipoverty pro-gram, the president rebuked those who asserted the federal government's unconditional duty to end poverty: "Federal funds or services, and the opportunities they provide, cannot permanently free a man from the trap of poverty if he does not want to be free. He must use the ladders that circum-stance, native ability, and his nation may create."[14]

161

SEARCH FOR A NEW POLITICS

At the beginning of 1967, Senator Joseph S. Clark (D-Pa.), chairman of the Labor and Public Welfare Committee, alarmed White House officials by announcing his intention to launch a full and impartial investigation of the War on Poverty during the forthcoming legislative session. The administration's displeasure focused on two aspects of this prospective examination, namely the political vulnerability of the OEO, and the likelihood that Clark—like Abraham Ribicoff before him—would use the hearings to exploit Johnson's unpopularity in pursuit of personal interest.

The results of the midterm elections of November 1966 had posed a threat to the very survival of the War on Poverty. Donald Radler, a congressional liaison officer, warned Marvin Watson, special assistant to the president, that the program was in "desperate jeopardy." He had heard "an increasing amount of talk . . . on the Hill to the effect that the 90th Congress will dismember OEO."[15] Moreover, House critics now included a number of powerful conservative Democrats whose previous support had greatly assisted the Economic Opportunity Act's legislative passage. The two most notable members of this group were Wilbur Mills of Arkansas, chairman of the Ways and Means Committee, and George Mahon of Texas, chairman of the Appropriations Committee.

The dramatic consequences of Mills's sensitivity to popular conservatism did not become apparent until the summer of 1967, but Congressman Mahon's increased hostility to Great Society liberalism was clear from the outset of the legislative session. Concerned by the Texan's evident disenchantment, Douglass Cater, Johnson's adviser on health and education matters, worried that recent congressional testimony by Walter Reuther in favor of increased domestic spending might backfire, angering Mahon and thereby enhancing the danger of "severe cuts in the Appropriation Committee." Responding to this concern, AFL-CIO President George Meany was struck by "how much trouble the president was having with Mahon." An administration loyalist, unlike the leader of the autoworkers, Meany pointed out that he had defended Johnson's spending priorities (thereby incurring Reuther's disapproval) but that labor leaders tended to believe that "Mahon was going to try to gut the program no matter what they said."[16]

As a senator, Joseph Clark was less obviously affected by the midterm election results of 1966 than were his embattled liberal colleagues in the House. Nevertheless, Donald Radler cautioned that even the Senate's support for the Economic Opportunity Act could not be taken for granted, given "the generally unfavorable national image of the War on Poverty."[17] According to Mike Manatos, the senator sensed that he was "in deep trouble in Pennsylvania in 1968," and expected political gains from "a frontal attack on the 'maladministration' of the Poverty Program." Manatos, however, feared "that Clark would be his usual bull-in-the-china-closet self" and that "the reaction on [sic] Democrats could be serious."[18]

It is significant, if unsurprising, that Senator Clark's political vulnerability should have led him to distance himself from the Johnson administration. While Johnson hoped to combat recent political reverses by convincing erstwhile liberal allies in Congress of "the urgency of a team effort," Clark had little reason to share the president's enthusiasm for closer relations. The most obvious reasons for detachment were Johnson's growing unpopularity and his identification with the deepening quagmire in Vietnam. In a revealing memo to Robert Kennedy in November 1966, Adam Walinsky suggested a number of reasons for high profile disengagement from a fatally weakened administration. For one, he reported that the president was "disbelieved and detested by all" and warned that "he who stands with LBJ now goes into eclipse—perhaps irretrievably." He also doubted the reliability of polls that suggested continuing public support for the war: "The overwhelming majority of the American people just want out, on some barely face-saving basis." Finally, he did not think that anti-Johnson Democrats need worry about splitting the party, since "there is no Johnson party, no real national Democratic party anymore."[19]

All three of these contentions were debatable, but the president's loss of standing during the previous twelve months could scarcely be doubted and clearly lay at the heart of Joseph Clark's determination to appear independent of White House orthodoxy. Moreover, the Pennsylvanian's uphill battle for reelection required that he woo a nascent New Politics coalition whose leading representatives were uniformly hostile to the administration. Ideally, he hoped to retain the support of powerful traditionalist forces within his state (especially the labor unions, who remained loyal to Johnson) while simultaneously attracting antiwar insurgent groups that possessed increasing financial and organizational importance. Writing to J. K. Galbraith after Eugene McCarthy's entry into the 1968 presidential race, Senator Clark stated his dilemma: "Probably the most pressing matter is how to get the most amount out of my peace-minded friends for the coming campaign—which will be appallingly expensive—without, for the moment at least, deserting the Johnson-Humphrey ticket to which I am publicly committed despite some doubt which I am sure you share."[20]

Joseph Clark's desire to secure the trust and allegiance of New Politics insurgents (whose growing power within the Democratic Party during 1967–1968 is considered in the next chapter) may also have been influenced by the sense that a new liberalism with potential mass appeal was emerging from the wreckage of Vietnam, economic dislocation, and racial tension. If the midterm elections of 1966 had represented a startling repudiation of the president, then according to some optimists the prospects for liberalism in 1968 were less bleak. Joseph L. Rauh, a tribune of Americans for Democratic Action (ADA) liberalism, told one correspondent to resist "the ugly backlash visible in so many places." Comparing 1966 to the seemingly dispiriting midterm elections of Harry Truman's first term, he argued that "if we push President Johnson into urging strong domestic programs, 1968 will be as much a reversal of 1966 as '48 was of '46."[21] The formulation that responding to popular conservatism with more forthright liberalism would ensure political success might seem surprising. And given the ADA's hostility to Harry Truman during the mid-1940s, Rauh's choice of liberal hero is richly ironic. But amid the seemingly revolutionary times Senator Ribicoff had espied a few months earlier, it is not hard to understand Rauh's view that the new conservatism might be a transient phenomenon.

White House anxiety about the prospective antipoverty hearings was intensified by Senator Clark's long-standing hostility to the Vietnam War. Johnson was convinced that Democratic doves could not be depended upon as domestic allies; he tended to conceive of publicly expressed opposition to the war as indicative of more general disloyalty. The prospect of a Vietnam dove with domestic political problems undertaking a high-profile investigation of the War on Poverty therefore appalled Johnson, who met with Clark in early January in a vain attempt to defuse the senator's hostility. The president followed up with a rather lame conciliatory letter:

> I was . . . glad to have a chance to discuss with you the poverty program and where we go to make it work better. All of us who are deeply committed to what it stands for have got to stay close together in the days ahead to insure that it survives its infancy and moves forward with increased efficiency as a fundamental part of our society. After you left it occurred to me, Joe, that if you knew how much time and imagination and effort we are now putting in to trying to bring about peace in Viet Nam . . . you'd be awfully pleased.[22]

164

Senator Clark's public statements on Vietnam during the first half of 1967 gave few indications of such pleasure. Indeed, this was a period during which he and his liberal colleagues on the poverty subcommittee became increasingly outspoken in their condemnation of administration policy. At the ADA's annual meeting in March, Clark launched an outspoken and emotional assault on Johnson's leadership.[23] The organization overwhelmingly endorsed his call for a unilateral ceasefire. Clark blamed the war in Vietnam for the problems of the War on Poverty and asked:

> What price will we pay for the glory of marching triumphantly through a defoliated countryside and streets of burning ruins . . . , monarch of all we survey. . . . We will have achieved nothing but the destruction of a civilization different from our own. And the long, hard task of paying penance at enormous cost for the havoc we have created in the name of national honor and the "holy war against Godless Communism" will haunt the conscience of America for many a year.[24]

A month earlier, the ranking Republican on Clark's poverty subcommittee, Jacob Javits, had responded to the ending of a four-day bombing pause by breaking with his previous pro-Johnson position and urging the "unconditional cessation" of bombing in the North.[25] Meanwhile, Robert Kennedy was reported by the *New York Times* to have had a major private confrontation with President Johnson.[26] In March, the president's leading Democratic adversary unveiled a much-heralded three-point peace plan, which infuriated Johnson loyalists but delighted senatorial doves.[27]

There were several reasons why such disaffection could not be insulated from the domestic sphere. The most obvious concerned the credibility gap that was alleged to separate Johnson's version of the war from reality. In his ever more futile—if arguably unavoidable—attempt to reconcile his military strategy with the respective critiques of increasingly vocal hawks and doves, Johnson combined escalated bombing with assurances of peaceful intent in a way that satisfied neither set of adversaries. In January, John Roche warned fellow White House staffers that "the greatest political issue is [the] credibility of the Administration."[28] The following month, Walter Cronkite bolstered this view, telling a Baltimore audience that systematic distortion of casualty figures had contributed to "almost unparalleled cynicism," which threatened "faith in our democracy at home and in our integrity abroad."[29] By April, the Committee of the American Society of Newspaper Editors was chiding Johnson for "consistently trying to make the news sound or seem better than it is." The war had escalated "to the accompaniment of an almost unbroken succession of pronouncements that it was going in the opposite direction, or at least that something else was happening."[30] One poll reported that 65 percent of Americans believed Johnson was not "telling the public all they should know."[31]

Although the credibility gap was identified primarily with suspect casualty figures and allegedly disingenuous "peace feelers," it was hard for a president accused of duplicity in one sphere to escape broader charges of dishonesty. (This was a problem for Johnson, more than most, since political adversaries had questioned his probity at regular intervals throughout his career.) As liberals turned against the war during 1967, they felt increasingly free to accuse Johnson of using Vietnam as an excuse for his capitulation to the white backlash. An important landmark in this process came in March of that year, when Martin Luther King, Jr., announced his intention to take "a much stronger stand" against the war. Claiming that Johnson's "obsession" with the war was "playing . . . havoc with our domestic programs," King urged a fusion of the peace and civil right movements and warned that he might stand as a third party candidate in the 1968 presidential contest.[32] At New York's largest antiwar demonstration up to that time, the disciple of nonviolence made a dramatic platform appearance alongside Floyd McKissick and Stokely Carmichael. A disturbed Harry McPherson warned Johnson that King's message was an appealing one for liberal antagonists who would rather blame the ogre in the White House for America's domestic problems than confront more profound obstacles to effective public policy:

> Martin Luther King has become the crown prince of the Vietniks, and along with the ADA blames the war for our failure to remedy social ills. Though this will not bear scrutiny, it will gain currency the more it is repeated by the liberal and civil rights establishments. It is a lot easier to make Vietnam the villain than to face (1) the problems of managing the new social programs, (2) the apparent failure of Negroes and other minorities to make substantial gains, or (3) the reluctance of Congress and the voting public to support new programs, or adequate funds for existing programs.[33]

King's militant stance on the war was both worrying and misguided, according to a number of normally sympathetic observers. The moderate NAACP accused King of a "serious tactical mistake," while John Roche, a senior presidential adviser, told Johnson that "a group of non-Communist peace advocates including Norman Thomas, Bayard Rustin and several Quakers" had "spent hours trying to convince King not to make the speech."[34] But if King's move dismayed many of his allies, it also confirmed that the war was beginning to have a devastating impact on the Great Society coalition of 1964–1965. His threat to run against Johnson as a peace candidate was particularly alarming. Despite evidence that King was not likely to take many votes from the major parties, his intervention could conceivably provide the margin for Republican success in a three- or four-way contest.[35] Even more disturbing, such a move might well weaken black attachment to the Democratic Party in a way that threatened liberal officeholders throughout the nation.

Surveying this bleak picture in April, the ADA expressed "disenchantment and dismay over many aspects of administration policy in Viet Nam and the parallel retreat at home." It urged Johnson "to reappraise positions that are disrupting the historic liberal coalition that has always meant progress for the nation."[36] The charge that Johnson's anticommunism somehow offended the values of the ADA was historically surprising, given that the organization had—in opposition to Henry Wallace's Progressives—contributed so much to the ideology of Cold War liberalism. But Steven Gillon has shown that throughout the 1960s, the ADA was progressively more divided over foreign policy issues, with the Vietnam conflict dividing "traditionalist, moderate, and reform groups."[37] By 1967, the third group (ascendant in many local chapters for some time, and now most prominently represented by the student organizer Allard Lowenstein) was winning converts among the "moderates," whose ranks included such luminaries as Arthur Schlesinger, Jr., and J. K. Galbraith. At the heart of reform advocacy within the A.D.A. lay the strategic belief that "antiwar agitation" provided "an opportunity for liberals to reach out to [the] dissatisfied young, pull them into the political system, and create a new coalition that would endure for a generation."[38]

As the Clark committee commenced its spring investigation into the War on Poverty, Vietnam had weakened the Great Society coalition to a startling degree. Association with the White House now presented unacceptable political risks to many liberals who, until 1966, had been keen to endorse the domestic policies of the Johnson administration. However, it should be observed that the response of dissidents such as Ribicoff, Clark, and Kennedy to Johnson's vulnerability was not likely to enhance the appeal of the liberal tradition that the president was alleged to have betrayed.

It is not simply with hindsight that the reform liberals' quest for an enduring New Politics coalition energized by antiwar protest seems misconceived. Even at the time, poll data suggested that public hostility to antiwar advocacy substantially exceeded opposition to the war. One week before Robert Kennedy proposed an unconditional bombing halt in Vietnam, Gallup polls indicated that 67 percent of Americans continued to favor bombing. Asked to explain their viewpoint, respondents claimed variously that this was the only way to end the war, that "we can't back down now," that America should "blow them off the map," and that bombing pauses were always violated. Such responses cast doubt on Adam Walinsky's earlier assertion that Americans "just want out, on any barely face-saving basis." His other claim—that Johnson was a reviled lame-duck president—was also shown to be premature. Between January and March, Kennedy's lead over Johnson evaporated, as former supporters reacted against his outspoken opposition to the war. Asked to name their preferred Democratic candidate for 1968, Americans gave the following replies:[39]

		Kennedy (%)	*Johnson* (%)	*Swing to LBJ* (%)
Republicans	Jan. 29, 1967	42	42	
	March 26, 1967	31	48	+17
Democrats	Jan. 29, 1967	52	39	
	March 26, 1967	48	44	+ 9
Independents	Jan. 29, 1967	48	39	
	March 26, 1967	41	45	+13

Superficially at least, Robert Kennedy's peace plan represented a remarkable political miscalculation, but it should be recalled that his presidential ambitions were still focused on 1972 rather than 1968. Senator Javits told one Johnson aide of his junior colleague's belief that the president could still expect to secure reelection; consequently, he was "willing to stake his belief on what he thinks will be the majority opinion five years from now." Looking ahead, Kennedy calculated that frustration with a continuing stalemate would soon polarize popular perspectives in a way that stranded centrists such as Johnson, compelling politicians to make a basic choice between escalation and withdrawal. His decision to take the side of the doves was dictated, in Javits's view, by the belief that "the new left will be the centrist position in 1972."[40]

The outcome of the 1972 presidential election revealed the magnitude of this misjudgment, but Kennedy's first priority was to win the Democratic nomination, and by 1967 it was already clear that many party activists had little concern for such prosaic considerations as voter preference. In this sense, Kennedy's maneuverings were shrewd and prescient, for George McGovern's capture of the Democratic Party in 1972 would confirm the strength of the New Politics coalition. Additionally, it would be wrong to imply that the New York senator was oblivious to the continued importance of traditionalist Democratic constituencies. His peculiar advantage lay in a remarkable capacity to attract the admiration and respect of mutually antagonistic groupings. Adam Walinsky told Kennedy that "all the city bosses know that you're the only national Democrat who can beat the backlash issue," adding that if he could "add the anti-war sentiment" to his drive for the presidency, then any losses associated with his rebellious image would be comfortably exceeded by gains.[41]

The extent of Senator Kennedy's rebellious image during the final campaign that resulted from these deliberations should not be exaggerated. Reflecting on the tumultuous politics and cultural division of 1968, David Halberstam concludes that Kennedy was in fact a *centrist* bidding to heal the nation's wounds rather than an insurgent wooing the forces of dissent.[42] Similarly, Gary Hart, pondering the meaning of George McGovern's campaign in 1972, concluded that this had been "the first step in forging a new political 'center.'"[43] As was seen with respect to the Ribicoff hearings of 1966, those who challenged orthodoxy and voter sentiment during this period of flux were trying to anticipate the mood of a new center, which they felt must emerge from the nation's deepening crisis.

Addressing the ADA in September 1967, Daniel Patrick Moynihan launched a remarkably outspoken attack on what he called "ultra-liberalism." In his view, the architects of the emerging Democratic minority had gone too far. In particular, they should remember that, for all their self-righteous attacks on Lyndon Johnson's bellicosity, the Vietnam War had been "thought up and is being managed by the men John F. Kennedy brought to Washington." Domestically, the ADA might find it useful to rediscover its "essential interest . . . in the stability of the social order," in the process overcoming "the curious condescension which takes the form of sticking up for and explaining away anything, howsoever outrageous, which Negroes, individually or collectively, might do." Moynihan scorned the "ultra-liberals" who automatically condemned uncomfortable ideas about social dislocation, "undisturbed by the thought they might be wrong, or that the politics of stability might involve something more hard-headed than the untroubled indulgence of sado-masochistic fantasy."[44]

THE POLITICS OF POVERTY AND DEPENDENCY: SPRING 1967

As the administration had feared, Senator Clark's investigation into the War on Poverty rapidly exposed the program's growing vulnerability. The most serious damage was inflicted in April, when Clark and his colleagues encountered hitherto unpublicized conditions of extreme malnutrition in the Mississippi Delta during a visit to the region. The Johnson administration had shown little public interest in the problem of hunger, although a 1966 Task Force on Nutrition and Adequate Diets had estimated that 10 million poor people suffered from some form of malnutrition.[45] In part, this reflected the fact that the Department of Agriculture and the congressional agriculture committees (which administered and funded the food stamp and surplus commodity distribution programs) were geared to the economic needs of the farmers rather than the material plight of the poor. Joseph Califano complained to a White House assistant, "Agriculture is the worst department you could pick to handle food problems," adding that "it is hard to think how they could have been handled in a less compassionate manner than the bureaucracy over there have handled them in the past." While Secretary Orville Freeman was personally sympathetic to the plight of the rural poor, "his subalterns are basically owned by farmers."[46]

But Johnson's apparent indifference also reflected his fundamental suspicion of welfare programs. In the short term at least, hunger could only be relieved by expanding programs that increased dependency, thereby contradicting the mission of the Economic Opportunity Act. As early as 1965, one staffer had suggested to him that "the lack of proper diet for children may be related to school and job difficulties and even to the incidence of second-generation relief families."[47] But the White House proved unresponsive, and was therefore vulnerable to the assault that Senator Clark's subcommittee launched in the spring of 1967.

Headlines revealing problems in the United States of a similar nature to those in the Third World further damaged the convenient notion that education offers some universal panacea to problems of inequality of opportunity. Albert Britton, a physician and chairman of Mississippi's civil rights commission, told Clark of the conceptual inadequacy of existing antipoverty measures, insisting that "the Mississippi Negro's basic problem is poverty, not education."[48] This judgment contained the basic premise of the income strategy, namely, that poverty is caused by poverty. Having struggled with intractable problems of family structure, vocational immobility, and subcultural passivity for three years, legislators were told that *opportunity* had been the wrong target. Bayard Rustin stated the emergent orthodoxy with attractive simplicity: "There is only one reason for poverty—it is not that people are lazy or indiscreet, or that they have broken families, or that they once were in slavery. Fundamentally and simply, those people are poor who do not have any money, and those are rich who have it."[49]

On the other hand, Rustin's attitude toward poverty was rather more traditional than this bald statement would suggest. Although the two principal elements of his proposed Freedom Budget were full employment and the guaranteed income, he told Clark that the latter "must be only for those who are too old, too young, or too crippled to work."[50] This tension between traditional and new conceptions provided a persistent theme throughout the hearings. Just a few months before American liberalism was to make a striking break with its work-oriented tradition, its proponents were still restrained by orthodoxy.

Appearing before the poverty subcommittee during the same week as Rustin, a panel of poor people came out strongly opposed to the guaranteed income, despite the manifest inadequacy of existing programs. Alphonzo Morris of New Bern, North Carolina, thought it "bad, to give that way," adding that he "believed in giving a man an opportunity." Carl Johnson, a disabled Kentucky miner, warned Clark and his colleagues that "a lot of people, if they know they are going to get a certain amount of money, they are not going to work." Dora Moore of New Haven, Connecticut, was more blunt: "Giving money for people to do nothing is ridiculous."[51]

If such testimony was vexing for advocates of universal income entitlement, further discouragement came from within the Johnson administration. Willard Wirtz told the Joint Economic Committee of his fear that discussion of the guaranteed income would obstruct attempts to help the poor become self-supporting. The following day Wilbur Cohen, undersecretary of HEW, reminded legislators that such proposals "raise[d] fundamental questions in our wage-related incentive economy."[52] During the spring of 1967, Cohen's department was increasingly worried by "expressed concerns about the substantial growth of the AFDC Program . . . and the lack of effective, constructive measures to encourage independence rather than continuing dependency."[53] Considering ways in which the administration's welfare reform package could be adjusted in the light of such adverse sentiment, a HEW task force proposed that the federal government "require states to offer work training and work incentives to all persons on the ADC [sic] rolls who can reasonably be expected to enter the labor force and thus become independent or less dependent."[54]

Mounting attacks on AFDC during this period were not confined to the right. Robert Kennedy was one of a number of liberals who sought to capitalize on the universal unpopularity of the program, calling in May for a "virtual revolution" in a system "which damages and demeans its recipients."[55] Such comments seemed well calculated to exploit the respective critiques of both left and right, and were praised on this basis by Arthur Schlesinger: "I hope you continue to press this issue. It is sound on its merits and I am sure it is also sound politically, since a lot of people, from the far right to the far left, are dissatisfied with the present system."[56] Schlesinger had correctly identified an important policy convergence on the part of conservative, liberal, and radical critics of the New Deal welfare system. The basis and extent of this convergence will be considered in the final chapter.

Elsewhere in his remarks, it appeared that Senator Kennedy was primarily courting disaffected blacks and liberals. If the system were not changed, he warned, "the results could be the ripping asunder of the already thin fabric of American life." Having toured Manhattan's deprived lower east side with other committee members, he proclaimed, ". . . this cannot continue. All around our nation, Negroes and Puerto Ricans, Mexican-Americans and Indians, poor whites in Appalachia and in blighted city areas are waking up to what we have done." As a result, they were "demanding their rights as human beings. They are demanding what the rest of us take for granted," including "a sense of communication with those whom they have elected to govern them."[57]

On the same day, Lyndon Johnson expressed his fear that "we may never live to see an America without poverty."[58] His weary pessimism paid dramatic testament to two years of savage disappointment but contrasted markedly with the curious mixture of despair and buoyant reformist zeal that was characteristic of his liberal critics. When Kennedy's remarks were echoed by New York Commissioner of Welfare Mitchell Ginsberg during an appearance before the Clark committee, they provoked a sharp response from Senator Javits:

> If you begin to make sweeping, sensational and categorical statements about throwing out the welfare system, you will be surprised how fast it will get thrown out. Right now there is pending in Congress a supplemental appropriation bill to provide federal matching funds for welfare. There are lots of congressmen who would be delighted to kill that bill by quoting you and Senator Kennedy.[59]

Joseph Clark rebuked Javits for "taking off on the other Senator from New York in a way that is obviously going to make headlines," but Javits's warning appeared prescient in August, by which time the administration's proposal for liberalizing the welfare system had been eviscerated by Wilbur Mills.[60] In a June address, Javits regretted the prominence of "the fashionable debate on guaranteed income proposals," noting that it had tended to overlook "practical proposals for the improvement of the present system." He added:

> National reorganization or replacement of the present system is, simply, not very likely to happen. For one thing, very few of my colleagues on Capitol Hill are ready—or think the country is ready—for a new monetary subsidy system which might tend to undercut the traditional connection between work and income. . . . [Furthermore], most poor people do not like that concept and prefer instead the kind of self-help training and education programs the government is now pursuing.[61]

SOURCES OF THE MILLS BILL

Javits's warning about the implications of popular conservatism for welfare reform does not seem to have affected the Johnson administration's confidence regarding the fate of the Social Security Amendments of 1967. Responding to a query from the president, an optimistic Wilbur Cohen reported in mid-July that "a *very good* bill should be reported" by the House Ways and Means Committee "in about two weeks." Chairman Wilbur Mills had been "most cooperative," and his bill would "revise and strengthen the welfare programs to give a further forward thrust to *rehabilitation* and *work incentives.*" Cohen could detect "only a very few cutbacks," and suggested that the Senate was likely to produce a still more liberal bill. Mills had even taken this latter fact into account in adjusting the administration's bill, and had told Cohen "to get some of the other changes we want in the Senate." In conclusion, Cohen told Johnson, "I am confident that it will be a bill you will be very proud of and want to take credit for in 1968."[62]

Wilbur Mills did indeed complete executive sessions at the beginning of August, but the bill contained none of the modest liberalizations that the administration measure had contained, and whose retention Wilbur Cohen had anticipated. Where Johnson had sought minimum standards and the extension of the unemployed parent program, Mills proposed mandatory workfare and a ceiling on federal contributions. Before exploring the nature and consequences of these restrictive provisions, consideration must be given to the remarkably sudden crisis of national direction from which Mills's surprise crackdown emerged.

In a sense, this crisis had no decisive new elements. Its principal ingredients—Vietnam, racial tension, economic problems, the president's declining credibility and popularity—were already major sources of social disruption and political polarization prior to the summer of 1967. Throughout June 1967, Joseph Califano remembers, Congress had been "increasingly divided over racial issues, the Great Society, and Vietnam."[63] This was especially the case in the House of Representatives, which signaled its antagonistic temper by voting down the administration's routine bill to increase the debt limit. However, during the short period between Cohen's memo and the House of Representatives' endorsement of the Mills bill, all the elements of divisiveness had acquired new force and combined to create the climactic crisis of Great Society liberalism.

Previously, the war and the racial revolution in particular had been dynamics of disruption, significantly undermining the Johnson coalition without popularizing clear-cut alternatives. Now, those same sources of disaffection were becoming active dynamics of intellectual transformation, causing both liberals and conservatives to demand an end to the half measures and equivocation with which Johnson's cherished consensus was being associated. For liberalism, the consequences of this shift in thinking were particularly far-reaching, for it dealt heavy blows to two major tenets: anticommunism abroad, and individualism at home.

Above all, the Newark and Detroit riots, a further increase (to 525,000) in troop deployments to Vietnam, and the president's August 3 tax message served to destroy popular and political faith in Lyndon Johnson's leadership. Continuing in vain to steer a middle course between dramatically polarized perspectives on foreign policy and social welfare, the president was seen to temporize where decisiveness held more appeal. In practical terms, Johnson had no choice but to disregard the partisan counsel of legislators who, unlike him, did not have to wrestle with competing economic, political, and social exigencies, and produce a package that embodied some element of each.

For his detractors—who, observing the crisis of his presidency, sought to satisfy the particular constituencies with whom they associated personal political success—such constraints were of no consequence. Abraham Ribicoff was one liberal who willfully ignored the president's dilemma, demanding that he "end the eternal search for consensus and exercise real leader-ship."[64] Presumably the Connecticut senator's brand of "real leadership" would have featured a commitment to what Moynihan had termed ultra-liberal positions, whether or not they could conceivably secure congres-sional support. The practical relevance to Johnson of such counsel was mysterious, but it clearly meshed with the senator's own political needs.

Once liberals and conservatives started to forsake the center field for which they had previously competed, the process acquired an internal momentum of its own, as each group responded to the increasingly obnox-ious doctrines of the other. (A parallel relationship existed between liberals and the activists to their left: as welfare rights campaigners staked out pro-gressively more daring positions, what were once seen as advanced liberal positions began to seem conventional.) In the process, possibilities for leg-islative coalition-building (admittedly dim already) were destroyed, and the more dominant rightward impulse tended to prevail in Congress. At the same time, rhetorical commitment to the critique of the reform liberal bloc enhanced Ribicoff's image with the ADA and the nascent New Politics coali-tion, while his personal attack on Johnson's leadership implied that blame for America's crisis of national direction could be very simply apportioned.

In conversation with administration officials, Senator Ribicoff was happy to acknowledge his less-than-selfless attitude. Postmaster General Lawrence O'Brien, de facto head of the president's congressional liaison team, reported one conversation to Johnson: "A recent poll conducted in Con-necticut shows me [Ribicoff] in excellent shape and currently points out that the only problem that I could have next year would be association with the national ticket."[65]

In September 1967, *Time* magazine reported that "between Independ-ence Day and Labor Day a profound malaise has gripped the American people."[66] The two most significant elements of this pervasive condition were public frustration with the stalemate in Vietnam and the combina-tion of resentment and fear generated by a devastating sequence of sum-mer riots. Daniel Patrick Moynihan detected a widespread conviction that violence at home and violence abroad were "somehow interconnected," and that "in combination they have the potential for polarizing, then frac-turing, American society."[67] Such diverse figures as Stokely Carmichael and William J. Fulbright made the same connection, the former suggest-ing that skills acquired by black soldiers in Vietnam would assist the ghetto revolution at home, the latter blaming the war for "the corrosion of values in our own society."[68]

175

This period saw a decisive shift in popular attitudes toward a war whose resolution seemed further away the longer it proceeded. Opinion polls indicate that in mid-July, Americans rejected by 48 percent to 41 percent the suggestion that the nation had been mistaken to send troops to Vietnam; by October, a narrow plurality agreed with this proposition.[69] Between July and August, Johnson's overall approval rating collapsed from 52 percent (after the Six Day War and the Glassboro summit with Alexis Kosygin) to 39 percent:[70]

	July 5, 1967	*July 29, 1967*	*Aug. 13, 1967*
Approve	52%	47%	39%
Disapprove	35	39	47
No opinion	13	14	14

For some time, identification with Johnson's middle way had been a political liability for liberal Democrats, but as both dovish and hawkish sentiment increased, the disadvantages of moderation became more generally apparent. Harry McPherson reported a "long, dispiriting talk" with one administration loyalist, Senator Joseph Tydings of Maryland. Tydings feared that "people are so frustrated and negative in Maryland that any reasonably good Republican could clobber me this year and probably next." He did not blame Johnson for his problems but admitted that "every political advisor I have says the only way I can save myself is by attacking the President." Tydings was not prepared to do this, but McPherson reported that "Birch Bayh, Fred Harris, Ed Muskie, and Phil Hart [D-Mich.] all have the same story to tell about their states. It's Vietnam, Vietnam."[71]

The radicalization of the ADA during 1967 provides a particularly good example of the war's divisive impact within the liberal community. The previous year, Arthur Schlesinger had told Hubert Humphrey that he was "increasingly troubled . . . by the efforts of the conservative press to whip up fights within the liberal community over Vietnam. . . . This seems to me one of the most complex and difficult issues our country has faced for a long time—and therefore one on which men of good will, equal in liberalism and patriotism, can honestly reach contradictory conclusions." He further assured the vice president of the ADA's determination that "an intellectual disagreement over Vietnam" should not be "transformed into an emotional estrangement."[72]

By June 1967, Schlesinger had only withering contempt for those who retained the position he himself had enunciated the previous year. In May, the National Board had approved a resolution that, according to Steven Gillon, made "Vietnam the sole test of ADA support in 1968."[73] Members such as Paul H. Douglas and Gus Tyler, who remained attached to the association's anticommunist past and felt that Johnson's record on domestic issues warranted the ADA's backing, were outraged. Douglas, the distinguished former senator from Illinois, told J. K. Galbraith (the new national chairman of ADA) that he felt a "strong feeling of revulsion" and was considering resignation:

> I would do so reluctantly and with great pain over the dissolution of old ties which are very precious to me. I am certainly willing to tolerate great differences of opinion inside the ADA and to remain within the organization despite my disagreement on foreign policy with the dominant group; but I do not intend to participate in the sacrifice of our domestic program for what I regard as a mistaken foreign policy, nor can I oppose a backup in support of a policy of collective security and resistance to aggression.[74]

Tyler, head of the International Ladies Garment Workers Union, remarked that the resolution would oblige the ADA "to back a reactionary Republican isolationist against a liberal Democrat." He further accused supporters of the resolution of "monomania," an obsession with Vietnam destined to "isolate ADA not only from the mainstream of American politics, from the vast body of liberal voters in America, but even from the meaningful and influential elements that have been with ADA since its inception." In reply to this charge, James Loeb, a founding member of ADA, questioned Tyler's assumption "that the coalition of the past several decades will persist eternally," and emphasized the importance of courting disaffected youth.[75] Schlesinger was considerably more abrasive, clearly no longer viewing the war as a mere "intellectual" disagreement between friends, and warning Tyler that "the politics of sycophancy are played out." Espying in the labor leader's position a stance of unthinking fealty to administration policy, he noted that the ADA's role was as an "independent liberal movement."[76]

The implications of this rancorous dispute for the future of liberalism were momentous. The disappearance of the Cold War consensus was accompanied among deviants from its precepts by the sense that the political coalition it had supported was also unsustainable. This belief required that its adherents conceive new ideologies and alliances from the diverse dissenting agendas associated with the New Politics. Correspondingly, politicians and activists who remained convinced of the continuing resonance of traditional liberalism (President Johnson serving as a leading example) were anxious to demonstrate their loyalty to the values of Middle America, including anticommunism and individualism. In other words, the fissure that opened up within liberal ranks during the 1960s, and that reached its apogee with the battle for the Democratic presidential nomination in 1972, owed far more to the Vietnam War than to any other single factor. But it was the simultaneous emergence of a series of splits over issues of race, culture, and civil liberties (individual freedom and group rights) that encouraged the sense that a New Politics agenda was emerging from the ashes of New Deal-Cold War-Great Society liberalism. This conviction became considerably stronger once Eugene McCarthy launched his bid to prevent Lyndon Johnson from winning renomination in 1968.

But in the meantime, splits within liberal ranks were less wounding to the Johnson presidency and its domestic agenda than was polarization between left and right. Again, it is the Vietnam War that best illustrates the president's predicament. Convinced that the war was tearing the nation apart, but offering diametrically opposed roads to its resolution, doves and hawks concurred only in their hostility to President Johnson. Robert Kennedy, Jacob Javits, and Senator John Pastore (D-R.I.) were among those who urged the administration to use alleged electoral irregularities in South Vietnam as an excuse for unilateral withdrawal. Javits asked for "the beginning of an end [to] an undertaking which has created profound strains in our society and which offers no end if the past route is followed."[77] George Romney (who in the spring had suffered from the indecision of handlers who could not decide whether to package him as a hawk or a dove) offered the thought that "it would have been better if we had never become involved."[78] Mike Mansfield berated Johnson for a provocative bombing strategy, warning that World War III was "incubating in the ever-deepening struggle in Southeast Asia."[79]

Hawks provided the commander-in-chief with quite different advice. Congressman Robert Sikes (D-Fla.) commended Israel's prosecution of the Six Day War, noting that "they wasted no time with diplomatic talks or the endless cacophony of the United Nations." His colleague, George Andrews (D-Ala.), demanded the use of nuclear weapons in the event of continued stalemate.[80] John Stennis, speaking on behalf of the Senate Preparedness Investigating Subcommittee, demanded a sharp intensification in the air war, warning that another bombing suspension would be a "tragic and perhaps fatal mistake."[81] Even comparative moderates such as Gerald Ford questioned the continued validity of sending more ground troops to their deaths while bombing restrictions still applied in North Vietnam.[82] Frightened by talk of escalated bombing, Johnson reportedly told George Ball, a former undersecretary of state, that "hippies, students and Commies" could not do any real damage to America, but that "the terrible beast we have to fear is the right wing. . . . If they ever get the idea I am selling out Vietnam, they'll do horrible things to the country, and we'll be forced to escalate the war beyond anything you've ever thought about."[83]

Both conservative and liberal responses to the Vietnam War reflected the conviction that its continuation threatened domestic stability and economic prosperity. For conservatives, the latter view was reinforced by the president's tax message. In his January Economic Report, Johnson had recommended a 6 percent surtax on income and corporate profits, to become effective July 1. Postponed because of a nine-month slowdown in economic activity, the president's proposal was finally expanded to a 10 percent surtax, whose purpose was to fund the war, dampen an anticipated boom, and reduce a rapidly expanding budget deficit. The conservatives who dominated the House Ways and Means Committee were suspicious of two aspects of Johnson's proposal, namely, its reliance on projected economic performance rather than hard facts, and its failure to demand cuts in nondefense expenditures. The senior Republican on the committee, John Byrnes of Wisconsin, stated that "any tax increase must be accompanied by drastic measures to curtail government spending,"[84] while Minority Leader Gerald Ford declared that the budget could be balanced through domestic cuts.[85] Most ominous of all, Wilbur Mills told the administration that it had "simply got to make a choice between guns and butter."[86]

Many liberals were also suspicious of Johnson's tax message, but for very different reasons. The conviction that increased taxes would have been unnecessary, but for the administration's obsession with Vietnam, gained strength in the wake of the Newark and Detroit riots. John Conyers, a black congressman from Detroit, proposed a $30 billion omnibus domestic spending bill, to be funded not through additional taxation but by withdrawal from Southeast Asia.[87]

The Newark riot (resulting in 25 deaths and 725 injuries) reached its climax on July 15—one day after Cohen's welfare bulletin—while forty-three died in Detroit just one week before the Mills bill was reported from the Ways and Means committee.[88] During this tense and frightening period, both liberal and conservative perspectives on social policy were powerfully influenced by the riots. As with Vietnam and taxation, however, Johnson was left stranded as opinion polarized in favor of either repression or vastly expanded domestic spending. That the conservative response was the dominant one may be gauged from the House of Representative's approval—by 377 votes to 23—of a strong anticrime bill; meanwhile, an administration measure intended to eradicate rats from urban ghettos was derided by House conservatives as a "civil rats" bill.[89] Congressman George Mahon received heavy applause on the floor of the House after demanding that legislators "stop crouching in the corner" and face the fact that their earlier liberalism had contributed to unrest: "The more we have appropriated for these programs, the more violence we have [had]"; the keys to social order were "discipline, self-respect and law and order."[90] The Republican Coordinating Committee blamed the president in part for the fact that America was "rapidly approaching a state of anarchy." Johnson had "totally failed to recognize the problem" and had vetoed critical law-and-order legislation. Charges of police brutality were "usually nonsense," and recent judicial decisions had "helped tilt the scales against effective law enforcement."[91]

THE LIBERAL RESPONSE TO WILBUR MILLS

This was the setting in which Wilbur Mills surprised Wilbur Cohen by deciding to crack down on welfare abuse. Reporting the Social Security Amendments of 1967, the House Ways and Means Committee observed that welfare rolls had been rising dramatically and were projected to continue to do so, despite the rehabilitative intent of the 1962 amendments and the Economic Opportunity Act. The committee was "deeply concerned that such a large number of families have not achieved independence and self-support," generating "rapidly increasing costs to the taxpayers." Responding to public anxiety, it sought to curtail rising rolls in two dramatic ways. First, federal contributions to AFDC would be frozen at their present level. Second, all "appropriate" adult recipients would be required to accept opportunities for work or training. Failure to do so would result in loss of benefits.[92] The committee bill made no attempt to ease the desperate material plight of the dependent poor in low payment states, despite the fact that recent interest in malnutrition had done much to dramatize this problem. Commending the revised Social Security Amendments on August 15, the chairman of the Ways and Means Committee told colleagues that "we are rough in this bill—we intended to be."[93] The bill passed by 415 : 3, partly because liberals were intimidated by popular conservatism but mainly because the amendments retained large increases in social security benefits that legislators were loath to oppose.

Once the importance of the measure had begun to sink in, however, a powerful counterreaction emerged from black leaders and liberals who found the new restrictions both repugnant and—in the present climate of ghetto discontent—alarming. Whitney Young, Jr., told President Johnson that the National Urban League was "greatly disturbed" by the proposed bill, particularly by a freeze that "could easily lead welfare officials to exact harsh, inhuman standards."[94] Within the administration, Robert Levine, of the OEO, warned Joseph Califano that the Mills bill moved public assistance "toward being even more of a repressive system than it is currently, when we should be moving in the opposite direction." Mandatory work programs might be desirable under a more humane system, but at present they were likely to prove "disastrous" and "repressive"; the "administration bill, insofar as it tried to alleviate poverty, has been gutted."[95] HEW Secretary John Gardner complained that "children should [not] have to pay for the shortcomings and inequities of the society into which they were born," or "for the sins or supposed sins of their parents." It would be "short-sighted of a society to produce, by its neglect, a group of future citizens very likely to be unproductive and characterized by bitterness and alienation."[96]

But if the administration was immediately uncomfortable with both the symbolism and substance of the House bill, then political reality dictated caution. Mills possessed immense political power, his support for the administration's tax bill was desperately needed, and the AFDC proposal faithfully embodied a public anger about rising rolls that Johnson had to respect. Accordingly, far from confronting the chairman of Ways and Means, Wilbur Cohen and Robert Ball, the commissioner of Social Security, chose to thank him for his "wonderful success in getting the bill passed with only three dissenting votes."[97] Two days later, in a letter to Mills, the HEW undersecretary was angrily denying a *Washington Post* story that "attempted to make out a clash between you and us regarding the welfare program." Insisting that "nothing could be farther from the truth," Cohen regretted his inability to control such irresponsible speculation.[98]

Within Congress, liberal opposition to the Social Security Amendments of 1967 reached a crescendo a month later, when they came under the scrutiny of Russell Long's Senate Finance Committee. As conservatives and liberals denounced each others' perspectives in the most extreme terms, they simultaneously revealed and advanced a mutual detachment from the consensual position of 1964.

The liberal deviation was more striking, in that it so clearly ignored the prevailing mood of the nation. In reality, the Mills bill was far less restrictive than its enemies contended. States could make their own judgments about which adult recipients were appropriate candidates for work or training, and were also compelled to provide child care. Liberal senators, however, identified something much more sinister and repressive. Wilbur Cohen later recalled their reaction and its political context: "While on the whole this program may not have been a slave labor program, a later term, at the time it was passed by the House Ways and Means Committee, it seemed to bring many of the liberals, [and] minority groups such as the blacks, into a counter-alignment in [sic] the legislation, thus causing a great deal of trouble for both Mr. Gardner and myself, but to some extent for President Johnson."

Cohen went on to add that "these people" (i.e., opponents of HR. 12080) tended to see "any kind of work program" as "designed to be a repressive kind of intervention into the freedom of welfare clients."[99] The course of the Long hearings amply confirmed this judgment. In one representative outburst, Robert Kennedy denounced "a punitive attitude reminiscent of medieval poor law philosophy."[100] Meanwhile, Jacob Javits condemned "a punitive and coercive approach which seems founded upon the belief that welfare recipients are universally shiftless and satisfied with being dependent upon a dole." Compulsory work "cannot instill motivation, but instead is likely to increase hostility and resentment." Furthermore, the bill "dangerously misreads the climate in the ghettos and the depressed rural areas of this country." Javits added: "We are in the midst of a 'revolution' in which the poor of the nation, so long denied equal opportunity, are awakening to their rights and powers and are gaining in new self-confidence of self-assertiveness [sic]."[101] Clearly shaken by the events of the summer, Javits forgot his own previous strictures regarding public opinion and demanded an investigation into the "desirability of moving toward some kind of automatic, guaranteed income program."[102]

One of the most comprehensive denunciations of the House bill came from John V. Lindsay. The New York mayor found so many reasons why welfare recipients could not be expected to work that the very goal of rehabilitation seemed to be undermined. In his city, 79 percent of recipients were children, or adults caring for children. An additional 15 percent were aged, sick, or disabled, and another 2 percent were employed males with earnings below subsistence level. When Senator Albert Gore (D-Tenn.) asked about prospects for the remaining 4 percent, Lindsay pointed out that, while they were able-bodied working-age males, they suffered from severe problems, "whether it be a partial illness through narcotics, or whether it be some handicap by total absence of education as to have very limited ability to read or write."[103]

Liberal hostility to Mills's rather crude exploitation of popular antiwel-farism was eminently understandable, as was the fear that provocation of deprived minority groups might generate even greater levels of ghetto unrest. Nevertheless, statements such as those by Kennedy, Javits, and Lind-say provided perfect ammunition for conservative legislators who sought to accuse liberals of abandoning the national work ethic. Chairman Long was dismayed by Mayor Lindsay's all-encompassing defense of entitlement: "I just hope we never get to the point where everybody has a right—able-bod-ied people have a right—to expect welfare payments although they decline to work. It seems to me that the right to go hungry, if you don't want to work, should be preserved in this country."[104]

Reacting against a noisy protest by would-be witnesses representing the National Welfare Rights Organization, Long railed against "female brood-mares," and suggested that "people who have that much time available to them should have time to do some work."[105] Senator Curtis of Nebraska complained about programs that "appease . . . some people whose worthi-ness might be doubted," observing that "we are developing a very unfair sit-uation to some of our citizens."[106] Congresswoman Martha Griffiths (D-Mich.) confessed to finding the testimony of an earlier witness a little bewildering: "What he is really saying is that America should offer each per-son a choice: 'Either work, or if you don't like that, don't work, the rest of us will provide for you.' If every person chose not to work, we could all starve together. It is a form of togetherness that I oppose."[107] Long found Griffith's statement "magnificent" and "refreshing," adding:

> Some of this testimony causes me to wonder just who it is that is losing their
> minds around here. I have always supported the programs to provide assistance
> for those who, through no fault of their own, were unable to help themselves,
> but the idea of just doling out tens of millions or more to people as a substitute
> for doing their duty to themselves and their children to me is just patently
> ridiculous.[108]

That most of America shared this conclusion in the summer of 1967 could scarcely be doubted; indeed, rioting and rising welfare rolls had greatly increased popular hostility to AFDC during the three years since Lyndon Johnson's popular promise to eradicate the causes of dependency.

By the end of that turbulent summer, however, the prospect of electoral oblivion and the continuing popular strength of the individualist tradition no longer had the capacity to restrain liberals who were overwhelmed by the scale of black discontent and swept along by a polarized political environment in which old assumptions no longer retained their force. Liberal individualism lay in tatters, the fundamental assumptions of the entitlements revolution finally having penetrated a previously resistant Senate. Two months later, Senator Eugene McCarthy of Minnesota would launch a bid for the presidency, incorporating welfare rights advocacy into his New Politics agenda. And within six months, the Kerner Commission would issue a report whose impassioned denunciation of societal values symbolized a further abandonment of the search for consensus.

CHAPTER 8

Liberalism and Governance, 1967–1968

By the summer of 1967, it is doubtful that there remained a unifying liberal creed, such were the divisions over both philosophy and strategy that separated President Johnson from his detractors on the left. This chapter examines how the divide expressed itself in three public policy debates of 1967 and 1968: the continuing debate over welfare reform; the Economic Opportunity Amendments of 1967; and the report of the Kerner Commission. The intention is less to illustrate the philosophical rift within liberal ranks than to consider the divergent political calculations that led reformers to disagree, even on issues to which their visceral responses were the same.

In all three instances, the president shared the instinctive response of the wider liberal community: he had little sympathy for Wilbur Mills's proposed welfare reforms, favored the early expansion of what was after all his War on Poverty, and, in different circumstances, would clearly have endorsed at least some of the Kerner Report's recommendations. However, in each instance he was compelled by economic and political constraints to adopt a course more cautious than that advocated by his critics.

President Johnson differed from liberal detractors in Congress, the ADA, and within his own administration, not simply in philosophy but also in his response to practical political obstacles. He saw no virtue in sacrificing political strength for a cause that, however laudable, could not currently be advanced. (It should be noted, however, that Johnson remained willing to take some unpopular stances in the name of racial justice, most notably his support for open housing from 1966 to 1968.) In a sense, this was a lesson he had learned from recent experience. In November 1967 he told Joseph Califano, "I'm fearful we are overpromised, overextended, and overenthusiastic."[1] But it was also the product of a centrist, consensus-seeking political philosophy which was losing ground elsewhere within the liberal community.

As he sought to persuade true believers that pragmatic liberalism could achieve more for the poor than the bolder commitments they favored, Johnson encountered situations which to some extent paralleled his experience as Senate majority leader in the 1950s. Then, his willingness to accommodate the mood of Eisenhower's America had infuriated more confrontational Democrats, such as Paul Douglas and Herbert Lehman. Now, his attempt to defend the gains of the Great Society rather than sacrifice them in the name of ideological purity similarly irked Joseph Clark and Abraham Ribicoff. The difference was that dissenters attracted to the nascent New Politics of the later 1960s were becoming progressively more disdainful of the values of New Deal constituencies upon which they were electorally dependent.

RIOTS AND RETRENCHMENT: THE DILEMMA OF LIBERALISM

President Johnson's public response to the riots of 1967 was conditioned by two quite different and seemingly irreconcilable sets of imperatives. On the one hand, it was clearly necessary that his administration should appear responsive to the legitimate grievances of poor blacks, thereby reducing the likelihood of future disorder and easing the increasingly strained relationship between Johnson and the wider liberal community. On the other hand, the president had to avoid any appearance of rewarding rioters and was constrained to develop programmatic responses that could secure legislative approval in a clearly adverse political climate. Finally, this all-but-impossible balancing act had to be achieved in the context of a deteriorating economic and fiscal situation whose redress would require a comprehensive range of unpopular revenue-raising and expenditure-cutting measures, quite incompatible with the various Marshall Plans so favored by black leaders and congressional liberals.

This was the setting for Johnson's decision to appoint a National Advisory Commission on Civil Disorders. Admonishing the "apostles of violence, with their ugly drumbeat of hatred," the president nonetheless urged America not to turn away from social and racial justice:

This is not a time for angry reaction. It is a time for action: starting with legislative action to improve the life in our cities. . . . There is a danger that the worst toll of this tragedy will be counted in the hearts of Americans: in hatred, in insecurity, in fear, in heated words which will not end the conflict, but prolong it. So let us acknowledge the tragedy, but let us not exaggerate it.[2]

This last sentence applied not only to law-and-order conservatives but also to those liberal and black leaders whose response to unrest, if intemperate, might simply strengthen the right-wing backlash. The composition of the riot commission attested to Johnson's desire for politically responsible recommendations. Vice Chairman John V. Lindsay was a potentially risky selection, given his presidential ambitions, his outspoken opposition to the Vietnam War, and his talent for self-promotion, but Chairman Otto Kerner (Democratic governor of Illinois) was viewed as a reliable and pragmatic ally. Blacks were represented by Roy Wilkins and Senator Edward Brooke (R-Mass.), both racial moderates whose appointment generated immediate charges of a whitewash from more militant figures.[3] Senator Fred Harris was viewed as a capable and dependable friend of the administration (an assessment that was to change within weeks), while labor was represented by I. W. Abel, an archetype of the New Deal coalition. Business and the law enforcement agencies were represented by Charles B. Thornton (head of Litton Industries) and Police Chief Herbert Jenkins of Atlanta, respectively.

Douglass Cater, Johnson's chief adviser on health and education issues, told the president that the Kerner Commission could "have useful but only somewhat limited value in terms of dealing with [the] bigger problems of the cities." Its principal contributions should ideally be to "deal with the issue of whether or not a conspiracy existed to cause the riots" and to "provide general endorsement for keeping the heat on Congress not to run away from your programs." Cater did however warn of the "danger" that the commission "may try to brainstorm big new programs of its own"—clearly not a prospect the administration would welcome, given its existing fiscal and political problems.[4]

One of these problems was that the immediate crisis of riot-torn urban America tended to obscure the impressive record of liberal accomplishment that President Johnson had compiled during the previous four years. In the aftermath of the 1967 riots, the administration sought to convince critics of Johnson's continued loyalty to progressive causes. One memorandum for congressional liaison staff, entitled "The Four-Year Johnson Record in Human Terms," summarized recent achievements in education, health care, the economy, antipoverty programs, civil rights, housing, and rural development. Legislators were to be reminded, among other things, that 5.7 million Americans had been lifted above the poverty line since 1964, that federal grants and loans for education had increased fivefold, that the educational gap between black and white students had declined from two years to six months since 1961, and that the economy had been expanding for eighty-one consecutive months.[5]

In announcing that no new ideas on urban policy would be unveiled during the remainder of 1967, Johnson reminded liberal legislators that congressional intransigence rather than his alleged passivity lay at the heart of the Great Society's recent loss of momentum.[6] Rebuked by sections of the press for his supposed failure to develop a comprehensive Marshall Plan for the cities, an angry president observed that "someone should send them the Marshall Plan we already have."[7] At one news conference in August, Johnson questioned the political relevance of Congressman Conyers's $30 billion urban aid package, referring to the ignominious fate of open housing legislation, a modest rent supplements bill, the Model Cities program, and the rat bill in recent weeks. The president confessed that he would feel gratified if the remainder of the administration's 1967 program survived "without material reduction." If liberals would only display a modicum of patience, then "over the long run—many years ahead—I am confident that we will make substantial increases in our expenditures in the cities."[8] Addressing a similar gathering at the beginning of November, Johnson reminded his critics that the meager $200 million appropriation for the Model Cities program was at least "a beginning," while $10 million for rent supplements was inadequate but "better than nothing."[9]

The fate of the administration's tax surcharge proposal during the autumn of 1967 should have convinced even the most fervent liberal that Congress was not in the mood to consider new social welfare proposals. Johnson's economic advisers had warned that the budget deficit for the 1968 fiscal year might be as high as $29 billion but, far from strengthening support for the $7.4 billion revenue package, this prospect simply reinforced Wilbur Mills's conviction that taxes should be raised only as part of a more comprehensive proposal including substantial reductions in federal spending.[10]

On October 3, the House Ways and Means Committee voted by 20 to 5 to set the 10 percent surcharge to one side until the administration demonstrated a new willingness to make basic choices about federal spending priorities. Johnson was placed in an extremely difficult position. On the one hand, liberal sentiment favored massive increases in nondefense spending and would clearly be dismayed by any reduction. On the other hand, Gardner Ackley, chairman of the Council of Economic Advisors, was predicting "interest rates that will curl your hair, a new depression in housing, [and] a new surge in imports" if no action was taken on taxes in 1967.[11]

By November, a deteriorating inflationary picture and a surge of speculative pressure against the dollar compelled a reluctant Johnson to make some concession to the committee's terms. Mills had privately pledged to support a tax increase in return for a $4 billion cut in expenditures, and on November 29, hearings were reconvened on this basis. Treasury Secretary Henry Fowler expressed his "deep-seated, personal conviction" that "favorable action by the Congress on the proposals to be placed before you cannot be further deferred without undue and unacceptable risk to the nation's economic and financial structure and the international monetary system."[12] In the same vein, William McChesney Martin, chairman of the Federal Reserve Bank, warned Mills that "the entire world is looking to the United States to see if it has the capability, the will, and the determination to preserve and maintain this period of prosperity."[13] Mills, however, resisted these entreaties and indeed receded from his earlier pledge to cooperate, announcing that "we are making progress, but . . . still have some distance to go."[14] (Congress nevertheless went ahead with the expenditure reduction package that the administration had put together in response to Mills' earlier promise.)

Influenced by its manifest unpopularity, liberal legislators were slow to embrace the tax surcharge, or even to acknowledge that additional revenues would be necessary prerequisites for their ambitious Marshall Plans. Some went so far as actively to oppose Johnson's proposal. George McGovern contended that the surcharge was "to be used entirely for another ill-advised escalation of the Vietnam War"; there was "no other economic justification for a tax increase."[15] Robert Kennedy claimed that the measure would place "a particularly heavy burden on lower-income and middle-income people." He feared a rise in unemployment that would "fall particularly on the Negroes, the Puerto Ricans, and the Mexican Americans; those who are having a particularly difficult time at the moment."[16]

The failure of Congress in general, and the Ways and Means Committee in particular, to rally around the tax surcharge caused both anger and frustration in the White House. Aroused too by what he what he saw as the Republican leadership's economic irresponsibility, the president predicted that Wilbur Mills and Gerald Ford would "live to rue the day when they

189

made that . . . dangerous, unwise decision.[17] But within Johnson's own administration, there was growing unhappiness with his fiscal strategy. Joseph Califano, who in 1966 had seen no alternative to domestic cutbacks, now denied that domestic spending must be curtailed in order to facilitate enactment of the surcharge. His endorsement of a more aggressive line was the product of political rather than economic calculation.

Califano believed that the president's current problems stemmed from his perceived failure to provide decisive leadership at a time of national crisis. The need to secure Wilbur Mills's support for the tax surcharge had forced Johnson to curtail important Great Society programs, and the administration's current intention was to make further substantial reductions in the 1969 fiscal year. His chief domestic adviser was now convinced that this strategy was based on a false premise, namely, that Mills was willing to contemplate a tax increase if Johnson agreed to limited domestic cutbacks. In truth, Mills's price was "one which we are probably not prepared to pay. . . . Therefore, if there is to be a tax bill next year, we may well have to try to do it on the basis of an enormous struggle which would involve overriding Mills in some way or other."[18]

If this latter premise were correct, then Califano saw little value in proposing 1968 cutbacks that would further strain relations with the liberal community. An attractive alternative would be to "repackage the tax increase to raise even more revenues," present a budget that "eliminates what we consider to be . . . obsolete programs," and "go forward on a fairly substantial scale with new programs in the area of housing and jobs." Califano told Johnson that such a strategy would force Congress to take the blame for any failure to meet its domestic responsibilities. Furthermore, "it should appeal to the traditional sources of Democratic strength—the cities, the liberals, and the low-income individuals, white and Negro alike."[19]

Califano's anxiety was understandable, given his expressed fears that society was "coming apart at the seams," and that powerful elements of the Democratic Party would no longer tolerate the president's perceived lack of domestic leadership. Nevertheless, his advice revealed a questionable understanding of the "sources of Democratic strength." It is surprising that he could have equated his party's future success with grand legislative designs when Congress would clearly dismiss such activism out of hand; when the previous election had suggested that middle-class Americans were outraged by the riots and tired of social reform; when the Vietnam War was costing more than $25 billion per year; and when soaring interest rates, a plummeting dollar, rising prices, and a ballooning budget deficit threatened the nation's prosperity. When Califano spoke of the Democratic coalition, he was presumably thinking of such groups as ADA, Citizens' Crusade Against Poverty, and the Committee of Concerned Democrats, and of what Joseph L. Rauh had called the "large degree of built-in liberalism" in every Democratic National Convention—not the angry voting constituencies that had helped to sustain the New Deal electoral coalition for over three decades.[20]

Califano was not the only senior administration figure to urge a more aggressive presidential response to the crisis of urban America: indeed, Johnson's political isolation was taking on startling dimensions. Sargent Shriver told Johnson that "for all their destructiveness, I can but read the riots as a terrible call: the Negroes want equal access to the fruits of participating citizenship—the opportunity both to earn and to control their destiny."[21] Robert Weaver, secretary for Housing and Urban Development, warned Charles Schultze that "no matter how imaginative our proposals or how inspiring our goals, . . . those whom we invite to partnership can hardly be blamed if they discount the rhetoric of the future in terms of the ascertainable priorities of the present."[22] And one of Weaver's senior colleagues, Charles A. Haar, sent Califano a doom-filled document entitled "Thinking the Unthinkable About America's Cities," predicting further racial polarization as the price of present administration policies.[23]

RADICALIZATION OF BLACK PROTEST AND ITS IMPACT ON CONGRESSIONAL LIBERALS

Evidence of such polarization was not hard to find in the aftermath of this latest long hot summer. Clifford Alexander, the black chairman of the President's Equal Employment Opportunity Commission, had warned back in June of the undue influence of such black militants as Floyd McKissick and Stokely Carmichael, whose words had the power to strike fear into the hearts of white liberals: "White society has developed a new Amos and Andy team—Floyd and Stokely. Floyd and Stokely entertain the living daylights out of masochistic white liberals whom they beat over the back . . . and at the end of all that they have no program at all."[24]

During the course of 1967, Stokely Carmichael had in fact been replaced as chairman of the Student Nonviolent Coordinating Committee

(SNCC) by an even more alarming figure, H. Rap Brown. Of his successor, Carmichael joked that "you'll be happy to have me back when you hear from him. He's a bad man."[25] Members of the Senate Judiciary Committee heard extensive testimony about Brown's rabble-rousing activities in riot areas and were particularly shocked by a speech delivered in Cambridge, Maryland, in which he compared Johnson to Hitler and urged his audience—successfully—to "take your violence to the honkies."[26] In fact, such exhortations frequently failed to produce results. On one notable occasion, Brown had been publicly humiliated by Governor Claude Kirk of Florida's unwelcome appearance on the stage at a rally in Jacksonville. Kirk had interrupted Brown's chant of "get yourself some guns" in order to welcome the SNCC leader to Florida and admonish him, "I don't want any talk about guns." Earl Caldwell reported that "the crowd surged around Governor Kirk, shaking his hand and telling him its problems," while Rap Brown stood silently, ignored, in the background.[27] However, white legislators—whether they advocated repression or a Marshall Plan—often found instances of successful incitement more closely in accordance with their own vision of an America teetering on the brink of racial revolution.

Established black leaders also felt acutely threatened by Brown's ghetto appeal and made strenuous efforts to demonstrate anew their sensitivity to the plight of the urban poor. On July 27, Martin Luther King, Jr., Whitney Young, Jr., Roy Wilkins, and A. Philip Randolph had signed a joint statement condemning the riots and emphasizing the importance of effective law enforcement. But a few days later, King sought to correct any impression that he held the black community responsible for unrest. He told the *New York Times* of his fear that "in the effort to make an appeal to the Negro community to act with responsibility, an impression might be conveyed that principal culpability lies with Negroes." To the contrary, rioters had been sorely provoked by governmental indifference, for "to do too little to relieve the agony of Negro life is as inflammatory as inciting to riot." The Johnson administration's obsession with Vietnam was particularly "provocative" at a time when the prior claim of the poor upon the nation's conscience was so apparent. Rioting was wrong, but he argued that its causes resided outside the black community: "What of the blood on the hands of a Congress that sneered at a modest bill to control the rats that daily bite babies in the ghettos; that emasculated a Model Cities program; that killed rent subsidies; that with administration cooperation is more than halving desperately needed antipoverty programs?"[28]

192

Two weeks later, on August 15, King sought to channel the militancy and frustration of disaffected blacks in directions more productive than rioting by announcing plans "to cripple the operations of an oppressive society" with nonviolent demonstrations of civil disobedience.[29] Protesting that it was "purposeless to tell Negroes they should not be enraged when they should be," King explained that "mass civil disobedience can use rage as a constructive and creative force." This belief underlay the Poor People's Campaign, which he began to plan at this time: King argued that to "dislocate the functioning of a city without destroying it can be more effective than a riot because it can be longer-lasting, costly to the society but not wantonly destructive." While there was currently "no disposition by the administration nor Congress to seek fundamental remedies beyond police measures," the Southern Christian Leadership Conference (SCLC) could use militant methods to compel accedence to black demands.[30]

To the deeply disillusioned civil rights leader, city administrations and the federal government had emerged as obstructionist adversaries, immune to the dictates of morality and politically unwilling to advance the causes of economic and racial justice. Indeed, King's embittered rhetoric and militant tactics suggested that the SCLC now viewed the white power structure in the North as being almost equivalent to its counterpart in the segregationist South.

The most moderate black leaders found King's attitude unhelpful. Roy Wilkins remarked that blacks must "use the tools of the democratic society," even though the process was "slow and painful." In his syndicated newspaper column, Wilkins reminded readers that all of the president's recent antipoverty and civil rights initiatives had been "trimmed or killed."

> All this, of course, escapes the pound-and-yell crowd. . . . They are [more] interested in . . . blasting away at LBJ. It requires skill and toughness and persistence (backed by voting power) to shepherd legislation to passage. It requires only a closed mind and a loud voice to denounce the handiest target of all—the President of the United States.[31]

Nevertheless, in the wake of Newark and Detroit, liberals within Congress, too, were variously dismayed and angered by President Johnson's alleged lack of leadership. Senator Clifford Case (R-N.J.) remarked that "despite all the passionate-sounding words" the administration had "failed to face up to the dimensions of the problems that beset our cities." An alarming "vacuum of leadership" was particularly apparent from Johnson's "transparent attempts to make the Congress the scapegoat for past and present failures." The senator anticipated that the "American people and Congress will have to take the leadership since the President has failed to do so."[32]

Democrats such as Abraham Ribicoff had been making similar pleas for executive leadership for more than a year, declaiming their willingness to fill any continued vacuum. Together with their Republican counterparts, these impatient legislators responded to the 1967 riots with proposals for massive new employment and housing programs. A few months before his entry into the 1968 presidential contest, Eugene McCarthy contended that "this is a special kind of insurrection . . . by the poor and the exploited— those who have been denied their part in the American dream." Congress should remember that "everyone has some share in the guilt—all who have exploited the poor, all who have stood aside or looked the other way, all who have responded in anger or cynicism."[33] Similar warnings came from Senators Walter Mondale (D-Minn.) and Jacob Javits, the latter going on to claim that the "whole question of whether we 'can afford' the 'freedom budget' is a moral question and not an economic issue." Mondale believed that "we face today what may be the most grave social crisis confronting the United States in all its history," and demanded that the American people "take immediate action to isolate the underlying causes for rioting and obliterate them."[34]

ECONOMIC OPPORTUNITY AMENDMENTS OF 1967

A plethora of ambitious—not to mention politically impracticable—social welfare initiatives were proposed by liberal legislators in response to the recent wave of rioting. Yet their approach to the amendment of two existing pieces of legislation, namely, the Economic Opportunity Act of 1964 and the Social Security Act of 1935, was more practically consequential and provides an equally revealing insight into the dominant liberal mentality of the time. To reiterate a point made earlier, the purpose here is less to illuminate a divergence in social philosophy than to highlight the shift in political philosophy that allowed the orthodoxy of entitlement to gain ground.

The 1967 riots further jeopardized the future of the War on Poverty, whose legislative prospects had already been damaged by the results of the midterm elections some nine months earlier. Particularly harmful was the claim that employees of the Office of Economic Opportunity (OEO) had participated in civil disturbances. One especially embarrassing episode occurred in Houston, Texas, where the local Community Action Program (CAP) was found to have purchased telescopic sights for high-powered rifles, with the apparent blessing of the OEO regional office. CAP officials claimed that the equipment was intended for use in lieu of microscopes, but uncharitable local politicians found this explanation unconvincing. Congressman George Bush, a moderate Republican, was swift to acknowledge that the story had become greatly distorted, urging the voters of Houston "to forget the incident and get on with the business of combating poverty," but his magnanimity was not shared by Senator John Tower, and the case rapidly became a cause célèbre.[35] (In view of Bush's liberal perspective on the antipoverty effort on this occasion, it is noteworthy that as president in 1992 he should have blamed many of America's social problems on the Great Society's misguided activism.)[36]

Sargent Shriver spent much time trying to convince both Johnson and congressional skeptics that the agency's principal contribution to the recent riots had been to defuse rather than to increase tension, but even within the administration significant divisions had opened up regarding the proper role and activities of the OEO. Harry McPherson questioned the utility of the Community Action Program, suggesting to Johnson that he should consider "saving what is worth saving, and renouncing the rest."[37] Douglass Cater went still further, counseling outright elimination of the OEO. One option might be "shifting all the nondelegated functions of OEO over to HEW" and giving John Gardner (secretary of Health, Education and Welfare) the responsibility for "making the combined welfare, health, education and poverty programs into an effective weapon."[38]

More serious than these internal doubts was the external threat to the OEO's survival posed by recent bad publicity. When Congressman Carl Perkins (D-Ky.) wrote to eighty mayors and police chiefs in the aftermath of the unrest, seeking their impressions of the War on Poverty, he was shaken by the degree of their hostility.[39] Still more disturbing was the disillusionment of Congressman Phil Landrum, whose co-sponsorship of the 1964 bill had done so much to boost its appeal among conservatives. The Georgian pledged his continued enthusiasm for the stated mission of the original bill, but told Shriver that he was appalled by the incompetence of some of the agency's senior staff and doubtful about the continued credibility of the Job Corps and Community Action concepts. Unless the OEO was completely overhauled, "the legislative program being proposed is doomed to failure." Moreover, "as sad as it is for me to tell you, . . . I simply cannot continue to support the program with personnel in the organization allowing the tragic mistakes which are taking place."⁴⁰

The survival of the War on Poverty in these difficult circumstances represented the administration's greatest legislative achievement in 1967, and came mainly as a result of a successful campaign to win the support of House moderates and conservatives. This strategy had three principal components. First, OEO congressional liaison staff emphasized the traditional purposes of the Economic Opportunity Act. (One agency bulletin described the program's ultimate goal as being "to help more than 30 million Americans work their way out of poverty—off of welfare and on to the tax rolls.")⁴¹ Second, Sargent Shriver vigorously contested the damaging claim that his agency existed primarily to respond to the demands of black rioters. In a letter to Congressman Bush—who, along with three Republican colleagues had written to commend his party's favored Neighborhood Action Crusade—Shriver stated that he had, "since the inception of the Poverty Program, tried to make it abundantly clear that ours is not an anti-riot agency." He further admonished Bush and his colleagues that "the programs of OEO are directed at long-range solutions to the basic causes of poverty." Accordingly, they could "not be expected to constitute the sole remedy to the many current tensions which afflict our society."⁴²

Third, congressional liaison staff working for both the OEO and the White House gave tacit support to a controversial House amendment that allowed local elected officials to take control of privately run Community Action programs. In public, the administration resisted the proposal by the respected congresswoman Edith Green (D-Ore.) as a betrayal of the War on Poverty's participatory ethos. But behind the scenes, this same proposal was endorsed as a prerequisite for securing the support of conservative Democrats. Sam Gibbons (D-Fla.) warned Barefoot Sanders, a White House aide, that "it is impossible to pass the poverty program in the condition it is now in."⁴³ If the Education and Labor Committee opposed reform of the CAP, he might oppose the bill.⁴⁴

Opposition by Gibbons, who had shepherded the previous year's amendments through the House, would have been a shattering blow. Yet many House liberals continued to resist the notion that—as they saw it—the principles of the War on Poverty should be sacrificed in the name of political expediency. Sanders told the president that while "Mrs. Green is very competent and very shrewd, . . . unfortunately she is distrusted and disliked by the liberals."⁴⁵ Another memorandum reported a meeting between Shriver, Perkins, House Speaker Carl Albert, and various Southern conservatives (including Landrum) whose purpose was "to see whether further concessions should and could be made to round up Southern support." All were happy with the Green Amendment, but Landrum demanded major reforms in the Job Corps, including a $100 million cut in funding. Shriver indicated that he would be willing to meet Landrum's conditions, but Sanders reported "a major problem politically." There was no possibility of getting a more ambitious package through the House, but "many of the articulate liberal group are unhappy with its CAP provisions. If we publicly embrace the committee bill too enthusiastically they will be unhappy."[46]

Congressman John Dent (D-Pa.), a member of the House Education and Labor Committee, feared that the feelings of some colleagues on the majority side went beyond mere unhappiness. "Jim O'Hara [D-Mich.] and others are putting stories out about Edith Green and as a result, the whole committee could fall apart. And all we need to lose is three Democratic votes to lose the whole works." He added:

> I'm trying to stay in the middle—to keep Edith happy. She's vital. She can bring a lot of Southerners and conservatives with her who would laugh at the rest of us. . . .
>
> What the committee wants to do is put out a bill that the House can't pass. Then they think they can make political hay out of the defeat—like Truman did [with the "do-nothing" 80th Congress in 1948]. . . .
>
> The whole thing's sophomoric. We can't be like Truman because he had a Republican Congress and we've got a Democratic one.[47]

After a prolonged struggle, the compromise bill was eventually reported from the committee, and a Republican move on the floor to reduce the 1968 authorization figure to $1.4 billion (from the administration request of $2.06 billion) was defeated, thanks to the opposition of substantial numbers of Southern Democrats. The House finally provided $1.6 billion, which was increased to just under $2 billion in conference with the Senate.

SOCIAL SECURITY AMENDMENTS OF 1967:
FINAL ACT

The final phase of the struggle over the Social Security Amendments of 1967 revealed a parallel rift. Whereas the major test for the antipoverty program had come in the House, the key battle over welfare reform was fought out in the Senate, whose Finance Committee reported a liberalized version of the Mills bill in November. Following the rancorous debate explored in the last chapter, Russell Long's committee had decided that the mandatory character of the new work-training program should not apply to the mothers of preschool-age children. On the Senate floor the bill's restrictive features were modified still further. Among twenty-nine amendments approved during the course of a marathon debate, one introduced by Fred Harris made the unemployed parent program (AFDC-UP) compulsory and another, by Robert Kennedy, stated that benefits could not be withheld from the mothers of school-age children outside of school hours. Opposing the latter, Chairman Long—who nonetheless supported the revised bill— complained that a "mother would not have to do so much as swat a mosquito off her leg as a condition for getting aid from the government."[48]

Senate liberals were generally pleased with the amended Social Security bill. But in conference, every important Senate provision was deleted, while the restrictive character of the Mills bill was fully restored. Wilbur Cohen was deeply worried by the likely liberal response to this result, although he appreciated that the president would be reluctant to oppose legislation that still provided important benefits to the elderly. Writing to Congressman Mills, Cohen warned that were Congress to implement the restored AFDC "freeze" and the other restrictions, "the possibilities of political exploitation of the issues in an election year by the liberal Republicans and Democrats who are critical of President Johnson . . . are very great."[49]

Cohen was aware that the social welfare community viewed the Mills bill with intense dismay and anger. His old ally Elizabeth Wickenden had earlier anticipated "tragic results from its draconian provisions" and had told the director of the American Public Welfare Association that she felt "really overwhelmed" by its "totally catastrophic" nature.[50] And within his own department, John W. Gardner was under tremendous pressure to oppose the Mills bill. Its final passage prompted an angry petition from disgruntled HEW employees. In the accompanying text, they accused Gardner of having connived in Johnson's "posture of political expediency." Declaring their intention to release the statement and petition to the press, they added that "it is inconceivable that DHEW could administer legislation so completely contrary to the rights and dignity of human beings in this society."[51]

Ever the pragmatist (he was known as the "salami slicer" because of his gradualist approach to expanding the American welfare state), Cohen understood that Johnson might feel pressured to sign the offending legislation. (The Mills bill also contained historic increases in Social Security benefits for the elderly.) Referring to a promise that Johnson had made almost a year before, Cohen suggested that it might be wise to combine the signing ceremony with the appointment of the Income Maintenance Commission, a decision that might help "to take the sting out of the criticism."[52] Joseph Califano praised what he considered to be an "excellent recommendation," but the president was unimpressed with Cohen's advice. With respect to the latter's general qualms, Johnson told Califano, "Wilbur ought to go over all the good things in this bill—and we better take what we can get."[53]

The response of Senate liberals to the conference report was immediate and fiercely critical. Lee Metcalf (D-Mont.) asked if the Senate had become a mere consultative chamber like the House of Lords and condemned "this bad, evil House bill."[54] Fred Harris (D-Okla.) pronounced himself "disturbed and depressed," while Walter Mondale condemned it as "one of the most backward, repressive, medieval pieces of legislation we have seen in a long time."[55] Robert Kennedy viewed the conference bill as a "disgrace to all Americans," contending that it "seems to say to the poor person that we in the government simply do not care what happens to him if he is unable to support himself."[56]

Three days after Wilbur Cohen had revealed his fears to the president, both he and his superior, John Gardner, moved into open opposition to the conference bill, effectively endorsing Kennedy's view that "no bill at all would be preferable to this legislation."[57] Califano explained to Johnson that Cohen had "a deep concern that this will be regarded as an anti-Negro bill and . . . an excuse for rioting next summer." Furthermore, "he feels you will gain greater support among the liberals if you come out and criticize the conference report."[58] Gardner's recommendation, delivered "with all the urgency I can express," amounted to a plea. Johnson must strongly oppose the freeze on AFDC and the mandatory character of the WIN program. Better than that, he should oppose the conference report altogether. Like Cohen, Gardner believed that the welfare provisions would "be perceived as anti-Negro" and that they would "become celebrated issues in the liberal community." He argued, "It is no accident that Senator Robert Kennedy and Mayor Lindsay have seized on the issue so strongly. The possibilities of political exploitation of the issues are considerable. . . . I think it is extremely important to your own domestic position to be numbered among the explicit opponents of these provisions."[59]

Five days after the release of the conference report, Gardner's fears were confirmed. Fred Harris and Robert Kennedy announced their intention to filibuster the Social Security Amendments until the end of the congressional session. Mike Manatos, together with the Senate Democratic leadership, made strenuous attempts to avert this disastrous possibility, but was forced to report to Johnson that "following 48 hours of intensive negotiations . . . we are precisely where we were when all this began—nowhere." The president's chief Senate liaison aide feared that Harris had become "Bobby Kennedy's agent." Despite repeated entreaties from Majority Leader Mansfield, Harris insisted "his conscience must rule." Manatos commented that "Ed Muskie, who is no less interested in the problems of the poor than are Harris and Kennedy, believes that a filibuster gives us the worst of both worlds—it inflames the Negro militants, and alienates 24,000,000 old people."[60]

As in 1966, the position of Senate liberals on reform seemed guided in part by whether they had to face the voters in the next round of national elections. Having safely negotiated a tough reelection race the previous year, Harris presumably felt free to disregard the views of his constituents. Manatos highlighted the issue: "Despite the almost repetitious pleas of Mansfield and the expressed views of [Alan] Bible [D-Nev.], [Frank] Church [D-Idaho], McGovern and Mondale, who are candidates next year, that a filibuster would be hurtful, Harris has not swerved one iota from his 'conscience' position, which seems to take on renewed vigor following Kennedy consultations."[61]

As it happened, the threat of a filibuster was averted thanks only to the opportunism of Russell Long, who forced a critical procedural vote while the Kennedy group was out of the chamber. On his return, a furious Kennedy railed against a "retreat into brutality." While denying that he was "an alarmist," he predicted that the enacted amendments would "sow seeds of great despair, unhappiness, agony and pain among our fellow citizens."[62] Clifford Case was similarly exercised, insisting that his colleagues could no longer ignore "the deep and bitter feelings of frustration and despair of those trapped in the poverty cycle." The "punitive" character of the welfare amendments could "only exacerbate the tension in the ghettos."[63] Kennedy and Case were among fourteen liberals who opposed the measure that President Johnson signed into law on December 23 and who did not seem notably appeased by the belated appointment of the Commission on Income Maintenance chaired by the businessman Ben Heineman.

CHALLENGE OF THE NEW POLITICS

On November 30, Senator Eugene McCarthy announced his decision to challenge Lyndon Johnson for the Democratic Party's presidential nomination. Speaking of a "deepening moral crisis in America," he pledged to offer disaffected American youth "entrance back into the political process."[64] His candidacy is relevant to the present study for two reasons. First, that Allard Lowenstein and others could persuade McCarthy of the value of such a bid demonstrates the momentum that the New Politics had generated by the autumn of 1967. Reference to the records of his 1968 campaign reveals the impressive array of insurgent organizations that comprised his self-proclaimed "Constituency of Conscience." In addition to the ADA, McCarthy was assisted by supporters of such groups as the Committee for a New Politics, the Council for a Livable World, the Congressional Peace Campaign Committee, and the National Committee for an Effective Congress.[65] According to Jeremy Larner, a campaign speech writer, the candidate "knew as well as anyone that their purposes and values were not necessarily his," but their strength and vigor were both impressive and encouraging.[66]

Moreover, shared hostility to the war and to Lyndon Johnson allowed dissidents with very different ideological agendas to unite under a common banner. For some student radicals, the politics of liberalism during the 1960s had exposed that creed's fundamental moral bankruptcy. From the current crisis, however, might emerge a youthful new order (of the kind later envisaged by Charles Reich in *The Greening of America*).[67] But for such McCarthy supporters as Congressman Don Edwards (D-Cal.) the challenge was one of restoration rather than reconception. Addressing the Committee of Concerned Democrats in Chicago, Edwards told fellow antiwar liberals that "we are here today as loyal Democrats—seeking to return our party to the course of Franklin D. Roosevelt, Adlai E. Stevenson and John F. Kennedy." He had been elected in 1962 as a "liberal, Kennedy Democrat" and he remembered 1963 as having been "the year of hope." Under Kennedy's successor, however, the nation had become enmeshed in "the wicked war in Vietnam," Johnson having adopted the foreign policy views of the defeated Barry Goldwater. He described McCarthy, by contrast, as "a man who will embrace again the challenge and the spirit of hope of the New Frontier."[68]

Edwards's remarks confirm that the overwhelming issue for both McCarthy and his supporters was the war in Vietnam. The previous chapter suggested that by the summer of 1967, domestic and military sources of dislocation had fused to form a single crisis of national direction that all but destroyed President Johnson's remaining political authority. Yet the "dump Johnson" campaign that ensued was fueled almost solely by hostility to the president's Vietnam policy. Accordingly, Vietnam became the single criterion by which antiwar liberals identified their friends. (This allowed John Kennedy and even William J. Fulbright to enter the pantheon of liberal visionaries, while Lyndon Johnson found himself alongside Barry Goldwater.) Those ADA liberals who chose to back McCarthy did so despite reservations concerning his mediocre record on domestic policy.[69]

During the early weeks of McCarthy's campaign, however, allies were irked by their candidate's laid-back approach to his task. McCarthy failed to catch the public imagination and this, together with Robert Kennedy's apparent disavowal of a 1968 bid, left Johnson the likely nominee, despite his unpopularity. For his part, Johnson's political and legislative strategy for 1968 was conditioned less by the challenge of the New Politics than by the familiar and unyielding economic and political constraints. The 1968 State of the Union Address was that of a president whose room for maneuver had been eliminated by Vietnam and by a profound national disillusionment with social activism. New housing and employment measures were announced, but civil rights received only a sentence, while the war, economic problems, and the "restlessness" of the American people provided dominant themes. Johnson's February 22 message on the cities struck a similarly gloomy tone. Urban renewal, federal housing, and Model Cities had contributed much, but the nation's cities remained burdened with "staggering" and intractable human problems whose resolution was uncertain. The president stated, "No one can say how long it will take, or how much of our fortune will eventually be committed. For the problems we are dealing with are stubborn, entrenched, and slow to yield."[70]

With the Kerner Commission on the verge of delivering its much anticipated findings, Johnson was disturbed to receive a stinging attack on his record from the Citizen's Crusade Against Poverty. On February 19, the crusade released a polemic entitled "The War on Poverty—Do We Care?" Its principal message was that the administration was not "serious about supporting basic antipoverty programs."[71]

President Johnson was infuriated by the fact that a body whose board included so many prominent members of the liberal coalition, including Walter Reuther, I. W. Abel, A. Philip Randolph, and Whitney Young, Jr., could have shown so little comprehension of his problems and demanded that Joseph Califano "tell them to cut this stuff out."[72] More serious was mounting speculation that the Kerner Commission would show a similar lack of political realism. Toward the end of February, Johnson made his apprehension clear in a letter to Califano:

> Whatever the report recommends, I hope it will also contain recommendations to finance these proposals. Anyone can recommend spending, but preparing methods to fund the costs of new programs takes more ability. It has been my experience that spenders can always spend if they can find lenders to lend or taxpayers willing to be taxed. So, I hope those who are preparing the final report will be as imaginative on taxing as they are on spending.[73]

THE KERNER REPORT

In both programmatic and philosophical terms, the Kerner Report distilled the dominant sources of liberal discontent during the previous six months and produced findings that implicitly repudiated the record of the Johnson administration on social issues. Its key recommendations—the creation of 2 million jobs over the next three years, a massive school desegregation program, 600,000 housing starts, and endorsement of the guaranteed income—were as unrealistic as they were dramatic. Nevertheless, they lacked the power to shock, if only because they so precisely embodied the sort of approach that liberal legislators had been demanding ever since the Newark riot. Far more arresting than its programmatic recommendations were the report's controversial explanation for unrest and its periodically apocalyptic tone, striking even by the standards of the time.

Martha Derthick, who served on President Nixon's 1970 Presidential Commission on Campus Unrest, has suggested that such bodies suffer from inherent weaknesses as interpreters of complex social phemonena. Her observations on "commissionship" deserve consideration here, for they have particular resonance with regard to the Kerner Commission.

Derthick, writing in 1971, concluded that the political character of presidential commissions impaired their objectivity and rendered the pursuit of truth a subordinate goal. However, the problem did not lie in excessive deference to the president, for commissioners were not bound by constraints inherent in the exercise of executive power. The Commission on Campus Unrest, for example, actually "inverted what was probably the President's initial assumption." Although it was "expected to reach the public through the medium of the Presidency, it sought instead to reach the Presidency through a manifesto to the press and public."[74]

The tone of such a manifesto was, in Derthick's opinion, unlikely to be dispassionate: "To be believed, it is first necessary to be heard, and to be heard it is helpful to use passionate, extreme language. The organizational need to command attention impels the use of crisis rhetoric," particularly in the introduction to a report: "What will command attention depends partly on the prevailing style of public rhetoric, and the threshold was very high by the end of the 1960s. . . . Within the Commission on Campus Unrest, one argument against moderate, restrained language was that it would make the report seem a step backward from that of the Kerner Commission."[75]

It would have been difficult for the authors of the campus unrest report of 1970 to surpass the anguished tone of the Kerner Report's opening summation. For some time, commission liberals, particularly Lindsay and Harris, had been concerned that the relative conservatism of some of their colleagues might mitigate the forcefulness of the final report, which would thus fail to serve their political interests. At the commission's final meeting, Lindsay produced a summary of the proposed report, drafted by his personal assistant, Jay Kriegel. Both in tone and substance, the summary differed markedly from the report that it purported to abridge. Nevertheless, it was accepted by the commission after Lindsay threatened to issue a minority report if it were excluded. Predictably, media coverage focused heavily on the summary: Michael Lipsky and David Olson observe that "the first two days of commentary about the report were based exclusively on the summary, and it structured public perceptions of the entire document."[76]

The summary proceeds from the "basic conclusion" that "our nation is moving toward two societies: one black, one white—separate and unequal."[77] It states:

> Reaction to last summer's disorders has quickened the movement and deepened the division. Discrimination and segregation have long permeated much of American life; they now threaten the future of every American. . . . To pursue our present course will involve the continuing polarization of the American community and, ultimately, the destruction of basic democratic values.[78]

The commission clearly saw its main function as being to stir the nation's conscience and anxiety to the point where currently far-fetched liberal panaceas would become suddenly feasible. Kerner stated that a principal goal of the commission's hearings was "to educate the white, rather than the Negro."[79] The headline-grabbing tone that such a mission required did not facilitate a rigorous analytical approach to the problems of urban America. Moreover, if the Lindsay summary served to distort the findings of the

Kerner Commission, then throughout the main body of the report, bald statements about culpability and causation are contradicted, or at best unsubstantiated, by subsequent evidence. Blacks and whites are consistently judged by the different standards that the commission's simple categories of *oppressor* and *oppressed* appear to require, while fear of appearing racist frequently deterred its members from balanced analysis. Above all, the report fails to indicate how the white electorate might be persuaded that its fears and prejudices were unfounded and that it should vote for legislators who would implement and finance the commission's proposals.

These basic criticisms may readily be illustrated with reference to the text of the Kerner Report. Having stated initially that white racism was responsible for black poverty and the 1967 riots, the report discovers a rather more complex explanation. In a chapter entitled "Comparing the Immigrant and Negro Experience," the primary source of black poverty— and hence of the dissatisfaction from which unrest sprang—is identified as the fact that "the Negro migrant, unlike the immigrant, found little opportunity in the city; he had arrived too late, and the unskilled labor he had to offer was no longer needed."[80] Racial discrimination is "undoubtedly the second major reason why the Negro has been unable to escape from poverty"—but if not the first, how could the report justify the prominence accorded its earlier and simplistic verdict of white racism? The third cause, incidentally, was the decline of the political machine, which had deprived blacks of entry into the political system—again, not primarily a racial factor.[81]

So great was the Kerner Commission's determination to condemn white society and existing federal efforts, that the report derived sweeping conclusions from the most unsatisfactory evidence. Particularly noteworthy perhaps is its persistent tendency to criticize Great Society programs by referring to data from the 1960 census. No attempt was made to highlight the substantial economic gains blacks had made during the course of the Kennedy and Johnson administrations, although comprehensive data on this subject had been released by the Census Bureau in the autumn of 1967. In one footnote, the authors profess to be "keenly aware of difficulties involved in comparing 1967 programs with 1960 needs," but the main text neither details such problems nor qualifies its findings in response.[82]

Also revealing in this context is the report's critique of existing social programs. Despite the vigor with which it demanded bigger, better programs, the commission acknowledged that it had "not attempted to analyze the often substantial social and economic programs of [nonfederal] levels

205

of government," that it had restricted its focus to federal antipoverty programs in three riot cities, and that it had "not attempted the far more difficult task of evaluating the efficiency of the programs, or the quality of assistance provided to recipients, or its impact on their lives."[83] The commission's failure is not surprising, given time constraints and limited staff support. Less defensible is its extrapolation of unequivocal indictments from so limited an investigation.

JOHNSON ADMINISTRATION'S RESPONSE

The Kerner Report was enthusiastically received within the liberal community, and in all but ignoring release, President Johnson seems to have resisted the unanimous entreaties of his closest advisers. Joseph Califano recognized "its enormous cost and the unrealistic nature of its recommendations," but questioned the political wisdom of simply disregarding a report that he had after all commissioned.[84] He suggested that Johnson might at least like to issue a statement thanking members of the commission for their work and expressing the hope that it might become the basis for a national dialogue.[85]

Attorney General Ramsey Clark agreed that such a course would "show decisive action without subscribing to everything the report says."[86] And even as the degree of Johnson's hostility became clear, Douglass Cater suggested that "whether or not the president comments directly on the Kerner Commission Report, what about a statement of conscience?"[87] Louis Martin, of the Democratic National Committee, shared with other advisers a deep apprehension about the wider political dangers of ignoring the report, noting that it was "getting a great reception in the liberal community." Despite the president's understandable misgivings, "I do not want to lose any capital we may be building up with the liberal community by nit-picking the report. It seems to me the president might receive the report with praise and use the opportunity to point out that he has been moving in the right direction all along."[88]

Harry McPherson warned Johnson that "a cold reception to the Kerner Report is bad policy for us." After all, the commission had a diverse composition, including "even for God's sake the police chief of Atlanta." Members of the commission, including close friends and allies of the president, had been "stunned by the gravity and urgency of the Negro's problems." Mc-

Pherson concluded, "If our response is 'we'll study it,' what will people think? I don't mean bomb-throwing liberals, *New York Times* editorial writers, columnists, or militant Negroes. I mean ordinary, moderate people [who] are *also* concerned about finding some way out of the tragic tailspin we are in."[89]

McPherson was convinced that Johnson's political problems would only increase unless he met the report "squarely and affirmatively rather than coldly or evasively." However, draft letters he prepared, thanking members of the Kerner Commission for their efforts, received short shrift from the president: "I just can't sign this group of letters. I'd be a hypocrite. And I don't even want it let known that they got this far . . . otherwise somebody will leak that I wouldn't sign them. Just file them—or get rid of them."[90]

In public, Johnson maintained his stubborn refusal to comment on the Kerner Report. However, at an off-the-record meeting with black newspaper editors and publishers he did provide insight into his thinking. The report had "more good than bad," and many of its recommendations were clearly desirable. The main problem was that proposals such as "the public employment of everyone" were simply not practical. "The president cannot get that out of the Congress. The country will not vote $80 billion and there is no sense of holding out false hopes or expectations," Johnson told them, adding, "I am more practical than some of those who wrote the report and some of the staff who sent it to me. First thing we have got to do is find the money. They didn't touch upon that problem. It's like saying we need sirloin steak three nights a week, but only have the money to pay for two steaks."[91]

Just a fortnight before announcing his decision not to seek reelection, the tone of the riot commission's findings, Johnson's response to those findings, and the unanimity with which advisers had regretted that response all attest to his profound isolation. If the president was convinced of the impracticability of accelerated legislative activism in the present climate, then fellow Great Society liberals were unpersuaded. Echoing the advice Califano had offered a few months previously, Commissioner of Education Harold Howe told Wilbur Cohen that Johnson should move aggressively to mobilize a latent coalition for liberalism:

The riots in the summer of 1967 had the general effect of destroying public confidence in the administration, . . . and adding to the power of those who wanted to economize, curtail, and delay efforts on the domestic side. There was a possibility that last summer the president might have used the blowup in the cities to mount a totally new and adventurous attack on the problems of minority groups and poor people generally, or to add substantially to the attack he already had going. In effect he, at that time, could have "gone to the people" over the objections of Mills and Mahon.[92]

For Howe, the release of the Kerner Report presented a second such opportunity, but one which "won't last for long." In place of the present policy of "domestic appeasement," the president should make a "positive, direct, personal appeal to the masses of the people and to the economic, social, and political institutions of the country to contribute and to work for the solution of problems which will engulf them if they do not make some sacrifices." HEW's responsibility was "to communicate with the president and urge him not to join with the economy bloc in selling the country short."[93]

But by now Lyndon Johnson, who in any case would have found such counsel facile and unrealistic, was a dispirited and broken president. Four weeks before the release of the Kerner Report, the Tet offensive had destroyed the credibility of the administration's official optimism over Vietnam, setting in motion the reevaluation process that would culminate in the March 31 decision to oppose further escalation along lines requested by General Westmoreland. Then, in the aftermath of Tet, the president's reelection prospects had been dealt a shattering blow by McCarthy's strong showing in the New Hampshire Democratic primary. Finally, the Kerner Report's release had been swiftly followed by Robert Kennedy's belated decision to enter the contest, the new candidate explaining that it had finally become clear to him that Johnson had no intention of either ending the war or tackling the nation's domestic crisis.

His morale and vigor destroyed by this succession of blows, Johnson announced his withdrawal from the 1968 contest. Days later, what McPherson had referred to as the nation's "tragic tailspin" gained yet greater momentum with the assassination of Martin Luther King, Jr., and the riots that ensued. With much of downtown Washington in flames, and with White House business being conducted from underground bunkers, planning continued for the campaign King had conceived the previous autumn: the Poor People's March on Washington.

The campaign's titular leader was King's successor at the SCLC, Rev. Ralph Abernathy. But as apprehensive federal officials contemplated the marchers' arrival, it was the *absence* of leadership that caused the most alarm. Two weeks before the planned arrival of the marchers in the nation's capital, an advance guard met with HEW officials to discuss the campaign and its demands. George Wiley complained that "we have not had the support from the secretary's office or from the administration for a real income maintenance program," and four welfare mothers denounced the federal government in impassioned tones.[94] Mary Switzer, a senior HEW official, reported that the meeting was "a serious and moving experience for all of us."[95] Equally, however, both this occasion and the subsequent campaign (which featured a monthlong encampment of participants near the Lincoln Memorial) placed additional pressure on the administration to abandon the politics of consensus.

Johnson was hostile to the Poor People's Campaign and determined not to be seen to accede to its demands.[96] But elsewhere within the administration, there existed a strong measure of sympathy for the demonstrators, combined with qualms about the implications of any failure to respond.[97] Following a meeting with Marian Wright, one of the leaders of the march, Ralph Huitt of HEW was struck by how little control campaign organizers had over their followers:

> Miss Wright clearly recognizes the thinness of the leadership's control over the march. She said several times, in response to our suggestions, "If I said that to them I wouldn't be a leader anymore." She says the poor people themselves will decide whether our responses are adequate. . . . They let their people excoriate us because the marchers had to have an outlet.

Huitt identified "enormous danger in the situation now developing," warning:

> The members of the march are talking about drastic actions among themselves. The leaders are aware of that but not disturbed by it; "that is your problem"—as are the problems of a tax increase, fiscal pressures, congressional attitudes, and all. Miss Wright, like the others, seems to have unqualified confidence that they can force from the government whatever they want. The risk that violence will lead to repression seems not to disturb them.[98]

Huitt feared that it would be impossible to preserve democracy if minority groups "through threats of violence" could "dictate what the government must do." His hope was that "the poor will become an organized interest with professional leaders who work through regular channels."[99]

In terms of the development of the guaranteed income movement, the events considered here had mixed consequences. On the one hand, the forces of conservatism that constrained President Johnson during the final eighteen months of his term obviated dramatic, new social welfare ventures; indeed, the principal legislative development of this period had been the restrictive Mills bill. On the other hand, riots, a rising tide of activism among the poor, the political ambitions of liberals identified with the New Politics, the Kerner Report, and other pressures from the left were lending fresh impetus to the guaranteed income movement.

Such was the momentum developed by this movement by the middle of 1968 that it had all but conquered the executive branch. Johnson had been compelled to appoint a guaranteed income commission. The OEO had initiated experimental projects designed to test the impact of the negative income tax concept on work incentives. And, seemingly in response to the Poor People's Campaign, HEW had developed a bold income maintenance proposal with the intriguing acronym, BIG (Basic Income Guarantee).[100] Nevertheless, Lyndon Johnson staunchly resisted such schemes.[101] Paradoxically, and for reasons that are explored in the next chapter, the guaranteed income movement would attain its greatest momentum during the presidency of Richard Nixon.

CHAPTER 9

Zenith of the Entitlements Revolution: Liberalism and the Family Assistance Plan

If Republicans capture the center as Democrats go to the extreme, we may well see Republican Presidents in the White House for a generation.
—Richard Scammon and Ben Wattenberg, *The Real Majority*

By the time that Lyndon Johnson left office, the guaranteed income principle had gained widespread acceptance within his administration, despite the president's personal resistance. His isolation is all the more striking if one considers that the income strategy was also winning converts among conservatives. The journalist T. George Harris, writing in the spring of 1968, wondered at the "strangely mixed group of liberals, Negro mothers, conservatives and radicals" who were "moving right along to their common goal: to make Uncle Sam give poor families and their children cash enough to live in moderate ease—whether they work, loaf or riot."[1]

In truth, any such community of purpose was of a distinctly limited nature. Where some reformers were concerned for the rights of the poor, others remained preoccupied with their responsibilities, deprecating a current welfare system that penalized the working poor and fostered chronic dependency. And if most supporters of the negative income tax (the most frequently advocated income strategy) viewed it as a guaranteed income, others claimed that this label might more properly be attached to the existing structure. Still, if supporters of the income strategy had divergent objectives, they shared a common disillusionment with the service strategy of Lyndon Johnson's War on Poverty. Gaining ground within the federal

211

bureaucracy, academia, both political parties and the business community, this was—according to Daniel Patrick Moynihan, Richard Nixon's top domestic adviser—"an idea whose time has come."[2]

It is because of this convergence of the left and the right—over means if less frequently over ends—that the guaranteed income movement attained its maximum momentum during Richard Nixon's first term. In August 1969, the president unveiled a Family Assistance Plan (FAP) that would have guaranteed a modest income to every American family with children. The first part of this chapter explores the motivation of this proposal, suggesting that in addition to its social objectives, FAP was part of Nixon's bid to construct a New Republican Majority. The main discussion, however, is concerned with the liberal reaction to FAP. It was in response to Nixon's innovative proposal that the revolution in liberal perspectives on entitlement reached its zenith, culminating in George McGovern's decision to sponsor a $6,500 guaranteed income proposal during his 1972 presidential campaign.

Like Richard Nixon, Senator McGovern was endeavoring to build a new political coalition and believed that his proposals for welfare reform would advance that objective. Both candidates found their proposals frustrated, with the result that the universally disliked New Deal welfare system remained in place. Paradoxically, however, President Nixon gained more from the defeat of FAP than he would have gained from its success. As radicals and liberals (including McGovern) were driven to endorse ever more extravagant definitions of entitlement, the Democratic Party demonstrated its virtual abandonment of an individualist tradition and work ethic whose popular appeal remained undimmed. Conversely, as FAP ran into political trouble and his political enemies moved to the left, Nixon emphasized the Republican Party's claim to embody the values of middle America. The GOP's performance over the next two decades suggests that something like a New Republican Majority did indeed emerge at a presidential level, albeit partially by default. Meanwhile, the travail of liberalism indicates that the Democrats' liaison with the New Politics yielded disastrous consequences.

FAMILY ASSISTANCE PLAN

On 8 August 1969, President Richard Nixon addressed the nation on the perennially vexing subject of welfare dependency. The recent presidential campaign had featured strong Republican attacks on the indignity and excessive cost of relief, together with corresponding paeans to the work ethic. In this context, Nixon's decision to embrace the cause of reform was scarcely a surprise. The tone of the president's remarks, too, was what would be expected from the tribune of the Silent Majority. Nixon expressed his disgust for "any system which makes it more profitable for a man not to work than to work," and—in a typically Nixonian phrase—pledged his commitment to the "forgotten poor," who worked but were unable to escape material hardship: "Poverty must be conquered without sacrificing the will to work, for if we take the route of the permanent handout, the American character will itself be impoverished."[3]

But if the president's tone was unremarkable, the substance of his remarks was more arresting. Far from introducing new restrictions on welfare entitlement, along the lines of the WIN Amendments of 1967, Nixon proposed a Family Assistance Plan that would—at a conservative estimate—add $4.4 billion to the federal welfare budget for fiscal year 1971 and double eligibility.

FAP embodied a negative income tax (NIT) approach whose greatest virtues were simplicity and directness, particularly in contrast to the complex and unrewarding prescriptions of the Johnson antipoverty program. In essence, the NIT sought to redistribute income rather than opportunity, in the belief that the former goal represented both a more realistic approach to eliminating poverty and a prerequisite for equal opportunity. Where the Economic Opportunity Act, the Model Cities program, and the Elementary and Secondary Education Act had sought to provide rehabilitative tools, such as training and motivation, the NIT would simply supply cash via the computers of the Internal Revenue Service or the Social Security Administration.

Under the Family Assistance Plan, every American family was to be guaranteed an annual income of $500 for each of the first two members, and $300 for every additional member. The resulting figure of $1,600 for a family of four was lower than existing payments in all but six states, but high-payment states were required at least to maintain current levels, on the understanding that they would receive fiscal relief from the federal government.[4] The principal element of FAP's additional cost over Aid to Families with Dependent Children (AFDC) came not from the introduction of a federal floor for payments to existing welfare recipients, but from the extension of benefits to the working poor. Both philosophically desirable and politically unavoidable, this emphasis on work necessitated a low income floor for two reasons: first, a higher level would discourage work and disrupt the labor market; and second, a generous floor combined with the 50 percent tax on earnings that FAP employed would simply cost too much.[5]

The NIT sought a middle way between mutually inconsistent goals of adequate benefit levels and work incentives. Families would be entitled to retain the first $720 of any earnings, plus one half of additional income. Eligibility for FAP would only end when total income reached $3,920, that is, above the official poverty line. Yearly benefits and total income for a family of four under FAP were as follows:[6]

Family Earnings	Amount of Earnings Disregarded	FAP Payments	Total Family Income
$ 0	$ 0	$1,600	$1,600
500	500	1,600	2,100
1,000	860	1,460	2,460
1,500	1,100	1,210	2,710
2,000	1,360	960	2,960
2,500	1,610	710	3,210
3,000	1,860	460	3,460
3,500	2,110	210	3,710
4,000	2,360	0	4,000

It is useful at this point to consider why President Nixon supported so seemingly liberal a measure, a measure that (despite his protests) was immediately labeled a guaranteed income program. Writing to newly appointed staff members in January 1969, President-elect Nixon demanded a "thorough investigation" of the "welfare mess" in New York. In his view, this "mess" was "probably typical of a problem which exists all over the country."[7] Examining the internal debate over welfare which took place prior to the unveiling of FAP in August, it becomes clear that the president's unhappiness with the present system owed little to liberal impulses. First, he was vexed by rising AFDC costs and rolls, and reformers with fundamentally liberal intent, such as Daniel Patrick Moynihan, were able to present a compelling conservative case for the NIT (although Moynihan's personal preference was for a family allowance). Since the mid-1960s, dependency rates in cities such as New York had accelerated in what seemed to be an uncontrolled and remorseless fashion. As one businessman told Nixon, "the basic difficulty with present programs is that they have built-in growing mechanisms."[8] The following data indicate the growth in the number of AFDC recipients over a five-year period.[9]

	No. of Recipients (000s)	Percent Change
1966	4,666	+ 6%
1967	5,309	+14
1968	6,086	+15
1969	7,313	+20
1970	9,660	+32

Nixon had become increasingly impressed by the heterodox figure of Daniel Patrick Moynihan during the 1968 campaign, and with his election, the M.I.T. professor returned to government as head of a new Urban Affairs Council. Gilbert Steiner characterizes his role tellingly as "President Nixon's iconoclast-in-residence."[10] Exploiting the president's aversion to welfare and the welfare bureaucracy, Moynihan returned to a familiar subject: the social pathology of the dependent poor. Writing in May, he observed that the disturbing pattern he had first identified in his 1965 report, *The Negro Family* (rising dependency despite falling unemployment), had "continued in a most remarkable way." Evidently fascinated by the accompanying evidence, Nixon asked "Why did this happen?" and requested that his adviser furnish "a brief memo on the causes."[11] Eighteen months later, Moynihan still sensed the value of this line of attack, telling the president that "your original forecast of soaring welfare rolls in the absence of reform is turning out to be incredibly—impossibly—correct." When FAP was first proposed, there were 6.7 million AFDC recipients, but by September 1970, the figure had increased to 8.6 million.[12]

Nixon was also concerned that welfare penalized work. When Moynihan referred to the importance of helping the working poor, the president remarked, "excellent theme."[13] Secretary of Defense Melvin Laird stressed the benefits of a comprehensive overhaul. Contending that the existing system was "really nothing more than a Guaranteed Income Welfare Program," he was attracted to the notion of a "Work Incentive Welfare Program."[14] At an early briefing meeting for Republican skeptics, the president insisted that the existing system was a "disaster," for the very reason that Laird had mentioned. His arguments were recorded by Bryce Harlow, the press secretary: "He said that he is trying to accomplish two principal purposes—first, to stop the endless emigration of the poor into the cities from the rural areas and, second, to develop practical incentives to get people off of welfare rolls and onto payrolls."[15]

Although such conservative rationales for welfare reform were politically opportune, there is no reason to doubt their genuineness.[16] Nixon had told his key domestic advisers in January that "the American people are outraged and, in my view, they should be." His further remarks attest to another conservative rationale, namely an aversion to the welfare bureaucracy: "I do not want this swept under the rug or put aside on the ground that we want to have an 'era of good feeling' with the bureaucrats as we begin. This whole thing smells to high heaven and we should get charging on it immediately."[17] The plethora of new social welfare programs introduced during the 1960s had not only conspicuously failed to help the poor; they had, according to conservatives, extended the federal government's control over functions and decisions properly reserved for individuals, localities, and the states. An income strategy, if correctly employed, would enable the federal government to save money by dispensing with a whole range of costly and inefficient social welfare programs (AFDC, rent supplements, Model Cities, food stamps), together with the bureaucrats and social workers who dispensed them.

The Nixon administration was understandably anxious to distance the Family Assistance Plan from the philosophy of entitlement, and correspondingly happy to reveal that the father of the NIT concept was none other than Milton Friedman. In the March 1967 issue of *National Review*, the right-wing Chicago economist had told readers that the existing "grab bag of relief and welfare measures" in effect already amounted to "a governmentally guaranteed annual income." Unfortunately, the principal beneficiaries of the current system were neither the recipient nor the taxpayer, but rather the administrator:

> It involves a tremendous bureaucracy, widespread intervention into the operation of the market system in areas that have nothing to do with poverty, and inexcusable interferences with the individual freedom and dignity of the truly poor who receive assistance, let alone for the rest of us. Equally serious, it has the worst possible effect on incentives, because a dollar earned and revealed is a dollar of relief lost. It tends to produce poor people, and a permanent class of poor people living on welfare, rather than to help the unavoidably indigent.[18]

As has already been suggested, in terms of political calculation FAP was part of a wider bid to construct a New Republican Majority from the ruins of the New Deal Democratic order. If FAP is construed as a guaranteed income plan, then this seems somewhat curious, for surveys of public opinion reveal little enthusiasm for that concept. Asked in 1969 to adjudge a $3,200 guarantee, only 32 percent of Americans expressed support. The only group to support the plan were nonwhites, a group that Nixon did not in other respects seem particularly keen to woo. Even the poor expressed their opposition.[19] If one accepts, however, that Nixon conceived of FAP as something other than a guaranteed income, then his political equation becomes more comprehensible.

In 1969, the Republican strategist Kevin Phillips declared that "the election of Richard M. Nixon as president of the United States . . . bespoke the end of the New Deal Democratic hegemony and the beginning of a new era in American politics."[20] The Democrats had become imprisoned within an anachronistic and increasingly elitist New Deal ideology whose inevitable decline had been hastened by the excesses of liberalism in the 1960s. Phillips espied an "epochal shifting of national gears," derived from economic and demographic changes that had marginalized the traditional sources of Democratic strength:

> A generation ago, the coming of age of the working-class central cities condemned the Republican Party to minority status, but the new "urbanization"—suburbanization is often a better description—is a middle-class impetus shaping the same ignominy for the Democrats. All across the nation, the fastest growing urban areas are steadily increasing their *Republican* pluralities, while the old central cities—seat of the New Deal era—are casting steadily fewer votes for Democratic liberalism.[21]

If Nixon was enticed by this image of the *Emerging Republican Majority*, then he remained more persuaded than Phillips of the continuing appeal of aspects of the New Deal Democratic message. The resilience of traditional alignments had indeed been suggested by the outcome of the recent presidential contest. In August, Nixon had led Hubert Humphrey by as much as 24 percent, but by polling day, the Democrat's deficit was just 0.7 percent. If this comeback could be explained in substantial measure by Humphrey's belated decision to distance himself from "Johnson's War," then it also owed much to his aggressive defense of such popular Democratic social programs as social security and medicare. Only 29 percent of Americans considered themselves to be Republicans in 1969, compared to 42 percent who professed a Democratic allegiance.[22]

But voter disaffection with both Great Society liberalism and the New Politics was equally striking. Between 1963 and 1969, the number of Americans who identified themselves as liberals declined from 49 percent to 33 percent, a fact that clearly endangered the long dominance of the nation's more liberal political party.[23] Nixon was intrigued by the thesis of Richard Scammon and Ben Wattenberg, whose book *The Real Majority* posited the continued viability of New Deal liberalism. Advisers to President Johnson, the authors argued that the decline of *liberalism* owed more to the new associations of that term, than to a basic shift in the nation's ideology. Liberalism would not have been able to attract 49 percent of the American people in 1963 had that creed been identified with welfarism, antiwar protest, racial preference, and the rights of criminals. The successful politicians of the 1970s would be those who recognized that the average voter was "middle-income, middle-aged, middle-educated, and white."[24]

Nixon sought to exploit obvious sources of Democratic vulnerability (for example, by championing the cause of the "forgotten American"), while simultaneously appropriating the sources of its continuing strength. His attempt to reform the nation's welfare system provides a fascinating case study of both approaches. On the one hand, AFDC was a highly unpopular product of New Deal liberalism, and its abolition would win approval from the average American, whose backing Nixon sought. On the other hand, by replacing AFDC with a plan that extended aid to the working poor, included a work requirement, and raised benefits in low-payment states, the president could signal his solidarity with the plight of the deserving poor.

Again, the strongest advocate of welfare reform within the Nixon administration shrewdly exploited this wider political equation. Daniel Patrick Moynihan responded swiftly to the president's interest in a 1969 article in *New York* magazine entitled "The Revolt of the White Lower-Middle Class." Its author, Pete Hamill, was concerned with the recent alienation of white Brooklynites from the political system. Moynihan suggested that the Great Society's service strategy had "excluded the white working class" and fomented interracial and inter-class tensions. The principal beneficiaries of this strategy had been middle-class program administrators. Conversely, the poor gained little, but "the black poor *seem* to be being favored over the white near poor, the loud mouths get louder, and temperatures rise." By contrast, under the income strategy (comprising FAP, food stamps, revenue sharing, and tax reform) "the government does not seem to [be] playing favorites, by providing sumptuous special services for one group—public housing, welfare, compensatory education—while ignoring the needs of others who are only marginally better off."[25]

On another occasion, Moynihan reported a recent briefing that had left such powerful businessmen as Joseph Wilson of Xerox "immensely impressed" by HEW's proposed Family Security System (the forerunner to FAP):

On the way out, Arjay Miller of Ford took me aside and suggested I might tell you, for what it is worth, that in his opinion . . . if you can (1) get out of Vietnam, and (2) put through a Family Security System, the Republicans will become the majority party in the United States.

"You'll be in for twenty years," was his closing remark.[26]

LIBERALISM AND THE "WELFARE MESS"

Liberal and radical advocates of the income strategy concurred with Richard Nixon's sense that there existed a "welfare mess" and that the War on Poverty had largely failed. In their 1971 book *Freedom from Dependency*, Stanley and Glenn Esterly remark that Johnson's programs had amounted to "little more than a modestly financed skirmish." In their view, "the American public was oversold, and grossly so."[27] It had been "absurd" to argue "that the children of the poor can simply be educated out of poverty," when many Americans could not even afford a balanced diet.[28] The service strategy had its place, but income redistribution was a prerequisite to its success.

The logic of this position had of course become apparent to the antipoverty warriors at a very early stage—witness the number of income maintenance proposals that were submitted to President Johnson during the autumn of 1965. By the end of the decade, however, many liberals favored the NIT not as a means to an end but as an end in itself. Senator Fred Harris regretted the tendency to "forget that poverty, by definition, means lack of money." Existing policy was guided by "the idea that if we can just give enough advice and services to the poor, they will stop being poor," but in most cases "this myth is just not working." According to Harris's calculation, "two percent of the gross national product would bring everyone in the country up to a minimum standard of living and employment. This does not seem to be an improper or unreal goal."[29]

The magnitude of the philosophical shift embodied in Harris's 1970 position may be gauged from brief reference to the consensual assumptions of 1964. Then, Walter Heller, of the Council of Economic Advisors, had acknowledged that "one could conceive of a program which would tackle the problem simply by redistributing . . . less than 2 percent of our annual gross national product," but had gone on to remind congressmen considering the Economic Opportunity Act that "this would be an unacceptable 'solution' because it would leave the roots of poverty untouched and deal

219

only with its symptoms."[30] At the inception of the War on Poverty, this proposition had appeared self-evident to American liberalism, yet as policy-makers sought to assess the contribution of OEO programs six years later, the opposite conclusion seemed just as obvious. Two other prominent senators to address the same theme were Abraham Ribicoff and Jacob Javits, both enthusiastic advocates of self-help during the first half of the 1960s. Javits, appearing before a skeptical House Agriculture Committee in 1969, identified "a totally new approach to . . . helping the poor in this country" and celebrated "our new determination to put a floor under the income of the poor."[31] Ribicoff feared that "much of the money that is being spent to alleviate poverty does not bring a single person out of poverty." He was now prepared to countenance an income strategy that had seemed politically unrealistic to him in 1966: "We can . . . really take people out of poverty by providing them direct financial assistance."[32]

Ribicoff, like Harris, seems to have had no sense that he was not simply proposing new answers to an old question; rather, he was asking an entirely different question from the one posed in 1964. President Johnson had sought answers to the problem of inequality of opportunity rather than to that of inequality of material condition; indeed, the latter was only a problem insofar as it stemmed from blocked opportunity. Far from seeking to overturn the traditional undeserving/deserving poor dichotomy, he fully accepted its legitimacy. By contrast, the comprehensive income strategy to which liberals flocked during the late 1960s was predicated on the radical—not to mention unpopular—notion that individual behavior and status were not proper standards by which entitlement should be judged.

INITIAL RESPONSE TO FAP

President Nixon strove hard to present FAP as a new approach that nevertheless respected traditional values regarding work and self-support.[33] But a majority of Nixon's advisers remained suspicious of the initiative. Three months prior to its unveiling, Secretary of Commerce Maurice Stans insisted that HEW's proposal was "a covert adoption of the guaranteed income principle, which is objectionable on moral grounds and not supported by a majority of the public." He cautioned the president, "The reaction of the taxpaying public, particularly among those who supported you in 1968, would be overwhelmingly against giving money to people as a matter of right, without any question of their ability and willingness to work. The results, politically, could be very damaging."[34] Charles Colson warned that George Meany was "privately very much opposed to it and suspected that most rank and file labor opposed it." Accordingly, FAP was "counterproductive politically to our efforts with the average middle-class working man and the labor movement."[35] Responding to conservative apprehension, one administration official suggested that the plan be repackaged as the Christian Working Man's Anti-Communist National Defense Rivers and Harbors Act of 1969![36]

Ultimately, an inability to persuade sufficient numbers of conservatives of the merits of FAP would critically undermine the plan's prospects of success. Yet the short-term success of Nixon's strategy was evidenced by the generous responses of both politicians and the media to FAP. New York Mayor John Lindsay praised it as "the most important step forward by the federal government in its field for a generation," while another liberal Republican, Senator Edward Brooke of Massachusetts, hailed "the liberation of the poor from perpetual dependence on welfare."[37] From the conservative end of the spectrum, Wilbur Mills and his Republican counterpart on the Ways and Means Committee, John Byrnes—whose antipathy to welfare was well-known and whose support for FAP was essential to its passage through the House—were cautiously positive.[38] Even the *Wall Street Journal* tempered skepticism about the probable effectiveness of the work provisions with praise for the president's boldness in embracing the cause of radical reform.[39]

After eighteen days of hearings, the Ways and Means Committee in turn reported a largely intact administration bill by 21 votes to 3; the only opposition came from Phil Landrum, Omar Burleson (D-Tex.), and Al Ullman (D-Ore.). A few days later, on 16 April 1970, the bill secured House approval by the comfortable margin of 243 to 155, causing Gerald Ford to wonder at the "strong bipartisan support" which FAP was able to attract.[40]

Having steered FAP through the House, the bill's sponsors must have been confident about its chances of enactment. The uniform support of House liberals was particularly encouraging, given the relatively more progressive reputation of the Senate. Over the next few months, however, FAP was to suffer surprising and ultimately crippling blows from an incongruous alliance of liberals and conservatives on the Senate Finance Committee. The remainder of this chapter examines how liberal legislators whose support for FAP had appeared to be assured, came to be imprisoned by the ideology and interest groups to which they were beholden, such that in 1971 and 1972 they transferred their allegiance to a series of increasingly improbable radical alternatives, frequently—if absurdly—characterizing the Nixon bill as an "attack on the poor."

EARLY HOSTILITY FROM THE LEFT

Analysis of the politics of welfare reform during the Nixon years is complicated by the absence of discrete liberal and conservative positions on FAP. Nixon's eagerness to characterize his proposal as a blend of liberal and conservative perspectives created problems for partisan politicians who had acquired a taste for ideological purity over coalition-building during the previous few years. Vincent and Vee Burke, in their valuable account of the odyssey of FAP, propose a tripartite division between *reformers* (liberal and conservative supporters of FAP or some recognizably similar alternative), *antiwelfarists* (conservative enemies of FAP), and *antireformers* (liberal opponents of FAP).[41]

For the purposes of this chapter, the most salient distinction is between reformers and antireformers. The spectacle of liberal legislators taking the latter position because FAP represented an insufficient departure from the individualist tradition to which they, too, had previously subscribed—a stance that attempted to cast reformers as *traditionalists*—serves to illustrate starkly the scale and incongruity of the philosophical transformation with which this book is concerned.

An early indication that FAP might face serious opposition from the left came in December 1969, with the endorsement by the White House Conference on Food, Nutrition and Health of a $5,500 guaranteed annual income. President Nixon had convened the conference as a symbol of "the national commitment to put an end to hunger and malnutrition due to poverty in America," but delegates were stubbornly unimpressed by his recent and massive expansion of the food stamp program, accusing the administration of having failed to develop "any new or meaningful program."[42] The $5,500 alternative resulted from the intervention of the National Welfare Rights Organization (NWRO), which had responded to FAP with a "$5,500 or Fight" campaign, and whose activists disrupted the conference in a successful bid to further their cause. Hulbert Jones of the NWRO later recalled that the conference had been a significant "turning point" which gave the organization's position on FAP "a lot more support" within the liberal community.

The churlish response of the White House Conference to the Nixon welfare reform and hunger initiatives provides one more illustration of a recurrent theme of this period, namely that many self-identified liberals and radicals felt bound by both disposition and political necessity to take positions to the left of those who were not perceived as ideological comrades. Liberals who for three years had systematically distanced themselves from the social policies of Lyndon Johnson, despite the political impracticability of their preferred alternatives, were likely to find the prospect of rallying behind Richard Nixon even less attractive.[43] Whereas Johnson's brand of liberalism had elevated compromise and consensus, devotees of the new orthodoxy instinctively felt that any middle way must constitute a perfidious sellout. Frank Mankiewitz, who had worked for Robert Kennedy in 1968, observed that "the liberals and the welfare community, by and large, cannot take the Nixon reforms emotionally, and cannot afford them politically."[44] How much merit could there be in any proposal that was supported by Richard Nixon, Wilbur Mills, John Byrnes, and the National Association of Manufacturers, but opposed by the NWRO?

The response of the antireformers to FAP provides a good instance of this mentality. The administration bill, together with the new food stamps legislation, would have had a dramatic impact on malnutrition and poverty, particularly in the South, where the income of the typical eligible nonwhite family would have increased by more than $1,200.[45] Nevertheless, the White House Conference on Food, Nutrition, and Health felt justified in discounting the Nixon administration's actions in favor of an NWRO alternative whose cost was estimated by Charles Schultze at $71 billion per year and whose financing was calculated to require a surtax of 78 percent.[46]

The NWRO had good reason to promote a high income floor, and to view the failure of FAP with equanimity. Its members were, after all, located overwhelmingly in the ghettos of high-benefit Northern states. Although the organization was happy to exploit the hunger issue (as at the White House Conference), its principal policy mission was to protect the interests of constituents who would gain very little from FAP. (Indeed, FAP placed new restrictions on the rights of many AFDC recipients by requiring them to register for employment.)

Contributors to the White House Conference on Food, Nutrition and Health were not constrained in the same way, but presumably they viewed support for the NWRO proposal as evidence of their solidarity with the poor. Moynihan recalls that the $5,500 figure (upgraded to $6,500 in 1971) "became almost a talisman of advanced liberalism." Its proponents "were demanding economic ruin. But they did not know this, or if they knew it they did not care. The defeat of FAP became for many on the liberal left a truly impassioned cause, [evoking] an increasingly hysterical and irrational response."[47]

Vincent and Vee Burke attribute this response in part to the NWRO's ability to exploit the guilt that members of liberal pressure groups frequently felt "for being white and unpoor." They cite the example of the National Conference on Social Welfare, whose 1969 convention was disrupted by welfare rights militants, with the result that the conference awarded the NWRO a grant of $35,000.[48] Mitchell Ginsberg, former welfare commissioner for New York City, acknowledged that, as far as the National Association of Social Welfare was concerned, George Wiley's activists "can do no wrong. We can't take a position against NWRO. We *can't discuss* it."[49]

The unhappiness of some liberal legislators with the Nixon proposal became evident at an early stage in the battle for FAP. In January 1970, Senator George McGovern, chairman of the Senate's select committee on malnutrition and thus someone who might have been expected to welcome FAP, denounced Nixon's "poor people's approach" as one that would continue to stigmatize dependency. In its place, he proposed a four-part Human Security Plan, which featured a child allowance, a guaranteed jobs program, increased benefits for the elderly and disabled, and federal support for anyone in need who was not covered by the first three programs. Senator McGovern explained that his proposal "looks toward insuring each of our citizens against the risk of poverty, and doing so simply because we believe that this kind of minimum financial security should be a right of citizenship in our country." He envisaged "a fully federalized guaranteed income plan which dispenses a uniform national payment generous enough to lift every poor family out of poverty within a very few years."[50]

In the same month, Senator Fred Harris proposed a National Basic Income and Incentive Act, which proposed to guarantee every family an annual income of $3,600 at a cost of up to $20 billion per year. In justification for his proposal, Harris made the extraordinary claim that the Family Assistance Plan, "instead of raising families out of poverty, would mean for many a sad plunge into the lower depths of even greater poverty."[51] This remark referred to the $1,600 federal floor but ignored four simple facts about FAP: (1) the $1,600 would be supplemented by $800 worth of food stamps; (2) states with higher levels of AFDC benefits would be required to maintain existing payments (which they were not obliged to do under existing law); (3) existing benefits were even lower than $1,600 in six Southern states; and (4) Nixon's plan extended eligibility to millions of poor households headed by a low-income worker.

Senator Harris had for two years been engaged in a systematic bid to package himself as the tribune of the New Politics. As chairman of the Democratic National Committee after Larry O'Brien's resignation in 1968, Harris was responsible for the composition of the party's reform commission. During the 1968 campaign, he had been Hubert Humphrey's manager, but in its aftermath he concluded that his political interest was best served by wooing the forces of insurgency.[52]

Despite their votes in favor of FAP in April 1970, a number of House liberals voiced significant doubts, centering mainly on the alleged inadequacy of the income floor and the perceived inequity of the work requirement. The fiercest criticism came from Shirley Chisholm (D-N.Y.), the only black representative to oppose the bill in 1970. Charging that FAP "hedges on involuntary servitude with its compulsory work qualification," she contrasted its meager $1,600 allowance with the $42,000 salary that legislators had just approved for themselves.[53] William Ryan of New York was gracious in his praise for the president's boldness, but insisted that "a guaranteed annual income is not a privilege." Contrary to the administration's approach, "it should be a right to which every American is entitled."[54]

Congressman Ryan had proposed the first guaranteed income proposal to Congress in 1968, and in 1970—despite FAP—he chose to resubmit his Income Maintenance Act, with its guarantee set initially at $2,000 but designed to rise to the poverty level within five years. In addition to its higher benefit levels, the Ryan bill differed from FAP in including married couples without children and unattached individuals. Moreover, the Income Maintenance Act did not contain a work requirement, for its author believed that "forced work" was "alien to individual choice and freedom." The only concession that Ryan's bill would make to the work ethic— scarcely a harsh one—was to allow that "beneficiaries on a voluntary basis may request referral for participation in a work incentive program."[55] Defending his proposal before a dubious House Rules Committee, Ryan suggested that it was in fact a somewhat "modest" measure, and that "actually, $6,000 a year is the floor which the government ought to provide if we are really serious about solving the crisis in this country." He was not able to provide colleagues with an estimate as to the likely cost of his scheme.[56]

THE FALL OF FAP

On 29 April 1970, the Family Assistance Plan moved to the Senate Finance Committee, accompanied by the widespread feeling that the hardest part of the battle had been won. Almost immediately, however, the proposal suffered what proved to be a grievous blow, when Senator John J. Williams (R-Del.)—backed by Chairman Russell Long—launched a devastating attack on the likely effectiveness of its work incentives. In the middle of this assault from the right, Eugene McCarthy, also a member of the committee, elected to introduce the Senate to the NWRO's $5,500 guaranteed income proposal. The Minnesota Democrat gave two reasons why legislators should back its Adequate Income Act of 1970 in preference to FAP and similar proposals. First, "the projected income provided by many of these plans is too low to be adequate for families." Second, "the plans continue many traditional aspects of welfare programs which are not conducive to [the] freedom and self-respect of those who must use the system to survive."[57] Senator McCarthy anticipated that it would be "helpful and constructive" for the Finance Committee to have the opportunity to consider the NWRO's recommendations. Although "some aspects of the bill may be criticized as unrealistic," the "same may be said about the amounts provided under the proposals of President Nixon."[58]

On the other hand, the clear danger existed that uneasy conservative backers of FAP would turn against the cause of welfare reform, were they to conclude that Nixon's plan might become a Trojan horse for the more extravagant designs of the left. Many conservatives were already fearful that Nixon had been hoodwinked by Moynihan and HEW into backing FAP; some suspected that the president did not fully understand the fiscal and social implications of his own bill.[59] When administration representatives had met with welfare lobbyists in a bid to secure their early support for FAP, they had warned that demands for a more generous bill "would demonstrate to conservatives what they most fear—that benefits and coverage will grow, if this is enacted, until we do in fact have a very generous and costly guaranteed annual income."[60]

Four months later, FAP had successfully negotiated the House but was about to be frustrated in the Senate. One day after McCarthy had spoken out in favor of the $5,500 bill, the Finance Committee to which he belonged elected to return FAP to the administration for redrafting. But this move owed nothing to McCarthy's concerns, stemming instead from Long's fear that the proposal would create "notches" that made it more profitable to remain on welfare than to find work.[61] By the time hearings resumed in July to consider the administration's revised bill, the optimism of three months earlier had given way to a more sober appreciation of the threat posed to FAP by Finance Committee conservatives such as Long, Williams, and Herman Talmadge (D-Ga.). Such an appreciation did not prevent prominent liberals and black leaders from embracing ever more fanciful definitions of entitlement. Appearing before the Joint Economic Committee of Congress in June, Whitney Young—an archetype of black moderation—contended that FAP rested upon "a web of vengeful fantasies" together with "the relentless implication that the poor are shiftless, lazy, worthless and irresponsible, particularly toward each other, when, in truth, the poor are lacking in money." He added, "There is no acceptable rationale for establishing differentials among the poor. . . . A plan that would separate the working from the nonworking poor in terms of cash benefits . . . cannot be said to represent even-handed treatment of people equally in need."[62] Ironically, in view of the fact that he was testifying to the Joint Economic Committee's Subcommittee on Economy in Government, Young suggested that it was "fruitless to establish a grant at a level less than . . . $6,500 for a family of four."[63]

Although it is remarkable that the leader of the National Urban League should have combined so unrealistic a proposal with so comprehensive a misrepresentation of FAP, it should be recalled that Young's credibility as a spokesman for black America was significantly threatened by the growing power of the welfare rights militants. Similarly, in embracing proposals that had little chance of enactment—and, moreover, destroyed the legislative prospects of more modest versions—liberal legislators such as Eugene McCarthy, George McGovern, and Fred Harris were influenced by the growing political power of an increasingly cohesive New Politics coalition.

In 1968, the nascent New Politics agenda had been overwhelmingly dominated by the Vietnam War. By 1972, an extraordinarily diverse network of groups had developed, of which the NWRO was a part. When, in 1970, the organization occupied Secretary Finch's office at HEW, they reportedly demanded that "the Nixon Administration end its military activities in Cambodia and institute a guaranteed annual income of $5,500."[64] Reflecting the group's growing involvement in peace activities, George Wiley invited Benjamin Spock to speak at a forthcoming welfare rights rally in Boston. Wiley saw this as "an important step toward building nationwide grass roots pressure to change the nation's priorities, from an emphasis on death and destruction to one of peace and plenty." He told Spock that he hoped "this might be the beginning of a close working relationship with you and the interests you represent.[65]

Spock did indeed speak at the rally, and Wiley was able to inform the veteran peace campaigner that "our ladies were very turned on by you and your speech."[66] Further invitations followed, and by 1971 Spock was suggesting that the NWRO might care to help set up the New Party in California and an umbrella group called The Coalition, which comprised this venture and such other bodies as the Peace and Freedom Party and the D.C. Statehood Party.[67] Reference to George Wiley's papers for this period reveals that the NWRO had additional associations with Washington Area Citizens Against the ABM and the National Coalition on the Transportation Crisis.[68] Meanwhile, Aileen Hernandez, president of the National Organization of Women, expressed her keenness "to establish immediate and continuing liaison with the Welfare Rights Organization."[69]

The vigor, passion, funds, and networking ability of New Politics bodies commanded respect on the part of liberals with national political ambition, the more so since the old politics appeared discredited and lifeless by comparison. Following Lyndon Johnson's decision to stand down, traditional liberalism had finally prevailed over the insurgent forces of McCarthy and McGovern. Yet Hubert Humphrey's victory at Chicago had been a pyrrhic one, despite the closeness of the subsequent contest. Such was the momentum won by the antiwar forces, and so damaging were the machinations of the old guard at the national convention, that rebels were able to launch a Commission on Party Organization, headed by George McGovern. The implications of this development became apparent once campaigning for the 1972 Democratic nomination began in earnest.

In the meantime, the NWRO's increasing militancy, together with its impressive capacity to influence the policy positions of prominent liberal politicians, were dramatized anew in November 1970 when Russell Long—mindful, no doubt, of his 1967 confrontation with Wiley's welfare mothers—elected not to receive their testimony. Eager, like Young, to demonstrate his solidarity with the black poor, Eugene McCarthy responded by convening two days of highly publicized unofficial hearings on their behalf. The results were to prove disastrous for the cause of welfare reform.

Once Senator McCarthy had opted to oppose FAP, he was—in the view of Vincent and Vee Burke—"willing to do anything within reason to help NWRO's welfare mothers discredit it in the liberal community."[70] At the hearings, attended by ten liberal senators, angry welfare activists decried FAP as an attack on the poor and even as a "giant step backward." Nixon was intent on enslaving the black poor, but one mother told legislators that "we only want the kind of jobs that will pay $10,000 or $20,000. . . . We aren't going to do anybody's laundry or babysitting except for ourselves." Beulah Sanders, vice chairman of NWRO, insisted that "You can't force me to work! You'd better give me something better than I'm getting on welfare. I ain't taking it."[71] One welfare mother from Minnesota reportedly "said in a shaking voice that she would rather see her children *dead* than subject to the indignities of FAP."[72]

The McCarthy hearings were described by one columnist as a "lynching bee," but Nick Kotz, Moynihan, and the Burkes all believe that the NWRO's testimony played a decisive role in turning a majority of the liberal Democrats on the Finance Committee against FAP.[73] Fred Harris told the *New York Times* that "if [FAP's] bad features can't be eliminated, I think it ought to be killed, and we should start all over." The *Times* noted that the bill's enactment had been dependent on "solid support by liberals and moderates," and that even modest defections "appear[ed] almost certain to doom any such majority."[74] On 20 November 1970, FAP was duly defeated in committee by 10 votes to 6, with Abraham Ribicoff the only liberal to support the president. FAP's six conservative opponents were joined by Fred Harris, Eugene McCarthy, and Albert Gore (D-Tenn.).[75]

FAP AND THE 1972 PRESIDENTIAL CAMPAIGN

Despite the defeat of FAP in 1970, Nixon submitted a revised version the following year, presenting it as his "Number One legislative priority." Once again, the bill was approved by the House only to fail in the Senate. Yet its chances of enactment were never as good the second time around, and they diminished still further during the course of the 92d Congress. In August 1971, the bill suffered a serious loss of momentum when the president postponed the date of its intended introduction by twelve months as part of an economy package. The approach of the 1972 elections then played a further part in diminishing Nixon's enthusiasm for the cause of welfare reform, as did the increased association of that cause with radical doctrines of entitlement. Following the defeat of the first bill, influential liberal pressure groups, such as the Americans for Democratic Action and the National Council of Churches, moved from skepticism to outright opposition, while the NWRO launched an increasingly impassioned "Zap FAP" campaign.

When the House voted on H.R.1 (as the revised proposal was designated), the Congressional Black Caucus was almost unanimous in its opposition, despite the entreaties of black political leaders in the South.[76] Congressman Ron Dellums (D-N.Y.) denounced FAP as "racist and repressive," further contending that the reported committee bill "contains provisions which comprise a vicious attack on five million black women and children."[77] In April, all twelve members of the caucus, together with nine white legislators (five of them from New York), introduced the Adequate Income Act of 1971, featuring a guaranteed annual income of $6,500. And in its 1972 Black Declaration of Independence and Bill of Rights, the caucus demanded "that the Democratic Party oppose any welfare 'reform' program which fails to establish a one-year timetable for reaching a guaranteed adequate income system of a minimum of $6,500 a year for a family of four."[78]

In the Senate, the NWRO-drafted bill was introduced by George McGovern. Association with a proposal that set its income floor at twice the level resulting from a full-time minimum wage job was hardly likely to enhance his standing with those centrist Democrats whose support McGovern would be seeking in November 1972. Still, it would be quite wrong to ascribe his association with the bill either to the extremism of the true believer or the naïveté of a political novice. On the contrary, from the time when he announced his possible candidacy in 1969, McGovern was engaged in a highly calculated bid to assemble an initially unlikely winning coalition.

McGovern's welfare strategy provides an intriguing case study of this political calculation. He was already associated with the New Politics through his antiwar activism, his role in the 1968 campaign, and his chairmanship of the party reform commission. Byron Shafer explains that McGovern "believed that an eventual presidential nomination required the support of these reformers first, although he did not believe that they would be sufficient, and he did hope to blend them with party regulars once they had helped get his candidacy off the ground."[79] Addressing the reform commission in 1969, the candidate emphasized the insufficiency of the old politics:

> We in the Democratic Party know that something has gone very wrong. We understand (and surely the Republicans must too) that the quality of life we have always believed would one day be ours has eluded all of us—not just the poor in our ghettos or the young people who are showing us their rage and dismay—but businessmen, college professors, soldiers, factory workers and U.S. senators. All of us share the same sense of powerlessness and lack of control over our own destinies.[80]

For all its vagueness, this language faithfully echoed the existential voyages of such New Age sages as Charles Reich and Philip Slater. Moreover, it was calculated to appeal to a youth vote whose importance in the forthcoming contest was redoubled by demographic patterns and the reduction in the minimum age of voting from 21 to 18. In his 1970 book, *The Changing Sources of Power*, Frederick Dutton suggested that the baby boom generation (which would "soon be moving massively into the electorate") took prosperity for granted, and accordingly possessed values that were "less economic and more social." Increasingly, the salient political divide was not between liberals and conservatives but rather between "existentialists" and "philistines." The latter group was currently more numerous than the former and was composed, as Dutton dismissively noted, "of those who pursue the traditional 'American dream.'" But it was the existentialists who represented the wave of the future: "The existentialists are the vital, vocal elitists and activists of the new generation, very much the smaller of these two principal groups but the forward edge, 'the prophetic minority,' as they like to think of themselves."[81]

The mechanism by which courting this advance guard was to provide the basis for political success during the 1970s was not made clear, but presumably Dutton envisaged something like Jack Newfield's touted alliance of "campus, ghetto, and suburb."[82] Even if McGovern did not view this combination as sufficient, he clearly had to cement the allegiance of Dutton's enlightened existentialists. His 1972 campaign literature rejected the old politics in striking terms: "Labels such as liberal and conservative have clearly lost any meaning they might have had. The old ideologies of the last decade are no longer relevant. . . . The contest now is not liberal–conservative, but old–new, status quo–change."[83] In more concrete terms, appealing to the New Politics meant assuring its exponents that he embodied the full range of their preoccupations, and not simply their antiwar convictions. One campaign adviser was worried that McGovern came across as a one-issue candidate. If he wished to succeed, Ted Van Dyk argued, he must start debating a range of domestic issues: "In our discussions, quite frankly, I don't get much feeling that you really know or care too much about these things."[84] It was partly within this context that welfare rights advocacy assumed its importance.

But McGovern's candidacy was a long shot; he could not afford to alienate the conservative rural voters of his home state if he wished to retain his Senate seat. Accordingly, while assuring the NWRO of his abhorrence of even the most trivial work requirement, the senator shared with home-state correspondents his abiding distaste for welfare. McGovern's mail was filled with complaints from voters like Mrs. Louis Remnitz of Corsica, South Dakota, who was offended by his objections to FAP's modest work requirement: "I'm afraid an awful lot of us common people resent your statement that people are forced to take jobs beneath their dignity. Their [sic] just isn't such a thing."[85] Responding to such complaints, McGovern signed letters expressing the conviction that "there are far too many people who take advantage of the welfare program."[86] He shared his stern views on the subject with W. H. Sill, Jr., of Vermillion, South Dakota: "It is my view that we should move in the direction of reducing our welfare rolls to only those who are physically incapable of working."[87]

For the purposes of the 1972 primary campaign, however, McGovern seemed less attached to the work ethic. Interviewed by NBC in January, he said, "I would just provide that every person in this country is given a certain minimum income. If he wants to work in addition to that, he keeps what he earns," subject to taxation. But, as he told another interviewer in May, "You can't force somebody to work if they don't want to work."[88] This message proved offensive not just to voters in his home state but to traditional Democratic constituencies throughout the country.[89] Pondering the candidate's general detachment from mainstream sentiment, Ted Van Dyk found himself troubled by McGovern's forthright admission that he was not a centrist: "We've made a great deal recently of the nonexistence of any 'center' in American politics. Yet I'm sure the vast majority of voters perceive themselves as *centrist*."[90] If he were to win the primary campaign, however, McGovern had little choice but to woo the distinctly noncentrist constituencies that controlled the nominating process.

The centerpiece of McGovern's welfare program by this time was not the NWRO proposal but rather a "demogrant" proposal, under which "every man, woman and child" would receive an annual payment from the federal government, regardless of income. As one of three illustrations, he proposed a figure of $1,000 per person, to the delight of his rival for the Democratic nomination, Hubert Humphrey, who suggested in debate that such a scheme might cost upwards of $210 billion per year.[91] A bewildered Lyndon Johnson reportedly remarked, "It is a damn fool idea and probably is the best asset that Nixon has."[92] Similarly skeptical was an otherwise supportive economics professor from Minnesota who remarked dryly that "feelings are strong outside academia that the parasite option is intolerable."[93] McGovern himself reportedly told campaign organizers, "I wish that I had never heard of the goddamn idea."[94]

Having defeated Humphrey, the stubborn defender of New Deal liberalism, McGovern did make some effort to appease traditional Democrats. Indeed, during the fall campaign, he went so far as to castigate the Nixon administration for having added $5 billion to welfare rolls. Deploying rhetoric previously reserved for the voters of his home state, the senator insisted that "no one who can work should be on welfare."[95] But as with so many aspects of his ultimately disastrous campaign, he was unable to shed associations that had been forced upon him by the power of the New Politics insurgents within his party.

Meanwhile, the cause of welfare reform suffered a by now inevitable defeat. It is not possible to say that liberal hostility was primarily responsible for the death of the Family Assistance Plan: despite the conservative rationale outlined by Nixon, it was never going to be easy for the administration to present FAP as congruent with national attitudes toward work and dependency. Had FAP been proposed in 1964, as an alternative to the Economic Opportunity Act, it would have been dismissed with scorn by adherents to a liberal tradition that celebrated the nation's dominant individualism and understood its political importance. Six years later, the combined effects of policy failure, racial unrest, and the Vietnam War had so transformed the political landscape of America that FAP could not only be sponsored by Richard Nixon but could be assailed by the new liberal orthodoxy for excessive fealty to the individualist tradition.

CONCLUSION

Many liberals who had endorsed the self-help ethos of President Johnson's War on Poverty in 1964 came, by 1972, to embrace a very different approach, one that emphasized entitlement rather than opportunity. That their new orthodoxy represented the dominant strain was indicated by the liberal response to FAP. Nevertheless, the concept of an unconditional entitlement to income was singular in a number of respects. First, it boldly confronted notions of reciprocal responsibility that had been long-accepted and retained widespread support, even among the poor. Second, such proposals as the Adequate Income Act of 1972 rested on the assumption that the causes of poverty were inseparable from its consequences: poverty was caused as well as defined by inadequate income. Such a judgment validated the redistributionist approach that had been rejected in 1964.

Finally, the new liberal orthodoxy embodied entirely different conceptions of dignity and dependency than had the Economic Opportunity Act. In 1964, liberals had shared the general tendency to equate dignity with self-sufficiency and to define dependency as its destructive opposite: long-term reliance on federal support. The evidence of Senator McGovern's mail suggests that this remained the popular view. But by 1972, it had become more common for liberals to define dignity as freedom both from hardship and from the stigma hitherto attached to dependency. In turn, independence, far from connoting self-sufficiency in the conventional sense, meant freedom from want, however achieved. Dependency, in the old sense, was almost equated with independence in the new.[1]

The importance of entitlement liberalism does not lie in its policy accomplishments. Insofar as the doctrine had policy consequences, they

235

were the result of the reaction *against* a philosophy which never won much popular backing. The conservative reaction against the assumptions of the guaranteed income movement included a growing political interest in attaching work requirements to AFDC. This countertendency found substantive expression with Governor Reagan's "workfare" experiment in California and Senator Herman Talmadge's 1971 bid to improve the effectiveness of the Work Incentive Program.

During the 1970s, the traditional dichotomy between the deserving and undeserving poor, far from being erased (as entitlement liberals had hoped), was reinforced. Even as they consigned the Family Assistance Plan to defeat in October 1972, legislators simultaneously enacted the Supplemental Security Income program (SSI), guaranteeing an index-linked federal income to the aged, blind, and disabled. This was the first federal guarantee other than that for veterans, and it removed from state welfare rolls all of the categories covered by the Social Security Act (as amended), other than families with dependent children. By 1986, the federal government spent more on SSI than on AFDC,[2] yet the program's enactment was—as Wilbur Cohen marveled—"[not] even controversial."[3]

Four months prior to enacting SSI, Congress had approved a 20 percent increase in social security payments. In the view of Congressman Byrnes of Wisconsin, such an increase threatened the actuarial soundness of the program, yet in an election year the measure passed the Senate by 82 votes to 4, and the House by 302 to 35. Robert M. Ball, commissioner for Social Security, announced that "in truth we have a new social security program—a program that provides a new level of security to working people of all ages and to their families."[4] Martha Derthick observes that interest in poverty "lent momentum to welfare legislation generally, and because social security was the most popular and feasible form of such legislation, it won support when more controversial forms were stymied."[5] Secretary Elliot Richardson, like his recent predecessors at HEW, tended to "support big increases in social security because that was the only place where big increases in social welfare spending could easily be had."[6]

The principal beneficiaries of this turbulent period in social policy, therefore, were the elderly and the disabled. By contrast, those whom the entitlement liberals had endeavored to help, the "undeserving poor," were victims of a growing backlash. Three weeks after the death of FAP and one week after George McGovern's crushing defeat by President Nixon, Mitchell Ginsberg—former commissioner for welfare in New York City and an early disciple of entitlement—told the *Los Angeles Times* that "the hatred of welfare is unbelievable. There is a strong mood across the country to crack down, keep people off the rolls. Welfare reform is at a dead end. . . . We are now in the midst of a very sharp swing against doing something for the poor, for minorities." In recent years, Ginsberg had become increasingly insistent that the nation respect the rights of a newly assertive poor. (In 1967 he had warned Senator Joseph Clark's subcommittee of the need for a revolution in antipoverty strategy.) In effect, the failure of welfare reform allowed Ginsberg to rediscover the virtues of traditional liberalism, particularly the value of congruence with—and respect for—popular sentiment:

> It is clear that people like me who have been pushing for reform for years obviously haven't made too much progress. . . . We underestimated the depth of the opposition. We didn't pay enough attention to the concerns of people who were above the welfare line. The heart of the opposition to welfare comes from people just above it—blue-collar workers, trade unionists, though not labor leaders or high-level businessmen. It is the group below, the lower-middle-income worker. He's the guy who feels welfare is taking it away from him. We will have to pay attention to the ethnic groups who feel more threatened by "them."[7]

In the aftermath of the failure of the entitlement revolution, Ginsberg's new two-part antipoverty plan attested to his rediscovery of opportunity liberalism. First, he proposed the expansion of health programs, better education, and further social security increases. Second, he recommended tax credits as a way of assisting the working poor (a proposal that bore fruit with the enactment of the Earned Income Tax Credit). Above all, public policy had to embody a philosophy that Middle America found acceptable. "The alliance of welfare clients, social workers and minorities won't do it," Ginsberg said. "They don't have enough influence. We have to move out to some other groups that we have too often disregarded."[8]

Sobered by the lessons of the failed battle for welfare reform, growing numbers of liberals underwent the same process of education, relearning lessons about popular individualism that had only recently been self-evident. As the prospect for reform diminished in 1971, an aide suggested that Jacob Javits might want to rethink proposals that he had sponsored the previous year:

> I see that you had one to completely eliminate any work requirements for women with school-age children. While at first glance this appears to be a liberal position, I believe that we should stop thinking of work requirements as punitive, and instead think of the potential therein for lifting an entire family unit out of the demoralizing poverty-welfare cycle.

237

Part of the problem the working classes have with welfare is because liberals have created the impression that work is somehow punishment. They justifiably wonder why they are working (subject to "punishment") while the government seems to believe that it's unfair or unjust to require welfare recipients to work.[9]

In conclusion, Javits's aide asked, "Why aren't we saying that we're giving the unfortunate an opportunity to be trained, to gain self-respect and a sense of achievement—a job?" Such rationales would indeed be deployed in support of welfare reform packages later in the decade, most notably President Carter's Program for Better Jobs and Income.[10] More generally, the mid-1970s featured renewed liberal interest in proposals to guarantee a job to every American.[11] Correspondingly, talk of an unconditional right to income largely disappeared from the language of liberalism.

If the entitlement revolution failed to reap substantive legislative reward, then neither did it have any discernable impact on attitudes to dependency, save perhaps to reinforce the traditional animus to which Ginsberg referred. During the next two decades, poverty among the elderly underwent a sharp decline, thanks to social security and SSI, but the same years saw an alarming increase in the number of poor children. Daniel Patrick Moynihan observes that, in a historic reversal of traditional patterns, "the rate of poverty among the very young in the United States has become nearly seven times as great as among the old."[12] But despite the growth of poverty among youth, and the growing incidence of female-headed families, the number of children receiving AFDC actually declined after 1972, as did the real value of benefits to individual families. Between 1972 and 1987, welfare payments as a proportion of GNP fell from 0.60 percent to 0.36 percent.[13] And between 1972 and 1984, the combined average value of AFDC and food stamp payments to a family of four declined, in real terms, by 20 percent.[14]

In political terms, portentous—although more amorphous—legacies become apparent if one conceives of this abortive entitlement revolution as being part of a wider crisis of American liberalism. In this context, the costs of the Democratic Party's deviation from the New Deal tradition are readily apparent. Within eight years, the party of the "common man" underwent an astonishing transformation in ideology, such that by 1972 it could credibly be characterized by President Nixon and Vice President Spiro Agnew as the party of the "limousine liberals." This book has explored just one component of that metamorphosis, but the dynamics of change upon which it has focused have broader applicability.

For all its deviant qualities and unintended consequences, the entitlement revolution is susceptible to a rational explanation. Such an explanation must answer two related questions. First, why did policymakers on both the left and the right come to embrace the income maintenance response to poverty during the 1960s? And second, why did liberals do so to a degree that required them to endorse radically unpopular notions of unconditional entitlement? If the two questions are related, then the underlying dynamics are to some extent separable.

In intellectual terms, an important aspect of both problems is that the previously favored service strategy for combating deprivation simply became less plausible as the War on Poverty progressed. At the same time, its logical implausibility became politically problematic. The key factor in both instances was race. The Economic Opportunity Act of 1964 was founded on two vulnerable premises concerning the practicability of self-help. First, it tacitly assumed that the deserving poor could be raised to comfortable self-sufficiency were they furnished with appropriate skills and values (self-esteem, motivation, education, vocational skills). The War on Poverty thereby operated on the basis that the U.S. economic system was fundamentally beneficent. Second, the program was ostensibly colorblind; it proceeded from the claim that black and white poverty could be treated by the same individualistic methods.

The intellectual vulnerability of these claims was clear from the outset to many politicians, bureaucrats, and academics, but in terms of the political purpose of the War on Poverty in 1964, such vulnerability was not important. It gratified the crusading liberal impulse for such a war to be declared, but no immediate pressure for victory existed. More important, if some policymakers did worry about the peculiar nature of black poverty or the structural problems of the American economy, even they shared the overriding liberal conviction that any problem susceptible to definition had a solution. It was this hubristic conviction that underpinned the belief that liberal social engineers could exploit new knowledge to empower the individual and lessen his or her dependence on welfare.

By the summer of 1965, both of these fragile premises had suffered grievous blows, while the administration's political equation had also changed. In his Great Society address at Ann Arbor, President Johnson had seemed to envision a new "era of good feelings" based on the consensual pursuit of enlightened liberal goals. A year later, his commencement address at Howard University even sought to envelop an unprecedentedly ambitious civil rights agenda within that consensus. But the Watts riot both symbolized and accelerated a rising tide of militancy within black America, a tide that abruptly destroyed the luxury of autonomous activism that Johnson had hitherto enjoyed. From now until the end of his troubled presidency, Johnson would be responding to events that he was increasingly powerless to influence.

As racial tension increased, political pressures on the War on Poverty from both left and right mounted. Meanwhile, the intellectual basis for an unalloyed service strategy was greatly undermined. Within the administration, domestic policymakers devised new approaches to poverty that retained traditional objectives but incorporated a strong new income maintenance component; only when income were redistributed, it was now acknowledged, could opportunity be equalized. Outside the administration, vocal antipoverty activists and black militants were going much further, questioning the entire legitimacy of the Economic Opportunity Act's "blaming the victim" approach. In their response to the Moynihan Report, and with their contributions to the November 1965 planning conference "To Fulfill These Rights," such radicals developed a fundamentally new approach to tackling poverty: redistribute income and expect nothing in return.

With the War on Poverty now so strongly associated with the black struggle for equality, supporters of the Economic Opportunity Act felt inevitably reluctant to demand that the rights of the poor be contingent on their behavior. If through its social policy American society was atoning for 350 years of racial oppression (and President Johnson had implied such a connection at Howard University), how could it justly demand anything in return? Liberal guilt, uncertainty, and apprehension were to be shrewdly exploited in the years to come, as for example by the black-dominated National Welfare Rights Organization. Moreover, the success of George Wiley's campaign to organize welfare mothers in defense of their rights and in pursuit of a guaranteed income placed pressure on more traditional groups (such as the National Urban League) to move leftward.

The liberal constituency most obviously vulnerable to NWRO guaranteed income advocacy was the welfare bureaucracy. By the latter half of the Johnson presidency, both HEW and OEO administrators and social workers were demonstrably anxious to appease demands to which they were in some measure already drawn by preference. Elected politicians, however, were more resistant to the income strategy in general, and seemingly impervious to the argument that long-term dependency was an acceptable response to able-bodied poverty. From the vantage point of the presidency, budgetary and economic strains, together with the growing conservatism of Congress and the nation, limited Johnson's ability to respond to the ever more insistent demands of the radicals. In so suddenly adverse an environment, what could he do other than pursue the gradualist approach that alone could command legislative approval and public consent? In this context, the instinctive sympathy Johnson felt for traditional and limited definitions of income entitlement was compounded by political necessity.

Liberal legislators, too, were initially cautious in embracing radical critiques of Great Society liberalism. During the first half of 1966, serious criticism of the president's domestic policies did begin to materialize, but attacks tended to focus on the size of Great Society programs rather than on their orientation. As the year wore on, however, ambitious liberal senators, such as Robert Kennedy and Abraham Ribicoff, progressively sharpened their critiques, beginning to demand basic redirection. An important source of such disengagement and restlessness was political opportunism. President Johnson's political authority and personal popularity were being dramatically weakened as the war in Vietnam intensified.

Vietnam's importance to the entitlement revolution is profound, albeit indirect. First, the bitterness and ill will it generated within liberal ranks inevitably impeded cooperation on domestic matters, and not simply because the war diverted funds from Great Society programs. Second, the language and style of protest represented by the growing antiwar movement came to be viewed by some dissenting politicians as embodying a New Politics through which the progressive spirit might yet emerge ascendant from the ashes of 1960s liberalism. By 1968, and much more strongly so thereafter, the NWRO was part of an extraordinarily eclectic and energetic coalition of discontents.

When Robert Kennedy observed in 1967 that the perspective of the New Left would soon constitute accepted orthodoxy, he was pondering a political landscape in which war, youth, dissent, and rioting had seemingly destroyed the basis for Democratic dominance. Equally, he contemplated dislocating events at home whose projection into the future might render transient the repressive spirit abroad in the land in 1966–1967. And even were that not the case, the strength of the New Politics within the Democratic Party was such that any serious bid for the presidential nomination must necessarily court the forces of dissent.

Only in 1970 did radical definitions of income entitlement gain important support among liberals. Not surprisingly, their principal exponents were politically ambitious Democrats with particular reason to display fealty

to the New Politics coalition: Fred Harris, Eugene McCarthy, George Mc-
Govern. In a different political context, they might have responded to
ghetto unrest and the failure of the War on Poverty by proposing to guarantee work to every American, an approach that would have boosted family
income without offending the work-oriented values of the American public.
Cost was one inhibiting factor, and legacies from the 1940s (when full
employment liberalism had suffered a historically important defeat) may
have constituted a second.[15] Equally, however, retaining the link between
economic security and employment would have offended the welfare rights
lobby, which advocated a different form of entitlement: George Wiley had
declared his goal to be "a guarantee[d] minimum income for every citizen
without any exception, whether they work or not, whether they're able to
work or not."[16] Once George McGovern had won the Democratic nomination in 1972, thanks to the backing of a New Politics coalition which
included the NWRO, he did indeed emphasize the employment route to
economic security.

Yet by this time, the guaranteed income movement had deeper foundations than such unalloyed opportunism might imply. In addition to self-
interest dictated by the strength of the New Politics coalition, there had
occurred within liberal ranks a more general eroding of the traditional
emphasis on mutual obligation. As the poor ceased to be conceived as citizens with responsibilities and instead were cast in the role of societal victims,
obligations of citizenship that had been unquestioned in 1964 ceased to
seem appropriate.

President Johnson, despite himself, had contributed to this process with
the Howard University address. Subsequently, the 1966 report of his Advisory Council on Public Welfare boldly repudiated traditional expectations
regarding the dependent poor. Its title, "Having the Power, We Have the
Duty," may have been drawn from Lyndon Johnson's speech declaring war
on poverty just two years before, but the "duties" that the phrase denoted
were substantially enlarged. Meanwhile, within Congress, the furious reaction of some Senate liberals to the WIN Amendments of 1967 had attested
to their recent loss of interest in the principle of self-help. And in 1968, the
Kerner Commission's verdict on the previous summer's riots had apportioned rights and responsibilities in such a way that they appeared mutually
exclusive rather than complementary.

The sheer breadth of support for the income strategy by this stage
undoubtedly lent additional momentum to entitlement liberalism. Within
the federal bureaucracy, among academics, in the business community and

within both political parties, the manifest failings of the War on Poverty had produced the conviction that income maintenance represented a more realistic response to deprivation. As has been seen, this conviction had first appeared within the Johnson administration as early as 1965, but as a means to the rehabilitative end rather than as an end in itself. Similarly, for Richard Nixon and Wilbur Mills, FAP would ultimately ease chronic dependency and protect the work ethic by extending support to the working poor. In this context, despite widespread support for some version of the income strategy during the Nixon years, entitlement liberalism as embodied by the Adequate Income Act of 1972 remains a singular phenomenon.

Having reached its zenith in opposition to President Nixon's welfare reform proposal, entitlement liberalism disappeared from view during the course of the 1970s and 1980s without having achieved any of its objectives. Such historians as Alonzo Hamby, contemplating the odyssey of American liberalism since Roosevelt, have associated President Johnson with the "politics of excess," arguing that it was with his leadership that the New Deal liberal tradition reached and overstretched its limits. In a similar vein, contemporary politicians and political commentators tend to characterize President Clinton's pledge to "end welfare as we know it" as a retreat from the big government activism of the New Deal and the Great Society.

Yet the case of welfare policy suggests that such interpretations are fundamentally flawed. In truth, both Franklin Roosevelt and Lyndon Johnson shared a sensitivity to their nation's dominant social philosophy and consistently resisted the counsel of those who found the traditional connection between work and economic security anachronistic. It was Johnson's liberal detractors and successors who abandoned a venerable tradition of liberal individualism, and they did so with politically costly results. With the "New Covenant" that he unveiled in 1988 and subsequently invoked again as president, Bill Clinton simply rediscovered a temporarily discarded old covenant whose principles had been central to the Economic Opportunity Act of 1964.[17] The crusading optimism of the War on Poverty was conspicuously absent, and the question of how to restore the dependent poor to employment had yielded some different answers.[18] Still, the question was the same and, to an as yet unacknowledged degree, the politics of welfare had come full circle.

NOTES

Introduction

1. *Congressional Quarterly Almanac, 1988,* 349.

2. Lawrence Mead, *Beyond Entitlement* (New York: Free Press, 1986), 17.

3. *Views of the National Governors' Association on Major Legislative Proposals,* Hearings before House Committee on Ways and Means, House of Representatives, 100th Congress, 1st Session, 24 Feb. 1987, 5. (Together with all subsequently cited congressional hearings and reports, these hearings were published in Washington, D.C., by the Government Printing Office.) For an introduction to the work requirement of the Family Support Act and to its historical context, see Desmond S. King, "Citizenship as Obligation in the United States: Title II of the Family Support Act of 1988," in Ursula Vogel and Michael Moran, eds., *The Frontiers of Citizenship* (London: Macmillan, 1991), 1–31. For the impact of the Title II JOBS program, see Judith M. Gueron, "The Route to Welfare Reform: From Welfare to Work," *Brookings Review* 12 (Summer 1994), 14–17.

4. Quotes from *Congressional Record,* 15 Dec. 1987, 35693 (Dorgan); and ibid., 16 Dec. 1987, 35834 (Espy). For these and other statements of support and opposition see *Congressional Digest,* Feb. 1988, 40–63.

5. *Congressional Quarterly Weekly Report,* 18 July 1987, 1587.

6. For the historical antecedents of the ideas that constituted the welfare "consensus" of the 1980s, see Hugh Heclo, "Poverty Politics," in Sheldon H. Danziger, Gary D. Sandefur, and Daniel H. Weinberg, eds., *Confronting Poverty: Prescriptions for Change* (Cambridge, Mass.: Harvard University Press, 1994), 396–437.

7. For particularly incisive accounts of this process, see Daniel Patrick Moynihan, *The Politics of a Guaranteed Income* (New York: Random House, 1973); and James T. Patterson, *America's Struggle Against Poverty, 1900–1985* (Cambridge, Mass.: Harvard University Press, 1986).

8. See Robert A. Levine, *The Poor You Need Not Have with Ye: Lessons from the War on Poverty* (Cambridge, Mass.: M.I.T. Press, 1970); and Nicholas Lemann, *The Promised Land: The Great Migration and How It Changed America* (London: Macmillan, 1991).

9. Mead, *Beyond Entitlement,* chapters 2, 3, 5.

10. This view is perhaps most commonly associated with Frances Fox Piven and Richard A. Cloward, *Poor People's Movements: How They Succeed, Why They Fail* (New York: Vintage, 1977), chapter 5; and *Regulating the Poor: The Functions of Public Welfare* (New York: Vintage, 1971), chapters 8–10.

11. Lawrence Mead claims that "the economic approach to poverty was indifferent to the moralistic concerns that had animated earlier approaches to welfare" (Mead, *Beyond Entitlement,* 98). Other scholars who have stressed the role of social science and bureaucratic elites in the rise of the guaranteed income include Michael B. Katz, *The Undeserving Poor: From the War on Poverty to the War on Welfare* (New York: Pantheon, 1989), and Patterson, *America's Struggle.* Martin Anderson, recalling his own experience within the Nixon administration, ascribes FAP to a bureaucratic plot that ensnared an unsuspecting president. See Anderson, *Welfare: The Political Economy of Welfare Reform in the United States* (Stanford, Calif.: Hoover Institution Press, 1978).

12. See chapter 9.

13. An extensive political science literature considers the dynamics and effects of this process, contributing to a debate initially stirred by Kevin Phillips, Richard Scammon, and Ben Wattenberg. See, in particular, Thomas B. Edsall and Mary Edsall, *Chain Reaction: The Impact of Race, Rights, and Taxes on American Politics* (New York: Norton, 1991); Byron E. Shafer, *Quiet Revolution: The Struggle for the Democratic Party and the Shaping of Post-Reform Politics* (New York: Russell Sage Foundation, 1983); Jonathan Rieder, "The Rise of the Silent Majority," in Steve Fraser and Gary Gerstle, eds., *The Rise and Fall of the New Deal Order* (Princeton, N.J.: Princeton University Press, 1989), 243–268; James L. Sundquist, *The Dynamics of the Party Systems* (Washington, D.C.: Brookings Institution, 1973); Richard Scammon and Ben Wattenberg, *The Real Majority* (New York: Coward-McCann, 1970); and Kevin Phillips, *The Emerging Republican Majority* (New Rochelle, N.Y.: Arlington House, 1969).

14. Shafer, *Quiet Revolution,* 7.

15. See Katz, *Undeserving Poor,* and Lemann, *Promised Land.* Katz's analysis contains a valuable summary of changing intellectual conceptions of rights during this period, including welfare rights and the ideas of John Rawls and Charles Reich. Broader studies, which approach the question of expanding definitions of entitlement from different angles, include Henry Abraham, *Freedom and the Court: Civil Rights and Liberties in the United States,* 5th ed. (New York: Oxford University Press, 1988), and the epilogue to Daniel T. Rodgers, *Contested Truths: Keywords in American Politics Since Independence* (New York: Basic Books, 1987).

16. Mead, *Beyond Entitlement,* 33.

17. Their actual benefits, however, may have fallen primarily to the activists and bureaucrats who administered the antipoverty programs, as Daniel Patrick Moyni-

han contends in *Maximum Feasible Misunderstanding: Community Action in the War on Poverty* (New York: Free Press, 1969).

18. Important works that emphasize dynamics other than the individualistic ideal include Linda Gordon, *Pitied But Not Entitled: Single Mothers and the History of Welfare* (New York: Free Press, 1994); and Jill Quadagno, *The Color of Welfare: How Racism Undermined the War on Poverty* (New York: Oxford University Press, 1994). These works assert, respectively, that gender and race have been consistently important determinants of social policy. Meanwhile, Margaret Weir and Theda Skocpol each view the state as a powerful actor in its own right. See Weir, *Politics and Jobs: The Boundaries of Employment Policy in the United States* (Princeton, N.J.: Princeton University Press, 1992); and Skocpol, *Protecting Soldiers and Mothers: The Political Origins of Social Policy in the United States* (Cambridge, Mass.: Harvard University Press, 1992).

19. Mary Ann Glendon contends that Americans have always been more inclined to identify their rights than to acknowledge their responsibilities. See Glendon, *Rights Talk: The Impoverishment of Political Discourse* (New York: Free Press, 1988.)

20. Mead, *Beyond Entitlement,* 189.

21. Ibid., 213. Considering welfare rights advocacy in the context of a wider rights revolution, June Axinn and Herman Levin conclude that the "historical value of individualism had been broadened to a demand for group-determined rights," in *Social Welfare: A History of the American Response to Need,* 2nd ed. (New York: Longman, 1982), 287.

22. For characteristically existential versions of the New Politics credo, see Charles A. Reich, *The Greening of America* (New York: Random House, 1969); and Frederick G. Dutton, *The Changing Sources of Power: American Politics in the 1970s* (New York: McGraw-Hill, 1970). For a historical overview, see John Patrick Diggins, *The American Left in the Twentieth Century* (New York: Harcourt Brace Jovanovich, 1973); and Christopher Lasch, *The Agony of the American Left* (New York: Knopf, 1969). For a recent exploration of the contrast between the old politics and the new, see Steven Gillon, *The Democrats' Dilemma: Walter F. Mondale and the Liberal Legacy* (New York: Columbia University Press, 1992), especially 103.

23. William H. Chafe, *Never Stop Running: Allard Lowenstein and the Struggle to Save American Liberalism* (New York: Basic, 1993), xvi.

24. George H. Gallup, *The Gallup Poll, 1935–1971,* vol. 3 (New York: Random House, 1972), 2177. Any attempt to implement this preference would have conflicted with similarly strong feelings about such matters as taxation and the size of government. But the distinction between attitudes toward unconditional versus conditional income maintenance remains instructive.

1. Historical Context of the War on Poverty

1. For the nature and contradictions of American individualism see Yehoshua Arieli's invaluable book, *Individualism and Nationalism in American Ideology* (Cam-

bridge, Mass.: Harvard University Press, 1964), chapters 9 to 15. Also useful are J. R. Pole, *The Pursuit of Equality in American History* (Berkeley: University of California Press, 1978), chapter 5; and Robert N. Bellah et al., *Habits of the Heart: Individualism and Commitment in American Life* (New York: Harper & Row, 1986), chapters 2, 3, 6, and 7. Some helpful insights are to be found in Louis Hartz, *The Liberal Tradition in America* (New York: Harcourt Brace Jovanovich, 1955), chapters 1, 2, and 5; and in Seymour Martin Lipset, *The First New Nation* (New York: Doubleday, 1967), chapters 1 to 3. For a well-chosen selection of documents treating the history of American individualism, see Moses Rischin, ed., *The American Gospel of Success: Individualism and Beyond* (Chicago: Quadrangle, 1968).

2. For a magisterial introduction to early usages of the term individualism, see J. R. Pole, *American Individualism and the Promise of Progress* (New York: Oxford University Press, 1980). A stimulating analysis of the "permanent dualism" created by the simultaneous attachment of Americans to individualism and mutualism is provided by Hugh Heclo, "General Welfare and Two American Political Traditions," *Political Science Quarterly* 101 (Summer 1986), 179–196.

3. In addition to Bellah et al., *Habits of the Heart,* and Arieli, *Individualism and Nationalism,* see Nathan Hatch, *The Democratization of American Christianity* (New Haven: Yale University Press, 1988). Hatch shows that some popular religious movements of the period associated wealth with moral bankruptcy. See especially page 117 for his treatment of the early Mormon Church's attitude toward economic success.

4. Ralph Waldo Emerson, "Self Reliance," in Geoffrey Moore, ed., *American Literature: A Representative Anthology of American Writing from Colonial Times to the Present* (London: Faber & Faber, 1964), 242.

5. See, for example, Michael B. Katz, *In the Shadow of the Poorhouse: A Social History of Welfare in America* (New York: Basic Books, 1986); Stephan Thernstrom, *Poverty and Progress: Social Mobility in a Nineteenth Century City* (Cambridge, Mass.: Harvard University Press, 1964); Edward Pessen, "The Egalitarian Myth and the American Social Realities: Wealth, Mobility and Equality in the 'Era of the Common Man,'" *American Historical Review* 76 (Oct. 1971), 4; and Robert H. Bremner, *From the Depths: The Discovery of Poverty in the United States* (New York: New York University Press, 1956).

6. Pole, *Idea of Equality,* xi.

7. Richard Hofstadter, *The American Political Tradition* (New York: Vintage Books, 1974), xxxvii.

8. For a recent analysis of the deep historical roots of some contemporary aspects of American social philosophy, see Michael B. Katz, *Improving the Poor* (Princeton, N.J.: Princeton University Press, 1995).

9. Katz, *Poorhouse,* 17.

10. Ibid., 74.

11. Robert Hunter, *Poverty* (New York: Macmillan, 1904), 2.

12. Ibid., 75–76.

13. For a good account of the impact of economic modernization upon the individualist tradition, see Irvin G. Wyllie, *The Self-Made Man in America: The Myth of Rags to Riches* (New York: Free Press, 1954).

14. *New Republic,* 11 April 1983, 34.

15. Hofstadter, *American Political Tradition,* xxxv.

16. Arieli, *Individualism and Nationalism,* 341.

17. See, in particular, Ira Katznelson, "Was the Great Society a Lost Opportunity?" in Steve Fraser and Gary Gerstle, eds., *The Rise and Fall of the New Deal Order, 1930–1980* (Princeton, N.J.: Princeton University Press, 1989), 185–211; and Margaret Weir, *Politics and Jobs: The Boundaries of Employment Policy in the United States* (Princeton, N.J.: Princeton University Press, 1992).

18. Nelson Lichtenstein, "From Corporatism to Collective Bargaining: Organized Labor and the Eclipse of Social Democracy in the Postwar Era," in Fraser and Gerstle, eds., *New Deal Order,* 122–152. The quote is from page 122.

19. For Roosevelt's adherence to the "melting away" myth, see Frances Perkins, *The Roosevelt I Knew* (London: Hammond, Hammond & Co., 1946), 230.

20. Quoted in Robert Bremner, "The New Deal and Social Welfare," in Harvard Sitkoff, ed., *Fifty Years Later: The New Deal Evaluated* (New York: Knopf, 1985), 76.

21. James T. Patterson, *America's Struggle Against Poverty, 1900–1985* (Cambridge, Mass.: Harvard University Press, 1986), 76.

22. Edward D. Berkowitz, *America's Welfare State: From Roosevelt to Reagan* (Baltimore: Johns Hopkins University Press, 1991), 14.

23. Martha Derthick, *Policymaking for Social Security* (Washington, D.C.: Brookings Institution, 1979), 220. Had it not been coupled with Old Age Assistance (OAA), which delivered immediate federal relief to the aged on the basis of need, legislative prospects for social security in 1935 would have been negligible. Both the House Ways and Means Committee and the Senate Finance Committee came very close to voting against OAI. The contradictions and political vulnerability of OAI in 1935 are well summarized by Berkowitz, *America's Welfare State,* chapter 2. For a fuller account, see Derthick, chapters 2, 6, 8, 10, and 11.

24. Berkowitz, *America's Welfare State,* 41.

25. Rexford Tugwell, *The Democratic Roosevelt* (New York: Doubleday, 1957), 342.

26. Berkowitz, *America's Welfare State,* 15.

27. Franklin D. Roosevelt, "Annual Message to the Congress, 4 Jan. 1935, in Samuel I. Rosenman, ed., *The Public Papers and Addresses of Franklin D. Roosevelt,* vol. 4 (New York: Random House, 1938), 19, 20. For Hopkins's view, see Perkins, *The Roosevelt I Knew,* 230. See also Tugwell, *Democratic Roosevelt,* 342.

28. Roosevelt, "Annual Message," 20.

29. Cited in Bremner, "The New Deal and Social Welfare," 84.

30. Theodore Marmor, Jerry Mashaw, and Philip Harvey, *America's Misunderstood Welfare State: Persistent Myths, Enduring Realities* (New York: Basic Books, 1990), 33.

31. Martha Derthick, *Policymaking,* 217.

32. Ibid., 229. The CES had proposed a system of employer and employee contributions to a trust fund, administered by the federal government, and eventually to be supplemented by general revenues. By such a method, OAI could be presented as having the characteristics of a social insurance scheme, yet payroll taxes would never have to reach politically prohibitive levels. Roosevelt, however, insisted that the CES redraft its proposal, minus the general revenue clause.

33. Ibid., 231–232.

34. For a synthesis of much recent writing on the later New Deal, plus a significant original contribution, see Alan Brinkley, *The End of Reform: New Deal Liberalism in Recession and War* (New York: Knopf, 1995).

35. Alan Brinkley, "The Antimonopoly Ideal and the Liberal State: The Case of Thurman Arnold," *Journal of American History* 80 (Sept. 1993), 557–579.

36. Thurman Arnold, *The Folklore of Capitalism* (New Haven: Yale University Press, 1937), 339.

37. Ibid., 347.

38. Ibid., 349.

39. Alan Brinkley, "The New Deal and the Idea of the State," in Fraser and Gerstle, eds., *New Deal Order,* 85–121.

40. Brinkley, *End of Reform,* 164.

41. Two good recent treatments are Brinkley, *End of Reform,* 251–257; and John W. Jeffries, "The 'New' New Deal: FDR and American Liberalism, 1937–1945," *Political Science Quarterly* 105 (Fall 1990), 397–418.

42. Edwin Amenta and Theda Skocpol, "Redefining the New Deal: World War II and the Development of Social Provision in the United States," in Margaret Weir, Ann Shola Orloff, and Theda Skocpol, eds., *The Politics of Social Policy in the United States* (Princeton, N.J.: Princeton University Press, 1989), 81–122. Quote taken from page 87.

43. Ibid., 88. Emphasis in original.

44. Jeffries, "The 'New' New Deal," 399, 406–409.

45. Kim McQuaid records that Congress was so agitated that it ordered the Board's research materials "transferred to the National Archives for permanent political burial." McQuaid, *Big Business and Presidential Power: From FDR to Reagan* (New York: William Morrow, 1982), 108.

46. Franklin D. Roosevelt, "Annual Message to the Congress, 11 Jan. 1944," *New York Times,* 12 Jan. 1944, 12.

47. Alonzo Hamby, *Liberalism and Its Challengers: FDR to Reagan* (New York: Oxford University Press, 1985), 49.

48. Brinkley, *End of Reform,* 144.

49. Weir notes that liberal legislators were reluctant to endorse planning schemes that promised to center still greater federal power in the White House, at their expense. See Weir, *Politics and Jobs,* 47.

50. Laura Kalman, *Abe Fortas: A Biography* (New Haven: Yale University Press, 1990), 126. Fortas was Arnold's law partner.

51. John Kenneth Galbraith, *American Capitalism: The Concept of Countervailing Power* (Boston: Houghton Mifflin, 1952), 1.

52. Ibid., 113. Emphasis in original.

53. Ibid., 116, 118. For an equally celebratory view of postwar capitalism, see David M. Potter, *People of Plenty: Economic Abundance and the American Character* (Chicago: University of Chicago Press, 1954).

54. Brinkley, *End of Reform*, 269.

55. Margaret Weir contends, "Decisions about macroeconomic management made in the 1940s narrowed the possibilities for decisionmaking about labor market policy into the 1960s." Weir, *Politics and Jobs*, 8.

56. Despite his 1944 campaign, President Roosevelt seems to have had little respect for the NRPB. Following its disbandment, he referred to its "grandiose scheme . . . which nobody understood, perhaps not even the Board." See Jeffries, "The 'New' New Deal," 405. Roosevelt's sardonic remark brings to mind Frances Perkins's recollection that "some of the high-strung people who advised" FDR favored "great changes in the economic or political patterns of our life," but that "he always laughed them off" (Perkins, *The Roosevelt I Knew*, 267, 268).

57. See Amenta and Skocpol, "Redefining," 107–108.

58. For a useful essay on the early years of the board and its growing potency, see Brian Balogh, "Securing Support: The Emergence of the Social Security Board as a Political Actor, 1935–1939," in Donald T. Critchlow and Ellis W. Hawley, eds., *Federal Social Policy: The Historical Dimension* (University Park: Pennsylvania State University Press, 1988), 55–78.

59. Quoted in Derthick, *Policymaking*, 86.

60. Ibid., 31–32.

61. Ibid., 113–114.

62. Berkowitz, *America's Welfare State*, 64.

63. Quoted in Gilbert Y. Steiner, *Social Insecurity: The Politics of Welfare* (Chicago: Rand McNally, 1966), 34–35.

64. Haber was chairman of the NRPB committee that produced *Security, Work, and Relief Policies*. See Brinkley, *End of Reform*, 253.

65. Steiner, *Social Insecurity*, 34.

66. Until 1950, OAA benefits were considerably more generous than those of OAI. The exclusion of farmworkers, domestic workers, and the self-employed from receiving OAI benefits reduced the stake that legislators (particularly those representing rural areas) had in its continuation.

67. Quoted in Berkowitz, *America's Welfare State*, 57.

68. Ibid., 92.

69. Ibid., 57.

70. Derthick, *Policymaking*, 273.

71. Within Republican circles, reservations about social security, and doubts regarding its fealty to the principles of private insurance provision, persisted into the Eisenhower years. For correspondence articulating these concerns, see Boxes 842 and 848, White House Central Files (WHCF), Office Files (OF), Eisenhower Library, Abilene, Kansas (henceforth, DDEL). Wilbur Cohen, as chief researcher for the Social Security Administration, helped persuade the first Eisenhower administration that social security was more compatible with the free market than was the sort of need-based grant currently favored by the U.S. Chamber of Commerce. See Wilbur Cohen, Oral History, 21-22, DDEL.

For an authoritative scholarly treatment of the continuing struggle for social security during the 1950s, see Edward D. Berkowitz, *Mr. Social Security: The Life of Wilbur Cohen* (Lawrence: University Press of Kansas, 1995), chapter 4.

72. Steiner, *Social Insecurity*, 71.

73. Presentation on the Social Security System (Minutes), 9 Oct. 1956, delivered by Wilbur Cohen to Faculty Seminar on Income Maintenance, University of Michigan, Cohen Papers, State Historical Society of Wisconsin, Madison, Box 70.

74. Ibid.

75. "Discussion of Charles Metzner's Propositions," handout prepared for 21 November 1956 meeting of Faculty Seminar on Income Maintenance, University of Michigan, Cohen Papers, Box 70.

76. Berkowitz, *America's Welfare State*, 98.

77. See Berkowitz and McQuaid, *Creating the Welfare State*, 152–153.

78. Ibid., 170, 171.

79. Steiner, *Social Insecurity*, 3.

80. Paper presented by Margaret Barnard, 4 Dec. 1956, at the Biennial Round Table Conference of the American Public Welfare Association (APWA). Papers of the APWA, Social Welfare History Collection, University of Minnesota, Box 20.

81. This resulted in the Ann Arbor Faculty Seminar series previously cited. See letter, Wilbur Cohen to Gardiner Means (CED), 15 May 1956, replying to Means's letter of 4 May, which had suggested "the possibility of my preparing a background memorandum or report which will bring together the relevant facts about poverty in the United States and the best thinking available on how to eliminate it." Cohen papers, Box 69.

82. Marion B. Folsom, the new secretary of HEW, outlined his desire for a fresh start in welfare designed to shift the emphasis from "relief" to "prevention." See Sanford M. Jacoby, "Employers and the Welfare State: The Role of Marion B. Folsom," *Journal of American History* 80 (Sept. 1993), 555. For the similar concerns of Eisenhower's chief of staff, see letter, Sherman Adams to Marshall Field, 31 May 1956, WHCF, OF, Box 842, DDEL.

83. Steiner, *Social Insecurity*, 41.

84. "Planning for Services in Public Assistance," Speech by Eunice Mincer at APWA conference, 4–7 Dec. 1957, APWA Papers, Box 70.

85. Elaine Burgess, meeting of the Advisory Committee of the APWA, 28 Oct. 1961, APWA Papers, Box 33.

86. This celebrated episode has been recounted in a number of works. See, for example, Edgar May, *The Wasted Americans: Cost of Our Welfare Dilemma* (New York: Harper and Row, 1964), chapter 2; Joseph P. Ritz, *The Despised Poor: Newburgh's War on Welfare* (Boston: Beacon Press, 1966); James T. Patterson, *America's Struggle Against Poverty, 1900–1985* (Cambridge, Mass.: Harvard University Press, 1986), 107–110; and Edward Berkowitz, *America's Welfare State,* 103–106. The papers of the APWA, the National Social Welfare Association, and the National Urban League are replete with anguished first-hand reports on the "Battle of Newburgh."

87. All Newburgh quotes and data taken from Patterson, *America's Struggle,* 107–110.

88. "Report on Meeting of Ad Hoc Welfare Committee with Secretary Ribicoff on September 8, 1961," Cohen papers, Box 195.

89. Ibid.

90. Quoted in Steiner, *Social Insecurity,* 39.

91. "Report on Meeting . . . with Secretary Ribicoff."

92. Letter, Arthur Altmeyer to Elizabeth Wickenden, 10 Sept. 1962. Copy in Cohen Papers, Box 6.

2. War on Dependency: Liberal Individualism and the Economic Opportunity Act of 1964

1. For a classic and influential exploration of this consensual faith in a harmonious American Way, see Godfrey Hodgson, *America in Our Time* (New York: Vintage, 1976), chapters 3 and 4.

2. For an exploration of this spirit, see Robert M. Collins, "Growth Liberalism in the Sixties: Great Societies at Home and Grand Designs Abroad," in David Farber, ed., *The Sixties: From Memory to History* (Chapel Hill: University of North Carolina Press, 1994), especially 23–24.

3. Speech to NAACP, 24 June 1964. Text attached to memo, Hyman Bookbinder to Cenoria Johnson, 15 July 1964, Papers of National Urban League (NUL), Washington Bureau, Box 10, Library of Congress.

4. I am thinking in particular of the various contributions to Steve Fraser and Gary Gerstle, eds., *Rise and Fall of the New Deal Order* (Princeton, N.J.: Princeton University Press, 1989), referred to in the first chapter. See also Margaret Weir, *Politics and Jobs: The Boundaries of Employment Policy in the United States* (Princeton, N.J.: Princeton University Press, 1991).

5. The best account of Johnson's early political career is Robert Dallek, *Lone Star Rising: Lyndon Johnson and His Times, 1908–1960* (New York: Oxford University Press, 1991). Two older, useful accounts are Joe B. Frantz, "Opening a Curtain: The Meta-

morphosis of Lyndon B. Johnson," *Journal of Southern History* 45 (Feb. 1979), 3–26; and T. Harry Williams, "Huey, Lyndon and Southern Radicalism," *Journal of American History* 60 (Sept. 1973), 267–293.

6. James L. Sundquist, "Origins of the War on Poverty," in Sundquist, ed., *On Fighting Poverty: Perspectives from Experience* (New York: Basic Books, 1969), 49.

7. Robert Caro, *The Years of Lyndon Johnson: The Path to Power* (New York, Vintage, 1981), 167–169.

8. See William E. Leuchtenburg, *In the Shadow of FDR: From Harry Truman to Ronald Reagan* (New York: Oxford University Press, 1983), chapter 4, for an accessible introduction to the extent of the influence.

9. Walter Heller's confidential notes of a meeting with Johnson, 23 Nov. 1963, Heller Papers, Box 13, John F. Kennedy Library (henceforth, JFKL).

10. Dallek, *Lone Star Rising*, 107.

11. Ibid., 126.

12. Ibid., 132.

13. Ibid., 142.

14. Ibid., 169.

15. Ibid., 288. Emphasis in original.

16. Ibid.

17. Ibid., 140.

18. James C. Gaither, Oral History No. 3, 11, Lyndon B. Johnson Library, Austin (henceforth, LBJL).

19. Robert Lampman, Oral History No. 1, 13, LBJL.

20. Charles Schultze, Oral History No. 2, 61–62, LBJL. Schultze went on to observe that the additional problem the government had to address was what to do about the undeserving poor, a group whose existence Johnson did not doubt and with whom he had much less sympathy.

21. See Nicholas Lemann, *The Promised Land: The Great Black Migration and How It Changed America* (London: Macmillan, 1991), 149–150.

22. "Findings and Declaration of Purpose," Economic Opportunity Act of 1964 (H.R. 10440), sec.2, *U.S. Code Congressional and Administrative News*, 88th Congress, Second Session, vol. 1 (St. Paul, Minn.: West Publishing, 1964), 377.

23. Ibid., Title I, Part A, 586.

24. Lyndon B. Johnson, *Public Papers of the President, 1964*, vol. 1, 377.

25. *Congressional Record*, 23 July 1964, 16780.

26. Economic Opportunity Act of 1964, sec.201 and sec.205(d), *U.S. Code*, 595, 598.

27. Ibid., sec. 121, 599.

28. *Congressional Record*, 23 July 1964, 16781, 16783.

29. *Economic Report of the President, 1954* (Washington, D.C.: GPO, 1954), 113.

30. Walter Heller, Oral History No. 2, 17, LBJL.

31. Henry J. Aaron, *Politics and the Professors: The Great Society in Perspective* (Washington, D.C.: Brookings Institution, 1978), 16.

32. *Economic Report of the President, 1964* (Washington, D.C.: GPO, 1964), 60.

33. *Economic Opportunity Act of 1964,* Report of the Select Committee on Poverty of the Senate Committee on Labor and Public Welfare, June 1964, 6.

34. *Economic Report of the President, 1964,* 6.

35. Cited by Michael B. Katz, *The Undeserving Poor: From the War on Poverty to the War on Welfare* (New York: Pantheon, 1989), 92–93.

36. For the relationship between the War on Poverty and federal employment policy, see Margaret Weir, "The Federal Government and Unemployment: The Frustration of Policy Innovation from the New Deal to the Great Society," in Weir, Ann Shola Orloff, and Theda Skocpol, eds., *The Politics of Social Policy in the United States* (Princeton, N.J.: Princeton University Press, 1989), 149–190.

37. Gunnar Myrdal, "War on Poverty," *New Republic,* 8 Feb. 1964, 14.

38. *Congressional Record,* 5 Aug. 1964, 18206.

39. Ibid., 22 July 1964, 16632.

40. *Economic Opportunity Act of 1964,* Hearings before the Ad Hoc Committee on the War on Poverty of the House Committee on Education and Labor, 88th Congress, 2nd Session, on HR.10440, 67.

41. Allen J. Matusow, *The Unraveling of America: American Liberalism in the 1960s* (New York: Harper and Row, 1984), 103–104.

42. Ibid., 103.

43. Economic policy meeting, 25 Nov. 1963, reported in Walter Heller's confidential notes, Heller Papers, Box 12.

44. In his memoir, *In Retrospect: The Tragedy and Lessons of Vietnam* (New York: Times Books, 1995), 323, Robert McNamara cites this hubris as one of eleven reasons why America failed in Vietnam: "We failed to recognize that in international affairs, as in other aspects of life, there may be problems for which there are no immediate solutions."

45. Hubert H. Humphrey, *War on Poverty* (New York: McGraw-Hill, 1964), 132. Emphasis in original.

46. Daniel Patrick Moynihan, "The Professionalization of Reform," *Public Interest* 1 (Fall 1965), 16.

47. *Congressional Record,* 6 Aug. 1964, 18309.

48. *Economic Opportunity Act of 1964,* House Hearings, 423.

49. *Joint Economic Report,* together with Minority Views, of the Joint Economic Committee, on the Economic Report of the President, Jan. 1964, 43.

50. *Congressional Record,* 6 Aug. 1964, 18309.

51. Ibid., 22 July 1964, 16622.

52. Ibid., 23 July 1964, 16742.

53. President Johnson's remarks, Economic Opportunity Act of 1964 signing ceremony, 20 Aug. 1964. Cited in "Administrative History of the Office of Economic Opportunity," 52, LBJL.

54. *Congressional Record,* 6 Aug. 1964, 18325.

55. Minutes of the first meeting of the Advisory Council on Public Welfare, 23–24 July 1964, APWA Papers, Box 39.

56. Julius Horwitz, *The Inhabitants* (Cleveland, Ohio: World Publishing, 1960), 31. In 1962 the author appeared before Congress in support of the administration's Public Welfare Amendments. A widely publicized factual account of similar degradation, Harry Caudill's book *Night Comes to the Cumberlands* (Boston: Little, Brown, 1962) concerned the plight of the families of unemployed coal miners in Eastern Kentucky. A third book that emphasized the damaging effects of relief was written by the journalist Edgar May, who would soon find employment in the Office of Economic Opportunity. See *The Wasted Americans: Cost of Our Welfare Dilemma* (New York: Harper & Row, 1964).

57. *Congressional Record*, 5 Aug. 1964, 18208.

58. In 1964, average monthly AFDC payments totaled $140 per family, or less than 25 percent of average family earnings. Because the Social Security Act allows individual states to set benefits at whatever level they desire, payments varied from $212 per month in Illinois to as little as $39.47 in Mississippi. U.S. Department of Commerce, *Statistical Abstract of the United States, 1965*, 309. (For average family earnings see ibid., 40.)

59. For a useful account of the congressional debate produced by Byrd's investigation, see Gilbert Steiner, *Social Insecurity: The Politics of Welfare* (Washington, D.C.: Brookings Institution, 1966), 45–49.

60. See *Washington Post*, 26 Feb. 1964; letter, Elizabeth Wickenden to Willard Wirtz, 9 March 1964; reply, Willard Wirtz to Elizabeth Wickenden, 20 March 1964; memo, Daniel Patrick Moynihan to Willard Wirtz, 12 March 1964; *Congressional Record*, 1964, A1027. All are in records of U.S. Department of Labor, 1964, Box 179, National Archives, Washington, D.C.

61. *Congressional Record*, 22 July 1964, 16612.

62. Ibid., 5 Aug. 1964, 18298.

63. Ibid., 6 Aug. 1964, 18310.

64. Ibid., 23 July 1964, 16761.

65. Ibid., 190.

66. Cited by Arthur M. Schlesinger, Jr., *The Crisis of Confidence* (New York: Bantam, 1969), vii.

67. President's Commission on National Goals, *Goals for Americans: Programs for Action in the Sixties* (New York: Prentice-Hall, 1960), 1–2.

68. *Congressional Record*, 6 Aug. 1964, 18309.

69. Ibid., 5 Aug. 1964, 18302.

70. Letter, Adam Yarmolinsky to David Denker, 26 June 1964, Yarmolinsky Papers, Box 12, JFKL.

71. *Congressional Record*, 28 Jan. 1964, 1263.

72. This interpretation is most closely associated with Frances Fox Piven and Richard A. Cloward, *Regulating the Poor: The Functions of Public Welfare* (New York: Vintage, 1971).

73. Matusow, *Unraveling of America*, 119.

74. For a good analysis of the relationship, see Katz, *Undeserving Poor,* especially page 85.

75. See Rev. Martin Luther King, Jr., *Why We Can't Wait* (New York: Signet Books, 1964), and Whitney M. Young, Jr., *To Be Equal,* (New York: McGraw-Hill, 1964).

76. Memo, Willard Wirtz to Bill Moyers, 29 Feb. 1964, "Legislative History of the Economic Opportunity Act of 1964," Box 2, LBJL.

77. See, for example, William Francois, "Where Poverty Is Permanent," *Reporter,* 27 Apr. 1961, 38–39; Francois, "West Virginia: The First Front," *Reporter,* 13 Feb. 1964, 21, 34–35; John Ed Pearce, "The Superfluous People of Hazard, Kentucky," *Reporter,* 3 Jan. 1963, 33; Thomas B. Morgan, "Portrait of an Underdeveloped Country: Appalachia, U.S.A.," *Look,* 4 Dec. 1962, 25–33; "Poverty, U.S.A.," *Newsweek,* 17 Feb. 1964, 19–38; Michael Harrington, "Close-up on Poverty," *Look,* 25 Aug. 1964, 66–72; John Domins, "The Valley of Poverty," *Life,* 9 Oct. 1964, 54–65. For the Homer Bigart story, see "Kentucky Miners: A Grim Winter," *New York Times,* 20 Oct. 1963, 1, 79; and *New York Times,* 21 Oct. 1963, 21.

78. Meeting notes, 22 Oct. 1963, Heller Papers, Box 13. See also memo, Theodore Sorensen to Walter Heller, 28 Oct. 1963, Box 13. Further Appalachian material is to be found in Sorensen's own papers, especially Box 37, JFKL; and in the Presidential Office Files, Box 66a, JFKL.

79. *Economic Opportunity Act of 1964,* Senate Hearings, 207.

80. Text of address by Sargent Shriver to NAACP, 24 June 1964, Washington, D.C., attached to memo from Hyman Bookbinder to Cenoria Johnson, 15 July 1964, NUL Papers, Washington Bureau, Box 10.

81. Daniel Patrick Moynihan, *Maximum Feasible Misunderstanding: Community Action in the War on Poverty* (New York: Free Press, 1969), 24.

82. Adam Yarmolinsky, "The Beginnings of O.E.O.," in Sundquist, ed., *On Fighting Poverty,* 49.

83. Gunnar Myrdal, "The War on Poverty," in *New Republic,* 8 Feb. 1964, 15.

84. See Hugh Davis Graham, *The Civil Rights Era: Origins of National Policy* (New York: Oxford University Press, 1991), 120. Chapters 1 through 5 provide a detailed exploration of the ambivalence toward racial preference created both by political calculation and by the logic of the civil rights movement's long-running battle for nondiscrimination.

85. See, for example, letter, Adam Yarmolinsky to Richard Salzmann, 28 July 1964, in which Shriver's assistant denied that the War on Poverty is racially motivated and emphasizes the political damage that would result from such a public association. Yarmolinsky Papers, Box 12.

86. *Congressional Record,* 5 Aug. 1964, 18198.

87. Reported to John W. Carley, memo to Adam Yarmolinsky and Wilson McCarthy, 20 July 1964, Office Files of Bill Moyers, Box 38, LBJL.

88. Memo, John McMillan to Lyndon B. Johnson, 10 Aug. 1964, "Legislative History of the Economic Opportunity Act of 1964," Box 2, LBJL.

89. *New York Times,* 23 Mar. 1964, 1. The complete text of the committee's report may be found in the NUL Papers, Part II, Series 5, Box 48.

90. Michael D. Reagan, "For a Guaranteed Income," *New York Times Magazine,* 7 June 1964, 20.

91. *Economic Opportunity Act of 1964,* House Hearings, 429.

92. Ibid., 287.

93. *Economic Opportunity Act of 1964,* Senate Hearings, 327.

94. Elizabeth Wickenden, "What Can a Community Do About Poverty," 20 April 1964, in the papers of the National Social Welfare Assembly (NSWA), Box 53, Social Welfare History Archives, University of Minnesota, Minneapolis. See also "The Recurrent Crises of Public Welfare—Asset or Handicap," a paper based on Wickenden's presentation to the APWA, delivered May 1963 in Milwaukee, in the records for 1964 of the Department of Labor, Box 179.

95. *Economic Opportunity Act of 1964,* House Hearings, 287–288.

96. "Report No. 4, Resolutions Committee, U.A.W. Constitutional Convention, March 20–27, 1964," reprinted in *Economic Opportunity Act of 1964,* House Hearings, 453–463.

97. Michael Harrington, *The Other America* (New York: Penguin, 1963), 120.

98. Ibid., 175. See Katz, *Undeserving Poor,* 16–35, for a good explanation for why such left-wing scholars as Harrington and Oscar Lewis were attracted to "culture of poverty" arguments that subsequently became associated with the right.

99. Gunnar Myrdal, *Challenge to Affluence* (New York: Pantheon, 1962), 46.

100. Congressman Dave Martin (R-Nebr.) asked Robert F. Wagner, the Democratic mayor of New York City, whether he would support the notion of a $3,000 guaranteed annual income, helpfully observing that "we have this kind of plan worked out in Communist nations." Wagner demurred, remarking that all he wanted was "to give some people the opportunity to get some dignity." *Economic Opportunity Act of 1964,* House Hearings, 746–747.

101. For good accounts, see Matusow, *Unraveling of America;* and Peter Marris and Martin Rein, *Dilemmas of Social Reform: Poverty and Community Action in the United States* (Harmondsworth, Middlesex: Penguin, 1972).

102. Matusow, *Unraveling of America,* 126.

103. Memo, Willard Wirtz to Bill Moyers, 29 Feb. 1964, Department of Labor Records, 1964, Box 179.

104. Memo, Daniel Patrick Moynihan to Willard Wirtz, 20 April 1964, Department of Labor Records, 1964, Box 190.

105. Letter, Whitney Young, Jr., to Sargent Shriver, 31 March 1964, NUL Papers, Part II, Series I, Box 19. Young congratulated the antipoverty czar on his "excellent handling of a difficult subject on 'Meet the Press.' . . . I recall some of the concerns we discussed, but nowhere in your presentation were these evident; you had all the right answers."

106. Cited by Edward D. Berkowitz, *Mr. Social Security: The Life of Wilbur J. Cohen* (Lawrence: University Press of Kansas, 1995), 201. This source contains much valu-

able new material on intra-administration dissent regarding the Economic Opportunity Act.

107. For bureaucratic tensions between the Department of Labor and the OEO, see Katz, *Undeserving Poor,* 88–89; and Margaret Weir, *Politics and Jobs,* 78–79. For HEW's attitude toward the prospective new agency, see Berkowitz, *Mr. Social Security,* 194–200. One CEA official cited by Berkowitz described the contribution of the mainstream cabinet departments to the antipoverty task force as "garbage" (196).

108. For labor's preferences and its consequent hostility to the OEO, see Jill Quadagno, *The Color of Welfare: How Racism Undermined the War on Poverty* (New York: Oxford University Press, 1994), 34.

109. Berkowitz, *Mr. Social Security,* 192. In a 1962 book coauthored with colleagues from the University of Michigan, Wilbur Cohen emphasizes the distinction between the "short-run alleviation of poverty" and the long-run "elimination of dependency." See James N. Morgan, Martin H. David, Wilbur J. Cohen, and Harvey E. Brazer, *Income and Welfare in the United States* (New York: McGraw-Hill, 1962), 3.

110. Reported in memo from Lenore Epstein, deputy director, Division of Research and Statistics, to Robert Ball, Commissioner of Social Security, 29 July 1964, Cohen Papers, Box 188.

111. A. Smithies, "Criteria for Income Maintenance Programs," 29 August 1964, p. 7, Cohen Papers, Box 188.

112. Minutes of the first meeting of the Advisory Council on Public Welfare, 23–24 July 1964, APWA Papers, Box 39.

113. "Toward Greater Security and Opportunity for Americans," Report to the President by the Task Force on Income Maintenance, 14 Nov. 1964, 4, Cohen Papers, Box 189.

114. "Criteria for Income Maintenance Programs," 1.

115. 1964 Task Force on Income Maintenance, *Report,* 5, Cohen Papers, Box 188.

116. Ibid., 3, 7.

117. "Criteria for Income Maintenance Programs," 6, 9.

3. Race and Poverty: Redefining Equality, 1964–1965

1. See Samuel Lubell, *White and Black: Test of a Nation* (New York: Harper & Row, 1964), chapters 6 and 7, especially pp.128–129.

2. Jill Quadagno, *The Color of Welfare: How Racism Undermined the War on Poverty* (New York: Oxford University Press, 1994), 48.

3. See Nicholas Lemann, *The Promised Land: The Great Black Migration and How It Changed America* (London: Macmillan, 1991), 71–110; and Quadagno, *Color of Welfare,* 52–53.

4. See John Hart, "Kennedy, Congress, and Civil Rights," *Journal of American Studies,* 13 (Aug. 1979) 165–178.

5. Lemann, *Promised Land,* 111.

6. Nathan Glazer and Daniel Patrick Moynihan, *Beyond the Melting Pot: The Jews, Irish, Negroes and Puerto Ricans of New York City,* 2d ed. (New York: Basic Books, 1970), 51.

7. Ibid., 70, 71.

8. Ibid., 65. Even at the end of this troubled decade, at least one conservative academic retained the conviction that black migrants were just another immigrant group . Edward Banfield's controversial book, *The Unheavenly City* (1970) is analyzed by Michael B. Katz, *The Undeserving Poor: From the War on Poverty to the War on Welfare* (New York: Norton, 1989), 30–35.

9. Glazer and Moynihan, *Melting Pot,* ix–x.

10. NUL Papers, Part II, Series I, Box 38.

11. Resolution received 26 May 1964, to be submitted by Randolph to the 4th Annual Convention of the Negro American Labor Council, May 29–31, 1964, Cleveland, Ohio, NUL Papers, Part II, Series I, Box 19.

12. See Hugh Davis Graham, *The Civil Rights Era,* for a detailed analysis of how, after much soul-searching, the commitment to affirmative action came about.

13. King, *Why We Can't Wait* (New York: Harper Torchbooks, 1963), 138–139.

14. *U.S. News & World Report,* 24 Feb. 1964, 57.

15. Whitney M. Young, Jr., *To Be Equal* (New York: McGraw-Hill, 1964), 31.

16. King, *Why We Can't Wait,* 130.

17. *Congressional Record,* 23 April 1964, 8878.

18. *Congressional Record,* 30 March 1964, 6525.

19. Ibid., 3 March 1964, 4164.

20. Ibid., 21 April 1964, 8594.

21. Ibid., 8594.

22. *New Republic,* 11 April 1964, 2.

23. *Congressional Quarterly Almanac, 1964,* 373.

24. George H. Gallup, *The Gallup Poll: Public Opinion, 1935–1971,* vol. 3 (New York: Random House, 1972), 1881, 1884.

25. Senators Javits, Clark, and Case represented states that, despite heavy minority concentrations in such cities as New York (14.7 percent), Philadelphia (26.7 percent), and Newark (34.4 percent), possessed relatively small black populations. In New York, the ratio of black to white voting-age populations was 1:11, while the figures for Pennsylvania and New Jersey were 1:12 and 1:13, respectively. On the other hand, the significance of the black vote was enhanced by its tendency to vote as a bloc. The statistics come from *U.S. News and World Report,* 27 April 1964, 35; and from *SAUS: 1964,* Table No. 13. For bloc voting, see Lubell, *White and Black,* chapters 6 and 7.

26. William Brink and Louis Harris, *The Negro Revolution in America* (New York: Simon and Schuster, 1964), 138.

27. Ibid., 148.

28. *New York Times,* 23 April 1964, 10.

29. Telegram, Whitney Young, Jr., to Lyndon B. Johnson, 12 May 1964, NUL Papers, Part II, Series I, Box 55.

30. *U.S. News & World Report,* 15 June 1964, 43.

31. A particularly full and dramatic account of the riot appeared in *Newsweek,* 3 Aug. 1964.

32. Rioting also hit Philadelphia, Chicago, and the three New Jersey cities of Trenton, Jersey City, and Elizabeth.

33. Iinterview in *Playboy* magazine, February 1965, reprinted in J. M. Washington, ed., *A Testament of Hope: The Essential Writings of Martin Luther King, Jr.* (San Francisco: Harper and Row, 1986), 360.

34. Ibid., 366.

35. For the radicalization of CORE in the North, including the World's Fair demonstration cited previously, see August Meier and Elliott Rudwick, *CORE: A Study of the Civil Rights Movement* (Urbana: University of Illinois Press, 1975).

36. The Mississippi Freedom Democratic Party was offered only token representation. For a balanced account, see Godfrey Hodgson, *America in Our Time* (New York: Vintage Books, 1978), chapter 10.

37. Letter, A. Philip Randolph to Martin Luther King, Jr., Whitney Young, Jr., Roy Wilkins, John L. Lewis, and James Farmer, 7 April 1964. A. Philip Randolph Papers, microfilm, Reel 2, Box 2 (Bethesda, Md.: University Publications of America, 1990).

38. According to Lemann, one participant, the playwright Lorraine Hansberry, told Robert Kennedy that "she would like to arm blacks so that they could start shooting white people in the streets." *Promised Land,* 127.

39. *New York Times,* 22 July 1964, 18.

40. For a detailed report on the HARYOU-ACT experiment, see Kenneth B. Clark, *Dark Ghetto: Dilemmas of Social Power* (New York: Harper Torchbooks, 1965).

41. *Newsweek,* 3 Aug. 1964, 20.

42. *New York Times,* 22 July 1964, 18.

43. Clark, *Dark Ghetto,* 203.

44. Ibid., 232, 230.

45. *New York Times,* 4 Aug. 1964, 28.

46. Letter, Joseph P. Vaccarella to Willard Wirtz, 11 Aug. 1964, Department of Labor Records, 1964, Box 179.

47. *Congressional Record,* 24 July 1964, 16957, 16958.

48. U.S. Department of Labor, *Weekly News Digest,* 17 Aug. 1964.

49. Reported in *Washington Post,* 26 Feb. 1964, D1. Clipping in Department of Labor Records, 1964, Box 179.

50. Memo, Moynihan to Wirtz, 20 April 1964, Department of Labor Records, 1964, Box 190.

51. In support of his claim, Moynihan asserted that the Aid to Families with Dependent Children program was 50 percent black, and that the number of blacks on welfare in New York had increased by 73 percent since 1957. Memo, Daniel

Patrick Moynihan to Willard Wirtz, 6 May 1964, Department of Labor Records, Box 190.

52. *Washington Post,* 26 Feb. 1964, D3.

53. Lemann, *Promised Land,* 154–155.

54. Ibid., 28–32.

55. In *To Be Equal,* Whitney Young, Jr., declared that an overriding objective of federal social policy must be to "rehabilitate urban Negro families" plagued by "unstable family patterns" and illegitimacy (28–31). See also earlier drafts of the black Marshall Plan. NUL Papers, Part II, Series I, Box 38.

56. Interview in *Playboy* magazine, Feb. 1965, reprinted in Washington, ed., *Testament of Hope,* 360.

57. Office of Policy Planning and Research, U.S. Department of Labor, *The Negro Family: The Case for National Action* (Washington, D.C.: GPO, March 1965).

58. For a balanced summary and analysis of the Moynihan Report, see Katz, *Undeserving Poor,* 24–29.

59. George H. Gallup, *The Gallup Poll, 1935–1971,* vol. 3 (New York: Random House, 1972), 1949.

60. President Johnson, "Commencement Address at Howard University: To Fulfill These Rights," 4 June 1965, *Public Papers of the President: Lyndon B. Johnson, 1965,* vol. 2, 640.

61. Richard N. Goodwin, *Remembering America: A Voice from the Sixties* (Boston, Mass.: Little, Brown, 1988), 310, 343–344.

62. This and preceding quotes taken from Lyndon B. Johnson, "Commencement Address at Howard University," *Public Papers,* vol. 2, 636–640.

63. Lyndon B. Johnson, "Remarks in the Capitol Rotunda at the Signing of the Voting Rights Act, 6 Aug. 1965," *Public Papers, 1965,* vol. 2, 842.

64. "Conference Transcript of the American Academy Conference on the Negro American, May 14–15, 1965," *Daedalus* 95 (Winter 1966), 288.

65. Milton Friedman's view paralleled the perspective of Depression era conservatives who favored needs-based public assistance over universal social insurance on grounds of efficiency. His preferred "negative income tax" was intended to supplant rather than accompany the service approach. See *Business Week,* 1 Feb. 1964, 42.

66. "Conference Transcript," 303–310. Emphasis in original.

4. Watts and its Aftermath: Rise of the Income Strategy

1. Report of Outside Task Force on Education, 14 Nov. 1964, i, ii, LBJL.

2. Ibid, 6, 9.

3. Lyndon B. Johnson, *Public Papers of the President, 1965,* vol.1, 414.

4. For an introduction to the early tribulations of the Office of Economic Opportunity, see John Donovan, *The Politics of Poverty* (Indianapolis, Ind.: Pegasus,

1973), 49–61; and Robert A. Levine, *The Poor Ye Need Not Have with You: Lessons from the War on Poverty* (Cambridge, Mass.: M.I.T. Press, 1970), 53–65. The Levine quote is taken from *The Poor,* 58.

5. A Gallup poll conducted in September 1965 revealed that 60 percent of the respondents approved of the way Johnson was "handling our domestic problems." George H. Gallup, *The Gallup Poll, 1935–1971,* vol. 3 (New York: Random House, 1972), 1965.

6. Memo, Sargent Shriver to Lyndon B. Johnson, 20 July 1965, WHCF, WE 9, Box 26, LBJL. The OEO was particularly gratified by the support of the *New York Herald Tribune,* which had been banned from the Kennedy White House because of its hostility to liberal causes.

7. The conversation is reported by Levine, *The Poor,* 62.

8. Lyndon B. Johnson, *The Vantage Point* (New York: Holt, Rinehart and Winston, 1971), 322.

9. Ibid., 323.

10. William E. Leuchtenburg, "A Visit with LBJ," *American Heritage,* May/June 1990, 50.

11. Memo, McPherson to Johnson, 19 July 1965, McPherson Office Files, Box 52, LBJL.

12. Governor's Commission on the Los Angeles Riots, *Violence in the City—An End or a Beginning?* (Los Angeles: State of California, 2 Dec. 1965), 1.

13. Cited in Doris Kearns, *Lyndon Johnson and the American Dream* (London: Andre Deutsch, 1976), 305.

14. Memo, George Reedy to Lyndon B. Johnson, 22 Aug. 1965, Office Files of Harry M. McPherson, Box 21, LBJL.

15. See Joseph S. Califano, *The Triumph and Tragedy of Lyndon Johnson: The White House Years* (New York: Simon and Schuster, 1991), 63.

16. Report of the President's Task Force on the Los Angeles Riots, 17 Sept. 1965, 23, LBJL.

17. Ibid.

18. *New York Times,* 21 Aug. 1965, 1. See also Harry McPherson, *A Political Education* (Boston: Houghton Mifflin, 1988), 344.

19. Parker cited in Califano, *Triumph and Tragedy,* 59.

20. *New York Times,* 27 Aug. 1965, 1, 13.

21. Ibid., 27 Aug. 1965, 13.

22. Levine, *The Poor,* 56. For the dramatic and immediate impact of the rioting on federal spending priorities, see the panicky tone of a memorandum from Willard Wirtz to Joseph Califano on 23 August, which contains "a listing of specific activities under Labor Department programs [sic] which can be redirected, enlarged or expedited or launched quickly to ease unemployment pressures in Los Angeles, particularly in the Watts district." See Department of Labor Records, 1965, Box 218.

23. *New York Times,* 29 Aug. 1965, 54.

24. Lee Rainwater and William L. Yancey, *The Moynihan Report and the Politics of Controversy* (Cambridge, Mass.: M.I.T. Press, 1967), 193.

25. Memo, Roger Wilkins to John G. Stewart (Office of the Vice President), 15 March 1966, attached to memo, Roger Wilkins to Clifford Alexander (Deputy Special Counsel to the President), 23 March 1966, McPherson Office Files, Box 21, LBJL.

26. Cited by McPherson, *A Political Education,* 352.

27. Memo, George Reedy to Lyndon B. Johnson, 7 Sept. 1965, Office files of Lee White, Box 4, LBJL.

28. Ibid.

29. "Report of President's Task Force," 44–45.

30. Memo, Wirtz to Moyers, 23 March 1965, Labor Department Papers, 1965, Box 190. Emphasis in original. Years later, Wirtz recalled "the almost physical excitement of reading it." See Nicholas Lemann, *The Promised Land: The Great Black Migration and How It Changed America* (London: Macmillan, 1991), 174.

31. Letter, Lyndon B. Johnson to Mrs. Roy Wilkins, 31 July 1965, Confidential Files, HU2/MC, Box 22, LBJL.

32. Robert Carter, general counsel for the NAACP, cited in Rainwater and Yancey, *Politics of Controversy,* 188.

33. Confidential File, WHCF, Box 30, LBJL. Monroe Dowling, executive director of the NUL chapter in Englewood, N.J., wrote to Johnson on 9 Aug. 1965 to request another fifty copies "because the speech is so wonderful and of such outstanding pertinence to our present situation."

34. Memo, John W. Leslie to Frank Erwin, 30 July 1965, WHCF, SP 3-93, Box 172, LBJL.

35. Memo, Lee White to Bill Moyers, 12 Aug. 1965, Office Files of Lee White, Box 6, LBJL.

36. Cited in Rainwater and Yancey, *Politics of Controversy,* 200.

37. Ibid., 214.

38. Ibid., 221.

39. Memo, Daniel Patrick Moynihan to Willard Wirtz, 10 April 1964, Department of Labor Records, 1964, Box 190.

40. Daniel Patrick Moynihan "Three Problems in Combatting Poverty," proceedings of a national conference held at the University of California, Berkeley, 26–28 Feb. 1965. In Margaret S. Gordon, *Poverty in America* (San Francisco: Chandler, 1965), 49, 51.

41. All quoted material taken from letter, Daniel Patrick Moynihan to Harry McPherson, attached to memo, Harry McPherson to Jack Valenti, 6 Oct. 1965, WHCF, General WE, Box 5, LBJL.

42. U.S. Department of Labor, *The Negro Family: The Case for National Action* (Washington, D.C.: GPO, March 1965), 16.

43. Ibid., 35.

44. Ibid., 20.

45. Ibid., 19.

46. Ibid., 31, 30.

47. Lemann, *Promised Land,* 174–175.

48. All quoted material taken from letter, Daniel Patrick Moynihan to Harry McPherson, 22 Sept. 1966, McPherson Office Files, Box 22, LBJL. Here, Moynihan was explicitly adopting the thesis of the Rainwater and Yancey book, which was about to be published. For a useful treatment of the bureaucratic rivalries, see their *Politics of Controversy,* 166–187.

49. The poll was conducted from 29 Oct. to 2 Nov. 1965, and was released on 5 Nov. 1965. See Gallup, *Gallup Poll,* vol. 3, 1969.

50. Letter, Theodore McKeldin to Johnson, 20 Jan. 1965, Office Files of Bill Moyers, Box 56, LBJL. McKeldin was writing in his capacity as chairman of the U.S. Conference of Mayors.

51. Memo, Hubert Humphrey to Lyndon B. Johnson, 18 March 1965, Office Files of Marvin Watson, Box 31, LBJL.

52. *New York Times,* 24 June 1965, 13.

53. Memo, James Rowe to Lyndon B. Johnson, 29 June 1965, Moyers Office Files, Box 56, LBJL, with Johnson's handwritten instructions attached. Emphasis in original.

54. All the above references are to a memo, Schultze to Johnson, 18 Sept. 1965, WHCF, WE 9, Box 26, LBJL.

55. *De Facto School Segregation,* hearing before the Special Subcommittee of the House Committee on Education and Labor (June 1965), 89th Congress, 1st session. Furthermore, in the immediate aftermath of the Watts riot, Martin Luther King had announced that the SCLC would made Chicago the test case for its northern strategy.

56. Califano, *Triumph and Tragedy,* 72.

57. Ibid., 64.

58. See memo, Wilbur Cohen to Ellen Winston (commissioner of welfare), 29 June 1965, which cites Richard Goodwin as the source for the date, Cohen Papers, Box 113. For the intensive consultation with experts that took place in July, see White Office Files, Box 5, LBJL.

59. Douglass Cater was the president's adviser on health and education. Article from *Chicago Daily News,* 17 Jan. 1967, with Johnson's note (apparently addressed to Marvin Watson) attached, Daniel Patrick Moynihan Name File, LBJL.

60. Wire, Lee White to Marvin Watson, 12 Nov. 1965, Confidential File, HU2, Box 56, LBJL.

61. Memo, Berl Bernhard to Lee White and Clifford Alexander, 8 Oct. 1965, White Office Files, Box 5, LBJL.

62. Telegram, Joseph Califano to Lyndon B. Johnson, 24 Sept. 1965, Confidential File, Box 22, LBJL. Memo, Bayard Rustin to numerous civil rights leaders (containing Abrams's complaint), 18 Oct. 1965, Reel 26, Randolph Papers.

63. Memo, Bayard Rustin to various civil rights leaders, 18 Oct. 1965, Reel 26, Randolph Papers.

64. Letter, Daniel Patrick Moynihan to Harry McPherson, 15 April 1965, McPherson Office Files, Box 21, LBJL.

65. Letter, Daniel Patrick Moynihan to Harry McPherson, 15 April 1966, McPherson Office Files, Box 21, LBJL.

66. "The Family: Resources for Change," A Synopsis of the Panel Discussions on the Family, 17–18 Nov. 1965, Records of the White House Conference "To Fulfill These Rights," Box 4, LBJL.

67. See, for example, the contributions of Daniel Thompson, a professor of sociology at Dillard University, and of Herbert J. Gans, a Columbia University sociologist who also served as an adviser to CORE. Transcript of panel discussion, "The Family: Resources for Change," Conference Records, Box 22; and Synopsis of panel discussions, Box 4.

68. All Cloward quotes from transcript of the planning session, "The Community: Institutions and Social Action," Conference Records, Box 24, 204–216.

69. Ibid., 215.

70. Ibid., 231–233. Rounding off an extraordinary and conspiratorial attack on Great Society liberalism, Landry launched an even more egregious assault on the "white, Jewish influence" at the planning conference. Ironically, he had previously been condemning the endemic racism of American society.

71. In a fiery opening speech to the conference, A. Philip Randolph suggested that "the Negro civil rights revolution is writing a new, broader and bolder role of responsibility of the Federal Government for racial and social justice and protection and advancement of the black and white poor." See Conference Records, Box 22.

72. Elizabeth Wickenden, "Confidential Notes on the Planning Session for White House Conference 'To Fulfill These Rights,'" 23 Nov. 1965, Cohen Papers, Box 238.

73. Memo, Monroe E. Price to Willard Wirtz, 19 Nov. 1965, Department of Labor Records, 1965, Box 240.

74. McPherson, *A Political Education,* 341.

75. Wickenden, "Confidential Notes."

76. Gallup, *Gallup Poll,* vol. 3, 1965. The disapproval rate was 67 percent, with 14 percent undecided. Interviews were conducted in mid-September 1965, and the results were released on October 8.

77. "Report of President's Task Force on the Los Angeles Riots," 27.

78. Memo, Wilbur J. Cohen to Joseph Califano, 13 Sept. 1965, records of the Inter-Agency Task Force on Public Assistance, 1965, Task Force Collection, LBJL.

79. "Income and Resources of Needy People" records of the Inter-Agency Task Force, 7–8.

80. "Extension of Coverage for Public Assistance Programs" records of the Inter-Agency Task Force, 6.

81. Ibid.

82. Ibid., "Income and Resources of Needy People" 7.

83. Letter, Joseph Kershaw to George Hildebrand (professor of economics, Cornell University), 7 July 1965, OEO Records, Reel 1, LBJL.

84. "Report of the Working Group on a Negative Income Tax and Related Proposals," 3 Sept. 1965, OEO Records, Reel 1, LBJL.

85. Memo, Sargent Shriver to Lyndon B. Johnson, 20 Oct. 1965, WHCF, WE 9, Box 26, LBJL.

86. Ibid. Emphasis in original.

5. Vietnam, Black Power, and the Decline of the Great Society

1. 12 Jan. 1966, *Congressional Quarterly Almanac, 1966,* 1206.

2. Even the Americans for Democratic Action (an assertive liberal group that had viewed Johnson with suspicion since the days when he was a senator) felt impelled to acknowledge his contribution in working "unceasingly for the enactment of liberal measures." See *ADA World* 29 (Nov. 1965), 1.

3. George H. Gallup, *The Gallup Poll: Public Opinion, 1935–1971,* Vol. 3 (New York: Random House, 1972), 1977, 2011.

4. Memo, Gardner Ackley to Lyndon B. Johnson, 30 July 1965, CEA Administrative History, vol. 2, Documentary Supplement I, LBJL.

5. Arthur N. Okun, *The Political Economy of Prosperity* (New York: Norton, 1970), 64–65.

6. Budget Bureau Chief Charles Schultze maintains that "if in early 1966 the President had . . . wanted to take the chance of whipping the American people up for symbolic purposes, even slapping on wage and price controls and the whole paraphernalia of a war economy, he would have had, for a time, massive acceptance and at the same time risked here the danger of blowing that war up into something far beyond anything else." Schultze, Oral History No. 2, 16, LBJL.

7. Defense secretary Robert S. McNamara urged Johnson to submit a $60 billion defense estimate predicated on the budgetary assumption that the war would be over at the end of FY 1967, with the caveat that supplementary funding requests would be made when necessary. See Donald F. Kettl, "The Economic Education of Lyndon Johnson: Guns, Butter, and Taxes," in Robert Divine, ed., *The Johnson Years,* vol. 2 (Lawrence: University Press of Kansas, 1987), 60.

8. Okun, *Political Economy,* 71.

9. For Arthur N. Okun the taxation decision represented "the first defeat of the new economics by the old politics" during the Johnson years. For assessments of the decision's economic consequences see David Halberstam, "How the Economy Went Haywire," *Atlantic Monthly,* September 1972, 56–60; Donald F. Kettl, in Divine, ed., *Exploring the Johnson Years,* vol. 2, 60–64; James E. Anderson and Jared E. Hazleton, *Managing Macroeconomic Policy: The Johnson Presidency* (Austin: University of Texas Press, 1986),

35–37; Arthur N. Okun, *Political Economy,* 70–73; Philip Cagan et al., *Economic Policy and Inflation in the Sixties* (Washington, D.C.: American Enterprise Institute, 1972), 49–50.

10. *January 1966 Economic Report of the President,* Hearings before the Joint Economic Committee, 89th Congress, 2nd Session, 1 Feb. 1966, 12, 107.

11. Ibid., 4.

12. *Congressional Record,* 25 Jan. 1966, 1083.

13. 17 Jan. 1966 address, reprinted in *Congressional Record,* 26 Jan. 1966, 1154.

14. Reprinted in *Congressional Record,* 7 Feb. 1966, 2384.

15. Statement by Scheuer on behalf of the DSG's Full Employment Steering Committee. Papers of the Democratic Study Group, Box 77, Library of Congress.

16. *Elementary and Secondary Education Amendments of 1966,* General Subcommittee on Education of the House Committee on Education and Labor, 89th Congress, 2nd Session, Part I, 7–14 March 1966, 41–43.

17. Ibid., 77–78. Congressman Alphonzo Bell (D-Calif.) was similarly exercised by his state's grave educational crisis, telling John W. Gardner that "you can't come close to catching up with our need in California."

18. Ibid., 83, 85.

19. Ibid., 85.

20. Ibid., 95.

21. *U.S. News and World Report,* 5 July 1965, 40.

22. Rowland Evans and Robert Novak, *Lyndon B. Johnson: The Exercise of Power* (New York: National American Library, 1966), 520.

23. Letter, Joseph L. Rauh to the Editor, *Village Voice,* 12 July 1965. Rauh thought that "President Johnson is the one who would get the biggest kick out of Mr. Newfield's piece." See Rauh Papers, Box 11, Library of Congress.

24. *Elementary and Secondary Education Act of 1966,* Hearings before the subcommittee on Education of the Senate Committee on Labor and Public Welfare, 89th Congress, 2nd Session, 1 April 1966, 344.

25. See letter, Arthur M. Schlesinger, Jr., to Robert F. Kennedy, 15 Dec. 1963, Papers of Robert F. Kennedy, Personal Correspondence, Box 11, JFKL.

26. Memo, Harry McPherson to Lyndon B. Johnson, 24 June 1965, McPherson Office Files, Box 21, LBJL.

27. Writing to fellow officials of the ADA, Leon Shull, the organization's national director, described the bombing in Vietnam as "a form of brinkmanship that could be disastrous." See letter, Leon Shull to National Officers, National Board, Chapter Chairmen, 4 March 1965, ADA Supplemental Deposit (Unprocessed) M73-472, Carton 1, State Historical Society of Wisconsin, Madison.

28. Senator Mansfield's deeply pessimistic assessment of the war's likely outcome was the product of a December 1965 fact-finding mission to Vietnam. Senator Vance Hartke of Indiana was a one-time Johnson protégé.

29. Letter, Frederick Dutton to Robert F. Kennedy, 29 July 1965, Kennedy Papers, Senate Correspondence Files: Personal File, 1964–1968, Box 3.

30. Letter, Frederick Dutton to Robert F. Kennedy, 29 Nov. 1965, Kennedy Papers, Senate Correspondence Files: Personal File, 1964–1968, Box 3.

31. Letter, Schlesinger to Kennedy, 16 April 1965, Kennedy Papers, Senate Correspondence: Personal File, 1964–1968, Box 11. The stimulus for this advice was an invitation from the St. Louis ADA, which intended to hold a dinner in Kennedy's honor.

32. Letter, Richard Goodwin to Robert F. Kennedy, 2 Feb. 1966, Kennedy Papers, Senate Correspondence: Personal File, 1964–1968, Box 4.

33. Memo, Frederick Dutton to Robert F. Kennedy, 8 Feb. 1965, Kennedy Papers, Senate Correspondence Files: Personal Files, 1964–1968, Box 3. George Aiken was a moderate Republican senator from Vermont and an early critic of the war.

34. *Congressional Record*, 19 Jan. 1966, 698. The DSG went on to bemoan the fact that existing means-tested programs often served to "perpetuate dependency and poverty rather than provide the means and motivation to break the cycle."

35. James Scheuer's hope was that a comprehensive employment program would "demonstrate the falsity of the old canard that the unemployed actually don't want to work, that they somehow enjoy their careers on the welfare rolls. Let us offer them real options." Statement issued on behalf of the DSG Full Employment Steering Committee, 1 March 1966, DSG papers, Box 77.

36. *Congressional Record*, 19 Jan. 1966, 698–700.

37. National Commission on Technology, Automation and Economic Progress, *Technology and the American Economy*, vol. 1 (Washington, D.C.: GPO, February 1966), 27.

38. Ibid., 34–35.

39. Ibid., 39.

40. Ibid., vol.3, Appendix, 34.

41. Norman Hill, review of Daniel Patrick Moynihan, *Maximum Feasible Misunderstanding: Community Action and the War on Poverty*, in *Civil Rights Digest* 2 (Spring 1969), 49.

42. Mary Rabagliati and Ezra Birnbaum, "Organization of Welfare Clients," in Harold H. Weissman, ed., *Community Development in the Mobilization for Youth Experience* (New York: Association Press, 1969), 104–105.

43. Ibid., 113.

44. Ibid., 108. The name of the organizer is not recorded.

45. Ibid., 115.

46. Moynihan, *Maximum Feasible Misunderstanding*, 95.

47. Richard A. Cloward and Frances Fox Piven, "A Strategy to End Poverty," *Nation*, 2 May 1966, 510.

48. Ibid.

49. Cited in Nick Kotz and Mary Lynn Kotz, *A Passion for Equality* (New York: Norton, 1977), 183.

50. Letter, Boone to James Farmer, 15 Nov. 1965, Papers of George Wiley, Box 3, State Historical Society of Wisconsin, Madison. Suggested policy priorities were

housing provision, work and training, minimum wage levels, liberalized unemployment provision, aid for migrant workers, wider availability of food stamps, and home rule for the District of Columbia.

51. Cloward was "concerned about the problem of having a very piecemeal and discoordinated [sic] effort if someone did not pick up the ball and run with it." See Notes on Telephone Conversation with Richard Cloward, 27 March 1966, Wiley Papers, Box 3.

52. Memo, George Wiley to Richard Boone, 4 April 1966, Wiley Papers, Box 3.

53. For a full account of the conference, and for the Boone quote, see *National Observer,* 9 May 1966, 6. For the Conway and Blake quotes, see *New York Times,* 15 April 1966, 2.

54. Memo from Preston Wilcox (assistant professor of social work, Columbia University) to "Interested Observers," n.d., Wiley Papers, Box 3.

55. This view has been disputed by Gilbert Steiner, who is impressed more by the orthodoxy of the council's recommendations ("tinker with the system, but . . . preserve it," in his characterization) than by the radicalism and urgency of their tone (which he regards as "fuzzy"). See Steiner, *The State of Welfare* (Washington, D.C.: Brookings Institution, 1971), 107–110. This view is echoed by June Axinn and Herman Levin, *Social Welfare: A History of the American Response to Need,* 2nd ed. (New York: Longman, 1982), 259–260.

56. Loula Dunn, Oral History, 69, Columbia University Social Welfare project.

57. Confidential Memo, Robert Theobald to "Key Mailing List," 22 April 1966, Cohen Papers, Box 107.

58. Elizabeth Wickenden, "The Legal Right to a Minimum but Adequate Level of Living," delivered to the National Conference on Social Welfare, Chicago, 31 May 1966. See Wickenden Papers, Accession M73-482, folder titled "National Conference on Social Welfare, 1966."

59. Ibid. Emphasis in original.

60. Draft Report by the Advisory Council on Public Welfare, 4 Oct. 1965. American Public Welfare Association (APWA) Papers, Box 39.

61. Draft Report, 14 Jan. 1966, APWA Paper, Box 39.

62. Draft Report, April 1966, APWA Papers, Box 39.

63. Letter, Elizabeth Wickenden to Fedele Fauri, 10 May 1966, Wickenden Papers, Accession M73-482, folder headed "Advisory Council on Public Welfare, 1965–1966."

64. Ibid.

65. Advisory Council on Public Welfare, *Having the Power, We Have the Duty* (Washington, D.C.: GPO, June 1966), xii.

66. Ibid., xix.

67. Ibid., 10.

68. Ibid., 23, 21–23.

69. *Congressional Record,* 22 Sept. 1966, 23749.

270

70. Ibid., 9 June 1966, 12742.

71. Cited in "The Late, Great Society," *New Republic,* 9 April 1966.

72. *Congressional Record,* 23 Feb. 1966, 3844, 3855.

73. See *New Republic,* 26 March 1966, 9. Significantly however, most detractors favored a *harder* line.

74. TRB, *New Republic,* 19 Feb. 1966, 4.

75. Memo, Robert Kintner to Lyndon B. Johnson, 25 April 1966, Confidential File, FG1, Box 16, LBJL.

76. Memo, Robert Kintner to Bill Moyers, 30 April 1966, Confidential File, FG(RS)PR18 (1965), Box 18, LBJL.

77. The "nervous Nellies" remark, made in a Chicago speech on 17 May 1966, was a departure from the prepared text. The Hanoi bombing on 29 June 1966 met with international and domestic outrage.

78. For the administration's efforts to win the loyalty of younger senators, see memo, Jack Valenti to Lyndon B. Johnson, 8 March 1966, Muskie Name File, LBJL.

79. Memo, Harry McPherson to Lyndon B. Johnson, 18 May 1966, McPherson Office Files, Box 52. It can safely be assumed that McPherson did not in fact regard Bayard Rustin as a "far-out Negro leader" but had no option but to pander to his president's mounting bitterness and isolation.

80. *New York Times,* 27 July 1966, 1, 25.

81. Ibid., 6 Aug. 1966, 1.

82. Ibid., 27 Aug. 1966, 1.

83. "There is widespread agreement that riots are inevitable in many cities this summer in the absence of bold measures. This has led many groups to search for new strategies; it is now clear that some of them, e.g., CORE, Urban League, SCLC, as well as religious and other community organization groups will use this strategy [guaranteed income advocacy] to a greater or lesser extent during the summer." Confidential Memo, Robert Theobald to "Key Mailing List," 22 April 1966, Cohen Papers, Box 107.

84. *New York Times,* 9 Aug. 1966, 24.

85. *Congressional Record,* 25 May 1966, 11482; see also *Congressional Record,* 22 July 1966, 16764.

86. *New York Times,* 9 Aug. 1966, 24.

87. Memo, Roger Wilkins to Clifford Alexander (special counsel to the president), 23 March 1966, McPherson Office Files, Box 21, LBJL.

88. Memo, Milton Semer to Lyndon B. Johnson, 10 Aug. 1966, WHCF, WE, Box 1, LBJL.

89. Theobald memo, Cohen Papers.

90. *Public Papers of the President: 1966,* vol. 1, 571–575.

91. Memo, Robert Kintner to Hubert Humphrey, 18 June 1966, in Confidential File, HU, Box 55, LBJL.

92. Memo, Robert Kintner to Harry McPherson (author of the Rhode Island speech), 15 Aug. 1966, Confidential File, HU, Box 55, LBJL.

93. *Public Papers of the President: 1966,* vol. 2, 857–860.

6. Political Polarization and the Search for a New Liberalism

1. George H. Gallup, *The Gallup Poll, 1935–1971,* Vol. 3 (New York: Random House, 1972), 2021 and 2074 (polls dated 24 July 1966, and 13 Aug. 1967, respectively).

2. Ibid., 2031 and 2074 (polls dated 24 July 1966 and 30 July 1967, respectively).

3. Ibid., 2031 and 2087 (polls dated 30 Sept. 1966 and 25 Oct. 1967, respectively).

4. See Donald F. Kettl, "The Economic Education of Lyndon Johnson: Guns, Butter, and Taxes," in Robert Divine, ed., *The Johnson Years,* vol. 2 (Lawrence: University Press of Kansas, 1987), 63.

5. See Bureau of the Budget, Administrative History, vol. 2, 67, LBJL.

6. Arthur Okun, *The Political Economy of Prosperity* (New York: Norton, 1970), 78.

7. Statistics from Kettl, "Economic Education," 62; Okun, *Political Economy,* 73; and Phillip Cagan et al., *Economic Policy and Inflation in the Sixties* (Washington, D.C.: American Enterprise Institute, 1972), 46.

8. Cagan et al., *Economic Policy,* 46.

9. See Charles Schultze, Oral History No.2, 10, LBJL.

10. Ibid., 38–39.

11. Lyndon B. Johnson, *The Vantage Point: Perspectives on the Presidency* (New York: Holt, Rinehart and Wilson, 1971), 444–445.

12. Memo, Joseph Califano to Lyndon B. Johnson with Johnson's reply appended, 16 March 1966, Confidential File, HU2/MC, Box 22, LBJL.

13. See, for example, details of the 24 March, 1 April, and 17 May 1966 meetings, Cabinet Meetings Collection, Boxes 4–5, LBJL.

14. Memo, Robert Kintner to Lyndon B. Johnson, 14 May 1966, in preparation for cabinet meeting, 17 May 1966, Cabinet Meetings, Box 5, LBJL.

15. Memo, Joseph Califano to Lyndon B. Johnson, 16 June 1966, Confidential File, FI 11, Box 44, LBJL.

16. Memo, Joseph Califano to Lyndon B. Johnson, 1 Sept. 1966, Confidential File, FI 11, Box 44, LBJL.

17. Memo with poll data attached, Fred Panzer to Bill Moyers, 8 June 1966, McPherson Office Files, Box 57, LBJL.

18. Okun, *Political Economy,* 75.

19. National Advisory Commission on Civil Disorder, *The Kerner Report,* 20th anniversary ed. (New York: Pantheon Books, 1988), 38. Stokely Carmichael gained particular notoriety and prominence from his supposed role in the July 1966 Atlanta riot.

20. *Federal Role in Urban Affairs,* Hearings before the Subcommittee on Executive

Reorganization of the Senate Committee on Government Reorganization, 89th Congress, 2nd Session, 1160.

21. Ibid., 60.

22. Ibid., 95.

23. Gallup, *Gallup Poll*, vol. 3, 2038.

24. Senate Liaison Contact Sheet, August 1966, in Manatos Office Files, Box 19, LBJL. One of Mike Manatos's colleagues had earlier warned Johnson that Harris faced "a real hard-fought close battle. This is an extremely good man in jeopardy." See Clifton Carter to Lyndon B. Johnson, 3 Jan. 1966, in Marvin Watson Office Files, Box 23, LBJL.

25. Sidney Spector to Mike Manatos, 4 Aug. 1966, Manatos Office Files, Box 19, LBJL.

26. Memo, Sidney Spector to Mike Manatos, 27 June 1966, Manatos Office Files, Box 19, LBJL.

27. Wilbur Cohen, Oral History No. 5, 1, LBJL. His recollection is ironic in view of the fact that administrative inefficiency provided a principal weapon in Abraham Ribicoff's assault on HEW and other agencies.

28. Cited by Wayne Granquist (administrative assistant to Abraham Ribicoff, September 1964 to August 1969), Oral History, 5, Ribicoff Papers, Library of Congress. For Hubert Humphrey's efforts, see memo, Marvin Watson to Johnson, 28 July 1966, with appended note from Bill Moyers to Watson, 30 July 1966, WHCF, FG 431/G, Box 342, LBJL.

29. Granquist, Oral History, 4–5.

30. Ibid., 16, 22.

31. Memo, Joseph Califano to Lyndon B. Johnson, 30 September 1966, LE/LG, Box 139, LBJL.

32. Abraham Ribicoff told Secretary of the Treasury Henry Fowler that while "Bobby got a lot of publicity" from the City Hearings, he himself "did not seek any publicity." Memo, Henry Fowler to Lyndon B. Johnson, 23 Sept. 1966, LE/FI 11, Box 52, LBJL.

33. *Federal Role in Urban Affairs*, 1115.

34. Letter, Frederick Dutton to Robert F. Kennedy, 6 April 1966, Robert Kennedy Papers, Senate Collection: Personal Correspondence, 1964–1968, Box 3.

35. Ibid.

36. Memo, Adam Walinsky to Robert F. Kennedy, entitled "Campaign Themes," n.d. but marked 1966, Robert Kennedy Papers, Senate Collection: Personal Correspondence,1964–1968, Box 26.

37. Gallup, *Gallup Poll*, vol. 3, 2056.

38. 24 Feb. 1967, in Philadelphia; in *New Republic*, 11 March 1967, 11–12. Concerning anti-Vietnam sentiment, Robert Kennedy suggested that "when a hundred student body presidents and editors of college newspapers; hundreds of former Peace Corps volunteers; dozens of present Rhodes scholars question the basic premises of the war, they should not and cannot be ignored."

39. Letter, Arthur Schlesinger, Jr., to Robert F. Kennedy, 6 Dec. 1966, Kennedy Papers, Senate Collection: Personal Correspondence, 1964–1968, Box 11.

40. *Federal Role in Urban Affairs,* 2624.

41. Ibid., 2626.

42. Robert Kintner to Lyndon B. Johnson, 25 April 1966, Confidential File, FG 1, Box 16, LBJL.

43. *Federal Role in Urban Affairs,* 1152.

44. *Washington Post,* 17 Aug. 1966, 1.

45. *Los Angeles Times,* 17 Aug. 1966, 7.

46. *Federal Role in Urban Affairs,* 299. See also *Congressional Quarterly Weekly Report,* 26 Aug. 1966, 1839.

47. *Federal Role in Urban Affairs,* 336.

48. Ibid., 450.

49. Ibid., 517.

50. Ibid., 94–95.

51. Ibid., 355.

52. "Questions for Secretary Gardner—from Adam [Walinsky]." Kennedy Papers, Senate Legislative Subject File, Box 18.

53. Statistics from *Congressional Quarterly Almanac, 1966,* 1398. The most recent comparable contest, that of 1938, saw no fewer than eighty Republican gains. See the *Economist,* 20 Aug. 1966, 730.

54. Interview with George Gallup, *U.S. News and World Report,* 19 Sept. 1966, 50–54.

55. *Congressional Almanac Quarterly, 1966,* 387.

56. One economist writing at this time detected an important shift in the work-force's attitude toward money income, as inflation cut into real wages. Americans "no longer harbor the 'money illusion,' the belief that real income . . . necessarily rises as fast as dollar income." See Gibbet Burch, "Must Full Employment Mean Inflation?" *Fortune,* October 1966, 121.

57. *Congressional Quarterly Almanac, 1966,* 264.

58. For a valuable recent treatment of this pattern, see Thomas B. Edsall and Mary Edsall, *Chain Reaction: The Impact of Race, Rights, and Taxes on American Politics* (New York: Norton, 1991), chapter 3, especially pages 60–61.

59. *Congressional Quarterly Almanac, 1966,* 516.

60. Ibid., 98.

61. *U.S. News and World Report,* 19 Sept. 1966, 35. Six "riots" were recorded in California, where Ronald Reagan proved adept at exploiting the law-and-order issue in his successful gubernatorial race against incumbent Edmund Brown. In the crucial House electoral battleground of the Midwest, 15 disturbances were recorded. The Kerner Commission would later regret the media's role in fueling anxiety by including relatively minor disturbances and acts of violence in their tallies.

62. *New York Times,* 21 Sept. 1966, 33.

63. Memo, Harry McPherson to Nicholas Katzenbach, 20 Sept. 1966, McPherson Office Files, Box 22, LBJL.

64. Data selected from table contained in memo, Tad Cantril to Hayes Redmon, 5 Oct. 1966, Office Files of Fred Panzer, Box 330, LBJL.

65. *New York Times*, 21 Sept. 1966, 33.

66. Ibid.

67. Ibid.

68. Ibid.

69. Memo, Nicholas Katzenbach to Joseph Califano, 9 March 1966, Manatos Office Files, Box 4, LBJL. Katzenbach found similar sentiments among other Southern members of the House Judiciary Committee.

70. *New York Times*, 15 Sept. 1966, 1, 32.

71. Ibid., 16 June 1966.

72. Memo, Henry Wilson to Lyndon B. Johnson, 10 Dec. 1966, WHCF, WE 9, Box 26, LBJL.

73. Memo, Charles Schultze to Lyndon B. Johnson, 7 Nov. 1966, WHCF, WE 9, Box 23, LBJL. Emphasis in original.

74. Memo, James Gaither to Lyndon B. Johnson, WHCF, WE 9, Box 26, LBJL.

75. *Congressional Quarterly Almanac*, 1967, 107. *Congressional Quarterly* identified the conservative coalition as having operated when a majority of Republicans and Southern Democrats opposed a majority of Northern Democrats. This approach affords useful insights, but the limits to its utility may be gauged from the fact that Northern Republicans backed the coalition only 58 percent of the time in the House and 45 percent in the Senate during 1967.

76. *Public Papers of the President, 1966*, vol. 2, 13 Nov. 1966, 1377.

77. For the civil rights movement's displeasure at Johnson's apparent retreat, see *Washington Post*, 12 Jan. 1967, 1. The House of Representative's virtually simultaneous refusal to seat the controversial Adam Clayton Powell only added to the sense that white America was becoming less receptive to the cause of black advancement.

78. Memo, Mike Manatos to Lyndon B. Johnson, 2 Dec. 1966, WHCF, FG 431/D*, Box 341, LBJL.

79. Johnson's handwritten note, attached to memo, read "Excellent. Get M.M. to suggest this, also comm. chr. also liberal leaders."

80. *Federal Role in Urban Affairs*, 2645–2646.

81. Ibid., 2683.

82. Ibid., 2940.

83. Ibid., 2974.

84. Ibid., 2772.

85. Ibid., 2575.

86. Ibid., 2655–2656.

87. "Questions for A. Philip Randolph," 6 Dec. 1966, Kennedy Papers, Legislative Subject File, Box 18. The authorship of this counsel is unclear, but Peter Edelman

seems a likely source. The emphasis is in the original and clearly comes from the senator.

7. Welfare Reform and the Crisis of Liberalism: 1967

1. *Statistical Abstract of the United States, 1968* (Washington, D.C.: U.S. Department of Commerce, 1968), 298.

2. John McCone's investigation of Watts, undertaken at the behest of the California governor, Edmund Brown, had been relatively restrained, but—as with the Moynihan Report—it was susceptible to distortion by right-wing polemicists. For one particularly extreme example, see Earl Selby and Anne Selby, "Watts—Where Welfare Bred Violence," in *Reader's Digest*, May 1966, 67–71.

3. *America*, 26 Nov. 1966, 681.

4. *Wall Street Journal*, 27 Oct. 1966, cited in *America*, 26 Nov. 1966, 680.

5. Advisory Council on Public Welfare, *Having the Power, We Have the Duty* (Washington, D.C.: GPO, June 1966).

6. See Robert A. Levine, *The Poor Ye Need Not Have with You: Lessons from the War on Poverty* (Cambridge, Mass.: M.I.T. Press, 1970), 28–43.

7. *Report*, 1966 Inter-Agency Task Force on Income Maintenance, 9, LBJL.

8. *Social Security Amendments of 1967*, Hearings before Senate Finance Committee, 90th Congress, 1st Session, 216, 259.

9. Ibid., 261.

10. For a fuller account of the amendments, see Gilbert Steiner, *Social Insecurity: The Politics of Welfare* (Chicago: Rand-McNally, 1966).

11. *Economic Report of the President, 1967* (Washington, D.C.: GPO, Jan. 1967), 17.

12. Levine, *Poor*, 82.

13. Message delivered on 1 May 1967, reprinted in *Congressional Quarterly Weekly Report*, 26 May 1967, 906.

14. *Public Papers of the President, 1967*, vol. 1, 346.

15. Memo, Donald Radler to Marvin Watson, 6 Jan. 1967, Confidential File, FG11–15, Box 21, LBJL.

16. Memo, Douglass Cater to Lyndon B. Johnson, 17 March 1967, WHCF, FG 11–15, Box 125.

17. Memo, Donald Radler to Marvin Watson, 6 Jan. 1967, Confidential File, FG 11–15, Box 21, LBJL.

18. Memo, Mike Manatos to Lyndon B. Johnson, 18 Jan. 1967, Clark Name File, LBJL.

19. Memo, Adam Walinsky to Robert F. Kennedy, n.d., but listed as Nov. 1966. Kennedy Papers, Senate Correspondence: Personal File, 1964–1968, Box 26.

20. Letter, Joseph S. Clark to J. K. Galbraith, 13 Dec. 1967, Papers of Joseph S. Clark, Box 17 (A) [Correspondence, 1967], Pennsylvania State Historical Society, Philadelphia.

21. Letter, Joseph L. Rauh to Claudia Dreifus (National Chair, Campus ADA), 18 Nov. 1966, Rauh Papers, Box 11.

22. Letter, Lyndon B. Johnson to Joseph S. Clark, 7 Jan. 1967, Clark Name File, LBJL.

23. This was an important audience for Senator Clark given that, according to J. K. Galbraith, "the largest and most successful chapter of ADA over the years has been that in Philadelphia." See letter, J. K. Galbraith to Senator Edmund Muskie, 13 Nov. 1968, ADA Papers (Unprocessed) M73-472, Box 3.

24. Speech delivered 31 March 1967, reported in *ADA World,* May 1967, 1, 15.

25. Javits's evolving perspective on Vietnam is recorded in *Congressional Quarterly Weekly Report,* 18 Aug. 1967, 1605.

26. *New York Times,* 5 March 1967, IV, 1.

27. Favorable comment came from Senator Mike Mansfield, but a frustrated Dean Rusk observed that every element of Robert Kennedy's proposal had already been rejected by Hanoi. *Congressional Quarterly Weekly Report,* 10 March 1967, 356.

28. Cited in memo, Robert Kintner to Lyndon B. Johnson, 20 Jan. 1967, in Confidential File, WH 10, Box 99, LBJL.

29. *Baltimore Sun,* 10 Feb. 1967, in Office Files of Fred Panzer, Box 340, LBJL.

30. *New York Times,* 21 April 1967, in Office Files of Fred Panzer, Box 340, LBJL. For the standard treatment of Johnson's changing relationship with the press as the war deepened, see Kathleen J. Turner, *Lyndon Johnson's Dual War: Vietnam and the Press* (Chicago: University of Chicago Press, 1985).

31. Gallup poll, 9 April 1967, in George H. Gallup, *The Gallup Poll, 1935–1971,* vol. 3 (New York: Random House, 1972), 2058.

32. The quote is from *New York Times,* 24 March 1967, 1. For King's threat, see *Congressional Quarterly Weekly Report,* 21 April 1967, 647.

33. Memo, Harry McPherson to Lyndon B. Johnson, McPherson Office Files, Box 14, LBJL.

34. *Congressional Quarterly Weekly Report,* 21 April 1967, 647; Memo, John Roche to Lyndon B. Johnson, 5 April 1967, Confidential File, HU2, Box 56, LBJL.

35. One trial-heat undertaken by the Gallup organization in June indicated the following results in a four-way contest: Johnson, 41 percent; Romney, 39 percent; Wallace, 11 percent; King 2 percent. Gallup, *Gallup Poll,* 2063.

36. *Congressional Quarterly Weekly Report,* 7 April 1967, 534.

37. Steven M. Gillon, *Politics and Vision: The ADA and American Liberalism, 1947–1985* (New York: Oxford University Press, 1987), 180.

38. Ibid.

39. Gallup, *Gallup Poll,* 2052. Poll released on 26 Feb. 1967. Full figures: U.S. should continue bombing, 67 percent; U.S. should cease bombing, 24 percent; no opinion, 9 percent.

40. Memo, George Christian to Barefoot Sanders, 27 Oct. 1967, Javits Name File, LBJL.

41. Memo, Adam Walinsky to Robert F. Kennedy, n.d., but Nov. 1966. Kennedy Papers, Senate Correspondence: Personal File, 1964–1968, Box 26.

42. David Halberstam's view is cited by William H. Chafe, *Never Stop Running: Allard Lowenstein and the Struggle to Save American Liberalism* (New York: Basic Books, 1993), 311.

43. Gary Hart, *Right from the Start: A Chronicle of the McGovern Campaign* (New York: Quadrangle, 1973), 330.

44. Daniel P. Moynihan, "The Politics of Stability," speech to ADA National Board Meeting, 23 Sept. 1967, in McPherson Office Files, Box 57, LBJL.

45. 1966 Inter-Agency Task Force on Nutrition and Adequate Diets, Report (Part 1), 1, Task Force Collection, LBJL.

46. See memo, Joseph Califano to Charlie Murphy, 5 Oct. 1968, WHCF WE, Box 2, LBJL.

47. Memo, Richard Reuter to Lyndon B. Johnson, 27 July 1965, WHCF, WE9, Box 26, LBJL.

48. *Examination of the War on Poverty,* Hearings before the Subcommittee on Employment, Manpower and Poverty of the Senate Committee on Labor and Public Welfare, 90th Congress, 1st Session, April 1967, 555.

49. Ibid., 235.

50. Ibid., 236.

51. *New York Times,* 14 March 1967, 1.

52. Ibid., 8 Feb. 1967, 11; and 9 Feb. 1967, 23.

53. "Report of the Task Force on Aid to Families with Dependent Children Program," June 1967, Cohen Papers, Box 161.

54. "A Strengthened Program of Aid to Families with Dependent Children with Emphasis on Reducing Dependency," proposal dated 22 June 1967. Cohen Papers, Box 161.

55. *New York Times,* 9 May 1967, 1.

56. Letter, Arthur Schlesinger to Robert F. Kennedy, 15 May 1967, Kennedy Papers, Senate Correspondence: Personal File, 1964–1968, Box 11.

57. *New York Times,* 9 May 1967, 1, 24.

58. *New York Times,* 9 May 1967, 24.

59. *Examination of the War on Poverty,* 1933.

60. *New York Times,* 10 May 1967, 50.

61. Remarks of Senator Javits before the Community Council of Greater New York, 9 June 1967, reprinted in *Congressional Record,* 15 June 1967, 16033.

62. Memo, Wilbur Cohen to Lyndon B. Johnson, 14 July 1967, WHCF LE/WE, Box 164, LBJL. Emphasis in original.

63. Joseph S. Califano, *The Triumph and Tragedy of Lyndon Johnson: The White House Years* (New York: Simon and Schuster, 1991), 206.

64. Reported by Lawrence O'Brien, memo to Lyndon B. Johnson, 25 Aug. 1967, WHCF, HS3, Box 6, LBJL.

65. Ibid.

66. Cited in *Congressional Quarterly Weekly Report,* 22 Sept. 1967, 1866.

67. Daniel Patrick Moynihan Address, 23 Sept. 1967, transcript in McPherson Office Files, Box 57, LBJL.

68. *New York Times,* 9 Aug. 1967, 23; and 18 Aug. 1967, 17.

69. Gallup, *Gallup Poll,* 2074, 2087.

70. Ibid., 2071, 2073, 2075.

71. Memo, Harry McPherson to Lyndon B. Johnson, 25 Aug. 1967, in Fred Harris Name File, LBJL. For an excellent account of the impact that disillusionment with the Vietnam War had on the political equation with which legislators were confronted, see Don Oberdorfer, *Tet!* (Garden City, N.Y.: Doubleday, 1971).

72. Letter, Schlesinger to Humphrey, 25 March 1966, Rauh Papers, Box 11.

73. Gillon, *Politics and Vision,* 198.

74. Letter, Paul H. Douglas to J. K. Galbraith, 13 June 1967; attached to letter, Gus Tyler to ADA National Board, 26 June 1967, Rauh Papers, Box 11.

75. Quotes taken from Gillon, *Politics,* 198.

76. Ibid., 199.

77. *Congressional Quarterly Weekly Report,* 18 Aug. 1967, 1589.

78. See *New York Times,* 8 April 1967, 1; quote taken from *Congressional Quarterly Weekly Report,* 18 Aug. 1967, 1625.

79. *Congressional Quarterly Weekly Report,* 14 July 1967, 1201.

80. Ibid., 16 June 1967, 1001.

81. *New York Times,* 10 Aug. 1967, 1.

82. Ibid., 9 Aug. 1967, 1.

83. Cited in Merle Miller, *Lyndon: An Oral Biography* (New York: Ballantine, 1986), 625–626.

84. *New York Times,* 4 Aug. 1967, 1.

85. Ibid., 18 Aug. 1967, 14.

86. Reported in memo, Barefoot Sanders to Lyndon B. Johnson, 13 Sept. 1967, Wilbur Mills Name File, LBJL.

87. *New York Times,* 18 Aug. 1967, 14.

88. For dates and casualty figures, see National Advisory Commission on Civil Disorders, *Kerner Report* 20th anniversary ed. (New York: Pantheon Books, 1988), 62, 108.

89. *New York Times,* 9 Aug. 1967, 1; 15 Aug. 1967, 24.

90. Ibid., 1 Aug. 1967, 17.

91. Ibid., 25 July 1967, 1; and 26 July 1967, 26.

92. *Report of the House Committee on Ways and Means into H.R. 12080, the Social Security Amendments of 1967,* 90th Congress, 1st Session, 94–103.

93. *New York Times,* 16 Aug. 1967, 35.

94. Memo, Whitney Young, Jr., to Lyndon B. Johnson, 11 Aug. 1967, McPherson Office Files, Box 15, LBJL.

95. Memo, Robert Levine to Lyndon B. Johnson, 11 Aug. 1967, and attached memo, James Lyday to Robert Levine, 5 Aug. 1967, WHCF, LE/WE, Box 164, LBJL.

96. 15 Aug. 1967 speech by John Gardner, cited by Douglass Cater, memo to Lyndon B. Johnson, 16 Aug. 1967, WHCF, LE/WE, Box 164, LBJL.

97. Letter, Wilbur Cohen to Wilbur Mills, 21 Aug. 1967, Cohen Papers, Box 161. In the letter, Cohen refers to an unsuccessful attempt by himself and Ball to thank Mills in person.

98. Letter, Wilbur Cohen to Wilbur Mills, Aug. 23, 1967, Cohen Papers, Box 131. In truth, the author of the article, Eve Edstrom, was well acquainted with undersecretary Cohen and had close ties to the social welfare community in general.

99. Wilbur Cohen, Oral History, 200, Columbia University Oral History Project.

100. *Social Security Amendments of 1967*, Hearings before the Senate Finance Committee, 90th Congress, 1st Session, 776.

101. Ibid., 1398–1399.

102. Ibid., 1402.

103. Ibid., 1130, 1133.

104. Ibid., 1129.

105. Ibid., 1647, 1537.

106. Ibid., 807.

107. Ibid., 1812.

108. Ibid., 1814.

8. Liberalism and Governance, 1967–1968

1. Attached to memorandum recording status of current legislation, Joseph Califano to Lyndon B. Johnson, 3 Nov. 1967, Confidential File, WE/MC, Box 98, LBJL.

2. Address, 27 July 1967, reprinted in *Congressional Quarterly Almanac, 1967*, 152-A.

3. Transcript of President Johnson's news conference, 31 July 1967, in *Congressional Quarterly Almanac, 1967*, 153-A.

4. Memo, Douglass Cater to Lyndon B. Johnson, 28 July 1967, WHCF, HU2, Box 6, LBJL.

5. "The Four Year Record in Human Terms," attached to memo, Mike Manatos to Lyndon B. Johnson, 18 Nov. 1967, in Manatos Office Files, Box 5, LBJL.

6. *New York Times*, 20 Aug. 1967, 3.

7. Note attached to adverse press reports dated 28 Aug. 1967, WHCF, WE 9, Box 30, LBJL.

8. Transcript of news conference, 18 Aug. 1967, *Congressional Quarterly Almanac, 1967*, 162-A.

9. Transcript of news conference, 1 Nov. 1967, *Congressional Quarterly Almanac, 1967*, 180-A.

10. *Congressional Quarterly Almanac, 1967*, 643.

11. Cited by Donald F. Kettl, "The Economic Education of Lyndon Johnson: Guns, Butter, and Taxes," in Robert A. Divine, ed., *The Johnson Years,* vol. 2 (Lawrence: University Press of Kansas, 1987), 68.

12. *President's 1967 Surtax Proposal; Continuation of Hearings to Receive Further Administration Proposals Concerning Expenditure Cuts,* Hearings Before the House Committee on Ways and Means, 90th Congress, 1st Session, 29–30 Nov. 1967, 2.

13. Ibid., 38.

14. Ibid., 199.

15. *Congressional Record,* 19 Sept. 1967, 25935.

16. Interview on *Meet the Press,* transcript reproduced in *Congressional Record,* 7 Aug. 1967, 21593.

17. Transcipt of news conference, 17 Nov. 1967, *Congressional Quarterly Almanac, 1967,* 185-A.

18. Memo, Joseph Califano to Lyndon B. Johnson, 4 Dec. 1967, WHCF FI4, Box 24, LBJL.

19. Ibid.

20. Rauh quoted in Leon Shull, "A Liberal Looks at 1968," *ADA World,* Nov. 1967, 5.

21. Memo, Sargent Shriver to Lyndon B. Johnson, 4 Jan. 1968, WHCF FI4/FG11-15, Box 26, LBJL.

22. Memo, Robert Weaver to Charles Schultze, 11 Dec. 1967, in Gaither Office Files, Box 14, LBJL.

23. "Thinking the Unthinkable About America's Cities: A Scenario in Four Parts," 18 Oct. 1967, in Califano Office Files, Box 77, LBJL.

24. Speech to Long Island Negro Business and Professional Men's Association, June 1967, cited by the *New York Post,* 2 Aug. 1967, copy in Panzer Office Files, Box 331, LBJL.

25. *New York Times,* 13 Aug. 1967, IV, 3.

26. *Anti-Riot Bill, 1967,* Hearings before Senate Judiciary Committee, 90th Congress, 1st Session, 2 Aug. 1967, 34–35.

27. *New York Times,* 13 Aug. 1967, IV, 3.

28. Ibid., 2 Aug. 1967, 36.

29. Ibid., 17 Aug. 1967, 26.

30. Ibid., 16 Aug. 1967, 1, 29.

31. "LBJ's Programs Would Aid Negro," *Detroit News,* 26 Aug. 1967, in Panzer Office Files, Box 331, LBJL. See also "LBJ and the Negro," *New York Post,* 2 Dec. 1967, same box, which compares Johnson's civil rights record favorably with that of President Kennedy, particularly in the area of housing.

32. *Congressional Record,* 25 Sept. 1967, 26656–26658.

33. Ibid., 8 Aug. 1967, 21782.

34. Ibid., 10 Aug. 1967, 22226–22227.

35. See Memo, Sargent Shriver to Lyndon B. Johnson, 15 Sept. 1967, Confidential File, FG11-15, Box 21, LBJL.

36. For George Bush's later position, in response to the Los Angeles riot, see Roger Wilkins, "Don't Blame the Great Society," *The Progressive* 56 (July 1992), 16.

37. Memo, Harry McPherson to Lyndon B. Johnson, 10 Aug. 1967, WHCF, WE9, Box 30, LBJL.

38. Memo, Douglass Cater to Lyndon B. Johnson, 28 July 1967, WHCF, HU2, Box 6, LBJL.

39. See *New York Times,* 25 Dec. 1967, 26. The report describes how Perkins, chairman of the House Education and Labor Committee, delayed consideration of the Economic Opportunity Amendments of 1967 until the late autumn, by which time this intense hostility had dissipated.

40. Letter, Phil Landrum to Sargent Shriver, 22 Aug. 1967, in Personal Papers of Barefoot Sanders, Box 14, LBJL.

41. "OEO and the Strategy Against Poverty: A Program for All Americans," in Sanders Papers, Box 14, LBJL.

42. Letter, Sargent Shriver to Congressmen Bush, Cowger, Goodell, and Steiger, 31 July 1967, Sanders Papers, Box 14, LBJL.

43. Letter, Sam Gibbons to Barefoot Sanders, 24 Aug. 1967, in Sanders Papers, Box 14, LBJL.

44. Memo, Sherwin Markham to Barefoot Sanders, 10 Oct. 1967, Sanders Papers, Box 14, LBJL.

45. Memo, Barefoot Sanders to Lyndon B. Johnson, 25 Oct. 1967, Sanders Papers, Box 14, LBJL.

46. Ibid.

47. Remarks reported by Bob Hardesty, memo to Barefoot Sanders, 11 Oct. 1967, in Sanders Papers, Box 14, LBJL.

48. *Congressional Quarterly Weekly Report,* 24 Nov. 1967, 2366.

49. Letter, Wilbur Cohen to Wilbur Mills, 11 Dec. 1967, Cohen Papers, Box 161.

50. The first quote comes from a Wickenden bulletin dated 21 Aug. 1967, in Box 53 of the NSWA Papers. The other remarks are from a letter to Guy Justis, dated 14 Sept. 1967, in Box 57 of the same collection.

51. The petition statement, dated 15 Dec. 1967, is attached to a letter by eight HEW employees to John W. Gardner, dated 21 Dec. 1967. The letter reveals that "a significant number" of their colleagues shared the sentiments of the petition but "did not sign their names for fear of retaliation." Cohen Papers, Box 161.

52. Memo, Wilbur Cohen to Joseph Califano, 8 Dec. 1967, Confidential File, LE/WE 6, Box 64, LBJL.

53. Memo, Joseph Califano to Lyndon B. Johnson, 9 Dec. 1967, with Johnson's note attached, dated 10 Dec. 1967, Confidential File, LE/WE 6, Box 64, LBJL.

54. *Congressional Record,* 8 Dec. 1967, 35640; and 11 Dec. 1967, 35748.

55. Ibid., 8 Dec. 1967, 35640.

56. Ibid., 35641.

57. Ibid., 35640.

58. Memo, Joseph Califano to Lyndon B. Johnson, 11 Dec. 1967, WHCF LE/WE, Box 164, LBJL.

59. Memo, John W. Gardner to Lyndon B. Johnson, 11 Dec. 1967, enclosed in memo, Joseph Califano to Lyndon Johnson, 11 Dec. 1967, WHCF, LE/WE, Box 164, LBJL.

60. Memo, Mike Manatos to Lyndon B. Johnson, 13 Dec. 1967, WHCF, LE/WE, Box 164, LBJL.

61. Ibid.

62. *Congressional Record,* 14 Dec. 1967, 36783–36786.

63. Ibid., 36794.

64. John Morton Blum, *Years of Discord: American Politics and Society, 1961–1974* (New York: Norton, 1991), 290.

65. National Files of the McCarthy Historical Project, Box 1, Georgetown University, Washington, D.C.

66. Jeremy Larner, *Nobody Knows: Reflections on the McCarthy Campaign of 1968* (New York: Macmillan, 1970), 36. Larner believes that McCarthy was "a personally unusual but conventional politician, suddenly raised on high by a movement that was at once a vindication and an embarrassment." (Ibid., 9.)

67. Charles A. Reich, *The Greening of America* (New York: Random House, 1969).

68. Keynote address by Don Edwards to the Conference of Concerned Democrats, 2 Dec. 1967, McCarthy Historical Project, National Files, Box 1.

69. Marvin Rosenberg, a senior ADA moderate, was upset that McCarthy missed the crucial cloture vote over open housing in March 1968 for the second successive year. (The administration won by a single vote.) "I feel that ADA must protest Senator McCarthy's unconcern for this tremendous procedural and substantive situation, or are we to forgive him everything because he is 'right on Vietnam.'" Wire, Marvin Rosenberg to J. K. Galbraith, 5 March 1968. ADA Papers, Carton 3 (Unprocessed), Accession M73-472.

70. *Congressional Quarterly Almanac, 1968,* 54–55–A.

71. Citizen's Crusade Against Poverty, "The War on Poverty—Do We Care?" McPherson Office Files, Box 14, LBJL.

72. Message dated 3 March 1968, attached to memo, Marvin Watson to Lyndon B. Johnson, 27 Feb. 1968, WHCF, WE9, Box 31, LBJL.

73. Letter, Lyndon B. Johnson to Joseph Califano, 26 Feb. 1968, WHCF, FG 690, Box 387, LBJL.

74. Martha Derthick, "On Commissionship: Presidential Variety," *Public Policy* 20 (Sept. 1971), 626.

75. Ibid., 628.

76. Michael Lipsky and David J. Olson, *Commission Politics: The Processing of Racial Crisis in America* (New Brunswick, N.J.: Transaction, 1977), 132–135, and 216–217.

77. National Advisory Commission on Civil Disorders, *Kerner Report,* 20th anniversary ed. (New York: Pantheon, 1988), 10.

78. Ibid., 1.

79. Lipsky and Olson, *Commission Politics,* 127.

80. *Kerner Report,* 278.

81. Ibid., 279.

82. Ibid., footnote 186 to chapter 2, 186.

83. Ibid.

84. Memo, Joseph Califano to Lyndon B. Johnson, 28 Feb. 1968 in WHCF, FG 690, Box 387, LBJL.

85. Proposed statement appended to memo, Joseph Califano to Lyndon B. Johnson, 2 March 1968, WHCF, FG 690, Box 387, LBJL.

86. Memo, Ramsey Clark to Lyndon B. Johnson, 2 March 1968, WHCF, FG 690, Box 387, LBJL.

87. Memo, Douglass Cater to Harry McPherson, 13 March 68, WHCF, FG 690, Box 387, LBJL.

88. Memo, Louis Martin to Joseph Califano, forwarded to Lyndon B. Johnson, WHCF, FG 690, Box 387, LBJL.

89. Memo, Harry McPherson to Lyndon B. Johnson, 1 March 1968, Confidential File, FG 690, LBJL.

90. Johnson note attached to draft letters and memo, Harry McPherson to Lyndon B. Johnson, 1 March 1968, Confidential File, FG 690, LBJL.

91. Notes by James R. Jones on 15 March 1968 meeting, WHCF, FG 690, Box 387, LBJL.

92. Memo, Harold Howe to Wilbur Cohen, 5 March 1968, Cohen Papers, Box 108.

93. Ibid.

94. Transcript of 30 April 1968 meeting between Wilbur Cohen and representatives of the Poor People's March, Cohen Papers, Box 110.

95. Memo, Mary Switzer to State Administrators [of the Social Rehabilitation Service], 2 May 1968, HEW records, Box 12, LBJL.

96. See Joseph A. Califano, *The Triumph and Tragedy of Lyndon Johnson: The White House Years* (New York: Simon and Schuster, 1991), 286–287.

97. HEW's Social and Rehabilitation Service employees were encouraged to participate in the demonstration, despite the fact that the administration was a principal target. Mary Switzer, administrator of SRS, urged "all supervisors to be as liberal as possible . . . in granting annual leave to those employees who would like to participate in the PPC." Memo, Switzer to All SRS Employees, 10 May 1968, HEW papers, Box 12, LBJL.

98. Memo, Ralph Huitt to Wilbur Cohen, 6 May 1968, Cohen Papers, Box 110.

99. Ibid. Piven and Cloward believe that this is actually what happened with the National Welfare Rights Organization during the Nixon presidency. See their *Poor People's Movements: Why They Succeed, How They Fail* (New York: Vintage, 1967), chapter 5.

100. For drafts of the Basic Income Guarantee proposal, and for its reception within HEW, see Cohen Papers, Box 131.

101. Wilbur Cohen recalled that Johnson proved decidedly unenthusiastic about BIG. Cohen, Oral History, 103, Columbia University Oral History Project.

9. Zenith of the Entitlements Revolution:
Liberalism and the Family Assistance Plan

1. T. George Harris, "Do We Owe People a Living?" *Look,* 30 April 1968, 25.

2. Memo, Daniel Patrick Moynihan to Richard M. Nixon, 6 June 1969, WHCF, WE 10-5, Box 60, Nixon Presidential Project, Alexandria, Va.

3. Address to the Nation on Domestic Programs, 8 Aug. 1969, *Public Papers of Richard M. Nixon, 1969,* 637–645.

4. FAP was also expected to please Northern mayors and governors by reducing the incentive for welfare recipients in low-payment Southern states to move North. See Jill Quadagno, *The Color of Welfare: How Racism Destroyed the War on Poverty* (New York: Oxford University Press, 1994), 123.

5. Part of FAP's appeal to business came from the fact that it did not distort the labor market. In this respect, a modest guaranteed income, such as FAP or the Heineman Commission's proposal, was much preferable to the minimum wage or to in-kind services. See Michael B. Katz, *The Undeserving Poor: From the War on Poverty to the War on Welfare* (New York: Pantheon, 1989), 104–105.

6. M. Kenneth Bowler, *The Nixon Guaranteed Income Proposal: Substance and Process in Policy Change* (Cambridge, Mass.: Ballinger, 1974), 31.

7. For the political backlash generated by rising welfare rolls in New York in 1968–1969, see Edward Berkowitz, *Mr. Social Security: The Life of Wilbur J. Cohen* (Lawrence: University Press of Kansas, 1995), 282; Quadagno, *Color of Welfare,* 120–121.

8. Letter, Philip M. Klutznick (chairman, Urban Investment and Development Co.) to Richard M. Nixon, 14 July 1969, WHCF, WE 10-5, Box 60, Nixon Project.

9. HEW statistics referring to dependency levels in December of each year, cited by Bowler, *Nixon Guaranteed Income Proposal,* 36.

10. Gilbert Steiner, *The State of Welfare* (Washington, D.C.: Brookings Institution, 1971), 36. For an insightful analysis of Daniel Patrick Moynihan's relationship with Richard Nixon, see Nicholas Lemann, *The Promised Land: The Great Black Migration and How It Changed America* (London: Macmillan, 1991), 202–205.

11. Memo, Daniel Patrick Moynihan to Richard M. Nixon, 1 Feb. 1969, President's Office File (POF), Box 1, Nixon Project.

12. Memo, Moynihan to Nixon, 17 Nov. 1970, POF, Box 8, Nixon Project.

13. Memo, Moynihan to Nixon, 8 July 1969, WHCF, WE 10-5, Box 60, Nixon Project.

14. Memo, Melvin Laird to Nixon, 7 May 1969, WHCF, WE 10-5, Box 60, Nixon Project.

15. Memo, Bryce Harlow to Staff Secretary, 11 Aug. 1969, POF, Box 79, Nixon Project.

16. For the centrality of work incentives to Nixon's political calculation and reform agenda, see Quadagno, *Color of Welfare,* chapter 5.

17. Memo, Richard M. Nixon to John Mitchell, Bob Finch, Bryce Harlow, and Pat Moynihan, 15 Jan. 1969, White House Special Files (WHSF), Papers of Robert Haldeman, Box 49, Nixon Project.

18. Milton Friedman, "The Case for the Negative Income Tax," *National Review,* 7 March 1967, 239.

19. The relevant data was furnished to Nixon by Arthur Burns, a key domestic adviser and strong opponent of FAP. Among Americans with an annual family income of less than $3,000, 43 percent endorsed the $3,200 proposal, but 44 percent were opposed. See memo, Arthur Burns to Richard M. Nixon, 28 April 1969, WHCF, WE 10-5, Box 60, Nixon Project.

20. Kevin Phillips, *The Emerging Republican Majority* (New Rochelle, N.Y.: Arlington House, 1969), 25.

21. Ibid., 467.

22. Scammon and Wattenberg, *Real Majority,* 74.

23. Ibid., 72.

24. Ibid., 61.

25. Memo, Moynihan to Nixon, 17 May 1969, POF, Box 2, Nixon Project (emphasis in original). The same box contains Pete Hamill's article, "The Revolt of the White Lower Middle Class," *New York* magazine, 14 April 1969.

26. Memo, Daniel Patrick Moynihan to Richard M. Nixon, 26 June 1969, WHCF, WE 10-5, Box 60, Nixon Project.

27. Stanley Esterly and Glenn Esterly, *Freedom from Dependence: Welfare Reform as a Solution to Poverty* (Washington, D.C.: Public Affairs Press, 1971), 26.

28. Ibid., 40–41.

29. *Congressional Record,* 10 Feb. 1970, 3115.

30. *Economic Opportunity Act of 1964,* hearings before the Ad Hoc Subcommittee on the War on Poverty Program of the House Committee on Education and Labor, 88th Congress, 2d Session, 29.

31. *General Farm Program and Food Stamp Program,* hearings before the House Committee on Agriculture, 91st Congress, 1st Session, October, 1969, 793.

32. *Social Security Amendments of 1971,* hearings before Senate Committee on Finance, 91st Congress, 1st Session, 190.

33. In his August address, President Nixon took care to distinguish his proposal from the entitlements-based income maintenance schemes of the left: "This national floor under incomes for working or dependent families is not a 'guaranteed income.' Under the guaranteed income proposal everyone would be assured a mini-

mum income, regardless of how much he was capable of earning, regardless of what his need was, regardless of whether or not he was willing to work." Daniel Patrick Moynihan, *The Politics of a Guaranteed Income* (New York: Random House, 1973), 218.

34. Memo, Maurice Stans to Nixon, 7 May 1969, WHCF, WE 10-5, Box 60, Nixon Project.

35. Memo, Charles Colson to H. R. Haldeman, 7 Oct. 1970, Papers of Charles Colson, Box 63, Nixon Project.

36. Vincent J. Burke and Vee Burke, *Nixon's Good Deed: Welfare Reform* (New York: Columbia University Press, 1974), 62.

37. *New York Times,* 11 Aug. 1969, 26.

38. The *Wall Street Journal* had predicted back in March that these two legislators would pose the single most serious obstacle to any income maintenance strategy. As a revenue measure, FAP had to originate in the Ways and Means Committee, where Chairman Mills and Congressman Byrnes wielded generally decisive influence. Mills preferred to report legislation under a closed rule, which precluded amendments from the floor, and his committee's endorsement of FAP would almost certainly ensure its passage through the House, particularly since it was Title IV of the popular Social Security Amendments. For the operations of the House Ways and Means Committee, see Bowler, *Nixon Guaranteed Income Proposal,* 84–88.

39. Editorial, *Wall Street Journal,* 14 Aug. 1969, 8.

40. *Congressional Record,* 16 April 1970, 12064.

41. Burke and Burke, *Nixon's Good Deed,* 132–134.

42. Nixon quote and that of the conference task force are taken from *Congressional Record,* 16 April 1970, 12051.

43. Daniel Patrick Moynihan observes that "to a degree that could be obsessive, liberal Democrats had defined their beliefs and measured their worth in terms specifically opposed to those of Nixon." Moynihan, *Politics of a Guaranteed Income,* 353.

44. Ibid., 353.

45. Ibid., 386.

46. Ibid., 247–248.

47. Ibid., 250.

48. Burke and Burke, *Nixon's Good Deed,* 174–175.

49. Ibid., 176 (emphasis in citation).

50. George McGovern, Speech to Citizen's Committee for Children, 20 Jan. 1970, *Congressional Quarterly Weekly Report,* 2 April 1971, 763.

51. *Congressional Record,* 10 Feb. 1970, 3111.

52. Supporters of Humphrey suspected that Senator Harris "had no real concern with the party as an organization" and would harm their man's presidential prospects for 1972 in his own quest for leadership. Byron Shafer explains that "the checkered character of Harris's recent career in politics reinforced these fears. In a short period, Harris had moved from being the protégé of Senator Robert S. Kerr of

Oklahoma, to being a premier ally of Senator Robert F. Kennedy of New York, to being campaign manager for Vice President Hubert Humphrey—to some new, unpredictable set of loyalties." See Byron E. Shafer, *Quiet Revolution: The Struggle for the Democratic Party and the Shaping of Post-Reform Politics* (New York: Russell Sage Foundation, 1983), chapter 2, quote from page 50.

53. *Congressional Record,* 16 April 1970, 12091, 12097.

54. *Congressional Record,* 16 April 1970, 12048.

55. Ibid., 12050.

56. *Family Assistance Act of 1970,* hearings before House Committee on Rules, 91st Congress, 2d Session, 251.

57. Ibid., 30 April 1970, 13618.

58. Ibid.

59. Conservatives (and indeed the president) were frequently distrustful of both the HEW career bureaucracy and of Secretary Robert Finch. As FAP faced the scrutiny of the House Ways and Means Committee in January 1970, Congressman Byrnes was reported to be "ardently pleading for far more prominent involvement of Secretary of Labor Shultz, and less prominence for Finch." See memo, Bryce Harlow to Staff Secretary, 26 Jan. 1970, WHCF, WHSF, Box 61, Nixon Project.

As FAP began to run into political trouble, a member of Nixon's congressional liaison staff said that Republican senators on the Finance Committee "fear that Moynihan sold the program to the President without the President fully understanding it." See memo, Edward Morgan to John Ehrlichman, 16 July 1970, WHCF, WHSF, Box 61, Nixon Project.

60. Memo, Ed Morgan to Don Webster, 26 Feb. 1970, WHCF, WHSF, Box 61, Nixon Project.

61. The notch effect stemmed from the existence of in-kind benefits, such as public housing, Medicaid, and food stamps—particularly the first two—that lacked a sliding scale; instead they terminated abruptly, once income reached a certain level. See Burke and Burke, *Nixon's Good Deed,* 153–158, and Moynihan, *Politics of a Guaranteed Income,* 460–483, for good explanations of the notch effect and its consequences for FAP.

62. *Changing National Priorities,* hearings before the Subcommittee on Economy in Government of the Joint Economic Committee of Congress, 91st Congress, 2d Session, 559–562.

63. Ibid., 562.

64. Washington *Evening Star,* 13 May 1970, clipping in Papers of George Wiley, Box 32.

65. Letter, George Wiley to Benjamin Spock, 19 May 1969, Wiley Papers, Box 33.

66. Letter, Wiley to Spock, 23 July 1969, Wiley Papers, Box 33.

67. Letter, Spock to Wiley, 26 Feb. 1971; and letter, Spock to Beulah Sanders, 21 Oct. 1971. Both contained in Wiley Papers, Box 33.

68. See Box 34 of the Wiley Papers for details of June 1969 public hearings on the

ABM; see Box 21 for the National Coalition on the Transportation Crisis, and its campaign for free fares.

69. Letter, Aileen Hernandez to George Wiley, 15 Dec. 1970, Wiley Papers, Box 21.

70. Burke and Burke, *Nixon's Good Deed,* 153.

71. Ibid., 162.

72. Elizabeth Wickenden, "Report on Trip to Washington, D.C., November 18–19, 1970" (emphasis in original); attached to memo, Elizabeth Wickenden to George Wiley, 20 Nov. 1970, Wiley Papers, Box 34.

73. See Nick Kotz, *A Passion for Equality* (New York: Norton, 1977), 270, 273; Moynihan, *Politics of a Guaranteed Income,* 533; Burke and Burke, *Nixon's Good Deed,* 159, 161. The "lynching" remark is cited by Moynihan.

74. *New York Times,* 20 Nov. 1970, cited by Moynihan, *Politics of a Guaranteed Income,* 533.

75. The tenth negative vote came from Clinton Anderson (D-N.Mex.) whose decision was attributed by the Burkes to the influence of Senator Harris.

76. The only black congressman to support FAP in 1971 was Mayor Daley's Chicago placeman, Ralph Metcalf. For the attempt by four South Carolina black politicians to secure the CBC's backing for FAP, see Burke and Burke, *Nixon's Good Deed,* 131, 172.

77. Statement by Congressman Ron Dellums on Welfare Reform, 24 May 1971, Wiley Papers, Box 16.

78. Text in Wiley Papers, Box 16.

79. Shafer, *Quiet Revolution,* 68.

80. Statement to Hearings of Commission on Party Structure and Delegate Selection, Chicago, 7 June 1969, Papers of George McGovern, Accession Number 329-73-64, Box 19, Mudd Manuscript Library, Princeton, N.J.

81. Frederick Dutton, *The Changing Sources of Power: American Politics in the 1970s* (New York: McGraw-Hill, 1970), 15, 27, 52, 44.

82. Jack Newfield, *Robert Kennedy: A Memoir* (New York: Dutton, 1969), 188.

83. *News: McGovern for President,* Press Release, 6 April 1972, 1972 Campaign Files, McGovern Papers, Box 19.

84. Letter, Ted Van Dyk to George McGovern, 30 Nov. 1971. In papers of Frank Mankiewicz, Box 28, JFKL. Other advisers, however, felt that he must not be distracted from the Vietnam issue. Frederic Papert told McGovern that he was "being suckered by the polls into taking positions for which you have none of the zeal and commitment that are your real essence and your only chance of getting nominated and elected. George McGovern the economist is going to be a bore." Letter, Frederic Papert to George McGovern, 25 Aug. 1971, Papers of Frederic Papert, Box 13, JFKL.

85. Letter, Mrs. Louis Remnitz to George McGovern, n.d., but listed as March 1970, Box 47, Accession Number 329-73-64, McGovern Papers.

86. The senator went on to stress the importance of "making these people contributing members of society and reducing the tax burden for welfare payments." Letter, George McGovern to Gene Holsing (Wecota, S.Dak.), 22 Dec. 1970, McGovern Papers, Accession Number 329-73-64, Box 47.

87. Letter, George McGovern to W. H. Sill, Jr., 7 April 1971, McGovern Papers, Accession Number 329-73-64, Box 93.

88. Transcript of *The Tonight Show*, NBC, 28 Jan. 1972; transcript of *Thirty Minutes With . . .* , National Public Affairs Center for Television, 25 May 1972. McGovern Papers, 1972 Campaign Files, Box 12.

89. There is no reason to think that McGovern was unaware of this problem. One adviser was concerned by the reception which the candidate had received at a Wisconsin rally: "The guaranteed annual income idea is, in my view, anathema to most people, particularly wage earners, and more particularly to the kind of union members you spoke to in Madison, who seemed to feel that if they were struggling to make a living, and had done so all their lives, a handout for others (e.g., blacks) was inappropriate. To sell such an idea seems to require a lot more time." Letter, Frederic Papert to George McGovern, 25 Feb. 1972. Papert Papers, Box 13.

90. Letter, Ted Van Dyk to George McGovern, 1 May 1972. Mankiewicz Papers, Box 28. Emphasis in original.

91. Bowler *Nixon Guaranteed Income Proposal,* 140.

92. Jack Valenti, *A Very Human President* (New York: Norton, 1975), 386.

93. Letter, Harlan Smith to George McGovern, 31 May 1972, 1972 Campaign Files, McGovern Papers, Box 12.

94. Gary Hart, *Right from the Start: A Chronicle of the McGovern Campaign* (New York: Quadrangle, 1973), 190.

95. Television advertisement, 20 Oct. 1972, McGovern Papers, 1972 Campaign Files, Box 27.

Conclusion

1. This provides a good instance of Daniel Rodgers's thesis that the existence of a shared rhetoric of national keywords need not denote philosophical agreement. The Great Society era saw representatives of very different ideologies fighting over ownership of such concepts as individualism, independence, and dignity—universally applauded principles, and ones worth fighting over. For all that this period saw great divisions opening up concerning income entitlement, one searches in vain for explicit endorsements of the principle of 'dependency.' For Rodgers's shrewd analysis of historical debates concerning such keywords as 'natural rights,' 'the people,' and 'the interests,' see Daniel Rodgers, *Contested Truths: Keywords in American Politics Since Independence* (New York: Basic Books, 1987).

2. The figures were $10,515 million for SSI, and $9,536 million for AFDC. See

Theodore R. Marmor, Jerry L. Mashaw, and Philip L. Harvey, *America's Misunderstood Welfare State* (New York: Basic Books, 1990), 36.

3. Vincent Burke and Vee Burke, *Nixon's Good Deed: Welfare Reform* (New York: Columbia University Press, 1974), 188.

4. Martha Derthick, *Policymaking for Social Security* (Washington, D.C.: Brookings Institution, 1979), 339.

5. Ibid., 364.

6. Ibid.

7. *Los Angeles Times,* 9 Nov. 1972, II, 7.

8. Ibid.

9. Memo, Pat [Shakow?] to Jacob Javits, n.d., but listed as spring 1971. Series 1, Subseries 1, Papers of Jacob K. Javits, Box 122, State University of New York, Stony Brook.

10. For a detailed account of the rise and fall of the Program for Better Jobs and Income, see Laurence E. Lynn, Jr., and David deF. Whitman, *The President as Policy-Maker: Jimmy Carter and Welfare Reform* (Philadelphia, Pa.: Temple University Press, 1981).

11. See Margaret Weir, *Politics and Jobs: The Boundaries of Employment Policy in the United States* (Princeton, N.J.: Princeton University Press, 1992), chapters 4–5.

12. Daniel Patrick Moynihan, *Family and Nation* (New York: Harcourt Brace Jovanovich, 1986), 96.

13. Marmor et al., *America's Misunderstood Welfare State,* 85. More recently, welfare rolls have started to rise again, although their real value continues to diminish. See Douglas J. Besharov with Amy Fowler, "The End of Welfare as We Know It?" *Public Interest* 19 (Spring 1993), 97.

14. David T. Ellwood, *Poor Support: Poverty in the American Family* (New York: Basic Books, 1986), 60. The weakness of AFDC's political legitimacy in 1992 was illustrated by an opinion poll which revealed that, while two thirds of those surveyed felt more money should be spent on "assistance to the poor," only 23 percent believed that "welfare" spending should increase. *New York Times,* 5 July 1992, 16.

15. President Johnson's income-maintenance commission, which reported to his successor at the end of 1969, had considered an employment-based plan. Quadagno explains that this option was rejected because of cost and because it would do nothing for the working poor. Jill Quadagno, *The Color of Welfare: How Racism Destroyed the War on Poverty* (New York: Oxford University Press, 1994), 122.

16. Edward D. Berkowitz, *Mr. Social Security: The Life of Wilbur J. Cohen* (Lawrence: University Press of Kansas, 1995), 272.

17. For current definitions of the dependency problem, and for a brief analysis of the politics of welfare during the Clinton presidency, see Besharov with Fowler, "End of Welfare," 95–109; and especially Kent Weaver, "Old Traps, New Twists: Why Welfare Is So Hard to Reform in 1994," *Brookings Review* 12 (Summer 1994), 14–17. For

President Clinton's position on welfare reform, see his State of the Union Address of 25 Jan. 1994, reprinted in *Washington Post,* 26 Jan. 1994, A12.

18. Most obviously, the contemporary debate over welfare has featured an interest in work requirements that was absent in 1964. The specter of a subculturally detached underclass, resistant to government incentives and impervious to middle-class values, represents an important source of the contemporary penchant for "tough love." These developments lie beyond the scope of the present study, but are perceptively covered by, inter alia, Lawrence Mead, *Beyond Entitlement: The Social Obligations of Citizenship* (New York: Free Press, 1986); James T. Patterson, *America's Struggle Against Poverty, 1900–1985* (Cambridge, Mass.: Harvard University Press, 1986); and Michael B. Katz, *The Undeserving Poor: From the War on Poverty to the War on Welfare* (New York: Pantheon, 1989).

BIBLIOGRAPHY

Manuscript Collections: Presidential

Dwight D. Eisenhower Library, Abilene, Kansas:
   Oral Histories of Wilbur Cohen, Arthur Flemming, Marion Folsom, William Mitchell; Personal Papers of Arthur Burns; White House Central Files: Office Files; White House Confidential Files: Alphabetical Files; Ann Whitman File: Administrative Series and Cabinet Series.

John F. Kennedy Library, Boston, Massachusetts:
   Records of Department of Health, Education and Welfare (microfilm); Personal Papers of Walter Heller, Robert F. Kennedy (Senate Papers), Frank Mankiewicz, Frederic Papert, Theodore Sorensen, Willard Wirtz, Adam Yarmolinsky; President's Office Files: Office Files; White House Central Files: WE 6 (Welfare); White House Staff Files: Myer Feldman, Larry O'Brien (Congressional Liaison Office).

Lyndon B. Johnson Library, Austin, Texas:
   Administrative Histories: Bureau of the Budget, Council of Economic Advisors, Office of Economic Opportunity; Departmental and Agency Records: Department of Agriculture, Department of Health, Education and Welfare, Office of Economic Opportunity; Legislative Histories: Civil Rights Act of 1968, Economic Opportunity Act of 1964; Name Files: Senator Joseph Clark, Senator Fred Harris, Senator Jacob Javits, Congressman Wilbur Mills, Daniel Patrick Moynihan, Senator Edmund Muskie; Office Files: Joseph Califano, James C. Gaither, Harry McPherson, Mike Manatos, Bill Moyers, Fred Panzer, Marvin Watson, Lee White; Oral History Collection: Clifford Alexander, Joseph Califano, Wilbur J. Cohen, James C. Gaither, Ben W. Heineman, Walter Heller, Hubert H. Humphrey, Robert Lampman, Robert A. Levine, Louis Martin, Clarence Mitchell, Joseph L. Rauh, John P. Roche, Bayard Rustin, Charles L. Schultze, Hobart Taylor, Jr., Roy Wilkins, Whitney M. Young, Jr.; Personal Papers: Wilbur J. Cohen, Barefoot

Sanders; Task Force Reports: Education, 1964; Income Maintenance, 1966; Los Angeles Riots, 1965; Nutrition and Adequate Diets, 1966; Public Assistance, 1965; White House Central Files: AG (Agriculture), FG 11-15 (OEO), FG 690 (Kerner Commission), FI 4 (Finance-Budget), FI 4/FG 11-15 (Finance-OEO Budget), HU 2 (Equality of the Races), LE/FG 11-15 (Legislation-OEO), LE/HU 2 (Legislation-Equality of the Races), LE/WE 9 (Legislation-Poverty Program), WE (Welfare), WE 9 (Poverty Program); Cabinet Papers Collection; Records of the White House Conference "To Fulfill These Rights."

Richard M. Nixon Project, Alexandria, Virginia:
White House Central Files: FG 6-11-1 (Daniel Patrick Moynihan), FG 23 (Family Assistance Plan), WE 10-5 (Family Assistance Plan); White House Special Files: Charles Colson Files, Confidential Files, President's Office Files, H. R. Haldeman Files, Egil Krogh Files.

Manuscript Collections: Miscellaneous

Columbia University Oral History Project, Butler Library, New York:
Oral Histories of Wilbur S. Cohen, Loula Dunn, Fedele Fauri, Marjorie Hunter, Elizabeth Wickenden.

Historical Society of Pennsylvania, Philadelphia:
Joseph S. Clark Papers.

Seeley G. Mudd Manuscript Library, Princeton University, Princeton, New Jersey:
George S. McGovern Papers.

Frank Melville, Jr., Library, State University of New York, Stony Brook:
Jacob S. Javits Papers.

Georgetown University Library, Washington, D.C.:
Eugene McCarthy Historical Project.

Library of Congress, Washington, D.C.:
Papers of Democratic Study Group, Leadership Conference on Civil Rights, National Urban League, Joseph L. Rauh, Abraham Ribicoff.

National Archives, Washington, D.C.:
Records of U.S. Department of Labor, 1964–1969

Social Welfare History Project, University of Minnesota, Minneapolis:
Papers of American Public Welfare Association, National Social Welfare Assembly.

State Historical Society of Minnesota, St. Paul:
Hubert H. Humphrey Papers.

State Historical Society of Wisconsin, Madison:
Papers of Americans for Democratic Action, Wilbur J. Cohen, Elizabeth Wickenden, George Wiley.

Other Primary Sources

CONGRESSIONAL HEARINGS

January, 1966 Economic Report of the President. Hearings Before the Joint Economic Committee, 89th Congress, 2nd Session, 1 Feb. 1966.

Changing National Priorities. Hearings Before the Subcommittee on Economy in Government of the Joint Economic Committee of Congress, 91st Congress, 2nd Session, 1970.

Current Economic Situation and Short-Run Outlook. Hearings Before the Joint Economic Committee, 86th Congress, 2nd Session, 7 Dec. 1960.

De Facto School Segregation. Hearings Before Special Subcommittee of the House Committee on Education and Labor, 89th Congress, 1st Session, July 1965.

Economic Opportunity Act of 1964. Hearings Before the Ad Hoc Committee on the War on Poverty of the House Committee on Education and Labor, 88th Congress, 2nd Session, April 1964.

Economic Opportunity Act of 1964. Hearings Before the Select Committee on Poverty of the Senate Committee on Labor and Public Welfare, 88th Congress, 2nd Session, June 1964.

Elementary and Secondary Education Act of 1966. Hearings Before the General Subcommittee on Education of the House Committee on Education and Labor, 89th Congress, 2nd Session, part I, March 1966.

Elementary and Secondary Education Act of 1966. Hearings Before the Subcommittee on Education of the Senate Committee on Labor and Public Welfare, 89th Congress, 2nd Session, April 1966.

Examination of the War on Poverty. Hearings Before the Subcommittee on Employment, Manpower, and Poverty of the Senate Committee on Labor and Public Welfare, 90th Congress, 1st Session, March–August 1967.

Family Security Act of 1987. Hearings Before the Senate Finance Committee, 100th Congress, 1st Session, 1987.

Federal Role in Urban Affairs. Hearings Before the Subcommittee on Executive Reorganization of the Senate Committee on Government Reorganization, 89th Congress, 2nd Session, August–September and December 1966.

General Farm Program and Food Stamp Program. Hearings Before the House Committee on Agriculture, 91st Congress, 1st Session, October 1969.

President's 1967 Surtax Proposal; Continuation of Hearings to Receive Further Administration Proposal Concerning Expenditure Cuts. Hearings Before the House Committee on Ways and Means, 90th Congress, 1st Session, November 1967.

Social Security Amendments of 1967. Hearings Before the Senate Finance Committee, 90th Congress, 1st Session, September 1967.

Social Security Amendments of 1967. Hearings Before the Senate Finance Committee, 92nd Congress, 1st Session, 1971.

Views of the National Governor's Association on Major Legislative Proposals. Hearings Before the House Committee on Ways and Means, 100th Congress, 1st Session, February 1987.

FEDERAL GOVERNMENT REPORTS

Civil Rights U.S.A.: Public Schools, Cities in the North and West, 1962, New Rochelle. U.S. Commission on Civil Rights.

Economic Opportunity Act of 1964. Report of the Ad Hoc Committee on the War on Poverty of the House Committee on Education and Labor, April 1964.

Economic Opportunity Act of 1964. Report of the Select Committee on Poverty of the Senate Committee on Labor and Public Welfare, June 1964.

Economic Policies and Practices. Material Prepared for the Joint Economic Committee, 1968.

Economic Report of the President, 1964–1967.

Goals for Americans: Programs for Action in the Sixties. President's Commission on National Goals. New York: Prentice-Hall, 1960.

Having the Power, We Have the Duty. Report of the Advisory Council on Public Welfare, June 1966.

Joint Economic Report of the Joint Economic Committee on the January, 1964 Economic Report of the President. Joint Economic Committee of Congress, 1964.

The Kerner Report. Report of the National Advisory Commission on Civil Disorder, March 1968. 20th Anniversary Edition. New York: Pantheon Books, 1988.

The Negro Family: The Case for National Action. U.S. Department of Labor, Office of Policy Planning and Research, March 1965.

The Program For Better Jobs and Income—A Guide and Critique. Study prepared for the use of the Joint Economic Committee of Congress, October 1967.

Social Security Amendments of 1967. Report of House Committee on Ways and Means, August 1967.

Technology and the American Economy. Report of the National Commission on Technology, Automation and Economic Progress, February 1966.

Up from Dependency: A New National Public Assistance Strategy. Report to the President by the Domestic Policy Council, Low Income Opportunity Working Group, December 1986.

NEWSPAPERS AND JOURNALS

Newspapers:
  Chicago Tribune, Christian Science Monitor, Los Angeles Times, National Observer, New York Times, Wall Street Journal, Washington Post.

Journals:
  A.D.A. World, Business Weekly, Commentary, Commonweal, Fortune, Life, Look, Nation, National Review, New Leader, New Republic, Newsweek, The Progres-

sive, The Public Interest, Reader's Digest, Saturday Evening Post, Time, U.S. News and World Report.

MISCELLANEOUS

Congressional Digest. Washington, D.C.: Congressional Quarterly, February 1988.

Congressional Quarterly Almanac. Washington, D.C.: Congressional Quarterly, 1964–1972, 1987–88.

Congressional Quarterly Weekly Report. Washington, D.C.: Congressional Quarterly, 1964–1972, 1987–1988.

Congressional Record. 1964—1972.

George H. Gallup, *The Gallup Poll: Public Opinion, 1935—1971,* vol. 3. New York: Random House, 1972.

Monthly Labor Report. Washington, D.C.: U.S. Department of Labor, 1964.

Public Papers and Addresses of Franklin D. Roosevelt. Edited by Samuel I. Rosenman. New York: Random House, 1938.

Public Papers of the President: Lyndon B. Johnson. 1964–1968.

Statistical Abstract of the United States. Washington, D.C.: U.S. Department of Commerce, 1964–1976.

U.S. Code Congressional and Administrative News, 88th Congress, Second Session. St. Paul, Minn.: West Publishing, 1964.

Violence in the City: An End or a Beginning? Governor's Commission on the Los Angeles Riots. Los Angeles: State of California, 2 Dec. 1965.

Secondary Sources

Aaron, Henry J. *Politics and the Professors: The Great Society in Perspective.* Washington, D.C.: Brookings Institution, 1978.

Abraham, Henry J. *Freedom and the Court: Civil Rights and Liberties in the United States.* 5th ed. New York: Oxford University Press, 1988.

Anderson, James E., and Jared E. Hazleton. *Managing Macroeconomic Policy: The Johnson Presidency.* Austin: University of Texas Press, 1986.

Anderson, Martin. *Welfare: The Political Economy of Welfare Reform in the United States.* Stanford, Calif.: Hoover Institution Press, 1978.

Arieli, Yehoshua. *Individualism and Nationalism in American Ideology.* Cambridge, Mass.: Harvard University Press, 1964.

Arnold, Thurman. *The Folklore of Capitalism.* New Haven: Yale University Press, 1937.

Auletta, Kenneth. *The Underclass.* New York: Vintage, 1983.

Bellah, Robert N. et al. *Habits of the Heart: Individualism and Commitment in American Life.* New York: Harper & Row, 1986.

Berkowitz, Edward D. *America's Welfare State: From Roosevelt to Reagan.* Baltimore: Johns Hopkins University Press, 1991.

————. *Mr. Social Security: The Life of Wilbur J. Cohen.* Lawrence: University Press of Kansas, 1995.

Berkowitz, Edward D. and Kim McQuaid. *Creating the Welfare State: The Political Economy of 20th-Century Reform.* Lawrence: University Press of Kansas, 1992.

Besharov, Douglas J. with Amy Fowler. "The End of Welfare as We Know It?" *The Public Interest* 111 (Spring 1993), 95–108.

Blum, John Morton. *Years of Discord: American Politics and Society, 1961–1974.* New York: Norton, 1991.

Bowler, M. Kenneth. *The Nixon Guaranteed Income Proposal: Substance and Process in Policy Change.* Cambridge, Mass.: Ballinger, 1974.

Brauer, Carl M. "Kennedy, Johnson, and the War on Poverty," *Journal of American History* 69 (June 1982), 98–119.

Bremner, Robert H. *From the Depths: The Discovery of Poverty in the United States.* New York: New York University Press, 1986.

Brink, William and Louis Harris. *The Negro Revolution in America.* New York: Simon and Schuster, 1964.

Brinkley, Alan. "The Antimonopoly Ideal and the Liberal State: The Case of Thurman Arnold," *Journal of American History* 80 (Sept. 1993), 557–579.

————. *The End of Reform: New Deal Liberalism in Recession and War.* New York: Knopf, 1995.

Burke, Vincent and Vee J. Burke. *Nixon's Good Deed: Welfare Reform.* New York: Columbia University Press, 1974.

Burkhart, James A. and Frank J. Kendrick, eds. *The New Politics: Mood or Movement?* Englewood Cliffs, N.J.: Prentice-Hall, 1971.

Butler, Stuart and Anna Kondratas. *Out of the Poverty Trap: A Conservative Strategy for Welfare Reform.* New York: Free Press, 1987.

Cagan, Phillip et al. *Economic Policy and Inflation in the Sixties.* Washington, D.C.: American Enterprise Institute, 1972.

Califano, Joseph S. *The Triumph and Tragedy of Lyndon Johnson: The White House Years.* New York: Simon and Schuster, 1991.

Caro, Robert. *The Years of Lyndon Johnson: The Path to Power.* New York: Vintage, 1981.

————. *The Years of Lyndon Johnson: The Means of Ascent.* New York: Vintage, 1989.

Caudill, Harry. *Night Comes to the Cumberlands.* Boston: Little, Brown and Co., 1963.

Chafe, William H. *Never Stop Running: Allard Lowenstein and the Struggle to Save American Liberalism.* New York: Basic Books, 1993.

Clark, Kenneth B. *Dark Ghetto: Dilemmas of Social Power.* New York: Harper Torchbooks, 1965.

Conant, James B. *Slums and Suburbs: A Commentary on Schools in Metropolitan Areas.* New York: McGraw-Hill, 1961.

Critchlow, Donald T. and Ellis W. Hawley, eds. *Federal Social Policy: The Historical Dimension.* University Park: Pennsylvania State University Press, 1989.

Dallek, Robert. *Lone Star Rising: Lyndon Johnson and His Times, 1908–1960.* New York: Oxford University Press, 1991.

Danziger, Sheldon H., Gary D. Sandefur, and Daniel H. Weinberg, eds. *Confronting Poverty: Prescriptions for Change.* Cambridge, Mass.: Harvard University Press, 1994.

Davis, Lanny J. *The Emerging Democratic Majority: Lessons and Legacies from the New Politics.* New York: Stein and Day, 1974.

Degler, Carl N. *Out of Our Past: The Forces that Shaped Modern America.* New York: Harper Colophon, 1967.

Derthick, Martha. "On Commissionship: Presidential Variety," *Public Policy* 20 (September 1971), 123–138.

―――. *Policymaking for Social Security.* Washington, D.C.: Brookings Institution, 1979.

Diggins, John Patrick. *The American Left in the Twentieth Century.* New York: Harcourt Brace Jovanovich, 1973.

Divine, Robert, ed. *The Johnson Years, vol. 2.* Lawrence: University Press of Kansas, 1987.

Donovan, John. *The Politics of Poverty.* 2nd ed. Indianapolis, Ind.: Pegasus, 1973.

Duhl, Leonard J., ed. *The Urban Condition: People and Policy in the Metropolis.* New York: Basic Books, 1964.

Dutton, Frederick G. *Changing Sources of Power: American Politics in the 1970s.* New York: McGraw-Hill, 1970.

Edsall, Thomas B. and Mary D. Edsall. *Chain Reaction: The Impact of Race, Rights, and Taxes on American Politics.* New York: Norton, 1992.

Ekirch, Arthur. *Ideologies and Utopias: The Impact of the New Deal on American Thought.* Chicago: Quadrangle Books, 1969.

Ellwood, David T. *Poor Support: Poverty in the American Family.* New York: Basic Books, 1986.

Esterly, Stanley and Glenn Esterly. *Freedom from Dependence: Welfare Reform as a Solution to Poverty.* Washington, D.C.: Public Affairs Press, 1971.

Evans, Rowland and Robert Novak. *Lyndon B. Johnson: The Exercise of Power.* New York: National American Library, 1966.

Ferguson, Thomas and Joel Rogers. *Right Turn: The Decline of the Democrats and the Future of American Politics.* New York: Wang & Hill, 1986.

Frantz, Joe B. "Opening a Curtain: The Metamorphosis of Lyndon B. Johnson," *Journal of Southern History* 45 (February 1979), 3–26.

Fraser, Steve and Gary Gerstle, eds. *The Rise and Fall of the New Deal Order, 1930–1980.* Princeton, N.J.: Princeton University Press, 1989.

Galbraith, John Kenneth. *American Capitalism: The Concept of Countervailing Power.* Boston: Houghton Mifflin, 1952.

Gilder, George. *Wealth and Poverty.* New York: Bantam, 1981.

Gillon, Steven M. *The Democrats' Dilemma: Walter F. Mondale and the Liberal Legacy.* New York: Columbia University Press, 1992.

―――. *Politics and Vision: The ADA and American Liberalism, 1947–1985.* New York: Oxford University Press, 1987.

Ginzberg, Eli and Robert M. Solow, eds. *The Great Society: Lessons for the Future.* New York: Bantam, 1974.

Glazer, Nathan and Daniel Patrick Moynihan. *Beyond the Melting Pot: The Jews, Irish, Negroes and Puerto Ricans of New York City.* 2nd edition. New York: Basic Books, 1970.

Glendon, Mary Ann. *Rights Talk: The Impoverishment of Political Discourse.* New York: Free Press, 1988.

Goodwin, Richard N. *Remembering America: A Voice From the Sixties.* Boston: Little Brown and Co., 1988.

Gordon, Margaret S. *Poverty in America.* San Francisco: Chandler, 1965.

Graham, Hugh Davis. *The Civil Rights Era: Origins of National Policy.* New York: Oxford University Press, 1991.

Graham, Hugh Davis. *Uncertain Triumph: Federal Education Policy in the Kennedy and Johnson Years.* Chapel Hill: University of North Carolina Press, 1984.

Graham, Otis L., Jr. *Toward a Planned Society: From Roosevelt to Nixon.* New York: Oxford University Press, 1976.

Greenstein, Robert. "Losing Faith in 'Losing Ground'," *New Republic,* 25 March 1985.

Gueron, Judith M. "The Route to Welfare Reform: From Welfare to Work," *Brookings Review* 12 (Summer 1994), 14–17.

Hamby, Alonzo L. *Liberalism and Its Challengers: FDR to Reagan.* New York: Oxford University Press, 1985.

Handler, Joel and Yeheskel Hasenfeld. *The Moral Construction of Poverty: Welfare Reform in America.* Newbury Park, Cal.: Sage, 1991.

Harrington, Michael. *The New American Poverty.* London: Firethorn, 1985.

―――. *The Other America.* New York: Penguin Books, 1963.

Harris, Fred R. *Now Is the Time: A New Populist Call to Action.* New York: McGraw-Hill, 1971.

Hart, Gary. *Right From the Start: A Chronicle of the McGovern Campaign.* New York: Quadrangle, 1973.

Hart, John. "Kennedy, Congress, and Civil Rights," *Journal of American Studies* 13 (August 1979), 165–178.

Hartz, Louis. *The Liberal Tradition in America.* New York: Harcourt Brace Jovanovich, 1955.

Hatch, Nathan O. *The Democratization of American Christianity.* New Haven: Yale University Press, 1988.

Haveman, Robert, ed. *A Decade of Federal Antipoverty Programs: Achievements, Failures, and Lessons.* New York: Academic Press, 1977.

Heale, M. J. *The Making of American Politics, 1750–1850.* New York: Longman, 1977.

Heclo, Hugh. "General Welfare and Two American Political Traditions," *Political Science Quarterly* 101 (Summer 1986), 179–196.

Herzog, Arthur. *McCarthy for President.* New York: Viking, 1969.

Horwitz, Julius. *The Inhabitants.* Cleveland, Ohio: World Publishing, 1961.

Howe, Daniel Walker, ed. *Victorian America.* Philadelphia: University of Pennsylvania Press, 1976.

Higham, John. "From Boundlessness to Consolidation: The Transformation of American Cultures, 1848–1860." Reprint Series in American History. Indianapolis, Ind.: Bobbs-Merrill, 1969.

Hofstadter, Richard. *The American Political Tradition.* Vintage, New York, 1974.

Humphrey, Hubert H. *War on Poverty.* New York: McGraw-Hill, 1964.

Hunter, Robert. *Poverty.* New York: Macmillan, 1904.

Jacoby, Sanford M. "Employers and the Welfare State: The Role of Marion B. Folsom," *Journal of American History* 80 (Sept. 1993), 525–556.

Jeffries, John W. "The 'New' New Deal: FDR and American Liberalism, 1937–1945," *Political Science Quarterly* 105 (Fall 1990), 397–418.

Jencks, Christopher. "How Poor are the Poor?" *New York Review of Books,* 9 May 1985.

Johnson, Lyndon B. *The Vantage Point: Perspectives on the Presidency.* New York: Holt, Rinehart and Wilson, 1971.

Kalman, Laura. *Abe Fortas: A Biography.* New Haven: Yale University Press, 1990.

Karl, Barry. *The Uneasy State: The United States from 1915–1945.* Chicago: University of Chicago Press, 1983.

Katz, Michael B. *Improving Poor People: The Welfare State, The "Underclass," and Urban Schools as History.* Princeton, N.J.: Princeton University Press, 1995.

———. *In the Shadow of the Poor House: A Social History of Welfare in America.* New York: Basic Books, 1986.

———. *The Undeserving Poor: From the War on Poverty to the War on Welfare.* New York: Pantheon, 1989.

Kearns, Doris. *Lyndon Johnson and the American Dream.* London: Andre Deutsch, 1976.

King, Rev. Martin Luther, Jr. *Why We Can't Wait.* New York: Signet Books, 1964.

Kotz, Nick and Mary Lynn. *A Passion for Equality.* New York: Norton, 1977.

Larner, Jeremy. *Nobody Knows: Reflections on the McCarthy Campaign of 1968.* New York: Macmillan, 1970.

Lasch, Christopher. *The Agony of the American Left.* New York: Knopf, 1969.

Leman, Christopher. *The Collapse of Welfare Reform: Political Institutions, Policy, and the Poor in Canada and the United States.* Cambridge, Mass.: MIT Press, 1980.

Lemann, Nicholas. *The Promised Land: The Great Black Migration and How It Changed America.* London: Macmillan, 1991.

Leuchtenburg, William E. *In the Shadow of FDR: From Harry Truman to Ronald Reagan.* Ithaca, N.Y.: Cornell University Press, 1983.

———. "A Visit With LBJ," *American Heritage* 41 (May/June, 1990), 47–65.

Levine, Robert A. *The Poor Ye Need Not Have with Ye: Lessons from the War on Poverty.* Cambridge, Mass.: MIT Press, 1970.

Levitan, Sar A. *The Great Society's Poor Law: A New Approach to Poverty.* Baltimore, Md.: John Hopkins University Press, 1969.

Lipset, Seymour Martin. *The First New Nation.* New York: Doubleday, 1967.

Lipsky, Michael and David J. Olson. *Commission Politics: The Processing of Racial Crisis in America.* New Brunswick, N.J.: Transaction, 1977.

Lubell, Samuel. *White and Black: Test of a Nation.* New York: Harper and Row, 1964.

Lynn, Laurence E., Jr., and David deF. Whitman. *The President as Policy-Maker: Jimmy Carter and Welfare Reform.* Philadelphia: Temple University Press, 1981.

Marmor, Theodore, Jerry Maslow, and Philip L. Harvey. *America's Misunderstood Welfare State: Persistent Myths, Enduring Realities.* New York: Basic Books, 1990.

Marris, Peter and Martin Rein. *Dilemmas of Social Reform: Poverty and Community Action in the United States.* Harmondsworth, Middlesex [Eng.]: Penguin, 1972.

Matusow, Allen J. *The Unraveling of America: American Liberalism During the 1960s.* New York: Harper and Row, 1984.

May, Edgar. *The Wasted Americans: Cost of Our Welfare Dilemma.* New York: Harper and Row, 1964.

McNamara, Robert S. *In Retrospect: The Tragedy and Lesson of Vietnam.* New York: Times Books, 1995.

McPherson, Harry M. *A Political Education.* Boston: Houghton Mifflin, 1988.

McQuaid, Kim. *Big Business and Presidential Power: From FDR to Reagan.* New York: William Morrow, 1982.

Mead, Lawrence. *Beyond Entitlement: The Social Obligations of Citizenship.* New York: Free Press, 1986.

Meier, August and Elliott Rudwick. *CORE: A Study of the Civil Rights Movement.* Urbana: University of Illinois Press, 1975.

Miller, Merle. *Lyndon: An Oral Biography.* New York: Ballantine, 1986.

Moore, Geoffrey, ed. *American Literature: A Representative Anthology of American Writing from Colonial Times to the Present.* London: Faber and Faber, 1964.

Moynihan, Daniel Patrick. *Family and Nation.* New York: Harcourt Brace Jovanovich, 1986.

―――. *Maximum Feasible Misunderstanding: Community Action in the War on Poverty.* New York: Free Press, 1969.

―――, ed. *On Fighting Poverty: Perspectives from the Social Sciences.* New York: Basic Books, 1969.

―――. *The Politics of a Guaranteed Income.* New York: Basic Books, 1973.

Murray, Charles. *Losing Ground: American Social Policy, 1950–1980.* New York: Basic Books, 1984.

Myrdal, Gunnar. *Challenge to Affluence.* New York: Pantheon, 1962.

Novak, Michael, ed. *The New Consensus on Family and Welfare.* Washington, D.C.: American Enterprise Institute, 1987.

Oberdorfer, Don. *Tet!* Garden City, N.Y.: Doubleday, 1971.

302

Ohlin, Lloyd and Richard Cloward. *Delinquency and Opportunity: A Theory of Delinquent Gangs.* New York: Free Press 1960.

Okun, Arthur N. *The Political Economy of Prosperity.* New York: Norton, 1970.

Patterson, James T. *America's Struggle Against Poverty, 1900–1985.* Cambridge, Mass: Harvard University Press, 1986.

Perkins, Frances. *The Roosevelt I Knew.* London: Hammond, Hammond and Co., 1946.

Pessen, Edward. "The Egalitarian Myth and the American Social Realities: Wealth, Mobility and Equality in the 'Era of the Common Man,'" *American Historical Review* 76 (Oct. 1971), 989–1034.

Phillips, Kevin P. *The Emerging Republican Majority.* New Rochelle, N.Y.: Arlington House, 1969.

Piven, Frances Fox and Richard Cloward. *Poor People's Movements: Why They Succeed, How They Fail.* New York: Vintage, 1977.

————. *Regulating the Poor: The Functions of Public Welfare.* New York: Vintage, 1971.

Pole, J. R. *American Individualism and the Promise of Progress.* New York: Oxford University Press, 1980.

————. *The Pursuit of Equality in American History.* Berkeley: University of California Press, 1978.

Potter, David M. *People of Plenty: Economic Abundance and the American Character.* Chicago: University of Chicago Press, 1954.

Pressman, Jeffrey and Aaron Wildavsky. *Implementation.* Berkeley: University of California Press, 1973.

Quadagno, Jill. *The Color of Welfare: How Racism Undermined the War on Poverty.* New York: Oxford University Press, 1994.

Rainwater, Lee and William L. Yancey. *The Moynihan Report and the Politics of Controversy.* Cambridge, Mass.: MIT Press, 1967.

Reich, Charles A. *The Greening of America.* New York: Random House, 1969.

Rischin, Moses, ed. *The American Gospel of Success: Individualism and Beyond.* Chicago: Quadrangle, 1968.

Ritz, Joseph P. *The Despised Poor: Newburgh's War on Welfare.* Boston: Beacon Press, 1966.

Safire, William. *Before the Fall.* New York: Belmont Tower, 1975.

Scammon, Richard and Ben Wattenberg. *The Real Majority.* New York: Coward-McCann, 1970.

Schlesinger, Arthur M., Jr. *The Crisis of Confidence.* New York: Bantam Books, 1969.

————. *The Politics of Upheaval.* London: Heinemann, 1960.

Shafer, Byron E. *Quiet Revolution: The Struggle for the Democratic Party and the Shaping of Post-Reform Politics.* New York: Russell Sage Foundation, 1983.

Sitkoff, Harvard, ed. *Fifty Years Later: The New Deal Evaluated.* New York: Knopf, 1985.

Slater, Philip. *The Pursuit of Loneliness: American Culture at the Breaking Point.* Boston, Mass.: Beacon Press, 1970.

Sorensen, Theodore. *Kennedy.* London: Hodder and Stoughton, 1965.

Sproat, John G. *'The Best Men': Liberal Reformers in the Gilded Age*. New York: Oxford University Press, 1968.

Stavis, Ben. *We Were the Campaign: New Hampshire to Chicago for McCarthy*. Boston: Beacon Press, 1969.

Steiner, Gilbert Y. *Social Insecurity: The Politics of Welfare*. Chicago: Rand McNally, 1966.
———. *The State of Welfare*. Washington, D.C.: Brookings Institution, 1971.

Stern, Mark. *Calculating Visions: Kennedy, Johnson and Civil Rights*. Rutgers, N.J.: Rutgers University Press, 1991.

Sundquist, James L. *Dynamics of the Party System*. Washington, D.C.: Brookings Institution, 1973.

———, ed. *On Fighting Poverty: Perspectives from Experience*. New York: Basic Books, 1969.

Thernstrom, Stephan. *Poverty and Progress: Social Mobility in a Nineteenth-Century City*. Cambridge, Mass.: Harvard University Press, 1964.

Tugwell, Rexford G. *The Democratic Roosevelt*. New York: Doubleday, 1957.

Turner, Kathleen J. *Lyndon Johnson's Dual War: Vietnam and the Press*. Chicago: University of Chicago Press, 1985.

Valenti, Jack. *A Very Human President*. New York: Norton, 1975.

Vogel, Ursula and Michael Moran, eds. *The Frontiers of Citizenship*. London: Macmillan, 1991.

Weaver, Kent. "Old Traps, New Twists: Why Welfare Is So Hard to Reform in 1994," *Brookings Review* 12 (Summer 1994), 14–17.

Weil, Gordon Lee. *The Long Shot: George McGovern Runs for President*. New York: Norton, 1973.

Weir, Margaret. *Politics and Jobs: The Boundaries of Employment Policy in the United States*. Princeton, N.J.: Princeton University Press, 1992.

Weir, Margaret, Ann Shola Orloff, and Theda Skocpol, eds. *The Politics of Social Policy in the United States*. Princeton, N.J.: Princeton University Press, 1989.

Weissman, Harold H. *Community Development in the Mobilization for Youth Experience*. New York: Association Press, 1969.

White, Theodore H. *The Making of the President, 1972*. New York: Bantam, 1973.

Williams, T. Harry. "Huey, Lyndon and Southern Radicalism," *Journal of American History* 60 (September 1973), 267–293.

Wills, Garry. *Nixon Agonistes*. New York: New American Library, 1971.

Wilson, William Julius. *The Truly Disadvantaged: The Inner City, the Underclass, and Public Policy*. Chicago: University of Chicago Press, 1987.

Young, Whitney M., Jr. *To Be Equal*. New York: McGraw-Hill, 1964.

INDEX

Altmeyer, Arthur, 22, 29
Amenta, Edwin, 19
American Academy of Political and
    Social Science, 74
American Public Welfare Association
    (APWA), 28, 120–21
Americans for Democratic Action
    (ADA), 141, 164, 175, 191, 229
  perspective on poverty in 1964, 48, 49
  Vietnam and, 110, 167, 176–77, 202,
    267n27, 282n69
Andrews, George, 179
Apollo project, 38
Appalachia, poverty in, 45, 46
Arnall, Ellis, 150
Arnold, Thurman, 18, 20
Automation problem, 37–38, 76,
    113–15. *See also* Ad Hoc Committee
    on the Triple Revolution

Baker, Howard, 151
Baldwin, James, 64
Ball, George, 179
Ball, Robert M., 181, 235
Bayh, Birch, 176
Bell, Alphonzo, 266n17
Berkowitz, Edward D., 26
Bernhard, Berl, 94
Berry, Edwin C., 74
Beyond the Melting Pot (Glazer and
    Moynihan), 55
Bible, Alan, 200
Bigart, Homer, 45
Black Power, 126–28
Blake, Eugene Carson, 119
Boone, Richard, 50, 89, 118–19
Brademas, John, 108–9
Brinkley, Alan, 17–19
Britton, Albert, 170–71
Brooke, Edward, 151, 187, 221
Brown, Douglas, 22
Brown, Edmund G., 78–79, 273n61

Brown, H. "Rap," 192
Burke, Vee and Vincent, 222, 224, 228
Burleson, Omar, 221
Bush, George, 195, 196
Byrd, Harry S., 150
Byrd, Robert, 42
Byrnes, John, 221, 235

Califano, Joseph A., 94
  on congressional conservatism in 1967,
    174
  on Mayor Daley, 92
  on Democratic coalition, 190–91
  on hunger issue, 170
  on Johnson and Watts, 78
  on Kerner Report, 206
  urges domestic cutbacks in 1966, 134
  on WIN amendments of 1967, 199
Cantril, Tad, 148
Carey, Hugh, 44, 108–9
Carmichael, Stokely, 82, 166, 176, 191–92,
    271n19
Carter, Jimmy, 150
  Program for Better Jobs and Income,
    237
Case, Clifford, 61, 148, 193–94, 200–201
Cater, Douglass, 162
  on Kerner Commission, 187, 206
  proposes disbandment of OEO, 195
Celebrezze, Anthony, 41, 51–52
Chafe, William H., 8
Chisholm, Shirley, 225
Church, Frank, 200
Citizens' Crusade Against Poverty
    (CCAP), 89, 118–20, 191, 202–3
City Hearings
  initial sessions, 135–44
  late sessions, 154–56
Civil rights legislation
  1964 act, 58, 59
  1965 act, 72
  1966 act, 126–27, 149

Johnson, Lyndon B., *continued*
  liberal break with, over Vietnam,
    109–12, 131–32, 139, 163–65, 201–2
  liberal individualistic faith of, 32–34,
    40–41, 155, 161, 170
  liberal unhappiness with domestic
    policies of, 108–10, 135–44, 175,
    189, 194–96
  as majority leader of Senate, 186
  midterm elections of 1966 and,
    152–54
  New Deal Democratic coalition and,
    157
  political pragmatism of, 32, 33,
    185–210
  response to riots, 78, 186–88
  retreat from reform of, 128–29,
    132–35, 172, 188, 192–93, 202
  state of the union addresses of, 105,
    153, 202
  taxation policies of, 106–7, 134–35
  unpopularity with young voters of,
    140
  Vietnam and collapse in popularity of,
    105, 131, 146, 163, 174–79
  on Vietnam hawks, 179
  Voting Rights speech, 72
  WIN amendments of 1967, 198–200
  withdrawal from 1968 race, 208
  See also Great Society liberalism;
    Howard University speech; Task
    forces, Johnson administration
Jones, Hulbert, 222
Justice Department
  investigation of Watts riot, 79

Katzenbach, Nicholas, 143
  on Southern politics of race, 150
Keating, Kenneth, 59
Kennedy, Edward M., 127–28
Kennedy, John F.
  Appalachia and, 45

on Cold War, 43
economic philosophy of, 31
juvenile delinquency committee of,
  50, 115
as New Politics hero, 201–2
Vietnam policies of, 169
welfare policies of, 29
Kennedy, Robert F., 151, 189
  ADA and, 141
  on black poverty, 45, 172
  and City Hearings (1966), 136–44,
    154–56
  on income maintenance policy, 144,
    156, 172–73
  New Politics and, 140–41, 163, 168–69,
    240, 272n38
  1963 meeting with black leaders, 64,
    259n38
  presidential quest of, 110–12, 139–40,
    202, 240
  on Social Security Amendments of
    1967, 182–83, 198–200
  on Vietnam, 126, 165, 168, 178,
    275n27
Keppel, Francis, 92
Kerner, Otto, 187
Kerner Commission, 136, 184, 202
  appointment of, 186–87
  report, 204–8, 241
Kershaw, Joseph, 101
Keyserling, Leon, 31
King, Rev. Martin Luther, Jr., 45, 70, 81
  assassination, 208
  Chicago campaign (1966), 127
  endorses guaranteed income, 127, 155
  G.I. Bill of Rights plan of, 57–58, 67–68
  on riots, 63, 192–93
  on Vietnam, 166–67, 167n35
  See also Poor People's Campaign
Kintner, Robert, 125, 134
  on Javits, 142
Kirk, Claude, 192

O'Brien, Lawrence, 175, 225
Office of Economic Opportunity
    (OEO). *See* Economic Opportunity
    Act of 1964; War on Poverty
O'Hara, Jim, 197
Okun, Arthur, 106, 107, 133, 266n9
Opportunities Industrialization Center,
    155
Opportunity, equality of, 97
    as basis for War on Poverty, 33, 37–38,
        159
    Howard University address and, 71
    Johnson on, 33–34, 161
Opportunity theory, 50
Other America, The (Harrington), 47–48, 49

Panzer, Fred, 135
Papert, Frederic, 288n84, 288n89
Parker, William, 79, 80
Pastore, John, 178
Patten, Edward, 44
Patterson, James T., 28
Percy, Charles, 146, 148, 151
Perkins, Carl, 195, 196
Phillips, Kevin, 217
Piven, Frances Fox, 117–19
Pole, J. R., 11
Politics of Controversy, The (Rainwater and
    Yancey), 86, 93–95
Poor People's Campaign, 193, 209–10
Poverty
    Cold War and, 43–44
    as a cultural problem, 25, 49
    decline in, after 1964, 188
    deserving/undeserving distinction, 9,
        11–12, 34, 40, 160, 220, 235
    education as a response to, 76
    malnutrition, 170–71, 181, 222–23
    racial dimension of, 44–47, 54–74,
        77–104, 203–10
    rehabilitation as a response to, 25, 31,
        161

as a spiritual condition, 39, 49
See also Economic Opportunity Act of
    1964; War on Poverty
Poverty/Rights Action Committee. *See*
    National Welfare Rights
    Organization
Powell, Adam Clayton, 39, 48
Price, Monroe E., 98
Program for Better Jobs and Income, 237
Progressive Era, 12–13, 18, 26, 99
Public assistance. *See* Aid to Families with
    Dependent Children; Task forces,
    Johnson administration; Welfare
Public Welfare Amendments of 1962,
    161
Pucinski, Roman, 43, 149–50

Race
    and the declaration of War on
        Poverty, 44–47
    as factor in 1966 elections, 148–51
    de facto discrimination, 58–72
    in neighborhoods, 149–50
    and the Newburgh episode, 28–29
    in schooling, 92–93
    Vietnam and, 110, 166–67
    WIN amendments of 1967 and, 199
    See also Affirmative action; Black
        Power; Civil rights legislation; Civil
        rights movement; Kerner
        Commission; Liberalism, American;
        Moynihan Report; Poverty; Riots;
        "White backlash"; White House
        Conference "To Fulfill These
        Rights"; *individual groups and leaders*
Radler, Donald, 162
Randolph, A. Philip, 81–82, 192, 203
    on black militancy, 56–57, 63
    chairs 1965 White House Conference,
        94
    "Freedom Budget" proposal of, 132,
        171